Risk, Society and Policy Series

The Social Contours of Risk:

Publics, Risk Communication and the Social Amplification of Risk

Volume I

Risk, Society and Policy Series

The Social Contours of Risk:
Publics, Risk Communication and the Social Amplification of Risk

Volume I

Jeanne X. Kasperson and Roger E. Kasperson, with collaborators

with the assistance of
Mimi Berberian and Lu Ann Pacenka

London • Sterling, VA

First published by Earthscan in the UK and USA in 2005

ISBN: 1-84407-073-5   paperback
       1-84407-072-7   hardback

Typesetting by MapSet Ltd, Gateshead, UK
Printed and bound in the UK by Cromwell Press Ltd, Trowbridge
Cover design by Yvonne Booth

For a full list of publications please contact:

Earthscan
8–12 Camden High Street
London, NW1 0JH, UK
Tel: +44 (0)20 7387 8558
Fax: +44 (0)20 7387 8998
Email: earthinfo@earthscan.co.uk
Web: **www.earthscan.co.uk**

22883 Quicksilver Drive, Sterling, VA 20166-2012, USA

Earthscan is an imprint of James and James (Science Publishers) Ltd and
publishes in association with the International Institute for Environment and
Development

A catalogue record for this book is available from the British Library

Library of Congress Cataloging-in-Publication Data

The social contours of risk / by Jeanne X. Kasperson and Roger E. Kasperson,
with contributors, with the assistance of Mimi Berberian and Lu Ann Pacenka.
     p. cm. – (Risk, society, and policy series)
   Includes bibliographical references and index.
   ISBN 1-84407-073-5 (v. 1 : pbk.) – ISBN 1-84407-072-7 (v. 1 : hardback) –
ISBN 1-84407-175-8 (v. 2 : pbk.) – ISBN 1-84407-176-6 (v. 2 : hardback)
   1. Risk – Sociological aspects. 2. Environmental risk assessment. I. Kasperson,
Jeanne X. II. Kasperson, Roger E. III. Series.
HM1101.S635 2005
302'12–dc22

                                                                    2005003307

Printed on elemental chlorine-free paper

Contents

PART 1 COMMUNICATING RISK AND INVOLVING PUBLICS

PART 2 THE SOCIAL AMPLIFICATION OF RISK

PART 3 RISK AND ETHICS

List of Figures

List of Tables

List of Boxes

Acknowledgements

The intellectual debt of this book to colleagues, collaborators and friends over the past several decades is unusually large; in the 'Introduction and Overview' we try to note some of the more important of these. Beginning with graduate studies at the University of Chicago, Norton Ginsburg, Marvin Mikesell and Gilbert White were exemplary mentors. Our long professional collaboration and friendship with Robert Kates stimulated our interest in hazards research, led Jeanne to work on world hunger for ten years and enriched many of the studies reported on in this volume. Others at the George Perkins Marsh Institute at Clark University who have been important colleagues and collaborators over the years include Christoph Hohenemser, Rob Goble, Billie Turner, Patrick Derr, Dominic Golding, Sam Ratick, Halina Brown and Ortwin Renn. Outside of Clark, we have benefited greatly from our collaborators and friends Bert Bolin, Bill Clark, Kirstin Dow, James Flynn, Howard Kunreuther and Paul Slovic.

Mimi Berberian and Lu Ann Pacenka of the George Perkins Marsh Institute played central roles in the preparation of this book, and it would not have been possible without their generous effort and customary excellence in the multitude of tasks involved in the preparation of a volume for publication. Our good fortune to work with them over the past several decades is something we have valued greatly. Others who contributed significantly to the preparation of the book are Teresa Ogenstad and Erik Willis of the Stockholm Environment Institute.

The authors are also indebted to a variety of funding sources that supported the work in this volume over the years. We wish to note in particular the National Science Foundation, the Nevada Nuclear Waste Project (and particularly Joe Strolin), the United Nations University, the National Oceanic and Atmospheric Administration and the Environmental Protection Agency. The George Perkins Marsh Institute of Clark University and the Stockholm Environment Institute supported the preparation of the book in a variety of ways and we acknowledge our appreciation to them.

Finally, we note the continuing support and joy we have received from our children, Demetri and Kyra.

Roger E. Kasperson, on behalf of
Jeanne X. Kasperson and Roger E. Kasperson
Stockholm, Sweden
June, 2004

Acronyms and Abbreviations

ACGIH	American Conference of Governmental Industrial Hygienists
AE	architect-engineer
AIDS	acquired immune deficiency syndrome
AIR	*All India Reporter*
ALARA	as low as reasonably achievable
AOSIS	Alliance of Small Island States
ASARCO	American Smelting and Refining Company
ASSOCHAM	Associated Chambers of Commerce and Industry of India
BBC	British Broadcasting Corporation
BGH	bovine growth horomone
BRWM	Board on Radioactive Waste Management
BSE	bovine spongiform encephalopathy
BST	bovine somatotrophin
CAER	Community Awareness and Emergency Response
CEGB	Central Electricity Generating Board
CENTED	Center for Technology, Environment, and Development
CEO	Chief Executive Officer
CFC	chlorofluorocarbon
CIA	United States Central Intelligence Agency
CIIT	Chemical Industry Institute of Toxicology
CJD	Creutzfeldt–Jakob disease
CMA	Chemical Manufacturers Association
CPSC	Consumer Product Safety Commission
DAD	decide–announce–defend
DDT	dichlorodiphenyl-trichloroethane
DEA	data envelopment analysis
DFID	Department for International Development
DHHS	Department of Health and Human Services
DNA	deoxyribonucleic acid
DOE	Department of Energy
EDB	ethylene dibromide
EIA	environmental impact assessment
EK-A	Energikommissionens Expertgrupp fur Sakerhat och Miljo
ENSO	El Niño Southern Oscillation

EPA	Environmental Protection Agency
EPRI	Electric Power Research Institute
ERDA	Energy Research and Development Agency
ESRC	Economic and Social Research Council
EU	European Union
EVIST	Ethics and Values in Science and Technology
FAO	Food and Agriculture Organization
FEMA	Federal Emergency Management Agency
FEWS	famine early warning system
FIFRA	Federal Insecticide, Fungicide, Rodenticide Act
FIVIMS	food insecurity and vulnerability mapping system
GACGC	German Advisory Council on Global Change
GAO	General Accounting Office
GATT	General Agreement on Tariffs and Trade
GCMs	general circulation models
GM	genetically modified
GMO	genetically modified organism
GSS	general social survey
HIV	human immunodeficiency virus
HLNW	high-level nuclear wastes
IAEA	International Atomic Energy Agency
ICPS	International Trade Unions of Chemical, Oil and Allied Workers
ICSU	International Council of Scientific Unions
IEO	industry and environment
IFRC	International Federation of Red Cross and Red Crescent Societies
IGU	International Geographical Union
IHDP	International Human Dimensions Programme on Global Environmental Change
IIASA	International Institute for Applied Systems Analysis
IIED	International Institute for Environment and Development
ILO	International Labor Office
INPO	Institute of Nuclear Power Operations
IPAT	impact of population, affluence and technology
IPCC	Intergovernmental Panel on Climate Change
KBS	Kärn-Bränsle-Sakerhet
LISREL	linear structural relationships
LMO	living modified organism
LULUs	locally unwanted land uses
MEF	Ministry of Environment and Forests
MIC	methyl isocyanate
MRS	monitored retrievable storage
MSDSs	material safety data sheets
MTHM	metric tonnes of heavy metal

NACEC	North American Commission for Environmental Cooperation
NBC	National Broadcasting Company
NE NIGEC	Northeast Regional Center of the National Institutes for Global Environmental Change
NEPA	National Environmental Policy Act
NGO	non-governmental organization
NIMBY	not in my backyard
NIMTOF	not in my term of office
NNC	National Nuclear Corporation
NOAA	National Oceanographic and Atmospheric Administration
NORC	National Opinion Research Center
NRC	National Research Council
NRC	Nuclear Regulatory Commission
NSSS	nuclear steam system supplier
NWPA	Nuclear Waste Policy Act
OCRWM	Office of Civilian Radioactive Waste Management
OECD	Organisation for Economic Co-operation and Development
OFDA	Office of US Foreign Disaster Assistance
OMB	Office of Management and Budget
OPEC	Organization of Petroleum Exporting Countries
ORNL	Oak Ridge National Laboratory
OSHA	Occupational Safety and Health Administration
OTA	Office of Technology Assessment
PCB	polychlorinated biphenyl
PRA	probabilistic risk analysis
PWRS	pressurized water reactors
RAINS	Regional Acidification Information and Stimulation
rem	roentgen equivalent in man
R.I.P.	rest in peace
SARA	Superfund Amendments and Reauthorization Act
SARF	social amplification of risk framework
SEI	Stockholm Environment Institute
SEK	Swedish krona
SFFI	Shriram Food and Fertilizer Industries
SRA	Society for Risk Analysis
SSI	Swedish National Radiation Protection Institute
START	SysTem for Analysis, Research and Training
SUPRA	Scottish Universities Policy Research and Advice Network
TLV	Threshold Limit Value
TMI	Three Mile Island
TRIS	flame retardant chemical structure, (2, 3 dibromopropyl) phosphate
TSCA	Toxic Substances Control Act
UCIL	Union Carbide of India Limited

UCS	Union of Concerned Scientists
UN	United Nations
UNCED	United Nations Conference on Environment and Development
UNDP	United Nations Development Programme
UNDRO	United Nations Disaster Relief Organization
UNEP	United Nations Environment Programme
UNFCC	United Nations Frameworks Convention on Climate Change
UNICEF	United Nations International Children Emergency Fund
UNISDR	United Nations International Strategy for Disaster Reduction
UNLV	University of Nevada, Las Vegas
USNUREG	United States Nuclear Regulatory Commission
USOTA	United States Office of Technology Assessment
USSR	Union of Soviet Socialist Republics
VDT	visual display terminal
WBGU	Wissenschaftlicher Beirat Globale Umweltveränderungen
WCED	World Commission on Environment and Development
WHO	World Health Organization
WICEM	World Industry Conference on Environmental Management
WIPP	Waste Isolation Pilot Plant
WTO	World Trade Organization

Introduction and Overview[1]

History

Roger Kasperson and Jeanne Xanthakos met as first year students at Clark University in the autumn of 1955, beginning a college romance that resulted in their marriage in 1959 and what eventually also became a long scholarly collaboration. Loading their few personal belongings and a family cat, as it turned out, into a small U-Haul trailer, they set off for the University of Chicago, where Jeanne commenced graduate studies in English (receiving an MA in 1961), while also working in the University of Chicago Education Library and Roger began his graduate programme in the Geography Department (receiving his PhD in 1966). Geography at Chicago was a hotbed at that time, under the direction of Gilbert F. White, for the creation of a field of natural hazards research and cross-disciplinary research on environmental issues. While Roger was pursuing a programme focused on political geography, the tutelage of Marvin Mikesell, Norton S. Ginsburg and Gilbert White had an important and lasting influence on his interest in human nature studies, and introduced both Roger and Jeanne to a talented cadre of fellow graduate students (e.g. Robert Kates, Ian Burton and Tom Saarinen) who were pushing the boundaries of environmental geography. Meanwhile, Jeanne was also extending the library skills that eventually became a professional career track.

After stints at the Massachusetts State College at Bridgewater, the University of Connecticut and Michigan State University, where Jeanne held library and Roger teaching positions, and a brief stint at the University of Puerto Rico where both served as researchers, Roger accepted a joint position in government and geography at Clark University and Jeanne spent the next six years at home with two young children. It was at Clark that both Roger and Jeanne developed professional interests in risk research.

Entrance to risk work

It all began with an educational innovation. In the early 1970s, many colleges and universities instituted a brief term – January term – between the two semesters during which innovative teaching and learning experiences would occur. At Clark, this promised such inviting things as field research on environmental problems in Puerto Rico and the Virgin Islands (geographers know where to go during New England winters!). On this occasion, in 1972, Chris Hohenemser had challenged Robert Kates and Roger Kasperson to apply their natural hazards frameworks and thinking to 'a really complicated problem – the nuclear fuel cycle'. The result was an extremely rich dialogue between geographers and physicists that highlighted a host of risk issues and questions. When the Ford Foundation shortly thereafter, in 1973, announced a new research initiative centred on important interdisciplinary problems, the Clark group applied, won one of the several grants awarded, and a new collaboration on technological risk that was to last for several decades got off the ground.

While the nuclear fuel cycle work led to an important publication interpreting 'The distrust of nuclear power' in *Science* (Hohenemser et al, 1977), more importantly it revealed the need for stronger theoretical and analytical underpinnings to the young field of risk analysis. During the late 1970s, as Jeanne was joining the Clark risk group as its bibliographer and librarian, we applied to the new risk programme in the National Science Foundation and secured several grants to work on foundational ideas and approaches to the study of risk.

Using a style of working based on an interdisciplinary team, bridging the natural and social sciences, that was to become a hallmark of Clark risk research, we undertook analyses treating the causal structure of risk, a framework for analysing risk management, a taxonomy of technological risk and a large number of case studies to which these analytical structures were applied. *Perilous Progress: Managing the Hazards of Technology* (Kates et al, 1985), with Jeanne as co-editor and both of us as contributors to many of the individual chapters, brought together these results. In the two volumes that follow, several chapters emerge from this foundational work of the late 1970s and early 1980s. We took, for example, the pervasive question of the time: how safe is safe enough? We argued (Volume II, Chapter 1) that this is a normative question to which no simple answer suffices. What is 'acceptable' or 'tolerable' is essentially a decision problem in which broad considerations of risk, benefits, industrial structure, equity and technological development enter. Such problems are better treated from the standpoint of process than by such 'fixes' as '1 in 1 million risk' or 'best practicable technology'. With David Pijawka, we drew upon hazard frameworks to compare natural and technological hazards, especially the shifting patterns of risk apparent in both developed and developing societies, the greater difficulties that technological risks pose for management, and the potential role of the therapeutic community during risk emergencies (Volume II, Chapter 2). This chapter also explored the possibility of using common analytical approaches in some depth.

From this basic work on technological risks, we identified a number of new research directions. One that resulted in sustained work involved the intertwining of risk management with value and ethical questions, exploration of issues that were to continue to occupy our research attention to the current time and helped inform our later work, treated in detail in this volume (Volume I), on the social amplification of risk.

RISK, ETHICS AND VALUES

Our work on nuclear risks brought home the realization that the most difficult risk problems are nearly always heavily value laden. This even involves the definition of risk, something about which people tend not to agree. Early in its history the Society of Risk Analysis sponsored an effort to reach a consensual definition of 'risk', and commissioned a committee for that purpose. After a year of work it was apparent that defining risk was essentially a political act and the committee gave up on its effort. Indeed, risk controversies suggest that it is often not the magnitude or probabilities of specific risks upon which interested parties disagree, but more basically what the risk of concern in the panoply of effects should be and what sign (positive or negative) should be associated with certain postulated changes.

Work on the nuclear fuel cycle highlighted the problem of nuclear waste, an issue largely underestimated and neglected in the US and elsewhere. Alvin Weinberg (1977) was not alone in designating this problem as the one in the nuclear fuel cycle that he had most underestimated. Our work suggested strongly the need to tackle the underlying problems of what we termed 'locus' and 'legacy', how the value problems involved in putting waste in someone's backyard or exporting the risks and burdens of management to future generations could be overcome. These questions stimulated what was to be a decade of work on a series of projects supported by a new National Science Foundation programme: 'Ethics and Values in Science and Technology (EVIST)'. Specifically, the 'locus and legacy' effort addressed the issue of how wastes could be equitably stored at one place for the benefit of a large and diffuse population at many other places, as well as how the burdens and risks of waste management could be equitably distributed over this generation, which has made the decisions and reaped most of the benefits, and future generations, which have had no voice in decisions and will bear the long-term burdens.

This early foray into risk and equity issues led in two directions. Firstly, together with earlier work on the nuclear fuel cycle, we began an extended project on the complex of social, equity and risk questions contained in radioactive waste management. This resulted in a book on *Equity Issues in Radioactive Waste Management* (Kasperson, 1983a) in which we and others identified and assessed a number of equity problems, as well as explored alternative principles of social justice that could be brought to bear on them. One of us (R.E.K.), during this period, also served two terms on the

National Research Council's Board on Radioactive Waste Management and chaired the panel that produced the report *Social and Economic Aspects of Radioactive Waste Disposal* (United States National Research Council (USNRC), 1984b). Eventually, we and others at Clark participated as members of a remarkable team of social scientists assembled by the state of Nevada to assess the social and economic impacts of the proposed Yucca Mountain nuclear waste repository (see Chapter 8 of this volume). Then in Chapter 14 of this volume we summarize the history of the nuclear waste adventure and the social and value issues that have pervaded the siting process. Specifically, it criticizes the 'tunnel vision' that has been apparent in the repository developmental effort and the focus of this vision on technical issues to the exclusion of the equity and trust issues that have driven societal concern in Nevada and elsewhere. Chapter 15 (this volume) then generalizes these equity issues to a much broader array of siting undertakings, both in the US and other countries. The latter chapter assesses the underlying problems that have stalemated siting ventures in many countries, contrasts the major approaches that have evolved, and prescribes a series of innovations in process and substantive equity aimed at getting the process through 'roadblocks' and securing greater success in outcomes.

The second line of work involved uncovering new risk equity problems that needed consideration. While analysing the difference in radiation standards used for workers and publics, for example, we discovered that this was only one example of what we came to term the 'double standard' in risk protection, namely that it was legally permissible to expose workers to much higher levels of risk than publics. 'What ethical systems supported such a position?' we asked. Chapter 12 in this volume reports on the results of a National Science Foundation project that identified the moral arguments used to support differential protection and analyses and then tested the validity of each of these arguments and their assumptions. The chapter concludes that the assumptions supporting many of the propositions are flawed and based on incomplete or erroneous evidence, such as the view that workers are compensated for the higher risk and voluntarily undertake them, and argues that steps should be taken to narrow or eliminate the divergence in risk standards and to afford workers greater protection.

In the various case studies of different equity problems, it became apparent that a framework for analysing equity issues was badly needed. As a result, in 1991, working with Kirstin Dow in the context of global environmental problems, we formulated such a framework (see Chapter 13, this volume). It allows for the treatment of a number of equity problems, including both geographical equity (the not-in-my-backyard, or NIMBY, issue) and temporal equity (fairness over current and future generations). Since it combines an empirical analysis of the 'facts' of existing or projected inequities with the ability to apply different normative principles to the distributions, analysts or decision makers could use the framework drawing upon their own definitions of social justice. Finally, the framework provides for the application of different management systems for responding to the risk equity problems, including means for building greater procedural equity.

Finally, as part of a larger effort during the second half of the 1990s that concentrated on the most vulnerable peoples and places, we examined the global social justice problems that climate change may pose for international efforts to address global warming. In Chapter 16, this volume, we argue that the current Kyoto process fails to treat the range of equity issues involved and, as a result, is unlikely to be successful until such questions are internalized. This includes not only differential past and future greenhouse gas emissions, but also the distribution of impacts that have already begun and differing abilities to deal with such impacts. We set forth in this chapter both principles of social justice that should be recognized and a 'resilience strategy' to supplement initiatives aimed at reducing emissions worldwide.

CORPORATIONS AS RISK MANAGERS

Our studies of risk management during the late 1970s and early 1980s had convinced us and others in the Clark group that those closest to the technologies and production processes were in the best position to be able to manage risks, if only they could be trusted with the social mandate to protect the public and the environment. A study of the Bhopal accident, undertaken with B. Bowonder of the Administrative Staff College in Hyderabad, provided a dramatic and poignant case of how industrial management of risk can go wrong. The results of the post-mortem study of the accident are set forth in Volume II, Chapter 5. Bhopal revealed how essential management attention to both safety design and ongoing management systems and attention to risk 'vigilance' was, but how important safety culture, auditing and high-level management priority to risk were as well. Furthermore, Bhopal suggested the need for public authorities to exercise monitoring and control over what happens in individual corporations and plants. In a follow-up assessment (see Volume II, Chapter 8) some decades later with B. Bowonder, we assessed what had been learned from the accident and the extent to which India was better prepared to deal with future industrial risks and another possible Bhopal. As might be expected, the progress we saw was greatest at the level of policy and standards and weakest at the level of monitoring, implementation and enforcement.

Bhopal was not the only case of industrial disaster that drew our attention. Some years earlier the accident at the Three Mile Island nuclear plant in Pennsylvania had produced major concerns over the adequacy of emergency planning around nuclear plants in the US. With the aid of a grant from the public fund established in the aftermath of the Three Mile Island plant accident, we broadly assessed the state of emergency planning for nuclear plants in the US, the major results of which appear in Chapter 6, Volume II. The review was not reassuring as to management plans for emergency response. The general approach was to try to 'engineer' local responses to accidents, and as much as possible to use 'command-and-control' procedures built upon military models of communication and organization. In Chapter 6 (Volume II) we argue, by contrast, that emergency management designs should build upon the adaptive behaviour of people at risk and intentionally seek to create rich information environments that allow people to exercise informed judgements and adaptive behaviour as they select protective strategies. In short, the chapter is a call for a major overhaul of approaches to managing serious industrial accidents.

The Bhopal and Three Mile Island accidents, taken together with the many case studies of risk management appearing in *Perilous Progress*, pointed to the need for a deeper understanding of how corporations actually went about the task of managing risks. And so we initiated an effort in the mid-1980s to survey what was known about the corporate management of product and occupational risks. Chapter 4 in Volume II, taken from *Corporate Management of Health and Safety Hazards: A Comparison of Current Practice* (Kasperson et al, 1988a), argues that corporate risk management is 'terra incognita'. Despite an extensive industrial trade literature and numerous exposés of particular failures, little was known systematically about the structures, practices and resources employed by corporations in their risk work. But the chapter does report on a number of findings emerging from case studies and the secondary literature: that corporations vary widely in the types and effectiveness of their risk management efforts, that a variety of exogenous and endogenous factors helped to explain the variance, and that much more systematic and in-depth research was needed to fill out the many empty spaces in our current knowledge. The analysis also called attention to what might be termed the 'shadow' regulatory system that exists in corporations of processes that assess risk, set standards, audit performance and seek to ensure the implementation of decisions. But, again, research is needed to build upon the existing sketchy state of empirical understanding of what actually happens in corporations and how decisions are really made.

This general study of corporate risk management highlighted the role that corporate culture, sometimes termed 'safety culture', plays in risk management. In a project focused on the risk and ethical issues involved in the transfer of technology and the location of plants by multinational corporations in developing countries, we undertook a case study of DuPont Corporation – a firm noted for having one of the most advanced corporate safety cultures – in its location of a new plant in Thailand. The study, reported in Chapter 7 of Volume II, examined the literature on corporate culture and then analysed the extent to which corporate culture considerations actually entered into the location and development of the DuPont plant and how conflicting objectives were negotiated and resolved. While the seriousness of replicating DuPont safety goals and performance in Thailand was quite apparent, the case also indicates the challenges arising from cross-cultural contexts and ways in which corporate culture may interfere with other goals involved in technology transfer. This is an issue of considerable importance to sustainable development programmes globally.

RISK COMMUNICATION AND PUBLIC PARTICIPATION

As the recognition of the limits to risk regulation grew during the 1980s, interest increased in the possibilities for managing risk through better communication of risks to the public and through greater involvement of publics in risk decisions. This impetus received considerable motive force through the support of Williams Ruckelshaus in his second term as Administrator of the US Environmental Protection Agency, and his use of risk communication as a central ingredient in a regulatory decision involving the release of arsenic into the air by an American Smelting and Refining Company (ASARCO) smelter in Tacoma, Washington in 1983. While the results of this process were ambiguous and controversial, risk communication became a central topic of management interest, not only in the Environmental Protection Agency (EPA) but in private corporations and state environmental agencies as well. Risk communication rapidly became a dominant topic at annual meetings of the Society for Risk Analysis and the risk communication group became one of the Society's largest specialty groups. In 1986, the EPA sponsored the first National Conference on Risk Communication, attended by 500 delegates. Later, in a searching overall assessment of literature and experience, the National Research Council published *Improving Risk Communication* (USNRC, 1989).

In this first generation of risk communication studies during the 1980s, the orientation was both simplistic and specific. Drawing from advertising and public relations, the risk communication task was conceived of as identifying 'target audiences', designing the 'right messages' and using the 'right channels'. Public relations people were viewed as the relevant experts for the risk communication job, and the task of facilitating discourse about complex risks as being, intrinsically, no different to selling soap. And engineering risk communication 'targets', 'channels' and 'messages' were seen to be the approach.

Predictably, these first generation efforts produced meagre encouraging results and, by the end of the 1980s, the limits of risk communication programmes were becoming painfully evident. Obviously risk communication, heretofore the domain of advertising and public relations firms, needed to be informed by psychometric and cultural studies of risk perception and, equally importantly, communication needed to be integrated with empowering of those at risk and with more democratic procedures in risk decision making.

A recognition also grew that the primary risk communication problem involved the failure of risk managers to listen to those who were bearing the risks and to act upon their feedback. So the decade of infatuation with risk communication as a 'fix' to the management problem ran its course and more sophisticated approaches began to evolve, essentially the 'second generation' of risk studies.

The Clark group made several modest contributions to this evolution. First, with Ingar Palmlund, we proposed a framework for evaluating risk communication programmes (see Chapter 3, this volume). This format argued that evaluation needed to begin as soon, or even before, the communication programme began. And it needed to be collaborative, so that publics participated in defining what the programme goals would be and what outcomes should be pursued. Properly designed, we argued, evaluation should be integrated with the substance and procedures of the communication programme, so that mid-course corrections could be undertaken to continue to develop the programme as it moved forward.

But we were also concerned that risk communication be integrated more generally with efforts to empower publics and to enhance their participation in risk decision making. Much earlier, we had prepared a resource paper for the Association of American Geographers dealing with public participation and advocacy planning (Kasperson and Breitbart, 1974). We went back into the extensive literature that had developed during the 1970s and early 1980s to glean major propositions that were consensual findings from previous analyses and experience. Chapter 1 (this volume) provides the results of that foray, which were published in *Risk Analysis*.

Interestingly, as experience with risk communication grew during the second half of the 1980s and the 1990s, the appeal of risk communication as an answer to how the various problems of risk management might be resolved using non-regulatory approaches began to fade. The mixed success of risk communication experience contributed to this, as well as critiques of 'message engineering' from various precincts of the social sciences. And the pendulum swung to strategies aimed at what came to be termed 'stakeholder involvement', which was increasingly seen both as a principal mechanism for informing risk managers of public concerns and values and as a means for winning the support of various participants in the process. And soon, through various federal and state agencies, stakeholder involvement had replaced risk communication as the required ingredient of any risk management effort, and 'focus groups' had become the preferred tool. As with risk communication a decade earlier, little substantive engagement with the conflicting purposes and complexities in achieving effective public participation occurred, leading us to prepare a short cautionary statement on the euphoria for the 'stakeholder express', provided in Chapter 5 of this volume. Nonetheless, the uncritical embrace of stakeholder involvement continues at the time of writing, not only in the US and Europe but in developing countries as well, where it is supplemented by mandatory efforts at 'capacity building'.

It is still important, of course, to draw together what has been learned from a wide range of experience and scholarly analysis. We were asked in 1997 to take stock of the risk communication efforts of two decades as they bore upon industrial accidents and emergency planning. In Chapter 4, this volume, we reviewed the various approaches that had developed over time to risk communication, pointing to the strengths and limits of each. We then proposed, drawing upon our social amplification research discussed below, that an integrative approach needed to be taken to designing effective programmes. Using that as a base, we then proposed a series of practical guides or advice to corporate and government officials charged with developing and implementing risk communication with various publics.

THE SOCIAL AMPLIFICATION OF RISK

By the mid-1980s, risk studies had gone through a period of rapid foment and development. The Society for Risk Analysis had been created and enjoyed rapid growth, a new risk and decision programme had been established in the National Science Foundation, and the National Research Council had published an influential study, *Risk Assessment in the Federal Government: Managing the Process* that encouraged the use of risk analysis in support of regulatory decision making (USNRC, 1983). And yet, progress in conceptual approaches appeared limited due to the separation of natural and technological hazards, each of which had its own journals, professional societies, and annual meetings; social and technical analyses of risks that proceeded largely independently from one another; and the preoccupation among social scientists with quarrels over which risk approach (the psychometric model, cultural theory, or economic analysis) should be preferred. The risk field, in short, appeared hamstrung by fragmented thinking and the lack of overarching analysis.

It was also at this time (1986 to be exact) that we were drawn, with other risk scholars, into what would become a remarkable chapter in social science research. The state of Nevada was a candidate site for the development of a high-level nuclear waste repository and had decided to embark on a programme of social and economic studies to identify and assess what impacts the state might experience as a result of both the consideration process and then the development of the facility itself. The study team assembled boasted diverse experience and talents, and included such prominent risk scholars as Paul Slovic, Jim Flynn, Howard Kunreuther, Bill Freudenburg, Alvin Mushkatel and David Pijawka. But the state also assembled a remarkable technical review committee chaired by Gilbert F. White that included the likes of the economist Allen Kneese, the sociologist Kai Erikson and the anthropologist Roy Rappaport. The research group interacted intensely with these advisers over a decade of collaborative work, producing not only several hundred articles and technical reports but breaking new ground on a number of risk issues and constructs.

One of these was the social amplification of risk framework. In 1986, as part of our review of risk analyses performed in support of the US Department of Energy's (DOE's) high-level radioactive waste management programme, we were pondering what effects small accidents in the transportation or operational system at the repository, or perhaps even significant mishaps in management without major radiation releases, might have on the programme. From past work, we recognized that such risk events would be likely to receive high levels of media attention and close public scrutiny. Paul Slovic (1987) was developing the concept of 'risk signals', risk events or occurrences that suggest to the public that the risk is more serious or difficult to manage than had been previously assumed. So we began a discussion with Paul Slovic and his colleagues at Decision Research about how we might analyse such issues, and together we started to try to describe, in schematic or simple conceptual form, what processes would be likely to emerge where things go wrong concerning risks that are widely feared. The team at Clark that worked intensively on this was made up of the Kaspersons, Rob Goble, Sam Ratick, and Ortwin Renn. Alternative schematic frameworks flowed back and forth between Clark and Decision Research until the two groups reached agreement, in the form of an article for *Risk Analysis*. This piece, reproduced as Chapter 6 of this volume, stimulated lively debate from those who commented on it in the journal and also a vigorous exploration of the conceptual framework by not only the original authors but many others over the next 15 years. Indeed, in terms of our own work, we subsequently wrote some 17 published articles or book chapters expanding on the framework and applying it to a broad array of risk issues and situations.

'The social amplification of risk' sought to produce an integrative framework which could be used to integrate both technical and social aspects of risk, but would also bring under one roof the findings from a variety of theoretical and social science perspectives. The intention was to examine the major structures of society that enter into the processing of risk and risk events. This processing can be either proactive, in anticipation of risk events, or reactive to them. We define 'social stations' that are active in processing or augmenting the flow of risk 'signals' and interpreting their social meaning. The actions of these social stations may either dampen the flow of signals, as in risk *attenuation*, or amplify them, as in risk *amplification*. Both affect the rippling of consequences in time and space. Highly socially amplified risks have ripples that extend beyond the immediately affected persons or institutions, and may have large effects upon distant actors. Highly attenuated risks, by contrast, typically have low visibility, and concern and impacts are restricted to those most directly affected.

The social amplification framework proved to be highly useful not only for the various studies conducted in the Nevada project on high-level radioactive waste management but for other risk issues as well. In Chapter 7 of this volume, for example, we ask the question: 'how is it, given all the ongoing attention to risks in the media and elsewhere, that certain risks pass unnoticed or unattended, growing in size until they have taken a serious toll?' Using notions from the social amplification framework, we explored the phenomena of 'hidden hazards' and found a variety of causes and explanations. Some hazards, such as those we term 'global elusive hazards', remain hidden because of the nature of the risks themselves. Elusive global hazards, such as acid rain and global warming, for example, have widely diffuse effects that are difficult to pinpoint in particular times or places. Some risks, by contrast, are widely attenuated due to society's ideological structures, and so in the US occupational risks, for example, have often generated little concern. Other risks are concentrated among marginal peoples who have little access to political power or the media, therefore hunger and famines often grow in severity and scope before they are 'discovered' by society's watchdogs or monitoring institutions. Meanwhile, socially amplified and value-threatening hazards, such as genetically modified foods, spark social clashes and conflicts while attenuated hazards generate yawns over the breakfast table.

Risk signals occupy an important place in social amplification thinking. But except for Paul Slovic's hypothesis that particular risk events have high signal value, little attention had been given to the types of signals that exist or the effects they might have. Therefore, working with Betty Jean Perkins, Ortwin Renn and Allen White, as recounted in Chapter 8 of this volume, we undertook an analysis of the flow of risk signals related to the nuclear waste repository issue in the major newspaper of Las Vegas. This necessitated the development of a methodology for identifying and analysing risk signals. We also created a taxonomy of risk signals for classifying the kinds of interpretation and inferences involved. The analysis of the flow of signals in the major Las Vegas newspaper pointed clearly to a major shift in the focus of the Nevada nuclear waste repository debate, from one initially centred on traditional risk and benefit issues to one almost wholly preoccupied with equity, social trust and the use of political power. Risk signal analyses are a promising new approach to understanding the social contours of risk but have yet to be fully developed by us or other social risk analysts.

Another aspect of risk emerging from the Nevada studies and one closely related to the social amplification of risk is the concept of stigma. In the nuclear waste context, the intense media coverage of repository-related risks and the social conflict surrounding the repository siting process has a large potential to stigmatize places under consideration for repository sites (invariably termed as 'dumps') and perhaps the waste disposal technology itself. These issues are explored in depth in *Risk, Media and Stigma: Understanding Public Challenges to Modern Science and Technology* (Flynn et al, 2001). As part of the effort on the stigma issue, we were asked to apply the social amplification framework to the development of stigma. This analysis, reported in Chapter 9 of this volume, modified the social amplification framework to focus it directly on stigma evolution and effects. We give particular attention, drawing both on the stigma and amplification literatures, to how people, places, or technologies come to be 'marked', how this marking, over time, changes the identity by which people view themselves, and finally how identity changes in the perceptions of others. Clearly, the social amplification of risks can constitute a powerful process in marking and identity change. And stigma becomes not only a consequence and part of the 'rippling' of effects but also a causal factor in future amplification processes.

During the late 1990s, the UK Health and Safety Executive had become interested in the social amplification of risk framework and had instituted a research programme on that theme. In 1999, with Nick Pidgeon and Paul Slovic, we convened a workshop in the UK that brought together researchers who had been working on social amplification concepts, themes and applications, and a series of papers was subsequently published in *The Social Amplification of Risk* (Pidgeon et al, 2003). For the workshop and volume, we joined with Pidgeon and Slovic in a stocktaking of social amplification work over the past 15 years, as reported in Chapter 11 of this volume. This overview reviews the principal scholarly debates that have emerged around the social amplification framework, major findings from empirical research on the concepts, diverse applications that have been undertaken, and unresolved issues that remain to be addressed. Sessions at the World Congress on Risk in 2003 showcased yet another array of empirical and theoretical studies, indicating that the framework continues to be useful for a range of social studies of risk and policy applications.

THE GLOBALIZATION OF RISK

Global environmental risk, we have noted elsewhere (Kasperson and Kasperson 2001b), is the ultimate threat. What is at stake is the survival of the planet itself, and the life-support systems it provides for humans and other species. At the same time, the risks are highly uncertain, and only partially knowable and manageable. The risk portfolios of individual countries and places are also becoming progressively more global in their sources. And so the increasing globalization of risk confronts humans with some of their most challenging and perplexing risk problems.

For some time our interests in global risks had been growing, as reflected in our writings with B. Bowonder (Chapters 5, 8 and 9 of Volume II), our international studies of comparative management of the nuclear fuel cycle (Chapter 3 of Volume II), and the decade that one of us (J.X.K.) spent at the World Hunger Program at Brown University during the 1980s and 1990s (see Newman, 1990). But two events – one international and one local – accelerated our attention to the global arena. The World Commission on Environment and Development (WCED, 1987) report clearly demarcated the need for concerted attention to changes in the basic biogeochemical cycles of the earth and the threats that human activities posed for the long-term security and well-being of the planet. It also called for an international programme of risk research to build the necessary knowledge base. At about the same time, Clark University hosted a landmark international conference entitled 'The Earth as Transformed by Human Action' (Turner et al, 1990a) that documented and assessed human-driven changes in the planet over the last 300 years. At Clark, this led us to join forces with Bill Turner and his research group who were examining human transformation of the planet, particularly in terms of land use, land cover and agricultural systems.

The concrete result of this new collaboration was a major international project entitled 'Critical Environmental Zones', which was to occupy a decade of effort analysing nine high-risk regions of the world (the Olgallala aquifer, the Basin of Mexico, Amazonia, the North Sea, the Aral Sea, Ukambani in Kenya, the Ordos Plateau of China, the Middle Hills of Nepal, and the Sundaland area of Southeast Asia). The goals were unabashedly ambitious – to understand the principal human driving forces in each of these regions, the human and ecosystem vulnerabilities, and the patterns of human response that arose to deal with the risks and their effects. And, as with the social amplification work, we sought integrative frameworks crossing the natural and social sciences in each of the regions. The work was also avowedly collaborative in that scientists indigenous to the regions were involved in each of the regional assessments.

The project taught us a great deal, both about the challenges of integrative work and how comparative studies can actually be achieved when everyone has their own pet interests and differing theoretical perspectives. We particularly came to believe in the importance of process – the need to formulate team-oriented questions and formats, frequent project meetings where research designs and initial findings are presented and defended, and successive 'approximations' of what the emerging comparative findings are. Eventually over the ten years of effort, a major comparative volume (Kasperson et al, 1995) and five regional books (see Chapter 11 of Volume II) appeared. Although the regions had been selected because they were seriously environmentally threatened areas, the results were nonetheless sobering: each region had distinctive arrays of human driving forces; state policies and globalization processes were assuming increased importance; high vulnerability was apparent in many subgroups and marginal areas; and policy interventions aimed at controlling driving forces and mitigating impacts and vulnerabilities were lagging seriously behind the pace of environmental degradation. So, while the Earth Summit in Johannesburg in 2002 could point to many good works and scattered successes in the first generation of sustainability work, *Regions at Risk* details that, however commendable these efforts, evidence abounds that we are losing ground. Chapter 11 in Volume II details the major findings at some length.

As we worked on regional patterns of environmental change in different parts of the globe, vulnerability issues were assuming a growing prominence in our analyses. And, of course, our sustained work on equity issues had invariably involved questions of differential vulnerability to risk. In the mid-1990s vulnerability research showed many of the same patterns and characteristics that the risk field as a whole had a decade earlier. Despite the fact that vulnerability is an integral part of the risk – threat is an interaction between stresses and perturbation and the degree of vulnerability that exists among receptor systems to them – the social science community researching the risk field had not given concerted attention to the assessment of vulnerability. Such attention as had occurred had come largely from analysts working on natural hazards and climate impacts, but they were heavily divided between the ecological and social science communities, while, in addition, the social scientists themselves were fragmented into competing ideological and theoretical camps. Indeed, a common view during the 1990s was that 'social vulnerability' was what really mattered, and thus linkages and interactions with ecosystems and ecosystem services could be left to others. Meanwhile, a variety of international efforts, such as those on the Intergovernmental Panel on Climate Change, the International Human Dimensions Programme, the emerging Millennium Ecosystem Assessment, and agencies such as the United Nations Environment Programme and the United Nations Development Programme had identified vulnerability as a priority issue. Expectations were high for what vulnerability assessment could deliver. And so the time seemed right to convene some of the leaders in vulnerability research to take stock of the state of theory and research and to explore whether broad-based, more integrative approaches could be identified.

So, with support from the International Human Dimensions Programme and the Land Use, Land Cover Research Program, we convened a workshop at the Stockholm Environment Institute to assess research and practice in this field. The discussions indicated that, while many differences remained among competing approaches, it might indeed be possible to find a middle ground. Many agreed that a common conceptual framework, such as that presented by Clark and the Stockholm Environment Institute (Kasperson and Kasperson, 2001a, p16), was essential for greater cumulative progress in the field. But it was also apparent that two requirements in particular stood out: (1) whatever framework emerged needed to treat the basic receptor as a social-ecological system, as researchers in the Resilience Alliance had been doing (Berkes and Folke, 1998); and (2) that empirical applications and validation of any conceptual framework were high priorities.

Earlier, we (along with George Clark and others) had been part of an effort to assess human vulnerability to severe storms along the northeast coast of the US (see Chapter 12 of Volume II). This analysis sought to assess the multiple dimensions of vulnerability in the coastal community of Revere, Massachusetts and to integrate physical dimensions of risk with social vulnerabilities to them, drawing upon census data in particular for the latter. Data envelope analysis was then used to analyse the results and maps were prepared that captured the interactions between physical and social risk. Drawing upon that study and the workshop results, and collaborating with Bill Turner, Wen Hsieh and Andrew Schiller, we developed a lengthy analysis of the fundamental issues involved in vulnerability, with a particular focus on creating a sound conceptual framework that captured the essential elements and dynamics of vulnerability (Chapter 14, Volume II). This work also benefited greatly from interactions with a research team convened by Bill Clark at Harvard University and two intensive workshops held at Airlie House in the US that reviewed and contributed to our thinking in Chapter 14 (Volume II). Vulnerability analysis poses a major challenge in global change assessments and the need for sustained efforts on this in future research topics remains clear .

HUSBAND AND WIFE COLLABORATION

Over the past 25 years, as a husband and wife team, we have worked together on some 40–50 research projects, written or co-edited eight books and monographs, and co-authored some 50 articles, chapters and technical reports related to the subject of this book, *The Social Contours of Risk*. The question has been often posed to us – how do you work together so much and still manage to have dinner together every night? So some comments on this may be of interest to some of the readers of this volume.

Typically, we were both heavily involved, often along with other colleagues at Clark or elsewhere, in designing research projects. Since we almost invariably worked in a context of interdisciplinary collaborative research, we often sought to have something like a 'mini-seminar' to talk through a research issue with colleagues in order to determine what the central questions should be and how the research would be focused. Roger often played a role in helping to organize and structure these discussions; Jeanne was typically the expert on literature and bibliography and was always the meeting scribe. Jeanne also always sat quietly in a corner of the room, talking little but listening carefully and thus was always the best source as to who said what and why (a precious skill; we know how good most men are at the listening function!).

As for collaboration in writing, we would always talk through what the central questions for a particular piece would be, what the argument was that would run through the work, and how it would be organized. We would then prepare an outline on which we agreed. Roger would usually write the first draft. Jeanne would review the draft and then, armed with a host of questions and issues, discuss what she saw as the necessary revisions. After these had been talked through, Jeanne would write the revised version. Roger would review this, raise remaining issues, and Jeanne would subsequently write the final and polished draft for publication. Over time, we got quite good at this style of working and could be reasonably productive in our joint writing.

While we were both at the Stockholm Environment Institute, on leave from Clark in 2002, Jeanne died unexpectedly while this book was in process. The book is lovingly dedicated to her.

Roger E. Kasperson
Stockholm
June, 2004

NOTES

1   This Introduction and Overview, slightly modified, also appears in Volume II.

Part 1

Communicating Risk and Involving Publics

1 Six Propositions on Public Participation and Their Relevance for Risk Communication

Roger E. Kasperson

New societal obligations for communicating risk information are emerging in a variety of contexts. This chapter draws upon the lengthy societal experience with citizen participation programmes to identify how risk communication efforts may be effectively structured and implemented. Six major propositions address such themes as means/ends differences in expectations, the timing of the programme, the role of credibility and trust, the need for technical and analytical resources, differing thresholds of public involvement and limitations upon current understandings. Key conclusions for the design of risk communication programmes are set forth.

INTRODUCTION

A time of community right-to-know laws, burgeoning liability claims and expectations for citizen participation imposes new societal obligations for communicating about risk. The growing obligation for communication reflects not only an increasing public concern over hazards of technology, but also a long-term movement for public participation (which has its roots in the civil rights and environmental movements of the 1960s) and the associated values embodied in the National Environmental Policy Act, the Freedom of Information Act and right-to-know requirements of specific health and safety regulations.

Notable risk events have provided added impetus. Three Mile Island revealed serious deficiencies in the transfer of risk information from officials of the utility and the Nuclear Regulatory Commission to nearby publics. At Love Canal, widely conflicting and fluctuating reports of the

Note: Reprinted from *Risk Analysis*, vol 6, Kasperson, R. E., 'Six propositions on public participation and their relevance for risk communication', pp275–281, © (1986), with permission from Blackwell Publishing

potential danger of the wastes exacerbated the fears of residents. Efforts to site hazardous waste facilities have sparked emotional confrontations over risk questions across the nation. In 1985 the US Environmental Protection Agency (EPA) confessed its inadequate communication of risk to concerned individuals and public officials during the handling of the ethylene dibromide (EDB) controversy and has since enlisted science writers for a new programme to improve the agency's handling of risk communication (Friendly, 1985). The Seveso Directive in Europe and the Bhopal accident in India have led to new regulatory obligations and to newly perceived responsibilities by chemical companies to communicate to community officials and residents about chemical inventories and emergency response plans. This growing communication obligation is becoming institutionalized through state and local right-to-know ordinances, increased labelling responsibilities for consumer products, upgraded industry programmes for informing about chemical hazards and a generic hazard communication regulation to inform workers of risk. In short, a wide variety of arenas harbours a growing social imperative that those possessing special knowledge of risk will communicate it to potential risk bearers and other interested parties.

The expectation, alas, exceeds considerably the current knowledge of when, how, by whom, to whom, and under what conditions such communication should occur. Clearly, a pressing need exists to enlarge our understanding of effective risk communication through examination of relevant experience, situations and disciplinary perspectives. This discussion addresses a number of implications that the lengthy societal experience with citizen participation may have for new risk communication efforts. It does so through a consideration of six major propositions that are well established in the literature and experience of citizen participation. The selection of these particular propositions reflects a preference for well-established empirical generalizations, for grounding in conceptual structures, and for relevance to the risk communication problem.

PROPOSITION 1: Conflicts emerging in public participation efforts often centre upon means/ends differences in expectations

Different individuals bring different expectations to the participation (or risk consideration) enterprise. The public official tends to see an instrumental role for public participation – it is a means to accomplish particular ends, often those included in an agency mandate (protect health and safety) or those associated with bureaucratic objectives (e.g. build a base of support for agency plans, protect the agency from outside attacks). Thus, agency-designed participation efforts characteristically recognize goals such as 'correcting misperception', 'educating the public', 'reducing conflict', 'easing implementation' or 'increasing legitimacy'. Public participants, by contrast, tend to approach the participatory effort with an ends goal. In particular, if the prospective participant is also a risk bearer, the participation process characteristically involves a struggle not only over the level of risk that is appropriate (or tolerable), but how powers in the decision process will be allocated and who will make the decision. In such contexts, the communication of risk to the risk bearer becomes part of the political struggle – it inevitably stimulates escalating demands for more risk information and tends to be viewed as an invitation to discuss the ethics of risk imposition, the roles of the risk bearer and the risk allocator in deciding the level of risk to be tolerated, and means for redressing the risk allocation decision.

Two classic treatments of typologies of public participation nicely illustrate these differing approaches. Viewing participation from the stance of the bureaucrat, Edmund Burke (1968) sees the lay public as a resource for the agency, an instrument for improving intelligence, a means for maximizing rationality, a catalyst for implementing decisions. The preferred approach to public participation in this view involves 'behavioural change' (changing the attitudes and behaviour of the public through group involvement) and 'staff supplement' (supplementing the expertise of the organization with the knowledge and perspective of individual citizens). Sherry Arnstein, by contrast, in her well-known 'ladder of citizen participation', ranks participation strategies preferentially according to the amount of power accorded to members of the public (Arnstein, 1969). In essence, participation is a struggle by the 'have-nots' to wrest away power from the 'haves'.

Nowhere has this conflict in expectations been more apparent than in the Superfund hazardous waste clean-up. Inevitably, the EPA seeks to provide accurate information, including uncertainties as to the risks that the wastes pose to residents of nearby communities. Nearly always, the Agency operates with a limited base of information from which only guarded risk statements are possible. The Agency also inherits the legacy of how the problems were originally created, and the community tends to focus on the inadequacies in the process that generated the risks. The battles that flow are less about the exact magnitude of risk or even how 'clean is clean enough' than who will control decisions on the disposition of risk. In this context, risk communication becomes a vehicle of protest by which community groups create resources with which to bargain with government in the risk management process (Lipsky, 1968).

Communication with risk bearers must inevitably address the decision processes that must resolve or redress the risks. This suggests questions that need answers. How may the issues of risk communication and risk allocation be separated so they do not continually interact to impede and confuse well-intentioned efforts? Is it possible to gain an increased public understanding of risk if satisfaction is not forthcoming on the management process issues? What agency or private sector experience with risk communication has been most successful in separating these confounding arenas of concern?

PROPOSITION 2: Experience repeatedly demonstrates that a lack of early and continuing involvement is a characteristic source of failure for public participation programmes

The developer of a project, programme or facility often waits until late in the developmental process to involve the public. By that time, major choices have been made, options foreclosed, and the developer and (not infrequently) regulators are committed to the enterprise. Whether characterized as a 'decide, announce and defend' (Ducsik and Austin, 1979) or as a 'locational opportunism' (Kasperson, 1985) approach to siting, it has enjoyed wide practice, for example, in the siting of noxious facilities, and has elicited a number of searching critiques (Ebbin and Kasper, 1974; Stever, 1980). Such a siting process has also contributed, not infrequently, to rancorous conflict over risk and to distrust of risk managers. Thus, analysts of public participation generally agree that activities aimed at informing and involving the public should occur early in, and continue throughout, the consideration and decision process.

The timing of information may be expected to affect its utilization and impact on the decision process (Ingram and Ullery, 1977). Generally, information furnished early is likely to have the greatest potential impact on the substance of the decision. Information consumers, be they risk bearers or risk managers, will also be most receptive to information at that stage. Yet a number of factors militate against early provision of risk information: the scientific assessment of risk underlying the information tends to be less adequate, early generation and communication of information are often not cost effective because numerous candidates compete for attention, and early communication increases opportunities for opposition (Ingram and Ullery, 1977).

As suggested above, early provision of information entails a clear trade-off for the risk communicator. On the other hand, once a risk situation has been identified, the participation imperative calls for the immediate transfer of relevant information to prospective risk bearers. Failure to do so may lead to public perception of a lack of candour or an intent to cover up. On the other hand, there is a corresponding need for the risk manager to have as much accurate technical analysis in hand as is possible, as well as a considered means for translating the information (together with relevant contextual data) in a form comprehensible to the several publics involved. The unfolding events at Three Mile Island and Love Canal speak persuasively as to the damage that conflicting information can produce, particularly when the coverage by mass media is intense and pays undue attention to exaggerated claims (Mazur, 1984).

PROPOSITION 3: The believability of risk information is closely related to institutional credibility and trust

Where potential personal harm is concerned, the believability of information provided depends greatly on the degree of trust and confidence in the risk communicator. If the communicator is viewed as having a compromised mandate or a lack of competence, credence in information provided tends to be weakened accordingly. Or if the particular risk has been mismanaged or neglected in the past, scepticism and distrust may greet attempts to communicate risks.

Harris polls, for example, suggest that in 1966, 55 per cent of the public had a great deal of confidence in major business companies (Harris and Associates, 1980). By 1980 this had declined to 19 per cent. Over the same period, the overall composite rating of confidence in some nine major social institutions (television news, medicine, the military, the press, organized religion, major companies, Congress, the Executive Branch and organized labour) fell by 50 per cent (Harris and Associates, 1980). A recent survey of public attitudes toward the siting of hazardous waste facilities revealed a widespread belief that individuals could neither trust the management of companies that operate treatment facilities, nor rely on government officials to ensure proper procedures (Portney, 1983). After a searching analysis of the problems confronting the disposal of radioactive wastes, the US Office of Technology Assessment concluded '... the greatest single obstacle that a successful waste management program must overcome is the severe erosion of public confidence in the Federal Government' (USOTA, 1982a, p31).

Social trust is, of course, multidimensional. At minimum, it comprises a judgement of *competence* – the agency possesses a strong intelligence function and the requisite expertise and information to carry out its mission and to protect public health and safety. Secondly, the agency must be seen as unbiased, able to conduct its activities uncompromised by any hidden agenda or undue influence by particular interests. Finally, people must have confidence that the agency *cares about* those whom it serves, that it will use *due process* in arriving at decisions, and that it will provide adequate opportunities for individuals to make their concerns known. Loss in any one of these three dimensions compromises the trust an institution can command; loss in all three seriously impairs the ability to communicate with risk bearers.

Situations involving low levels of social trust require an explicit recognition that the agency faces short-run and long-run objectives that may be inconsistent and perhaps even in conflict. The short-run objective is to convey particular messages as efficiently as possible so that the institution or agency meets its obligation to inform. This may require extraordinary actions, such as creating new communication channels or enlisting the aid of independent information sources that command greater public trust. But the need also exists over the long run to recover social trust, a development almost certain to require extensive organizational and financial resources. Indeed, even the ability of an organization to speak with one voice is costly. Somehow the skirmishes of risk communication need to be woven into a larger design of recovering social trust.

PROPOSITION 4: Effective public participation depends substantially upon the development of indigenous technical and analytic resources and upon institutional means to act upon increased knowledge

Complex technological controversies (such as many risk problems) find publics at a distinct disadvantage, regardless of levels of interest and commitment. Technical experts are divided, risk assessments difficult to understand, value issues poorly defined and governmental agencies distrusted. It is not surprising that publics become fearful and risk averse. In such situations, the ability of risk bearers to reach informed judgements about risk is substantially enhanced if technical and other resources *under their control* are made available. Providing such capability is, of course, possible only in certain risk situations – where risk bearers are clearly identifiable, where the risk is concentrated rather than dispersed. But the harnessing of increased technical capability is vital to the social dynamic of risk consideration, as described by Perrow (1984).

The ability of risk bearers to respond to risk communication and to engage in a consideration of risk depends, then, upon the existence of technical resources and contexts in which the individual, social groups and the community can enlarge their analytical and communication capabilities. Sometimes this may involve simple means by which individuals can themselves monitor a risk, such as exposure badges on workers, radiation monitors disseminated around Three Mile Island or air pollution monitoring instruments in Los Angeles. On other occasions, it may involve financial and informational support to allow a community to establish its own citizen panel to identify environmental and social impacts associated with a particular development (as with the Alaska pipeline). In situations demanding high technical expertise, a panel of experts funded by the developer but appointed by and reporting to a population of risk bearers may, as indicated by the successful experience of the New Mexico Nuclear Waste Evaluation Committee, provide independent assurance of the effectiveness of risk assessment and management programmes.

It is also apparent that the more successful risk communication programmes are likely to be those in which increased information is linked to an enlarged capability to act upon that knowledge. Increased information without accompanying institutional mechanisms for action is ultimately frustrating and unlikely to generate individual motivation to acquire information. Worker participation in Sweden in health and safety matters is a good example of success – the coupling of ambitious and broad-based risk communication with an institutional structure of national research, worker education and training, local safety delegates and various means of worker recourse (Kasperson, 1983b). The community action programmes of the 1960s are a negative example, in which the lack of power ultimately detracted from the eroded participation programmes (Kasperson, 1977).

PROPOSITION 5: Members of the public differ in arenas and scope of involvement, suggesting differing 'thresholds' of involvement and differing communication strategies

In their important volume *Participation in America*, Verba and Nie (1972), after examining a wide array of participation data, classify public participants into six major types:

1   *The inactives* – citizens who engage in no political activity and who are also psychologically detached from politics.
2   *The voting specialists* – citizens who limit their political activity to voting and who are unlikely to take sides in community conflict and in issue extremity. Their activities are guided by national attachment to their political party.
3   *The parochial participants* – citizens whose political participation is focused on the narrow problems of their own personal lives. They tend to have somewhat more information than the average citizen but have a low level of psychological involvement.
4   *The communalists* – citizens who are heavily involved in activity that is relatively non-conflictual and aimed at the attainment of broad community goals. They tend to have above average psychological involvement in politics, levels of information and sense of efficacy.
5   *The campaign activists* – citizens who are the opposite of the communalists – they have strong partisan affiliations, readily take sides in community conflict and have relatively extreme issue positions.
6   *The complete activists* – citizens who are the mirror image of the inactives; they rate high on all participation orientations and are involved in conflict and cleavage but also have a sense of contribution to the community at large (Verba and Nie, 1972).

The attitudinal and behavioural orientations that underlie this typology provide content to the frequent observation that there is not one but many publics. Individuals tend to specialize in types of policy issues and arenas of public involvement. Accordingly, they present different priority problems and may require different strategies of risk communication to reach the spectrum of social groups in a particular community. Each group, in short, has its own appeal and incentives and its own 'thresholds' of involvement for varying risk issues. Typologies of participation explain in part the existence of the 'participation paradox' – those most often affected by a particular risk or prospective development may be the most uninvolved and difficult to reach. Depending upon the 'fit' of the risk to the 'participation domain' of the individual or group, publics may be readily involved or, alternatively, quite resistant to communication and involvement efforts. Even 'stakeholders' will not all be responsive to a given approach to risk communication.

Much of the current understanding of public response to risk rests upon the concerted efforts of an international group of able psychologists. These insights into individual behaviour, undoubtedly valuable, need to be augmented by a corresponding knowledge of risk consideration, debate and opinion formation as they occur *in situ*, in the social groups and communities in which individuals live, during actual events and controversies. Confronted by a risk situation, most individuals do not function in isolation but seek out additional information, contexts by which to interpret, peer groups to validate perceptions, relevant experience which may exist in the community and potential linkages with other social issues. What are the key sources of information in such cases? How do communication channels function? How are perceptions validated (if at all)? What credence is attached to what kinds of information? What is the impact of unfolding events? The research agenda is rich and needs to be tackled seriously if risk communication programmes are to be anchored in something more than trial-and-error experience and folk practitioner do's and don'ts.

PROPOSITION 6: Although a large array of participation techniques exists, current knowledge does not allow for successful prediction as to which are likely to be effective under what conditions

Much of the public participation literature deals with discussion, in case study context, of techniques that can be used to involve and communicate with 'the public' and the merits and demerits of each. The US Federal Highway Administration (1970), for example, has provided an exhaustive inventory. Rosener (1975) discusses some 42 techniques, ranging from interactive cable TV-based participation to 'fishbowl' planning, in a piece appropriately entitled 'A Cafeteria of Techniques and Critiques'. The treatment generally centres upon common sense observations garnered from experience, or, put differently, lessons from war stories.

One finding endorsed by all is the ineffectiveness, and often alienating effect, of communication and involvement through public hearings. The problems are manifold: communication to the public is often in technical language difficult for lay publics to understand, any two-way exchange of information is constrained by strict procedural rules, those attending the hearing are often unrepresentative of the area population and the information gleaned tends to have little impact on agency decisions (Sinclair, 1977; Checkoway, 1981). Indeed, public hearings, whatever their intent, tend to be used to satisfy minimal legal requirements and to solve agency goals, for example by building support for agency plans and for diffusing existing or potential antagonism.

Given the limited state of understanding, programmes for risk communication should: (1) be treated as research problems for which a limited knowledge base now exists; (2) involve the use of diverse mechanisms for any given set of programme objectives; (3) employ control groups wherever possible; and (4) undergo rigorous evaluation. Although this is a straightforward social science recipe, it is remarkable how little of this occurs as well-intentioned efforts work their way through governmental agencies and trickle down to implementation. Part of this failure in design and implementation occurs because participation (and risk communication) programmes are rarely subjected to searching ongoing and retrospective evaluation. As a result, evaluation strategies are likely to need substantial attention and investment, involving the definition of adequate baseline studies, measures of the cognitive changes that occur in risk perception, isolating planned from unplanned communication, and causally linking messages with observed behavioural outcomes in a messy and changing information environment.

CONCLUSIONS

Key conclusions for risk communication efforts emerging from this review of public participation research are:

- The public consideration of risk characteristically occurs in a social group or community context, consisting of multiple sources and channels of information, peer groups, and an agenda of other ongoing social issues. Much more is known about the response to risk by members of the public as individuals than as members of social groups. Improved understanding is needed of the social dynamic of risk consideration in the context of actual controversies and community processes.
- 'Tolerable' risk level issues are inextricably linked with the process by which the risk was allocated or imposed. For that reason, risk communication often becomes a vehicle of conflict by which community groups seek to create resources with which to bargain in risk management decisions.

- The timing of risk communication entails a difficult trade-off between the social imperative to inform without delay and the need for full scientific information and analysis. Improved understanding is needed of effective ways to communicate in a timely manner while minimizing potential errors or subsequent conflicting information.
- Members of the public tend to specialize their participation in types of social issues and arenas of involvement, suggesting the need to develop different communication packages and strategies to reach the attention of and afford maximum assistance to different social groups.
- The success of a risk communication programme will often depend heavily upon (1) the provision, or development, of an indigenous technical capability by which expertise under the control of risk bearers can be brought to bear on complex problems, and (2) institutional means by which the public can act on the enlarged information.
- A long-term erosion of social trust for many of the institutions, and particularly large corporations, responsible for risk management has greatly complicated the difficulties in risk communication, suggesting the need for innovative programmes to achieve a short-run dissemination of information to the public in given situations coupled with a long-run strategy aimed at the recovery of social trust.
- The present state of knowledge does not permit authoritative statements about which participation techniques are likely to be successful in given situations, for specific groups, and for particular communities. Accordingly, public participation efforts need to employ a wide array of methods, to be treated as research designs, and to include careful ongoing and retrospective evaluation. Risk communication efforts may be expected to share these attributes.

2

Social Distrust as a Factor in Siting Hazardous Facilities and Communicating Risks

Roger E. Kasperson, Dominic Golding and Seth Tuler

INTRODUCTION

Conflicts regarding the siting of hazardous facilities in the US have often led to an impasse due to numerous problems, including, in particular, social distrust. To address this situation, this chapter proposes a multidimensional conception of trust, including cognitive, emotional and behavioural aspects, and involving themes of expectations about others, subjective perceptions of situations and an awareness of taking risks. Four key dimensions of trust are: (1) perceptions of commitment, (2) competence, (3) caring and (4) predictability. Distrust arises from violations of expectations that people have in social relations. Research has shown a broad loss of trust in leaders and in major social institutions in the US since the 1960s, together with growing public concern over health, safety and environmental protection. These trends combine to make hazardous-facility siting highly controversial. This chapter recommends a number of key steps in risk communication and hazardous-facility siting that are aimed at dealing as effectively as possible with social distrust.

Siting conflicts are as much a part of organized human experience as politics itself. Historically, such conflicts typically centred upon competition among places to obtain desired functions, as with the location of railroads and state capitals in early American political history, or the siting of national capitals elsewhere (e.g. Brasilia or Islamabad), or *desired* facilities (e.g. 'clean' industries in residential suburbs), or sometimes federal contracts or grant awards. More recently, disagreement and controversy have erupted over where to locate facilities or functions such as prisons, cemeteries, taverns, 'adult' bookstores, drug treatment centres or town dumps with *undesired* (or risky) characteristics. With widespread

Note: Reprinted from *Journal of Social Issues*, vol 48, Kasperson, R. E., Goldiing, D. and Tuler, S., 'Social distrust as a factor in siting hazardous facilities and communicating risks', pp161–187, © (1992), with permission from Blackwell Publishing

urbanization and technological development, with increasing pressure upon land use, and with growing concern over environmental and health protection, siting controversial facilities of all sizes and kinds has become increasingly difficult, and has emerged as a national policy problem of major significance (Popper, 1983). Nowhere are the difficulties greater than with the perplexing issue of how and where to locate radioactive and other hazardous waste storage and disposal facilities.

The public policy stakes should not be underestimated. After four decades of the commercial use of nuclear power, the failure to put into operation a smoothly functioning disposal 'back end' of the nuclear fuel cycle continues to haunt the prospects for one of the nation's major energy sources and to threaten international security in a petroleum-scarce world. Spent nuclear fuel is accumulating in the US at 110 operating commercial reactors and threatens to exceed the capacity of available on-site temporary storage space at some nuclear plants. Meanwhile, concern over radioactive waste stands at the top of public misgivings about nuclear power. Even when the wastes involved are low-level radioactive wastes, prospective waste site developers are confronted by angry local opponents, buttressed by widespread public anxiety over the potential risks, linkages with national opposition groups and traditions of local control over land use in the US. Meanwhile, public opposition in Nevada has delayed, if not stymied, the national programme for high level waste disposal.

The situation with hazardous wastes, and perhaps even non-hazardous solid wastes, is equally serious. With 66,000 hazardous waste generators and 50,000 hazardous waste shipments per year (Piasecki and Davis, 1987), it is clear that, even with major strides in waste reduction and recycling, numerous new land disposal facilities will be needed. Yet the recent record of siting efforts for such facilities affords little optimism. A national survey by the New York Legislative Commission on Toxic Substances and Hazardous Wastes (1987) revealed an unsuccessful record of outcomes: only 1 of 33 existing commercial landfills had been given an operating permit since 1980; only 1 commercial hazardous waste incinerator had received a permit and become operational since 1980; and, of 81 applications for waste management facilities received since 1980, only 6 had been successful. Meanwhile a national survey by Cambridge Reports (1990) revealed that a 62 per cent majority of respondents opposed placing a new landfill site in their community and a 53 per cent majority believed current landfill technologies were unable to protect groundwater supplies.

This siting impasse has been the subject of substantial diagnosis and analysis (O'Hare et al, 1983; Greenberg et al, 1984; Kasperson, 1986; English and Davis, 1987; Colglazier and Langum, 1988). While the specific items vary somewhat by analyst, key aspects of the siting problem include those in the following list:

- *Lack of a systems approach.* No less than waste management itself, facility siting is part of a system's activity. It involves a network of waste generators, treatment, processing, storage and disposal facilities, interconnected by waste transportation links. And, of course, other unwanted facilities are also being sited. Whereas the developer sees waste facility siting in terms of the individual facility, publics see it in the context of other facilities and previous locational decisions.

- *Risks and uncertainty.* While considerable consensus exists that well-designed and well-managed waste management facilities pose only limited risks to nearby publics, residual risks and associated uncertainties do exist. The long duration of the hazard and the presence of irreducible uncertainties make risk communication very difficult. Compounding the uncertainties is the generally inadequate knowledge base used to decide which locations are generally best for specific hazardous wastes (USOTA, 1982b, p20).

- *Public perceptions of risks.* Whatever the actual public health and environmental risks posed by new and potentially hazardous facilities, they pale in comparison with public perceptions of them. National public opinion polls taken throughout the 1980s consistently revealed hazardous wastes to be at or near the top of the public's agenda of serious environmental concerns (Kasperson et al, 1990). Indeed, a 1980 national poll that found only 10–12 per cent of the American public was willing to live a mile or less from either a nuclear power plant or a hazardous waste site (US Council on Environmental Quality, 1980) is a figure that remains remarkably contemporaneous over a decade later. A recent national survey, for example, found that the closest that a facility could be built to respondents before they said they would actively protest or move to another location was a median distance of 60 miles for nuclear plants, 100 miles for a chemical waste landfill and 200 miles for an underground nuclear waste repository (Flynn, 1990, p6). The factors underlying these perceptions of danger have been quite extensively charted in psychometric research, and include such considerations as the perceived 'newness' and 'dread' of the associated hazard, its 'severity' and 'catastrophic potential', and the extensive media coverage and 'memorability' (Slovic et al, 1982a; Slovic, 1987b). Increasing evidence suggests that these perceptions are contributing to a stigmatization of the places and communities where such wastes are found (Edelstein 1988).

- *Inequity in risk allocation.* Exacerbating these concerns is the mismatch between the concentration of risks and burdens in the host community for a noxious facility and the diffuse distribution of benefits. In one of the few thorough empirical analyses of distributional equity at a hazardous waste site (in West Valley, NY), Kates and Braine (1983) painted a complex picture of gains and losses over more than a dozen locations stretching across the US, and a concentration of losses in the host community and region. The degree of mismatch can reach quite

Source: Data from Rasky, 1987

Figure 2.1 *Locations and projected volumes of spent nuclear fuel through the year 2000*

dramatic proportions, as is evident in the distribution of locations of nuclear high-level waste generation in relation to their potential disposal site in Nevada (Figure 2.1). This lack of concordance between benefits and burden is compounded by the opportunism frequently exhibited by those siting facilities in locating unwanted facilities in 'down and out' communities where high unemployment rates and limited access to political power undermine community opposition (USGAO, 1983; Greenberg et al, 1984).

- *Social distrust.* The complexity of the above problems points to the need for high levels of public trust and confidence in the institutions and people responsible for siting hazardous facilities and managing the risks. It is quite apparent, however, that the requisite social trust rarely exists. Where prospective risk bearers harbour suspicions over the fairness of the siting process and doubt the trustworthiness of those responsible for protecting them, the conditions exist for intense conflict and impasse. Because of the far-reaching impacts of social distrust on prospective solutions, this article examines more fully its meaning and ramifications before exploring how siting and risk communication strategies might better address it.

THE CONCEPT OF TRUST

Trust is a concept widely identified as important to social interactions, but rarely well defined or characterized. The social importance of trust stems, in large part, from its contribution to cooperative behaviour and information flow. Intellectual perspectives on trust emanate from diverse academic quarters – psychology, sociology, political science, economics and mass communication. Theoretical conceptualizations from these disciplinary perspectives share a number of common features and dimensions, as well as a considerable amount of loose use. The commonalities can shed light on different types of trust and how they develop among people in social interactions. Trust has been defined in several distinctly different ways:

- 'A generalized expectancy held by an individual that the word, promise, oral or written statement of another individual or group can be relied on' (Rotter, 1980, p1).
- 'The degree of confidence you feel when you think about a relationship' (Rempel and Holmes, 1986, p28).
- 'The generalized expectancy that a message received is true and reliable and the communicator demonstrates competence and honesty by conveying accurate, objective and complete information' (Renn and Levine, 1991, p181).
- 'A set of expectations shared by all those involved in an exchange' (Zucker, 1986, p54).
- 'Members of that system act according to and are secure in the expected futures constituted by the presence of each other or their symbolic representations' (Lewis and Weigert, 1985, p975).
- 'A person's expectation that an interaction partner is able and willing to behave promotively toward the person even when the interaction partner is free to choose among alternative behaviours that could lead to negative consequences for the person' (Koller, 1988, p266).

These definitions share some general themes, suggesting the need for a broad-based, multidimensional conception of trust. Important attributes of trust include the following:

- *Expectations about others and orientations toward the future.* Trust allows people to interact and cooperate without full knowledge about others and future uncertainties.
- *A notion of chance or risk taking.* To trust also implies that one has confidence that others will act voluntarily in a manner that is beneficial, even if not certain.
- *Subjective perceptions about others and situations.* These include perceptions of the intentions and attributes of others (e.g. commitment, competence, consistency, integrity, honesty), their motivations, qualities of the situation (e.g. the availability and accuracy of information), risks and uncertainties. In risk communication programmes, trustworthiness can depend on judgements about the quality of a message, its source, and the structure and performance of institutions (Midden, 1988).

The literature treating the concept of 'trust' provides a number of possible conceptualizations of its functions and dynamics. Social psychological research on trust, for example, typically focuses on behavioural and cognitive aspects of people's interactions. Researchers seek to identify situational variables that affect levels of trust among people. This approach is closely related to discussions of trust from the perspectives of economics and political science (e.g. Deutsch, 1973; Butler, 1983). On the other hand, personality theorists have conceptualized trust as something internal to an individual (e.g. Rotter, 1980; Blakeney, 1986). Here, trust is viewed as a psychological construct or trait that individuals develop, depending on their personal experiences and prior socialization (Lewis and Weigert, 1985, p975). Trust, then, is clearly linked to the degree of confidence, predictability, faith or cooperation that prevails in a given situation.

Sociologists, by contrast, have approached trust as a property of groups or collectives. In this view, the primary function of trust is not psychological, because, aside from its role in social relationships, individuals would have no innate need to trust (Lewis and Weigert, 1985). Moreover, when trust is regarded as a purely psychological state, it is easily confused with other psychological states (hope, faith, behavioural prediction) and is dealt with by methods that have reductionistic consequences, in that they substitute individual behaviour for more complex, interactive social phenomena (Lewis and Weigert, 1985, p976).

In both the psychological and sociological approaches, trust is viewed as an important prerequisite for effective orientation and action at both the inter-individual and societal levels of interaction. For example, trust allows one to predict a partner's intentions in both familiar and novel uncertain situations. Political and economic exchange relies to a large degree on the trust that reduces complexity in social interactions by limiting the number of legitimate or acceptable options among persons (Luhmann, 1980; Bradach and Eccles, 1989).

At the level of larger social groups and societal processes, such 'background' factors as social norms, rules, shared symbols and interpretive frames, and structural properties of institutions have been identified as important to the development of trust. Approaches to the study of these issues are based on research in other areas, including persuasion (Renn and Levine, 1991), economic and political behaviour (Lewis and Weigert, 1985; Zucker, 1986; Bradach and Eccles, 1989), organizational development (Dwivedi, 1988) and organizational communication from a transactional perspective (Blakeney, 1986).

To a large degree, trust as a psychological and sociological orientation relies on faith, and faith is an orientation that involves emotions. Faith is important to procedural justice, for example, because trust involves beliefs about neutrality, benevolence and fairness even in situations where they are not required (Tyler, 1989). However, many psychological, political and economic perspectives conceptualize trust very narrowly in terms of individual cognition and rational, calculative behaviour. In our view, trust needs to be seen as a social phenomenon, composed of multiple dimensions, each possessing distinct cognitive, affective, behavioural and situational manifestations (Lewis and Weigert, 1985; Koller, 1988). Thus, it is possible to conceptualize different types of trust:

- *Cognitive trust* provides a foundation upon which an individual can discriminate among those perceived to be trustworthy, distrusted or unknown. Since such trust requires a degree of familiarity with situations that lie between total ignorance and total understanding (Luhmann, 1980), some cognitive leap of faith is involved.
- *Emotional trust* provides a basis for this cognitive leap of faith. Its contribution consists of an emotional bond among those participating in a relationship, which is strongest in close primary relationships (e.g. love and friendship).
- *Behavioural trust* is a behavioural enactment in social relationships. To trust is to act as if the uncertain future actions of others were certain and predictable, even where the violation of these expectations may produce negative consequences (Lewis and Weigert, 1985). Behavioural acts can influence cognitive and emotional trust. Cognitive trust, for example, may grow with increasing behavioural enactments of trust.

These different types of trust reflect varying combinations of rationality and emotion. The emotional content of trust, for example, is presumably higher and more important in primary than in secondary group relations. By contrast, in secondary group situations, social trust depends more on rationality because of the widespread anonymity of individuals in demographically large and structurally complicated social systems. The mix of the emotional and rational contents of trust may thus affect the development and loss of trust. The stronger the emotional content of trust relative to the cognitive content, for example, the less likely it is that contrary behavioural evidence may weaken the existing pattern of trust (Lewis and Weigert, 1985, p972).

    While a number of functional theories attempt to explain what trust is, few provide insight into the dynamics of trust at the level of society. Many argue that trust is gained slowly through incremental increases stemming from properly conceived and timed acts on the part of each person in a relationship (Shapiro, 1987). The general social climate also structures the conditions under which institutions must operate to gain or sustain trust. In a positive social climate, people may invest more trust in institutions from the beginning and may be more forgiving when this trust is abused. In a negative social climate, by contrast, people may be very cautious in investing trust in any social institution (Renn and Levine, 1991, p205). Social change and disruption associated with immigration, internal migration, economic instability and social conflict can disrupt and change expectations and the bases of social trust (Zucker, 1986).

Trust also depends heavily on the performance of social institutions. The characterization of trust as a complex interaction of cognitive, emotional and behavioural properties underscores the important contributions of individual or group perceptions as well as their interaction with macrosocial forces. Luhmann (1980) contrasted the *interpersonal trust* that prevails in small, relatively undifferentiated societies with the *system trust* that prevails in the bureaucratic institutions of modern, complex societies; he argued that the shifting nature of trust from the former to the latter is one of the hallmarks of our times. It is also probably the case that trust in larger, more complex societies rests on higher levels of cognitive trust, whereas trust in smaller, more immediate groups rests on higher levels of emotional trust (Lewis and Weigert, 1985).

These conceptions contribute to several insights into the nature of *social distrust*. Distrust appears to arise from violations of expectations that people have in social relations, and it occurs on cognitive, affective or behavioural levels. Violations of expectation, in turn, occur at both the individual level (such as in close interpersonal relationships) and the social level (as when politicians violate constituent expectations). In general, the literature suggests that trust is hard to gain and easy to lose (Rothbart and Park, 1986). Slovic et al (1991b) noted, for example, that a single act of embezzlement is sufficient to convince us that an accountant is untrustworthy, and that even 100 subsequent honest actions may do little to restore our trust in the individual. A recent National Research Council panel on risk communication, viewing the 'tremendous' credibility problems of the Department of Energy, concluded that 'one year of being honest with the public is not enough' (USNRC, 1989, p120). On the individual psychological level, Rempel et al (1985) have argued that trust may be lost in the reverse order or sequence from that in which it developed.

Trust is probably never completely or permanently attained, but instead requires continuous maintenance and reinforcement. Distrust reflects the suspicion that violated expectations in one exchange may generalize to other transactions. To distrust, then, involves an attribution of intentionality that spreads from limited cases through a broader realm of interactions or exchanges. Renn and Levine (1991) distinguished five analytical levels related to trust and confidence that vary in degree of complexity and abstraction: trust involving a message, personal appeal, institutional perception, institutional climate or sociopolitical climate. They argued that the lower levels (i.e. message, personal appeal) are embedded in the higher ones (i.e. institutional perception, institutional performance) and that conditions that operate on the higher levels also affect lower levels of trust and confidence. Thus, consistent violations of trust at lower levels will, they argued, eventually affect the next higher level. Similarly, distrust at the higher levels will tend to shape options for gaining or sustaining trust at the lower levels.

A CHARACTERIZATION OF SOCIAL TRUST

Drawing upon these previous writings, we define *social trust* as a person's expectation that other persons and institutions in a social relationship can be relied upon to act in ways that are competent, predictable and caring. *Social distrust*, therefore, is a person's expectation that other persons and institutions in a social relationship are likely to act in ways that are incompetent, unpredictable, uncaring and thus probably inimical.

Four key dimensions of social trust, in our view, are essential to capture the range and depth of trust-related behaviour. Each dimension is necessary and plays an important role in the development and maintenance of social trust; none is sufficient in itself, however, to assure the existence of such trust. These four dimensions are as follows:

1   *Commitment.* To trust implies a certain degree of vulnerability of one individual to another or others, to an institution, or to the broader social and political system. Thus, trust relies on perceptions of uncompromised commitment to a mission or goal (such as protection of the public health), and fulfilment of fiduciary obligations or other social norms. Perceptions of commitment rest on perceptions of objectivity and fairness in decision processes, and the provision of accurate information. Commitment, however, does not entail blind progress toward predefined goals, nor insufficient awareness of and response to changing circumstances.

2   *Competence.* Trust is gained only when the individual or institution in a social relationship is judged to be reasonably competent in its actions over time. While expectations may not be violated if these individuals or institutions are occasionally wrong, consistent failures and discoveries of unexpected incompetence and inadequacies can lead to a loss of trust. In particular, risk managers and institutions must show that they are technically competent in their mandated area of responsibility.

3   *Caring.* Perceptions that an individual or institution will act in a way that shows concern for and beneficence to trusting individuals are critical. Perceptions of a caring attitude are an especially important ingredient where dependent individuals rely upon others with greater control or authority over the situation and the individual's opportunities and well-being.

4   *Predictability.* Trust rests on the fulfilment of expectations and faith. Consistent violations of expectations nearly always result in distrust. It should be noted, however, that predictability does not necessarily require consistency of behaviour. Complete consistency of behaviour would require unchanging actions or beliefs, even in the face of contradictory information, and also more consistency in values and related behaviour than most individuals, groups or institutions possess.

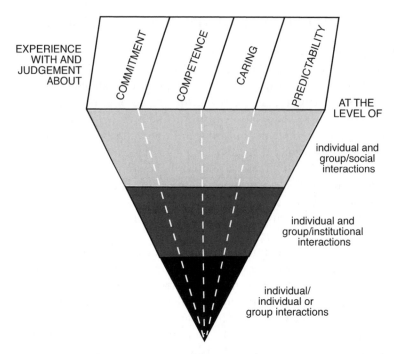

EXPERIENCE WITH AND JUDGEMENT ABOUT

COMMITMENT

COMPETENCE

CARING

PREDICTABILITY

AT THE LEVEL OF

individual and group/social interactions

individual and group/institutional interactions

individual/ individual or group interactions

Figure 2.2 *Nested hierarchy of social trust and distrust dynamics*

This conceptualization of trust emphasizes that individual perceptions, specific situational or institutional contexts, and general societal and systemic factors all play important roles in the development of different types, levels and nuances of social trust (Figure 2.2). Thus, the nature of an individual's or a group's interaction with individual members of organizations, with institutions as a whole, as well as their experience in society more generally, all affect the 'goal' of social trust. This suggests a 'nested hierarchy' for analysing the dynamics of social trust and distrust in any given situation (illustrated in Figure 2.2), in which both vertical and horizontal flow constantly occurs. Trust, in our view, operates simultaneously at the cognitive, emotional and behavioural levels. Fulfilment and maintenance of trust, accordingly, requires that these dimensions be validated at all three levels by the personal observation and experience of the trusting individual. Thus, general societal processes, situation-specific experiences, and continuing validation affect the levels of trust or distrust in institutions, and, by extension, influence the possibility of developing or recovering trust. These issues are addressed later in this chapter when policy and procedural implications are examined.

The unpleasant reality must be noted that actions to build trust on one dimension or level may entail a corresponding loss of trust on another dimension or level. To improve public perceptions of caring, for example, an institution could increase the openness of its decision process and information. Yet, since scientific research often proceeds through incomplete results, false starts and gradually developing databases, openness of information that proves to be in error could increase public perceptions of science's unreliability or lack of competence, leading to decreased levels of social trust. In fact, substantial uncertainty exists as to whether improvements along one dimension of trust will outweigh decreases in trust along another. Similar observations could be made about compatibilities among levels of trust. Such is the paradox for the facility developer or the risk communicator!

OBSERVATIONS FROM EXPERIENCE

Empirical studies lend credence to the above conceptual discussion and to the nested hierarchy of social trust dynamics just described. It is apparent from this research that important changes in social trust have occurred over time at the societal level in the US and that these changes establish an important context in which institutions concerned with the processing and handling of environmental risk issues and the siting of risk facilities must function. Three observations are particularly germane.

Observation 1. A broad-based loss of trust in the leaders of major social institutions and in the institutions themselves has occurred over the past three decades. Following World War II, public opinion surveys revealed a general rise in public confidence in various social institutions and their leaders to a peak in the early to mid-1960s. Over the next decade, however, public confidence dropped precipitously, to expressed levels of confidence that were only about half of what they had been a decade earlier (Figure 2.3). Since that time, public confidence has oscillated in response to important events but has generally remained at a low level, and all social institutions have been affected (Figure 2.4). The factors contributing to these long-term declines are imperfectly understood but are thought to include the Vietnam War, the revelations of environmental degradation in the late 1960s and 1970s, social protest, the Watergate scandal and the energy crises and economic recessions of the 1970s (Rourke et al 1976; Lipset and Schneider 1983). Lipset and Schneider (1983, p66) concluded that unemployment and inflation particularly affect levels of social trust, and that business and government bear the brunt of the public disaffection. Even the optimism of the early Reagan years was unable to restore the levels of public confidence that prevailed during the early 1960s or to reverse the long-term erosion of the 1965–1980 period.

It is highly likely, however, that these events are embedded in, and contribute to, a broader web of basic attitude and aspiration changes in American society. Thus, better education and greater affluence increased people's aspirations concerning their desired share of public resources and

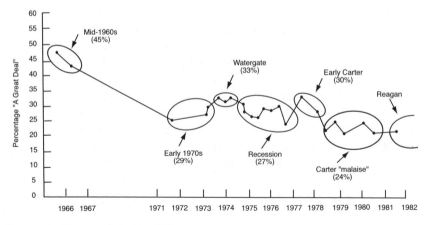

Source: After Lipset and Schneider, 1983

Figure 2.3 *Confidence in institutional leadership in seven periods from 1966 to 1982, from 24 Louis Harris and National Opinion Research Center surveys. Figures in parentheses show the average percentage expressing 'a great deal of confidence' in the leadership of ten institutions, averaged across all polls taken in that period.*

welfare, while the increased complexity of social issues and the pluralization of values and lifestyles may have contributed to a growing dissatisfaction with the performance of social institutions (Renn and Levine, 1991). Then too, the apparent broadening and deepening of environmental values and the growing public concerns over the risks of technology during the past two decades have had their impact; indeed some see the changed aspirations and growing social disaffection in the US as the reflection of basic changes in American culture (Douglas and Wildavsky, 1982; Wildavsky and Dake, 1990). Others (Lipset and Schneider, 1983) attribute falling confidence to a suspicion of those in power, based upon a rational public assessment of the actual performance of institutions. At the same time, it is notable that the disenchantment with institutions and their leaders (level 2 in Figure 2.2) has not translated into systemic distrust; dissatisfaction with the performance of institutions has not yet led to support for fundamental changes in the economy, government or social processes in the US. Moreover, people's personal experiences with institutions appear more positive than the generalized assessment of the institutions (Lipset and Schneider, 1983).

Observation 2. Growing public concern over health, safety, and environmental protection has accompanied the erosion of social trust. The 1970s were also a decade during which the environmental movement spread throughout the various regions and social groupings of American society. Prior to 1970, the environmental movement was strongly elitist in its base, but by the end of the 1970s all major social and economic groups espoused environmental

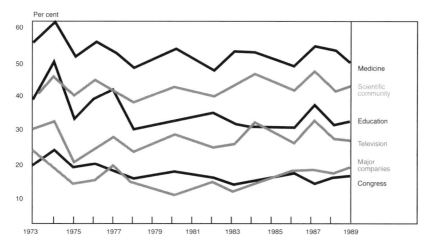

Source: Data from Cambridge Reports, 1990

Figure 2.4 *Public confidence in six institutions, 1973–1989. Figures are percentages of respondents who have a high degree of confidence in each institution*

values (US Council on Environmental Quality, 1980). Similar patterns were apparent in changing attitudes toward technology and health risks (Harris and Associates, 1980; Weinstein, 1988). Many authors have noted that, as Americans have increased their longevity and enjoyed declining risks from accidents and natural hazards, they have paradoxically become more concerned about their health and safety. An active environmental and public-interest community and increasingly sophisticated mass media have assiduously detailed the 'downside' of technology and the many failures of regulatory agencies. It may be that the greater affluence of post-industrial society has shifted the 'worry beads' of society away from those primary concerns of eking out an economic subsistence and the familiar threats of famine and pestilence, toward heightened concern with the more subtle threats of chemicals in the environment and unhealthy diets and lifestyles (Kates, 1986). Whatever the causes, some risk analysts (e.g. Wildavsky, 1988; Lewis, 1990) by the 1980s began to fret over whether the US was becoming a 'nation of hypochondriacs', and the USEPA (1987, 1990) sought to reduce the extent to which public concern rather than expert knowledge drove its agenda of effort and allocation of resources.

Observation 3. Both of the above processes interact and reach particularly intense expression in hazardous-facility siting and controversial risk management. The public concern over threats to health and safety and the lack of social trust in risk managers interact to spark intense public opposition and protest in hazardous-facility siting. The litany of public response to hazardous facilities is now a familiar one: a public agency or private developer announces a site search and screening process, candidate sites are chosen, local opposition erupts in the prospective site communities, and eventually the siting process is immobilized and the search is delayed or discontinued. The search for a low-level radioactive waste site in New York State illustrated this sequence when, in 1990, a 'posse' of local opponents swept down on state officials engaged in site characterization, while elderly local residents chained themselves to a bridge in protest. Such actions in response to potential facilities, widely viewed by experts as posing only very minimal threats to their host communities, have been characterized by an alphabet soup of acronyms (LULUs – locally unwanted land uses; NIMBY – not in my backyard; NIMTOF – not in my term of office), which suggest selfish behaviour on the part of publics seeking to escape social responsibility or impelled to hysterical reactions to risks conjured up by fertile imaginations.

In fact, such acronyms are both misleading and self-serving. Controversies over hazardous-facility siting, and over some well-publicized risks (such as ethylene dibromide, EDB, in food and Alar on apples), are less about risk than they are about institutions. They are, in essence, 'social trust crises'. Where publics are highly concerned over potential risks, there must be trust that decisions will be made with scrupulous fairness and uncompromised commitment to the protection of the public if potential risk bearers are to accept, or at least tolerate, the imposition of risk. The lack of such trust is quite apparent in the results of surveys taken during siting controversies. In Nevada, for example, where a high-level nuclear waste repository is under investigation at Yucca Mountain, a 1988 survey of residents in the Las Vegas metropolitan area (Mushkatel et al, 1990) found that none of the institutions involved in the siting process received strong trust ratings (see Table 2.1). Respondents judged the Governor of Nevada as most trustworthy (40 per cent for trust categories 6 and 7), whereas they viewed the president and Congress of the US with a substantial mix of trust and distrust.

Two years later in the siting controversy, social trust had apparently eroded still further. A 1990 poll of Nevada residents by the *Las Vegas Review-Journal* found that only 29 per cent of respondents agreed or agreed strongly with the statement that 'the federal government will be honest in the scientific research it does to determine if nuclear wastes can be safely stored at Yucca Mountain', whereas 68 per cent disagreed or disagreed strongly. In regard to trust in the objectivity of the developers, 52 per cent of respondents agreed or agreed strongly with the statement that 'the nuclear waste facility will be built at Yucca Mountain no matter what the scientific research shows'. Several interviews reported by the newspaper (*Las Vegas Review-Journal*, 1990) suggest issues bearing upon social distrust:

Table 2.1 *Percentage of respondents expressing various degrees of trust that officials' decisions will protect the public safely (n > 535)*

Trust level		President	Congress	Governor	State legislature	City/county
No trust	1	9	6	6	3	5
	2	7	7	5	6	8
	3	9	15	7	9	14
	4	17	26	20	25	25
	5	24	28	24	31	28
	6	22	14	26	20	15
Complete trust	7	12	4	14	6	6

Source: Mushkatel et al, 1990, p95

I don't trust any government agency, explicitly... Our government agencies have a history of not being honest and keeping information from us; they think it's best we do not know. (Faye Duncan-Daniel, adult-education teacher)

I do have some difficulty with DOE's credibility, primarily because they are extremely influenced by Congress, and Senator Bennett Johnson (D-LA) has been very, very adamant about the nuclear waste repository. And I think this has biased the DOE... It's my feeling from newspapers and magazines the process has been politicized. So we're not looking at developing an independent scientific review. Instead, we're looking at mandating a political solution. (Jon Wellinghoff, private attorney and former state consumer advocate on utility issues)

I don't know whether I trust DOE. But I know one thing, they are failing miserably to communicate all the facts to the public. (B. Mahlon Brown III, private attorney and former US Attorney for Nevada)

The Government didn't do Love Canal safely, so why should I trust them? (Ann Vigue, personnel manager for a food distribution company)

It is instructive that the newspaper ran its eight-part series (21–28 October, 1990) on the proposed repository under the heading 'Yucca Mountain: A Question of Credibility'. Professional analysts and scholars appear to agree. In its assessment of the nuclear waste programme, the USOTA (1985a, p10) found a lack of public confidence to be 'the single greatest obstacle' to further progress, while such experienced analysts as Luther Carter (1987) and Slovic et al (1991b) have reached similar conclusions as to the 'crisis of confidence' that pervades the nuclear (and other hazardous) waste siting programme.

Given the high conditions of social distrust that characterize the arenas in which hazardous-facility siting and communication about risk occur, what can be done?

DECISION PROCESSES GEARED TO SOCIAL DISTRUST

The basic answer to this question by most practitioners, often supported by social analysts, is to work harder to undo this distrust. This resolve finds additional energy in the frustration over the discrepancy between expert and public assessment of risk, where experts, propelled by a technical focus on the health risk, cannot help but believe that the public would change 'if only they knew the facts!' And, of course, officials are convinced that 'when people see that I am not like my predecessors, they will come to believe me'. And, thus, photocopy machines work overtime to produce information, brochures aim at reassuring sceptical publics, 'public information' budgets proliferate, 'public relations' staffs grow, and non-stop public meetings occur to carry forth the new 'openness' of the agency.

Attempts to communicate about controversial risks or to site hazardous facilities predicated upon well-intentioned efforts to regain social trust are, in our view, naive at best and self-defeating at worst. As indicated above, the loss of social trust is a broad, fundamental societal phenomenon that affects all social institutions and public orientations toward particular policies or decision arenas. Secondly, the burden on social trust is unusually demanding in risk communication and hazardous-facility siting cases because of the inevitable technical uncertainties, expert disagreements, and deep-rooted concern over the risks. Thirdly, social trust is multidimensional in its content so that views on various attributes of managerial 'trustworthiness' are involved. Finally, while the dynamics of trust recovery are not well understood, it appears that the rebuilding process, once social trust is lost, may require a lengthy process of confirmatory experience along multiple dimensions of performance. Even minor trust-eroding events or slips of the tongue may impede substantial progress in procedures or cases that merit trust.

Thus, the allure of recovered trust misleads. Instead, a clear-eyed approach is needed that explicitly recognizes that the recovery of social trust is probably impossible within the time frame of most risk communication and facility-siting efforts. An explicit assumption that high levels of social distrust will continue despite the best of efforts could lead to very different, and more effective, decision processes. Accordingly, the remainder of this article explores the implications of a redefined context and a different set of assumptions for risk communication and hazardous-facility siting.

Risk communication

In situations of high social distrust, any narrow conception of risk communication will almost certainly be inadequate. The goal of risk communication cannot be merely the transmission of factual information, nor can it be the narrow aim of enlightenment or the promotion of behavioural change. Since doubts may exist about some or all of the dimensions of trust – commitment, competence, caring and predictability – risk communicators should seek broad public participation. In particular, they should aim to mobilize the personal and institutional experiences and judgements of risk bearers and other interested parties, as well as to make use of multiple communication sources and channels (Sorensen, 1984). The risk communicator will need to develop a strong listening capacity in order to discern issues about the distribution of risks and benefits, the adequacy of proposed solutions in socioeconomic terms, and potential vested interests. Social debate about proposed facilities or controversial risks typically stretches beyond institutional issues to tap more fundamental concerns about underlying values and overall worldviews (see Chapter 3).

Thus, the risk communicator must be sensitive to the social fabric of participants and the symbolic meanings embedded in discourse and language (Kasperson et al, 1988e; Short, 1984). Also, it is important to recognize that purposeful risk communication occurs in a context of multiple and diffuse social communication (Krimsky and Plough, 1988). The key task for the communicator is to foster the growth of an environment in which exchanges of information and ideas can take place in a meaningful fashion, and interested participants can make their own evaluations and judgements. Two-way communication, widely espoused but rarely achieved, is essential in identifying any consensus or key points of contention.

Key elements in the design of a risk communication programme, then, will include the following five aspects, which are discussed further below: identifying the needs that risk communication should address; assessing the content of the debate (facts, distrust of institutions, values/ worldview); developing an overall process for the communication effort, including attention to the roles and capacities of the communicator and the participants; designing the risk communication strategies and techniques (e.g. messages); and adopting an ongoing monitoring and evaluation system.

A *needs assessment* is the first step. The need to know cannot be defined solely by the expert or the communicator. Rather, an open process of two-way exchange of information is necessary to elicit what various publics believe they need and want to know. Such a process will reveal that there is no 'monolithic' public, of course, but a number of interested publics with differing concerns, expectations and cultural agendas (Rayner and Cantor, 1987, see also Chapter 1). The assessment must be sufficiently flexible and broad based to accommodate the full range of public concerns, which do not necessarily relate narrowly to risk and are often neglected in traditional, technical risk assessments. They include such issues as losses in property values and quality of life, erosion of the sense of community, disrupted social relations and stigma. In needs assessments, the analyst should err on the side of inclusiveness of issues and needs, recognizing the imperfections in the methodologies of risk assessment and social impact analysis, and the high levels of irreducible uncertainty surrounding expert judgements (Freudenburg, 1988). An openness to criticism and a transparency in decisions can improve perceptions of caring and commitment.

The *content of the risk debate* may be expected to go beyond even these broad issues of risk and impact, and to include questions of means and ends (Chapter 1). For developers or communicators, public participation is primarily a means to accomplish a particular end; for members of the public, participation is often an end in itself. Social conflict over facilities and risks is often not a conflict over risk per se, but rather a political conflict over access to power and resources, and who will allocate how much risk to whom. Debates over risk are thus typically debates about technology and ethics in their broad social context, and about the roles to be played by risk and risk managers in a democracy (Otway, 1987; Ruckelshaus, 1985). These are issues critical to public perceptions of an uncompromised commitment to safety.

The *design of the risk communication process* should, as suggested above, explicitly recognize the levels of social distrust that exist. The key to the design of a process geared to social distrust is the sharing of power, that is the empowerment of risk bearers, in the management of the risk or the facility. Power sharing can positively affect trust along all four of its key dimensions. Sandman (1985) made several suggestions directly relevant to this goal. Firstly, the communicator or developer must acknowledge that the host community or region has substantial power to prevent or delay the siting process, even though members of the public (and perhaps developers) may believe otherwise. Such acknowledgement may help to reduce community feelings of anger and resentment, and put the dialogue on a more equal footing. Secondly, the community must be involved in all negotiations from the beginning and throughout the process, and all plans and positions should be presented as provisional. The traditional approach to siting – decide, announce and defend – will serve only to generate conflict, anger and additional distrust. Presenting positions as provisional removes some of the burden on social trust, allows all parties the freedom to manoeuvre and provides members of the public with the knowledge that they do have power over the process and the ultimate decision.

The process should incorporate indigenous and independent expertise as well as the means to act on this information (Chapter 1). Providing the risk bearers with the ability to appoint their own independent experts to interpret and validate risk assessments and to develop risk monitoring programmes will enhance their sense of control. Independent verification of the claims of the developer and the siting authority removes the need for trust in others in order for the process to go forward.

The process in conditions of high social distrust must, therefore, be 'information rich' at all times. As much relevant information as possible should be available to the public from the beginning, with ready access to experts and policy makers for clarification and elaboration. And the agency or corporation should err on the side of presenting too much information. 'Failure to disclose a relevant fact can poison the entire process once the information has wormed its way out – as it invariably does... Any information that would be embarrassing if disclosed later, should be disclosed now' (Sandman, 1985, pp460–461). In the absence of provided information, the public will actively seek answers from other (often unreliable) sources to fill the 'information void'. Responsible agencies and developers will have little or no control over the quality of such information, while the failure to provide desired information will lead to public perceptions of a cover-up (or, in our terms, a lack of uncompromised commitment). Although the early release of still-developing information can also lead to problems and erode trust (as noted above), on balance, damage associated with openness is easier to address than damage associated with concealment.

In regard to *risk communication strategies and methods*, it is essential to recognize that since many different publics exist, a variety of strategies will be necessary to reach the full spectrum of social groups. Paradoxically, those most affected by the risk may be the least likely to participate in the process and may possess the fewest resources to protect themselves. Special attention is required, therefore, to ensure that their concerns are fully addressed. A wide variety of risk communication techniques exists, each relevant to particular risk and social circumstances. But it is difficult to predict which participatory technique may be most effective in a given situation. There is a general consensus, however, that public hearings are ineffective, alienating and often erosive of social trust (Checkoway, 1981). Other more promising methods exist, including Delphi procedures, role playing, gaming simulation, focus groups and planning cells. Each of these provides an opportunity for diverse interests to participate in focused processing in informal settings, where issues can be confronted and explored in some depth. Throughout, negotiation is the central process for reconciling conflicts. Risk communicators must be acutely aware that publics and experts see risk through different lenses. The task of the risk communicator is thus not to pass judgement nor to approve or disapprove of public perceptions, but to recognize the reasons for the divergences and to act on them.

Finally, *monitoring and evaluation* are indispensable resources in a process adapted to social distrust. In environments of high distrust, interpreting what is happening and how multiple interests are responding is highly problematic and prone to failures. Thus, it is essential to mount an ambitious programme of participatory evaluation that begins even before the initiation of the communication or siting programme, so that appropriate baseline information and broadly agreed-upon procedures can be established. Ongoing evaluation can be structured as another form of responsibility and power sharing, and can be closely linked to a dynamically changing communication programme linked to evaluation results (see Chapter 3).

Hazardous-facility siting

Given that host publics typically have strong fears about the hazards associated with noxious facilities, that inequities are difficult to overcome and that high levels of social distrust exist, a process is needed that has sufficient robustness to address squarely the public concerns and yet deliver a needed facility site. In our view, the intertwining of risk, equity and distrust calls for a process that is hierarchical in content, sequential in design and plural in power sharing.

Resolution of the safety issues is the first and most basic task confronting facility siting and development. From previous risk and facility siting studies, it is apparent that efforts to proceed based on a technical assessment of risk (i.e. 'our risk assessment shows that we will meet the emission standard') and to attempt to win public confidence are destined to failure in most cases. The crux of the issue here is the large difference between the technical and public assessments of risk, often exacerbated by the inevitable equity problems that arise (Freudenburg, 1988). Reassurances about risk in a climate of social distrust are unlikely to be convincing, and indeed may be alienating. The alternative is to take steps to resolve the safety concerns among risk bearers and host community publics as much as can reasonably be done, whether they are warranted or not by a purely technical assessment. The definition of concerns to be addressed should be sufficiently broad to capture those that may arise from the interaction between technical risk considerations and social processes (Kasperson et al, 1988e). This is likely to involve 'overbuilding' the safety systems of the facility and including concerned publics in the content of that overbuilding. Negotiation over the facility design and the selection of the contractor and operator, as well as independent community review of the planned facility, are all helpful. If some particular issue emerges (e.g. what are the safeguards in case of an earthquake?) that becomes a driver of public concerns, an independent study by a jointly selected expert may be undertaken. An agreement might also be developed by which a host community has the capability to monitor facility performance and to have recourse under specific conditions to seeking facility shutdown if emission standards are violated. The recommended strategy, in essence, is to resolve as broad a range of public concerns over risk as is reasonable. Such an approach does not, of course, guarantee that a site will be successfully agreed upon, but it does provide facility developers a seat at the table so that the other issues can be discussed. This approach has been a central part of the success in Sweden in siting various nuclear facilities (Parker et al, 1986), and in the Oak Ridge negotiation with Tennessee over interim nuclear waste storage facilities (Peele, 1987). Until important progress has been made on the risk issue, a dialogue with host publics about other issues is not possible (Creighton, 1990).

In this strategy, it is essential that a *systems and historical perspective* be maintained. While developers generally see the siting process as a here-and-now, single-facility problem, publics typically have long memories and employ broader contexts. So the locations of previous controversial facilities and the sites of facilities generating wastes (for example) become important ingredients in shaping public responses. Thus, approaches to facility siting will assist in developing a dialogue if they can demonstrate that the burden of hazardous facilities will be shared over time by the whole population of the political jurisdiction, and that the location of the last controversial facility provides a context for the current decision.

If the risk issues have been effectively engaged (if not totally resolved), then the *equity problems* can be addressed. These problems will involve both procedural and outcome equity issues. In both cases, the emphasis should preferably be on reducing the inequity wherever possible, for it is morally better to avoid harm and injustice than to compensate for it (Derr et al, 1986). This emphasis is also critical for perceptions of caring and of commitment to public protection. Key procedural aspects that are needed to assure basic procedural equity have been noted above. To them should be added efforts to achieve *evidentiary equity* – that is, steps taken to assure that host-community publics possess needed information and independent analytical resources, and that the burden of proof for demonstrating safety and the suitability of the site rests upon the developer and not the potential risk bearers (Colglazier, 1991). In regard to *outcome equity*, the distribution of benefits and burdens will be critical, since host communities for hazardous facilities characteristically experience a disproportion of harms and burdens in relation to benefits. In particular, steps may be taken to reduce potential harms through the provision of planning resources and property value guarantees, while benefits can be enlarged through preferential employment and purchasing practices. A well-conceived programme of inequity reduction can do much to narrow the net level of negative impacts and to increase the social acceptability of the site.

It is at this juncture, and only at this point in the sequence, that the *use of resources for compensation and incentive* becomes appropriate. The failure to recognize that compensation cannot substitute for safety assurance and inequity reduction has contributed to the design of socially unacceptable siting programmes, such as those involving auction and bidding schemes, in which prospective host communities are asked to bid a dollar price at which they would be willing to accept the facility. Inevitably, the approach of compensating for risk rather than reducing risk greatly exacerbates social distrust by its adverse effects on perceptions of two of the four dimensions of trust – uncompromised commitment to health and safety, and caring about local persons. If, on the other hand, determined efforts involving the community have been made to reduce risks and adverse impacts and to narrow uncertainties, compensation for the remaining adverse burden and incentives for the community to help society solve a problem become acceptable. The level of compensation should be administratively set to avoid prolonged and often alienating bargaining, but the form and content of the compensation package should be negotiated with host-region publics to assure its maximum social value and acceptance. If a voluntary solicitation for sites is part of the siting process, consideration should be given to providing a right to 'opt out' at any time in the process, as an incentive for candidate communities to stay involved, and to provide time for full community consideration to occur and for local advocates to emerge.

FINAL OBSERVATION

While successful risk communication and siting programmes will always depend upon both historical experience and the regional political culture and institutions, the strategies outlined above are sensitive to a context of high social distrust and provide some potential for success under what are inevitably very inimical conditions for addressing controversial public (or private) decisions. Initiatives based upon the explicit recognition of high social distrust may, through empowerment, risk clarification and negotiation, ultimately prove to be much more effective in the long-term recovery of social trust than approaches that assert that such trust is merited a priori, and that an attempt to combat long-term trends and convert ingrained attitudes in the relatively short time periods that characterize siting decisions.

3 Evaluating Risk Communication

Roger E. Kasperson and Ingar Palmlund

INTRODUCTION

This chapter inquires into the potential and limits of evaluation as a component of risk communication programmes in diverse institutional settings. We begin by discussing the roles of institutional setting and government in risk communication. Then we ask why risk communication programmes need to be evaluated and what assessments may contribute. We next inquire into the ways in which implicit models and paradigms of risk communication influence the way we think about objectives and approaches. We examine the evaluation process for an insight into effective means for organizing and conducting the assessment. Finally, we propose specific criteria to guide the evaluation of risk communication programmes.

INSTITUTIONAL SETTING

Risk communication is all about us. It enters our lives in a multitude of forms, sometimes in the imagery of advertising, sometimes in a whisper in the back row of a public hearing, sometimes in a local corporation's formal statement. Sometimes it fails to say anything, as in certain multi-volumed and impenetrable technical risk assessments. Even when government is the risk communicator, the objective is, alternatively, to inform, to incite to action, to reassure, to co-opt or to overpower. This suggests not one risk communication problem but many. It also suggests that evaluating risk communication is fraught with difficulty because the meaning of success – or, for that matter, failure – will be elusive.

What is certain is that the institutional setting of risk is important. Risks of concern and controversy characteristically involve asymmetric distributions of responsibility and power. Risk in the doctor's office is

Note: Reprinted from *Effective Risk Communication: The Role and Responsibility of Goverrrnment*, Covello, V., McCallum, D. and Pavlova, M. (eds), 'Evaluating risk communication', Kasperson, K. E. and Palmlund, I., pp143–160, © (1989), with permission from Kluwer Academic/Plenum Press

intensely personal, and regulatory agencies have generally avoided intruding on the sanctity of the doctor/patient relationship. The risk communication problem here is to change long-standing patterns of behaviour and for individuals to assume greater responsibility for personal health decisions.

Risk in the workplace occurs in a setting where the risk generator is also the risk manager, and where the risk bearer has few options for avoiding the risk. Here the risk communication problems are many:

1   How to encourage the full dissemination of information about risk when such information may stimulate labour problems or subsequent legal action.
2   How to encourage workers to learn about risk when they usually can do little in the short run to change the basic risk conditions.
3   How to raise worker consciousness about actions that can be taken to limit and prevent risks in the long run.

Risk in the community setting is different still. Here the individual is beset with multiple and conflicting sources of information and uneven access to local and distant authorities.

Whatever the institutional setting, government is frequently called on to intervene in risk issues. The challenge is nearly always fraught with conflicting goals and diverse interests.

GOVERNMENTS AND RISK COMMUNICATION

In most cases, risk communication occurs outside the scope of governmental influence and control; indeed, risk communication is part of the social processes that, only in certain instances, creep into governmental agendas. The conflicts of interest between risk generators and risk bearers is the milieu in which government mediates disputes, formulates norms for determining acceptable risk and fashions measures to reduce risk.

Governments initiate risk communication for three main reasons: to determine the range where a lack of consensus prevails as to the acceptability of risks; to mediate among conflicting interests or to persuade those concerned that the actions decided on by government are appropriate and equitable; or to induce the general public to act individually or collectively to reduce its risk.

To communicate means either to impart information (i.e. it is a one-way process) or to have an interchange of ideas whereby more than one party actively gives information (i.e. it is a two-way process). Requirements that consumers of pharmaceuticals or workers be provided with information about risks are examples of one-way communication. Environmental impact statements or public inquiries on major installations affecting the physical environment, the public discussion of such evidence and the public hearings regarding regulatory measures concerning risk management are two-way communication processes.

Government programmes for risk communication involve both form and content. Such programmes may aim only at establishing the forms of communication that should be observed by risk generators in their interaction with risk bearers. An example of this is the requirement in Sweden that a safety committee be set up in each workplace that has more than 50 workers, with both employers and employees participating, as a forum for handling occupational risks. Government programmes for risk communication may also aim at establishing only the content of risk communication, leaving the definition of appropriate forms to others. Requirements that drivers know about and comply with traffic rules for highway safety is an example of this. Typically, however, government involvement in risk communication concerns both form and content, as in the mandatory labelling of pharmaceuticals.

The role of government in communicating risk becomes especially important during emergencies and crises. Major industrial accidents – such as those at the Three Mile Island nuclear power plant, the pesticide factories in Seveso, Italy and Bhopal, India, and the 1986 accident at the nuclear power plant at Chernobyl – are challenges to any governmental bureaucracy. In such emergencies, government is expected to provide the correct interpretation of what is happening, to create conditions for preventing harm and provide relief for those at risk, and to compensate for material and physical loss. For governments not used to sudden disasters, but accustomed to ample time for planning and carefully considered action, this is an unusual situation.

Risk communication is often a direct invitation or an incitement to action by those exposed to risk. When government communicates risk without also providing advice on remedies or opportunities for protection, it creates an incentive for converting risk situations into political campaigns. Risk is not only an objectively verifiable element of a situation; it is also a culturally defined phenomenon that reflects the distribution of power, the political atmosphere, and societal values and conflicts.

Evaluation of government programmes often aims to investigate how faithfully specific rules, objectives or directives have been implemented. In such evaluations, the investigator can retain the politically defined intention or assess how the results correspond with what was desired by various political interests. If the aim of the evaluation, however, is to decide which programmes – public or private – best contribute to solving the problem at hand, the situation becomes one of policy formulation. Policies are expressions of the intentions or rationales that guide people's behaviour in specific situations. Evaluation in situations of policy formulation requires a conscious search for clear objectives, an open declaration of the values used in measuring success, and an assessment of the different activities that may synergistically contribute to the problem to be solved.

PURPOSES AND MOTIVATIONS: Why evaluate risk communication programmes?

The urge to evaluate is rooted in a view of human progress as a process of trial and error. Evaluation, however, is a matter of values, of political agenda and, perhaps, of taste. Therefore, evaluation depends critically on who orders the assessment, how the risk communication problem is constructed, and what measuring rod is used. These aspects depend, in turn, on the motivation for evaluation. In the discussion to follow, we identify five distinct motivations for evaluation.

Evaluation as commodity marketing

Many risk communications have a product, service or idea to market. The commodity is often a government or industry risk management programme, such as the Environmental Protection Agency's Superfund programme or a post-Bhopal Union Carbide, seeking to restore its credibility as a manager of health and safety. Evaluation in this situation becomes an indispensable tool to allow the organization to assemble documentation to demonstrate that efforts are working and merit continued support, and that government goals and the public interest are being met. Organizations tend to be very resistant to information that runs counter to organizational goals, so that selective use, or distortion, of information emerging from evaluations is not uncommon (Wilensky, 1967). Throughout, this self-evaluation tends to serve the central purpose of solidifying, justifying or extending the risk management or technology programme.

Evaluation as mandated accountability

In mandatory accountability, evaluation is a pro forma means of verifying compliance with requirements placed on the organization by the external environment. These evaluations can be used to modify and further develop the risk communication performance. Affirming that material safety data sheets (MSDSs) are being used as a means of complying with the rule of the Occupational Safety and Health Administration on hazard communication is one example. In other cases, the evaluation itself may either be a requisite for programme continuation or a part of regulatory compliance.

Evaluation as programme development

Frequently, the organization is uncertain about its performance, threatened by failures or outside criticism, or involved in decisions concerned with allocating scarce resources. The scope of the evaluations can include the revision of implementing strategies or even goal reassessment. Evaluation tends to be more open-ended and to make greater use of independent, outside evaluators. The risk communicator may be more open to information critical of organizational performance, unless the core of organizational activity is at stake. This type of evaluation is, therefore, more likely to be found in newer organizations whose programmes are still in flux or the more peripheral programmes in well-established organizations.

Evaluation as a safety valve

When confronted by crisis in their risk management and communication programmes, organizations seek ways of diverting public pressure and gaining time to marshal resources and to formulate responses. Stimulated by such motivation, evaluation not only has a factual but also a symbolic role – in demonstrating interest in what went wrong, in seeking solutions, in making concessions to outside critics, and in allocating blame and responsibility. Since legitimacy is frequently at issue, the institutional process and the composition of the evaluators become essential. Evaluation, as the Kemeny Commission (Kemeny et al, 1979) and the Challenger Commission (US Presidential Commission, 1986) suggest, may also provide an opportunity to resolve internal conflicts.

Evaluation as a war tool

This motivation for evaluation is the converse of commodity marketing. A higher level of bureaucracy, a legislative oversight committee or an external opponent may seek to weaken or destroy a particular organization or to dissolve its risk management programme. Sometimes the evaluation is conducted by the hostile party; on other occasions an external, and unfriendly, evaluator is enlisted. The process of evaluation, providing the opportunity for 'leaks' to the media, can be as important, and damaging, as the evaluation product itself.

These differing motivations will largely determine how managers define risk communication problems, how they conceptualize success and how they use the results. Thus, the purposes of evaluation need to be clear.

IMPLICIT PARADIGMS

Different approaches to evaluation have evolved over time. Here we describe several of the major types and suggest how they enter into the underlying assumptions and substance of evaluation programmes. They are essentially implicit paradigms of risk communication that are sometimes complementary, sometimes conflictual.

Information systems

One common approach to communication research arises from the field of information systems, in which interest focuses on such concepts as sender, receiver, messages, information channels, channel density, target audiences and information overloads. These concepts have enjoyed wide use in communication engineering, which structures the communications process as (1) the communication source; (2) the message; (3) the communication channels; and (4) the receivers. The source relates to the attributes of the sender of information (e.g. credibility). The message involves the specific package of information used to accomplish a particular purpose; it may be factual or emotional in appeal and may use or avoid symbols. As noted earlier, in risk situations, the intent may be to incite to action, warn, inform or reassure. Lee (1986) notes that message variables include such factors as emotional versus logical presentation; fear appeals; message style; implicit versus explicit conclusions; placing explicit conclusion first versus last; how opposition arguments are addressed; and where the message is pitched.

Communication channels include not only, prominently, the mass media, but other interpersonal and intergroup networks as well. The receivers are those for whom the messages are designed: alternatively the risk bearer, the risk manager or the general public. Variables of the receiver include prior experience with the risk, group membership, education and personality. Evaluation, in the information systems context, tends to focus on four components – source, message, channel and receiver. The assumption is that the key to success is the timely and efficient flow of messages from source to receiver, along diverse channels, with as little loss of information as possible.

Marketing

The marketing approach to risk communication consists of a diverse set of methods and strategies that have evolved in advertising and marketing products to consumers. In this view, risk communication is not conceptually distinct from the selling of soap. Central concepts, which include consumer information processing and market segmentation, have been reviewed by Earle and Cvetkovich (1984). Research on consumer information processing recognizes the various limitations that exist for prospective consumers of information. The difficulty of consumer choice, for example, relates to the number of alternatives that exist and the extent to which information formats facilitate comparisons. The amount of time available for processing information suggests that some media are preferable to others. The information format chosen can either facilitate or impede the amount and type of information processing.

The concept of market segmentation recognizes the basic fact of individual differences in interest and need. The goal of segmentation is to produce the most efficient groupings of people (i.e. disaggregation of the market) so that marketing may target its message to particular consumer groups.

Much of this risk communication paradigm derives from the 'do's and don'ts' emerging from the practical experience of advertising and marketing, as suggested in Lesly's (1982) guides for effective communication.

Psychometric research

If information systems highlight message flows and marketing approaches emphasize consumer behaviour, then psychometric studies centre on the 'receiver', now characterized as an individual coping with alternative decision situations and making judgements based on perceptions and values. The psychometric paradigm uses psychophysical scaling and multivariate analysis techniques to produce quantitative representations, or 'cognitive maps', of risk attitudes and perceptions (Slovic et al, 1986). Within this paradigm, people are asked to make quantitative judgements about the existing and desired riskiness of different hazards and the desirable level of regulation for each. These judgements are then related to such issues as (1) the attributes of the hazard (e.g. voluntariness, dread, knowledge); (2) the benefits accompanying the hazard; (3) the number of deaths caused by the hazard in a disastrous year; and (4) the seriousness of each death from a particular hazard relative to deaths from other causes (Slovic et al, 1986). This work has led to important conclusions, as articulated by Baruch Fischhoff (1985), directly relevant to risk communication efforts:

- In order to cope with decision and information overloads, people simplify.
- Once people's minds are made up, it is difficult to change them.
- People remember what they see. For most people, the primary sources of information about risk are what they see or hear in the news media and what they observe in everyday life.
- People cannot readily detect omissions in the evidence they receive. As a result, their risk perceptions can be manipulated.
- People disagree more about what risk is than about how large it is. Lay people and risk managers use the term 'risk' differently.
- People have difficulty detecting inconsistencies in risk disputes. As a result, risk communication needs to provide people with alternative perspectives.
- People have difficulty evaluating expertise.

The cultural hypothesis of risk

This approach to risk begins with the premise that different institutional cultures exist with their own characteristic views of the world, or cultural biases, including viewpoints on risk and danger (Douglas and Wildavsky, 1982). Underlying this notion of cultural bias is the premise that in order to steer through the daily social maze, an individual's ideas must be generally consistent with the social constraints on interactions arising from organizational and institutional contexts. Thus, individuals structure their worldviews in ways that are consistent with their shared, daily social experience. It has been argued (Rayner, 1984; Rayner and Cantor, 1987) that there may be as few as four basic ways of structuring a worldview, according to what has been termed the 'grid' and 'group' variables of organizational life. Grid refers to the degree of constraint that exists on individual interaction; group refers to the range of social interaction. These dimensions can be used to generate different prototypical visions of social life. Seen this way, risk is a way of classifying a whole series of complex interactions and relationships between people, as well as between man and nature (Rayner, 1984). This perspective on risk has generated a number of propositions relevant to risk communication:

- Culture is the coding principle by which hazards are recognized. The community sets up the individual's model of the world and the scale of values by which different consequences are reckoned grave or trivial (Douglas, 1985).
- A polymorphous definition of risk is needed that encompasses purely societal concerns about equity as well as concerns about the probability and magnitude of adverse consequences.
- Technology options must be debated on the explicit basis of trust and equity rather than on rival estimates of quantitative risk.
- Different institutional cultures engaged in controversies over technological risk have great difficulty in understanding the fears and objections of others.

Public participation

Since the early 1960s, new expectations for the right of citizens to know about and to participate in public decisions that affect their lives have become quite apparent. This change in social responsibilities has its roots in the civil rights, anti-war, consumer and environmental movements. In Europe, the Seveso accident had far-reaching implications for the European Community in the form of the Seveso Directive, which imposed obligations for both the assessment of risk and its communication to responsible authorities and the public. In the US, the Occupational Safety and Health Administration's hazard communication rule has set new expectations, and responsibilities, for informing those at risk. The 1987 Superfund amendments not only expand hazard communication responsibilities but substantially increase local participation on hazard assessment as well.

Experience with public participation over several decades has afforded a variety of insights into both the nature of the obstacles and realistic expectations of what is possible. In Chapter 1, R. Kasperson has identified a number of different propositions, emerging from several decades of public participation research, for formulating risk communication programmes. These include:

- Conflicts emerging in public participation often centre on means/ends differences in expectation. Citizens will see programmes as an invitation to share power, to participate in defining ends. The agency managers, by contrast, will see it as having only an instrumental function, a means, say, to realize established health and safety objectives.
- A lack of early and continuing involvement of the public is a characteristic source of failure.
- The believability of risk information is clearly related to institutional credibility and trust.
- Effective public participation depends substantially on the development of indigenous resources and the technical means to act on and assess increased knowledge.
- Members of the public differ in the arenas and scope of their involvement, suggesting the need for differing communication strategies.
- Although a large array of participation exists, current knowledge, especially about risk communication, does not allow for successful predictions as to which forms of participation are likely to be most effective under different conditions.

RISK COMMUNICATION IN SWEDEN IN THE WAKE OF THE CHERNOBYL ACCIDENT

On 28 April, 1986, headlines in the Swedish newspapers warned that something was wrong with one of the nuclear reactors in the Stockholm region. The news the following day revealed that the radioactivity had emanated from a nuclear reactor failure in the Soviet Union.

The subsequent day, the headline in one of the major newspapers was: 2,000 DEAD IN THE ACCIDENT, THE SOVIET UNION ASKS FOR HELP, coupled with NO DANGER IN SWEDEN in smaller print. That was the first communication from the Swedish National Radiation Protection Institute (SSI) concerning the risks following the Chernobyl accident.

During the following days, measurements of radiation showed values at a level about ten times higher than the natural radiation from the ground in an area along the northeastern coastal region. That was a level, however, far below the point at which emergency measures would be deemed necessary. Authorities advised that the drinking water could be used as usual but that people should not use rainwater. Some independent physicians recommended that parents not allow small children to play in sand or mud puddles for a few days. No special recommendations regarding animals were necessary, according to SSI. Milk had been measured for radioactivity, but no high values had been encountered. The SSI also announced that it would not be necessary to take iodine tablets.

So people gathered for their Valborgsmass festivities and traditional 1 May national holiday with no apparent worry about radiation hazards.

But before long other orders were forthcoming. Farmers were forbidden to release their cattle for grazing until the regions where they lived had been classified as safe. Milk showing high levels of radiation had to be poured on the ground. Farmers were told to cut their grass but not to store it in heaps. The farmers' organizations protested that compliance with the rules would mean considerable financial loss for the farming community. Eventually, the government promised full economic compensation to farmers for the extra costs caused by the prohibitions. Gradually, through May, the restrictions on grazing cattle were lifted, first in the southern regions, then gradually further north as values from radiation measurements got lower.

The SSI also soon warned that people should avoid eating the traditional spring food, young nettles, as well as rhubarb and other leafy vegetables. Later, meat from cattle and reindeer in the regions of heavy fallout was found to have been contaminated so it could not be allowed on the market, which meant an erosion of the economic basis of the ethnic Lapp minority. By the end of May, some areas around the town of Gaevle in Sweden had some of the highest levels of radioactive caesium (137,000 becquerels) in Western Europe. While no acute damage to humans was involved, cancer and genetic damage rates are expected to increase slightly over the long term.

The Swedish government agencies in charge of the assessment and communication of risks generally did a good job under the circumstances. Their stance seemed to aim at avoiding unnecessary anxiety while openly informing the public of what they knew. The authorities did what they could to make the technical information comprehensible, comparing radiation levels from the fallout to those experienced during X-ray examination. Most people responded with a quiet sadness, but some had the following criticisms: Kiev had lower levels of radioactivity than Sweden. Yet why were women and children evacuated from Kiev but not from Gaevle? Why were the Swedish people initially informed that there was no danger, when later the government decided on many restrictions for grazing cattle? Were they hiding something? Questions also arose in the media and in the Swedish Parliament.

The Chernobyl accident carries a number of lessons in risk communication. Early reassurances in risk events may not always be the best strategy for a government, but balancing warning and reassurance appropriately is difficult. Openness and candour are critical if trust is to be built. Providing the contexts whereby information can be interpreted may be as important as the risk data themselves. A single source of authoritative information helps to prevent confusion.

THE PROCESS OF EVALUATION

Simplified models of organizational decision making envision a sequence of activities, typically including a statement of objectives, a search for information and options, formal decision making, implementation, evaluation and feedback. In this context, evaluation has the same function as it does in experimental research – to assess the value of the experiment that has been performed. When government or other interests intervene to disseminate information or to initiate a dialogue with risk bearers over health and environmental impacts, the experimental research analogue breaks down. Science is no longer the objective, the role of the analyst changes, and evaluation takes on political meaning. Evaluation of risk communication should include the considerations discussed in the following subsections.

The formulation of objectives

Which are the stated and which the real purposes of evaluation? As noted above, the motivations for evaluation are diverse. Assessing efficiency, that is, carrying out programmes in a cost-effective manner, is one common objective. Investigating effectiveness, that is, the accomplishment of goals regardless of cost, is another.

The locus of evaluation

Should the evaluation be organized in-house or should external evaluators be brought in? Generally, the ethics of auditing prohibit the persons responsible for the accounts from auditing their own performance. In organizational activities, separating these roles and minimizing potential conflict of interest is no less important. However, much depends on the organizational motivation for the evaluation. An external evaluation can be very helpful if the goal is commodity marketing. Such an evaluation may bring new knowledge or a valuable perspective, thereby redefining the problem or offering new solutions.

However, if the administrator of the risk communication programme opposes the evaluation, it is likely that the evaluation will have little overall impact. The programme administrator has many reasons to resist outside evaluation. Risk communication is a highly uncertain activity with high visibility and political stakes. The simple fact of the matter is that we know relatively little about how best to communicate complex risk issues. The external evaluator typically has little first-hand knowledge of the trials and tribulations of the risk communication practitioner.

Evaluations located in-house have their own advantages and prices. The internal evaluator is highly knowledgeable about the organization, the programme and constraints. However, the evaluation runs the risk of being partial and distorted, so as not to threaten agency or department goals. Data may be suppressed or selectively interpreted. While in-house evaluation may be more closely geared to agency goals and cognizant of constraints, it may also be safely ignored. In short, differing loci of evaluation shape the evaluation and its ultimate impact.

Timing

Whether an evaluation is foreseen and planned before the activity to be evaluated starts (*ex ante*), or undertaken after the fact (*ex post*), is extremely important. Characteristically, evaluation is retrospective. The timing of an evaluation may coincide with budgetary review to determine if the risk communication programme is an appropriate reason for the expenditure of funds. The evaluation may seek to document the agency's risk management programme, or it may serve as a map for avoiding the minefields of wrong turns in communication process. *Ex post* evaluation involves a number of serious problems:

- Relevant data may no longer be available, particularly if the need for evaluation was not anticipated at programme inception.
- Participants or risk bearers may be difficult to locate.
- Evaluation may not be available in time to correct programme deficiencies.
- The purpose of the evaluation may influence the results.
- Programme managers may be suspicious of an evaluator who arrives after the fact to assess a programme in which he was not involved.
- Changes in programme operation or impacts may be difficult to discern after the programme is completed (Morgenstern et al, 1980).

It can be argued, correspondingly, that *ex ante* (planned, ongoing) evaluation also has its problems, particularly in the intrusion of the evaluator and the potential disruption that could occur. The essential point is that evaluation should be used to inform, and improve, the communication process as it unfolds. A well-founded evaluation effort will also incorporate baseline data obtained at the beginning of the process so that changes can be accurately assessed.

Training and monitoring of evaluators

Too often, overburdened programme staff carry out the evaluation effort, with little training in evaluation and little monitoring of their performance. For many of the staff, evaluation will be less important than communicating the risks, and they will allocate their scarce time and resources accordingly (Comfort, 1980). Searching evaluation requires that different members of the programme reflect sensitively and thoughtfully on their performance. In this way, the evaluation process becomes a central means by which the organization develops the skills of its staff in the performance of risk communication.

The role of the individual in risk communication

What should be the role of those for whom the risk communication programme is intended – the 'target groups' in marketing terminology? Should their role be restricted to providing information to the evaluators or should they contribute to the design of the evaluation process and instruments? Differing parties in the risk communication programme will clearly ask different questions and desire different kinds of data in an evaluation.

If the risk communication programme is designed to be interactive in nature and to serve multiple needs, then public or risk bearer participation in the formulation of evaluation programmes seems to be particularly essential. In all cases, the degree of expressed public satisfaction with the programme is one appropriate measure of success.

Boundaries of the evaluation

We live in a time when the scope of risk is increasingly transnational, sometimes even global, while government remains national. Technology and products are disseminated globally, carrying benefits and risk into a space that is far broader than any government can control. Chernobyl, Bhopal, fluorocarbons, and the 1986 Rhine pollution all suggest the internationalization of risk. If the boundaries of goals and evaluations are drawn too narrowly, comfortable results may ensue but may correspond badly to the real risk problems.

The measurement trap

A classic anecdote recounts how a man searching on a dark night for his lost key concentrates on the illuminated circle under the lamppost, since that is where the key would be most easily found. The focus and scope of evaluation are often defined less by what we most need to know than by what can be measured easily or by a favourite measuring tool. Risk communication programmes need to be seen, given the current state of knowledge, as exploratory and experimental; in short, as serious research ventures using the most appropriate yardsticks, qualitative as well as quantitative. Learning from experience, then, will require substantial methodological investment and resources, so that thoughtful questions are asked and causality is pursued with determination.

TEN CRITERIA FOR EVALUATING RISK COMMUNICATION PROGRAMMES

Based on the discussions above, we propose ten criteria for evaluating risk communication programmes. In doing so, we recognize that such criteria rely on normative conceptions of success in risk management and that debate over such propositions will continue in the coming years.

Needs appraisal

Risk communication should not be based solely on assumptions by the risk manager of what risk bearers need to know about risks. Rather, a careful appraisal should be made of the risk bearers' needs and how they might best be met. Such judgements should be based on information from both expert and lay opinion. It should also include the identification of groups who are especially affected by the risks and how communication can be tailored to reach them in depth. An explicit formulation of concrete objectives of risk communication is an essential prerequisite for performing an honest evaluation of the results.

Risk complexity and social pluralism

Despite the propensity to convey risk in one-dimensional terms (reduced life expectancy, lifetime fatality risk, etc), risk, as we know, is multidimensional. Technologies have a broad range of consequences; defining the particular consequence to be assessed is a decision of importance and often a political act. The qualitative attributes of risk – voluntariness, catastrophic potential, and degree of familiarity – affect our responses to them. Then, too, cultural groups define risks differently, attach different values to them, and incorporate them into differing sociopolitical agenda. A primary challenge in risk communication is making complex phenomena understandable to non-technical people while simultaneously capturing the major attributes of concern to a highly variegated public. In such situations, it is important to err on the side of multiple perspectives, differing characterizations of risk, and richness in communication approaches.

Risk in context

Technological risk is a complex phenomenon, at once technical, uncertain, probabilistic and value laden. Provision of information needs to be accompanied by efforts to assist individuals in comprehending the risk. Types of contextual information include comparisons with other relevant risks (which need to be done with intelligence and sensitivity); comparisons with benefits of the activity or technology; comparisons with regulatory standards or natural background levels, etc; and comparisons of ways in which the risk can be reduced and what it would require in resources. Invariably, individuals also desire, and may demand, full information on the process that generated the risk – why it occurred, what is being done to reduce it, and why this was not done before.

A management prospectus

As suggested by Baruch Fischhoff (1985), risk managers should develop a protocol that ensures that all relevant information concerning the risk management programme is communicated to the public. Such a prospectus would include how the manager sees the facts, what options the manager is legally empowered to consider, what the manager considers to be the public interest, how the decision was (or will be) made, and with what envisioned results. A well-thought-out treatment is greatly preferable to speculation on such matters by the mass media or piecemeal construction of the picture over time. Prompt provision of such information will also head off fears that the agency is withholding relevant facts or has hidden motivations.

Timeliness

Risk communication should be timely, meaning that it should occur early enough in the process to alert the individual to the risk so that any available actions can be taken to avoid it or to minimize its consequences. The common error is for risk managers to withhold information until late in the process, when information and evidence are more complete and control strategies and supporting rationales more fully developed. It is possible, however, for communication to be premature, thereby eliciting unwarranted fear or unnecessary protective actions. Repeated over-reactive warnings to evacuate in the face of a predicted natural hazard (e.g. an earthquake) or industrial accident (e.g. a chemical release) may result in decreased credibility and, thus, increased risk.

Iterative interaction

Although there may be special circumstances in which risk communication involves only a single transaction or message, multiple or continuous interaction is nearly always necessary to ensure a flow of relevant risk information. Interaction implies the two-way flow of information, with learning by all those participating in the process. Very few risk communication programmes build in the means to listen to or to initiate public response, which should be a requisite to developing the communication programme and gauging its effectiveness.

Empowerment

Risk information unaccompanied by power and the means to act on the expanded knowledge is ultimately frustrating. Clearly, it reduces the incentive to acquire risk information and causes the audience to ask 'If I can't do anything about it, why are you telling me?' Wherever possible, risk communication should be embedded in a broader approach that empowers those at risk to act in their own protection or to influence those who act on their behalf. The effectiveness of the Swedish information programme on workplace hazards is connected in no small part to worker participation in risk management programmes. Similarly, the recent success in community consideration of a monitored retrievable storage facility for radioactive wastes in Tennessee was associated with the power the community of Oak Ridge was able to assume.

Credibility

Success in risk communication depends heavily on the confidence individuals place on the sources of information. Credibility is multidimensional, involving perceived competence, commitment to public health and safety, and caring about those who bear the risks.

Ethical sensitivity

The current risk communication initiatives that have been started by a broad array of institutions assure that a great many campaigns will soon be in place and that experience will grow rapidly. Safeguards are needed that reflect thoughtful deliberations on the ethical issues involved, including:

- identification of unintended adverse consequences in programmes and structured means for avoiding them;
- respect for the autonomy of the individual and avoidance of paternalism;
- recognition of potential self-interest or bias in the institution acting as risk communicator;
- respect for the rights of those bearing the risks so that programmes will be responsive to them;
- means to ensure that risk communication will be compassionate and respectful of those addressed by the communication;
- avoidance of undue worry and fear;
- assurance that agency staff will have the right to refuse to engage in unethical conduct.

To assure that these ethical issues are addressed, the creation of codes of conduct for risk communicators would be helpful.

Resiliency

Given our limited understanding of risk communication, false steps and approaches are nearly certain. A well-designed risk communication programme should therefore assume surprises and failures, and plan accordingly. Programmes should include conflict among information sources; unforeseen events; potential blockages in information channels; inadequate identification of interested groups and citizens; unidentified value structures and community agenda; higher levels of distrust than assumed; and substantial departure in expert and lay risk judgements. The objective of attempting to anticipate failure should be to make the communication process resilient, so that accurate information gets through, sensitivity is developed, interaction occurs, and credibility grows in the face of adversity and the unexpected.

CONCLUSION

Communicating risk is an emerging major activity of institutions responsible for managing risks. It requires a sensitive balance between providing factual information on risk and avoiding undue anxiety. Evaluation provides a central means for assuring appropriate goals, content and outcomes of such programmes. Such evaluation will have the potential for both good and harm, and requires clear criteria by which success can be measured, the good maximized and the harm avoided. Most of all, evaluation must be taken seriously as a central part of risk communication programmes, and not merely an activity to conduct if sufficient funds are left when the programme is ended.

4 Considerations and Principles for Risk Communication for Industrial Accidents

Roger E. Kasperson and Jeanne X. Kasperson

INTRODUCTION

In 1988, the Organisation for Economic Co-operation and Development (OECD) adopted Council Act C(88)85, aimed at 'the provision of information to the public and public participation in decision-making processes related to the prevention of, and response to, accidents involving hazardous substances' (OECD, 1990, p10). This Act recognized the rights of potentially affected publics to information regarding hazardous installations and accidents that might occur at such installations. A 1990 workshop in Stockholm addressed the provision of information to the public and a subsequent meeting in Boston in the same year dealt with emergency preparedness and response. Meanwhile, extensive developments have occurred in risk communication in individual European countries and in the US over the past decade (Baram, 1993; Gow and Otway, 1990; Kasperson and Stallen, 1991; Pidgeon et al, 1992).

This discussion builds upon these earlier treatments as well as the growing, and now quite substantial, body of research on risk communication. There is now, as well, substantial accumulated experience with industrial accidents and even a journal, *Environmental and Industrial Crisis Management*, that focuses on research on this topic. In this assessment, we begin with a discussion of the challenges facing those responsible for designing and implementing risk communication programmes. We then review the major approaches that have evolved to accomplish this task, and consider in some detail one integrative approach – the 'social amplification of risk' – to guide studies of risk and risk communication. Tapping research on risk perception and risk

Note: Reprinted from *Report of the OECD Workshop on Risk Assessment and Risk Communication in the Context of Chemical Accident Preparedness and Response*, Kasperson, R. E. and Kasperson, J. X., 'Considerations and principles for risk communication for industrial accidents', pp63–90, © (1997), with permission from OECD

communication, we identify potential guides for designing communication programmes and assess the particular issues posed by emergency situations. Finally, the paper addresses how success or failure in risk communication may be evaluated. The intent throughout, it is important to emphasize, is to be suggestive rather than to be prescriptive.

THE CHALLENGES OF RISK COMMUNICATION

Just as many types of risk communication are continuously at work in society (see the discussion of the 'social amplification of risk' below), so too are diverse challenges that risk communication must overcome – before, during and after accidents – to be successful. Prominent among these are the distributed decision setting, the nature of public perceptions and concerns, and the need for flexibility and resilience.

The setting. Distributed decision systems

Emergency responses to industrial accidents necessarily involve integrating information and action across a wide variety of expertise, public and private sectors, differing levels and agencies of government, responsible officials and numerous publics. Major accidents call for what Lagadec (1987, p29) terms 'organizational defense in depth'. It is estimated that the response to the Three Mile Island accident involved up to 1000 different decision makers, not counting the publics. Assuring the timely flow of information and coordinating efforts in such a widely dispersed decision structure can be a Herculean problem that harbours countless opportunities for failure. Another key problem is that emergencies frequently necessitate that organizations assume roles and responsibilities that are unfamiliar and that they interact with other organizations with which they do not normally interact. Organizational coordination and performance are central factors in the success or failure of emergency response during accidents.

Distributed decision structures raise a series of intrinsic problems that are not easily overcome. The agencies involved have competing missions and priorities and, not infrequently, rivalries. Crises are not only substantive problems requiring solutions but opportunities for settling old scores, enlarging funding sources, and changing organizational mandates and programmes. Problems tend to be defined in different ways and information often carries conflicting meaning.

It is not uncommon for emergency planners and risk communicators to seek answers to institutional fragmentation in command-and-control structures, often modelled on the military (Quarantelli, 1988). The command-and-control structures that have evolved do have a number of attributes responsive to emergency situations. Ordinarily, such structures provide a clear delineation and enumeration of tasks. A strong vertical organization with well-developed channels of communication facilitates the rapid dissemination of information. To a varying degree, the inclusion of back-up systems permits accommodation should particular links in the system fail. Overall, such structures attempt to deal with the authority dispersion problem by imposing a detailed articulation of roles and tasks and by invoking predefined categories of accidents and emergency response. At their best, such structures are capable of rapid diagnosis, complex task accomplishment, and timely response.

However, they are also prone to failures. The intelligence system depends heavily upon the accuracy of assumptions and diagnosis at the apex of the system, for the upward flow of communication is characteristically weak. Even when signals come in from outlying areas, the command function often has difficulty interpreting or assigning priority to them. Command-and-control structures also tend to develop rigor mortis as guidelines become regulations, assumptions reality, and broad categories substitute for rich variance. As a consequence, unexpected situations that do not fit preconceived structures can easily result in a delayed or maladaptive response. Meanwhile, participants all too often know only their specific roles and have little sense of the response system as a whole.

So risk communicators confront a central problem – how to ensure a timely and effective response from multiple and dispersed decision makers on the one hand and how to maximize local knowledge and adaptiveness by publics on the other. A central problem is how to make accident response processes resilient to surprise and failure.

Public perceptions and behaviour

The success of risk communication programmes also depends upon their sensitivity to the perceptions of risk and the behaviour of various publics before, during and after an accident. Much knowledge exists about how various publics view different types of risk, about the elements of a warning system that will facilitate effective public responses, and about likely public behaviours under situations of high stress.

Yet stereotypes and misconceptions abound. Many emergency planners fret about the panic they regard as almost certain to erupt during an emergency, despite the rarity of such instances. Others seek plans to overcome the likelihood that emergency workers will fail to perform their specified duties, although cases of emergency role abandonment are almost totally absent in disaster experience. Still others worry about overwhelming the public with information, although experience suggests that publics seek and can process an extraordinary amount of information during serious emergencies. Even human nature comes into question, with managers' fears over antisocial behaviour at odds with the observed tendency for widespread altruistic actions by publics. Major improvements in risk communication and emergency planning are possible by narrowing the gaps between what is known, what is practised and what is assumed by the professionals.

Beyond that, we do, of course, need to know more. The social amplification of risk (see Chapters 6–11) that trails in the wake of accidents is a major driving force in defining the requirements for emergency planning. How prepared should society be for rare but catastrophic industrial accidents? What contribution can risk communication make to assure safety for any given facility? How much of society's scarce resources should be allocated to communication programmes? How much variation exists among various publics in their reactions to different accident events?

Flexible and resilient risk communication

Improved emergency preparedness places heavy burdens on effective communication of risk information prior to, during and after accidents. The communication needs exist at multiple levels – the risk assessor must inform the industrial manager and the emergency planner, representatives of the mass media must be knowledgeable, information must flow effectively throughout the overall emergency organization, and publics need some understanding of potential accidents as well as available means for protecting themselves. The accumulated experience with industrial emergencies increasingly points to an environment rich in timely and accurate information as perhaps the most precious of all emergency resources. At the same time, the Bhopal, Mexico City, Chernobyl, Three Mile Island and Rhine spill accidents suggest how vulnerable risk communication systems can be to communication breakdowns and distortions.

We have gained much useful knowledge of communication and educational systems for preparing communities and local publics for accidents at industrial facilities. Yet many risk communicators are still reluctant to trot out all of the bad things that could potentially happen at plants that want to be seen as 'good neighbours'. Local government officials are sometimes loathe to assume new burdens that they are ill-equipped and poorly supported to carry out. And always lurking is the ever-present fear that frank talk about potential accidents may spark overreaction by ill-informed publics and media representatives and prompt mischief by miscreants who are potential opponents of the plants. Overcoming the reluctance of those who possess knowledge of the risk to share it openly with those who are at risk is an essential task of risk communication.

Complicating the task at hand are the difficult questions regarding what should be communicated. The public information brochures that have been prepared for nuclear and chemical emergencies tend to concentrate more on what publics need to do than why they need to do it. These brochures are directive and prescriptive but often not pedagogic. Improved approaches will need to go well beyond producing prescriptive action guides to constituting broad programmes aimed at enhancing local knowledge about risks and at enlarging the basic capabilities of various publics to protect themselves from industrial accidents. Such programmes will involve not only brochures and pamphlets but also training, risk education, study circles and participation in emergency response simulations and exercises.

Communication during crises requires special handling, for time is characteristically short, stress high and confusion abundant. Experience speaks to the need for multiple channels of communication, the use of credible sources of information, the importance of care in designing messages, the frequency of message transmission, the need for message validation, consistency among message sources, prior training of mass-media representatives, redundancy in communication mechanisms, and effective rumour control. It is also apparent that the characteristics of the risk event (e.g. rapid onset, the persistence of the consequences) as well as the levels of public concerns are important considerations in the design of effective risk communication programmes.

Given our still-limited understanding of how to design and implement effective risk communication programmes, false steps and approaches are nearly certain. A well-designed risk communication programme should therefore assume that surprises and failures will occur, and plan accordingly. Programmes should, thus, anticipate conflict among information sources; unforeseen events; potential blockages in information channels; inadequate identification of interested groups and citizens; unidentified value structures and community agenda; higher levels of distrust than assumed; and substantial divergence in the risk judgements of experts and lay persons. The objective of anticipating failure should be to make the communication process resilient, so that accurate information gets through, local knowledge develops, interaction occurs and credibility grows in the face of adversity and the unexpected.

APPROACHES TO RISK COMMUNICATION

Different approaches to risk communication have evolved over time. What follows are several major types and how they reflect communication objectives and underlying assumptions. They are essentially implicit notions of risk communication that are sometimes complementary, sometimes inconsistent, sometimes in conflict.

The information systems approach

One common approach to risk communication arises from the field of information systems, which focuses on such concepts as sender, receiver, messages, information channels, channel density, target audiences and information overloads. These concepts have enjoyed wide use in communication engineering, which structures the communications process as: (1) the communication source; (2) the message; (3) the communication channels; and (4) the receivers. The *source* refers to sender of information (e.g. credibility). The *message* involves the specific package of information used to accomplish a particular purpose; it may be factual or emotional in appeal and may use or avoid symbols. The goal may be, alternatively, to incite to action, warn, inform, change behaviour or reassure. Lee (1986) notes that designing messages needs to address such factors as emotional versus logical presentation; appeals to fear; message style; implicit versus explicit conclusions; placing explicit conclusions first versus last; and where the message is pitched.

Communication *channels* include not only, prominently, the mass media, but other interpersonal and intergroup networks as well. The *receivers* in this approach are those for whom the messages are designed – the risk bearer, the risk manager, the general public or publics with special needs. The design of the risk communication system focuses on four components – source, message, channel and receiver. The assumption is that the key to success is the timely and efficient flow of messages from source to receiver, through diverse channels, with as little loss of information as possible.

The marketing approach

The marketing approach to risk communication consists of a diverse set of methods and strategies that have evolved in advertising and marketing products to consumers. In this view, risk communication is essentially no different from the selling of soap.

Research on consumer information recognizes the various limitations that confront prospective consumers of information. The difficulty of consumer choice, for example, relates to the number of alternatives that exist and the extent to which information formats actually facilitate comparisons. The amount of time available for processing information suggests that some media are preferable to others. The information format chosen can either facilitate or impede the amount and type of information processing that is possible.

The concept of market segmentation recognizes the basic fact of individual differences in interest and need. The goal of segmentation is to produce the most efficient groupings of people (i.e. disaggregation of the market) so that marketing may target its message to particular consumer groups.

Much of this risk communication approach derives from the 'do's and don'ts' emerging from the practical experience of advertising and marketing, as suggested in Lesly's (1982) guides for effective communication.

The psychometric approach

If information systems highlight message flows and marketing approaches emphasize consumer behaviour, then psychometric studies centre on the 'receiver' – the individual who is coping with alternative decision situations and making judgements based on perceptions and values. The psychometric paradigm uses analytical techniques to produce representations, or 'cognitive maps', of risk attitudes and perceptions (Slovic et al, 1986). In this approach, people are asked to make judgements about the riskiness of different risks and the desirable level of regulation for each. The judgements are then related to such issues as (1) attributes of the risks (e.g. voluntariness, dread, knowledge); (2) benefits accompanying the risk; (3) number of deaths caused by the hazard in a disastrous year; and (4) the seriousness of each death from a particular risk relative to deaths from other causes (Slovic et al, 1986).

This work has led to important conclusions directly relevant to risk communication efforts, namely that:

- to cope with decision and information overloads, people simplify;
- once people's minds are made up, it is difficult to change them;
- people remember what they see; for most people, the primary sources of information about risk are what they see or hear in the news media and what they observe in everyday life;
- people cannot readily detect omissions in the evidence they receive; as a result, their risk perceptions can be easily manipulated;
- people disagree more about what risk is than about how large it is; ordinary people and risk managers typically use the term 'risk' very differently;
- people have difficulty detecting inconsistencies in conflicting risk information; as a result, risk communication needs to provide people with alternative perspectives;
- people have difficulty evaluating expertise (i.e. who is an 'expert' and who is not).

The cultural approach

This approach to risk communication begins with the premise that different cultures exist in society, each with its own characteristic view of the world or cultural bias, including viewpoints on risk and danger (Douglas and Wildavsky, 1982). People structure their worldviews in ways that are consistent with their shared, daily social experience. It has been argued (Rayner, 1984; Rayner and Cantor, 1987) that there may be as few as four basic ways of structuring a worldview, according to what has been termed the 'grid' and 'group' variables of organizational life. Grid refers to the degree of constraint that exists on individual interaction; group refers to the range of social interaction. These dimensions can be used to generate different prototypical visions of social life. Seen this way, risk is a way of classifying a whole series of complex interactions and relationships between people, as well as between people and nature (Rayner, 1984). This perspective on risk has generated a number of propositions relevant to risk communication:

- Culture is the framework by which people recognize risks. The community is the context for the individual's view of the world and the scale of values by which different risk consequences are reckoned grave or trivial (Douglas, 1985).
- A broad definition of risk is needed that encompasses concerns about equity and values as well as concerns about the probability and magnitude of adverse consequences.
- Technology options must be debated on the explicit basis of trust and equity rather than simply rival estimates of quantitative risk.
- Different corporate and governmental cultures engaged in controversies over risk have great difficulty in understanding the fears and objections of others.

The public participation approach

The 1980s and 1990s have witnessed increased expectations by citizens of their right to know and to participate in public decisions that affect their lives. In Europe, the Seveso accident had far-reaching implications for the European Community in the form of the Seveso Directive, which imposed obligations for both the assessment of risk and its communication to responsible authorities and the public. The OECD Council Act C(88)85 establishes that potentially affected publics have a right to, as well as a need for, information regarding hazardous installations. In the US, the Occupational Safety and Health Administration's hazard communication rule set forth new expectations and responsibilities for informing those at risk. The 1987 US Superfund amendments not only expanded hazard communication responsibilities but substantially increased local participation in hazard assessment as well.

Experience with public participation over several decades has afforded a variety of insights into both the nature of the obstacles and realistic expectations of what is possible. Research on public participation offers some guidelines for formulating risk communication programmes:

- Conflicts emerging in public participation often centre on means/ends differences in expectation. Publics often see programmes as an invitation to share power, to participate in defining goals. Managers, by contrast, often see it as having primarily an instrumental function, a means to realize established health and safety objectives.
- A lack of early and continuing involvement of the public is a characteristic source of failure.
- The believability of risk information is clearly related to institutional credibility and trust.
- Effective public participation depends substantially on the development of resources and the means to act on and assess increased knowledge.
- Members of the public differ from country to country and from culture to culture, suggesting the need for differing communication strategies.

- Although a large array of participation programmes exists, current knowledge, especially about risk communication, does not allow for successful prediction as to which forms of participation are likely to be most effective under different conditions and in different communities or cultural settings.

An integrative approach:
The social amplification of risk

The differing approaches to risk and risk communication outlined above suggest the need for an integrative framework. The social amplification of risk framework is based on the thesis that accidents and other risk events interact with psychological, social, institutional and cultural processes in ways that can heighten or attenuate perceptions of risk and shape risk behaviour (Figure 4.1). Public responses, in turn, generate secondary social or economic consequences. These consequences extend far beyond direct harm to human health or the environment to include significant indirect impact such as liability, insurance costs, loss of confidence in institutions, stigmatization or alienation from community affairs (see Chapter 6).

Such secondary effects often (in the case of risk amplification) trigger demands for additional institutional responses and protective actions, or, conversely (in the case of risk attenuation), place impediments in the path of necessary protective action. In our usage, 'amplification' includes both intensifying and attenuating signals about risk. Thus, alleged 'overreactions' of people and organizations receive the same attention in this framework as alleged 'downplaying'.

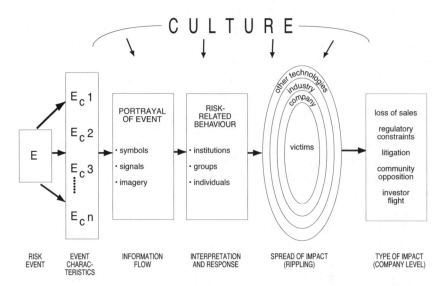

Figure 4.1 *Highly simplified representation of the social amplification of risk and potential impacts on a corporation*

Some terms used in this concept need further explanation. Risk, in this view, is in part an objective threat of harm to people and in part a product of culture and social experience. Hence, risk events are 'real'. They involve transformations of the physical environment or human health as a result of continuous or sudden (accidental) releases of energy, matter or information or involve perturbations in social and value structures. These events remain limited in the social context unless they are observed by human beings and communicated to others (Luhmann, 1986, p63). The consequences of this communication may lead to other physical transformations, such as changes in technologies. The public experience of risk is, therefore, both an experience of physical harm and the result of cultural and social processes by which individuals or groups interpret risks. These interpretations provide rules about how to select, order and explain signals from the physical world. Additionally, each cultural or social group selects certain risks to worry about even as it dismisses other risks as not meriting immediate concern.

The amplification process starts with either a physical event (such as an accident) or a report on environmental or technological risk (see Chapters 6 and 9 for a fuller discussion of what follows). Some groups and individuals also, of course, search for risk events related to their agenda of concern. In both cases, individuals or groups select specific characteristics of these events and interpret them according to their perceptions and values. They also communicate these interpretations to other individuals and groups and receive interpretations in return. Social groups and individuals process the information, locate it in their agenda of concerns, and may feel compelled to respond. Some may change their previously held beliefs, gain additional knowledge and insights, and be motivated to take action. Others may use the opportunity to compose new interpretations that they send to the original sources or other interested parties. Still others find the added information as confirming long-held views of the world and its order.

The individuals or groups who collect information about risks communicate with others and thus act as *amplification stations*. Amplification stations can be individuals, groups or institutions. Amplification may differ among individuals in their roles as private citizens and in their roles as employees or members of organizations.

Membership in social groups affects what risk information the individual regards as significant. Information that is inconsistent with previous beliefs or that contradicts the person's values is often ignored or attenuated. It is intensified if the opposite is true. Individuals act as members of cultural groups and organizations, which also determine how people process and respond to accidents. In this framework, we term these as *social stations of amplification*. Thus, publics perceive risk information and messages and construct the risk 'problem' according to their cultural biases and the views of their organization or group (Johnson and Covello, 1987).

The information flow depicting the accident or risk event and the actions of social amplification stations generate secondary effects that extend beyond the people directly affected by the accident. Secondary impacts include such effects as:

- enduring mental perceptions, images and attitudes (e.g. anti-technology attitudes, alienation from physical environment, social apathy or distrust of risk management institutions);
- impacts on the local or regional economy (e.g. reduced business sales, declines in residential property values, drops in tourism);
- political and social pressure (e.g. political demands, changes in political climate and culture);
- social disorder (e.g. protesting, rioting, sabotage, terrorism);
- changes in risk monitoring and regulation;
- increased liability and insurance costs;
- repercussions on other technologies (e.g. lower levels of public acceptance) and on social institutions (e.g. erosion of public trust).

Secondary impacts are, in turn, watched by social groups and individuals so that additional stages of amplification may occur to produce higher-order impacts. The impacts thereby may spread, or 'ripple', to other parties, distant locations, or future generations. Each order of impact will not only disseminate impacts but may also trigger (in risk amplification) or hinder (in risk attenuation) positive forces for risk reduction. The concept of social amplification of risk is hence dynamic, taking into account the continuing learning by society in the experience with risk (as detailed in Chapter 6).

The analogy of dropping a stone into a pond (see Figure 4.1) illustrates the spread of these higher-order impacts associated with the social amplification of risk. The ripples spread outward, first encompassing the directly affected victims or the first group to be notified, then touching the next higher institutional level (a company or an agency), and, in more extreme cases, reaching other parts of the industry. This rippling of impacts is an important element of risk amplification since it suggests that the processes can extend (in risk amplification) or constrain (in risk attenuation) the temporal and geographical scale of impacts associated with an accident.

GUIDES FOR THE RISK COMMUNICATOR

Every day members of the public in OECD countries are bombarded by risk information. Daily experience carries its arsenal of threats – from industrial accidents, falls on slippery bathroom floors, house fires from faulty wiring, infection by AIDS and the potential of nuclear war. The mass media abound with accounts of extreme natural events (e.g. hurricanes, tornadoes, floods) or the failures of technology (e.g. airplane crashes or

WHAT IS RISKY?
> Key terminology and concepts
>> Hazard, exposure, probability, sensitivity, individual risk, population risk, distribution of risk, unattainability of zero risk
>
> Qualitative attributes
>> Voluntariness, catastrophic potential, dreadedness, lethality, controllability, familiarity, latency

WHAT DOES RISK ASSESSMENT CONTRIBUTE?
> Quantification
>> Quality, completeness, uncertainty, confidence
>
> Scientific and policy inferences
>> Assumptions, assessment of benefits, risk management choices

WHAT IS THE ROLE OF THE RISK COMMUNICATION PROCESS?
> Setting
>> Public debate about decisions, informing or influencing personal action
>
> Purpose
>> Messages can inform, influence, or deceive
>
> Interaction among participants
>> Contending conclusions, justification, credibility, and records

HOW CAN YOU FIND OUT WHAT YOU NEED TO KNOW?
> Technical content
>> Demystifying jargon, comparing relevant risks, finding trusted interpreters
>
> Independent sources
>> Information clearinghouses, academic or public service sources

HOW CAN YOU PARTICIPATE EFFECTIVELY?
> Finding the right arena
>> Identifying the responsible decision-maker, getting on the agenda
>
> Intervention
>> Identifying points and times for intervention, marshalling support

HOW CAN YOU EVALUATE THE MESSAGES AND THE COMMUNICATORS?
> Accuracy
>> Factual base, track record, consistency, self-serving framing, use of influence techniques, misleading risk comparisons
>
> Legitimacy
>> Standing, access, review, due process justification
>
> Interpreting advocacy
>> Comparing competing arguments, seeing where information has been omitted, questioning messages sources

---

Source: USNRC, 1989, p179

Figure 4.2 *A consumer's guide to risk and risk communication*

near-collisions, toxic wastes or the carcinogen *du jour* in the environment). Confronted by this myriad of threats and dangers, publics must somehow navigate their daily existence, choosing which information and events to heed and which to ignore. Since ordinary people have ordinary skills and knowledge, making sense of all of this is no simple task.

Nor is it simple to be the communicator. It is now known that the ways by which risk information is presented can greatly affect public response. Risk communicators are key 'stations' in the social amplification process, shaping the nature of public concerns and placing risks on society's agenda. Which risks should be covered, which ignored? How much coverage should be devoted to a particular accident? Since subtle differences in the presentation of information (framing effects) can elicit very different responses from publics, how may risk informing be effectively accomplished while minimizing exaggeration, misinformation or unintended manipulation? When should the communicator provoke, and when soothe? Figure 4.2 provides an overview of what the 'consumers' of risk information are looking for in risk communication programmes.

The discussion that follows presents general guidelines intended to assist risk communicators in being sensitive to the implications of alternatives ways of communicating risk The intent is to demarcate potential pitfalls and problems, and to suggest means for avoiding them (where possible). The suggested guidelines seek throughout to contribute to more accurate and helpful risk communication and to better informed and prepared publics.

Choose a good risk measure (or, preferably, several measures). Any given risk or risk event can be measured in multiple ways. Thus, industrial accidents can be characterized by:

- the number of events or releases;
- the number of people (drivers, passengers, victims, bystanders) exposed;
- the number of deaths and injuries;
- the number affected who require medical attention; or
- the number affected who file insurance claims.

Confusion and debates about risk are often the product of differing, perhaps conflicting, measures and numbers. So some observers cite the tens of thousands of persons around the Three Mile Island nuclear plant who received 'above normal' (as compared with background levels) radiation doses, whereas others note that the eventual fatalities were probably near zero.

Viewed systematically, the measure of risk can treat different stages in the evolution of the hazard, as shown in Table 4.1.

Obviously, risk communication that is comprehensive (i.e. that treats data characterizing the different stages of hazard) is preferable to coverage

Table 4.1 *Stages in the evolution of a hazard*

Accidents--->	Releases--->	Exposure --->	Consequences
Number of failures	Number of off-site releases	Number of persons exposed	Deaths, injuries, hospitalizations, insurance claims, property damage, loss of trust

that treats only a single stage (e.g. releases). In particular, risk communicators should avoid confusing jumps, or discordant data, among different stages.

Reporting on toxic wastes illustrates well the misleading potential involved in dwelling upon one, or perhaps two, stages of risk. Characteristically, the many stories focus upon the amount of wastes at a particular disposal site, the large number of disposal sites or the numbers of people exposed. The numbers involved are usually frightening. If, however, measures of *consequences* (i.e. harm) are used, the numbers are often very small.

Different measures of risk emerging from the *scope of the risk* category also need careful sorting. The unit of measure can be altered according to whether only *acute* effects (immediate deaths, injuries) are included or if *latent* effects (illnesses, deaths from disease, genetic effects) are also treated. A classic misrepresentation of risk in an important scientific risk document occurred in the so-called Rasmussen Report, the US Nuclear Regulatory Commission study (USNUREG, 1975) of nuclear plant risks, where the *Executive Summary* reported only acute risks, despite their being only one-tenth as high as the latent risk.

In short, the numerator of risk really matters.

Include the risk denominator

The measure of risk (i.e. the risk numerator) always relates (often implicitly) to a particular population or aggregate (an exposed group, air travellers, a period of activity or a measure of production) or the *denominator*. People may use aggregate data to draw unwarranted implications about individual risk. Evaluating the numbers provided by different expert sources, and depicting the risk to publics, requires careful attention to the denominator. Take the case of coal mining in the US. Statistics show that accidental deaths *per million tons of coal* mined have decreased steadily over time. The inference may be drawn that the industry is becoming safer. Data also show, however, that accidental deaths per *1000 coal mine employees* have increased. This time, the inference may be drawn that the industry is becoming more dangerous. Neither is the 'right' measure; each tells only part of the story (Slovic, 1986, p406).

The denominator issue is apparent in environmental hazards whose effects accrue over very long time periods. The environmental standard of protection for high-level radioactive wastes is based upon a 10,000-year time duration and a goal, in the US, that no more than 1000 fatalities should be associated with all exposures to waste disposal. The use of absolute numbers – '1000 people may die from nuclear wastes' – conveys a level of risk very different from the communication that links the fatalities to the large denominator of time – 'on the average, no more than one person may die every ten years'. If the projection notes (which it cannot, with precision) the very large estimated population for the nation, the effect of the risk communication would be quite different again.

Help people to think about probabilities

Most people do not readily think in terms of probabilities and so may be expected to have difficulty interpreting quantitative risk information that contains probabilities. The problems arise from various human limitations in dealing with uncertainty. It is a natural human tendency, for example, when confronted by a threat to one's health and safety, to wish to have definite or deterministic statements – 'Am I safe or not?' is the recurring question in risk situations – in essence an attempt to impose a binary categorization on a spectrum of probabilities of harm. When individuals have to make decisions that must be made on the basis of probabilistic information, errors are common. Often this involves a failure to recognize the random nature of events or the lack of connectedness in particular occurrences ('Storms run in cycles – we get one every 10 years' or 'We had a 100-year flood failure years ago, so we are not in danger for many years yet!'). This is sometimes the result of the so-called 'gambler's fallacy' of misunderstanding randomness; on other occasions it reflects an individual's imposing order on uncertainty.

A related problem arises from human limits on processing quantitative data. Probabilistic information that involves very large or very small numbers is particularly problematic; some risk communication research suggests that people may compress scales that range over a very large spread of numbers. In an experiment at Decision Research in the US, lay people were asked to estimate the number of fatalities associated with a wide range of hazards. The results (Figure 4.3) indicate that people use 'heuristics' (simplifying mechanisms) to deal with complex risk data. Respondents frequently overestimate the number of deaths from rare but vivid hazards (eg, botulism) but underestimate the deaths from chronic, commonplace diseases (eg, cancer, heart disease). Press coverage of rare and vivid events as compared with more routine and chronic risks may be an important source of public misperceptions.

What do these problems with probabilities suggest for the risk communicator? First, simply announcing the risk probabilities provided by scientists will certainly not be very helpful. People need assistance in interpreting risk probabilities. One approach is to compare a particular

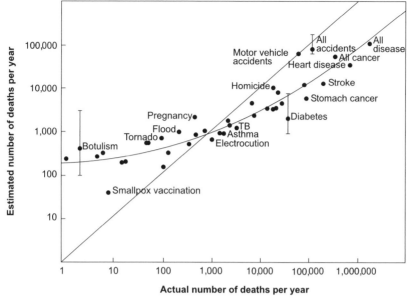

Source: After Lichtenstein et al, 1978

Figure 4.3 *Relation between judged frequency and the actual number of deaths per year for 41 cases of death*

probability to events in the public's experience with other risks. Thus, a risk of accidental death of one in a million for a year of exposure might be compared to the risk of being killed by lightning, or, for the frequent air traveller, of being killed in an air crash. A graphical representation of the risk may also be helpful.

Be sure to state the uncertainties

The very concept of risk implies uncertainty. It is a common failing to assume that estimates of risk are true representations (which they are not) of what will actually occur. Estimates of risk, since they project what is expected to happen in the future under some assumed conditions, abound with arbitrary assumptions, imperfect data and imperfect scientific understanding. For acute hazards where the causality of risks is well understood and where a strong actuarial database exists, predicting risk is nonetheless risky. For chronic hazards – subject to poorly understood dose–response relationships, inadequate exposure data, confounding variables, potential synergistic effects and imperfect measurement techniques – risk estimates can (and do) vary dramatically. Simply using alternative extrapolation models of possible effects of exposure to a carcinogen in rats to humans, for example, can produce estimates of risk that can vary by as much as a factor of 10,000 (USNRC, 1983, p26).

Given this situation, the risk communicator should beware of point estimates of risk. In communicating the risk, it is essential to begin by stating clearly that the estimate is uncertain. Next, the extent of the uncertainty should be noted. The risk estimate is often best expressed with error bars, or uncertainty limits, that suggest the credible range, as well as the most likely estimate, of the risk. Since most risk estimates are built upon an edifice of assumptions and data, they too need to be made explicit in the communication of the risk. Uncertainty connected with the method, such as in the extrapolation model, should also be specifically noted. A major service that the risk communicator can provide is to bracket the range of credible risk estimation, to indicate the major sources of uncertainty, and (if possible) to state the sensitivity of the estimate to each of the major types of uncertainty.

Give the best case as much attention as the worst

The constant temptation exists to describe risk as the worst it can be. Risk is danger, so one clear need is to know the worst possible danger. The worst case also makes news – it is the attention grabber. Defining the 'worst', of course, is difficult in itself, because if one is willing to conjure up very rare occurrences, then the worst case quickly becomes incredible. So the selection of a 'reasonable' worst case is a contentious issue.

But if only the worst case is presented, the public has been poorly served. As Alvin Weinberg (1977, p54) has pointed out, 'unscaring people' is much more difficult than scaring them. The tendency for reification of a worst case estimate needs consideration. Once the worst case estimate is reported, it often becomes *the* (rather than *one*) risk estimate, crowding out subsequent competing estimates. This suggests the need for an even-handed approach, treating the best case as well as the worst case. Even then, the human propensity may well be to recall the worst case rather than the best. But the risk communicator can, by presenting the best case, the most likely case and the worst case at once, bracket the credible range of the risk for the public.

Note the impact on vulnerable groups as well as 'average' people

Risks are not democratic – they do not recognize equality in producing their victims. Some people, because of greater vulnerability, are at greater risk than others (see Chapter 16). The reasons are both scientific and social, and they are an important part of the risk communication problem.

Quantitative risk estimates typically convey a human toll in the form of abstract representation (numbers). Those numbers generally convey the size and intensity of effect but rarely who the people are. Often the numbers are an aggregate, or address the 'average' person, as in occupational health standards. In fact, a given exposure to a harmful substance may affect persons very differently. Increasingly, it is apparent that some persons are much more susceptible (by as much as a factor of 10 or 100) than others to a given hazard. Lead in the environment takes a greater toll on children than on adults. The foetus is often highly susceptible to harm from toxic materials, tobacco or alcohol. Previous experience with lower back pain tends to make a person at higher risk from lifting and even some sedentary activities. Genetic make-up can increase susceptibility to a variety of diseases.

Individuals may also be socially vulnerable to risks. Many risks are 'hidden' because they affect groups or individuals who are marginal to society, politically powerless or both (see the extended treatment of such hazards in Chapter 7). Classic cases include the belated discovery of the Sahelian famine in the 1980s, the toll on workers from asbestos exposure, oestrogen hazards to women or the delayed response to the HIV/AIDS virus.

So, the microscope through which risk numbers are examined needs to include a social lens that lays bare the susceptibility of, or impact on, differing racial, gender and social groups. The communication of risk, accordingly, needs to delineate the spectrum of impact, with particular attention given to the most vulnerable.

Be sensitive to the qualitative aspects of the risk

Studies of public perceptions of risk reveal that experts and publics often evaluate the same risk very differently. Although the reasons are not entirely clear, the charge of 'ignorance' or 'emotionalism' in the public is not the answer. Rather, it is now clear from risk perception research that members of the public apparently take a broader approach than do technical experts in evaluating risk. Characteristics of risk – newness, catastrophic potential and familiarity – are important considerations in the public assessment of risk. Simple quantitative measures of expected fatalities or days lost from work tend to miss these qualitative dimensions of risk. The clearest example of risk qualities that affect concern is the degree to which the risk is voluntary or imposed. If one is injured when skiing or skydiving, the response is very different from the reaction to the discovery of toxic chemicals in one's backyard. If risks have been concealed and if one's exposure is involuntary, such threats cause highly amplified concern over the risks.

Thus, risk communication needs to be sensitive to the fact that purely quantitative expression of risk may miss what most concerns people. The risk communicator should note carefully the qualities that may socially amplify the risk. Figure 4.4 provides a useful list of qualities that merit attention.

Include all the consequences that concern people

Just as a hazard event has multiple causes, it also has multiple effects. Accident consequences may be numerous and synergistic, ranging over health effects to worker and publics, losses to the employer, effects on families of those harmed, and perhaps even broader social impacts on the

Risk assumed voluntarily	Risk borne involuntarily
Effect immediate	Effect delayed
No alternatives available	Many alternatives available
Risk known with certainty	Risk not known
Exposure is an essential	Exposure is a luxury
Encountered occupationally	Encountered non-occupationally
Common hazard	"Dread" hazard
Affects average people	Affects especially sensitive people
Will be used as intended	Likely to be misused
Consequences reversible	Consequences irreversible
Risk assumed voluntarily	Risk borne involuntarily

Source: Lowrance, 1976, p87

Figure 4.4 *An array of considerations influencing safety judgements*

community and society (as through stigmatization of places). For technologies such as chemicals, nuclear power and recombinant DNA, the risks apparently touch basic human values. Narrow quantitative portrayals of risk miss the consequences about which people are most upset.

Thus, risk communication needs to address the broad range of potential consequences rather than a *single* consequence measure of risk. In addition, it should be appreciated that many risk debates fluctuate among different consequences, and the intensity and rhetoric of the conflict may obscure the real problems. Effective risk communication involves assuring that: (1) the same consequences are actually the focus of debate, and that (2) all consequences of concern to the public have been included.

Good comparisons help, but poor comparisons mislead and confuse

Because quantitative measures of risk are difficult for most people to decipher and interpret, comparisons are essential. But comparisons may be extraordinarily helpful or extraordinarily misleading. Since every comparison necessarily reveals and conceals at the same time, selection of comparisons must be undertaken very carefully.

In the past, risk analysts have published the risks of widely disparate activities, all of which are standardized to the common metric of increasing one's chance of death during any year by one in a million (Wilson, 1979). These lists (see, for example, Figure 4.5) have appeared widely in newspapers and popular magazines. Although such comparisons may provide insight and perspective, they can also be quite misleading. The lists include risks (e.g. flying 1000 miles by jet) for which the understanding of the risk is high and a substantial actuarial database exists, but also include risks (living two days in New York or Boston) that are poorly understood, whose uncertainties are enormous, and for which few sound databases exist.

Activity	Cause of Death
Smoking 1.4 cigarettes	Cancer, heart disease
Spending 1 hour in a coal mine	Black lung disease
Living 2 days in New York or Boston	Air pollution
Traveling 10 miles by bicycle	Accident
Flying 1,000 miles by jet	Accident
Living 2 months in Denver on vacation from New York	Cancer caused by cosmic radiation
One chest X-ray taken in a good hospital	Cancer caused by radiation
Eating 40 tablespoons of peanut butter	Liver toxin caused by Aflatoxin B
Drinking 30 12-oz. cans of diet soda	Cancer caused by saccharin
Drinking 1,000 24-oz. soft drinks from recently banned plastic bottles	Cancer from acrylonitrile monomer
Living 150 years within 20 miles of a nuclear power plant	Cancer caused by radiation
Risk of accident by living within 5 miles of a nuclear reactor for 50 years	Cancer caused by radiation

Source: Wilson, 1979, p45. Republished with permission of MIT Press, from *Technology Review*, vol 81, pp41–46, February, Wilson, R., 'Analysing the daily risks of life', 1979, permission conveyed through Copyright Clearance Center Inc

Figure 4.5 *Risks estimated to increase the chance of death in any year by 0.000001 (one part in one million)*

Other essential aspects of the risks – voluntariness, distributional effects, susceptibility to risk reduction, newness – do not make their way onto such lists. Generally, only a single consequence is treated. Sometimes it is suggested (or it is implicit) that such lists can be used to guide social action by suggesting which risks are small and which large. Other versions attempt to portray risks by citing the cost of reducing the risk by one fatality per year, with a similar unstated social imperative as to which risks most need to be addressed. Such simplistic, undiscriminating lists are capable of great mischief in misleading the public and can lead to anger against those who provide such poorly formulated comparisons.

Several considerations may help in the selection of appropriate risk comparisons. Comparisons *within* a risk category (e.g. radiation risks) are more germane than *between* categories. Risk comparisons *for technologies for a particular use* (e.g. generation of electricity, pesticides), which have similar purposes and benefits, have more direct policy relevance. Certain comparisons – such as those that indiscriminately lump together voluntary and involuntary risks or risks affecting different generations – should be avoided. Similarly, statements that compare events involving loss of life from small repeated events with events involving catastrophes are likely to be misleading.

Risk communication is a potentially important aid in assisting publics to understand the risks involved in diverse human activities and

INFORMATION ABOUT THE NATURE OF RISKS

1. What are the hazards of concern?
2. What is the probability of exposure to each hazard?
3. What is the distribution of exposure?
4. What is the probability of each type of harm from a given exposure to each hazard?
5. What are the sensitivities of different populations to each hazard?
6. How do exposures interact with exposures to other hazards?
7. What are the qualities of the hazard?
8. What is the total population risk?

INFORMATION ABOUT THE NATURE OF BENEFITS

1. What are the benefits associated with the hazard?
2. What is the probability that the projected benefit will actually follow the activity in question?
3. What are the qualities of the benefits?
4. Who benefits and in what ways?
5. How many people benefit and how long do benefits last?
6. Which groups get a disproportionate share of the benefits?
7. What is the total benefit?

INFORMATION ON ALTERNATIVES

1. What are the alternatives to the hazard in question?
2. What is the effectiveness of each alternative?
3. What are the risks and benefits of alternative actions and of not acting?
4. What are the costs and benefits of each alternative and how are they distributed?

UNCERTAINTIES IN KNOWLEDGE ABOUT RISKS

1. What are the weaknesses of available data?
2. What are the assumptions on which estimates are based?
3. How sensitive are the estimates to changes in assumptions?
4. How sensitive is the decision to changes in the estimates?
5. What other risk and risk control assessments have been made and why are they different from those now being offered?

INFORMATION ON MANAGEMENT

1. Who is responsible for the decision?
2. What issues have legal importance?
3. What constrains the decision?
4. What resources are available?

Source: USNRC, 1989, p175

Figure 4.6 *A risk message checklist*

technologies. The risk communicator carries a particular obligation to present this information in ways that enlighten rather than confuse, that clarify rather than conceal important properties of the risk, that aid rather than impede valid inferences from the data, and that serve those at risk rather than the managers. Figure 4.6 provides a checklist of considerations relevant in the design of risk messages. This task calls for recognition that although publics have many shortcomings in their grasp of complexity and uncertainty, most ordinary people manage to navigate their health and safety reasonably well in the uncertain and messy risk domain of advanced industrial societies. They are also, on the whole, quite rational in their response to risk, as risk perception studies have repeatedly confirmed. That fact merits respect in designing risk communication programmes that genuinely respect the capabilities of publics and that seek to inform rather than prescribe.

A robust emergency communication system is one that achieves a continuous, two-way flow of information. All people in the emergency response network, and members of the public, should have as much information as possible, including:

- the current conditions at the plant;
- the movement of any plume or release;
- the current off-site conditions, including local weather and traffic conditions;
- the necessity for certain protective actions; and
- the availability of emergency resources.

At the same time, the authority managing the emergency response should coordinate the gathering of information from

- the plant and government officials: concerning plant status and possible accident sequences;
- industrial and government environmental monitoring teams: concerning weather conditions and any contamination;
- emergency workers: concerning traffic and road conditions, problems at mass-care centres and decontamination stations, and the public response in general; and
- institutions, such as prisons, hospitals, nursing homes, schools, and colleges: concerning their special needs and problems.

A centralized computer system, with back-up computer and manual systems, may be useful to assist in gathering, evaluating and disseminating information about on-site and off-site conditions. Multiple redundant communication channels, including microwave transmission with a relay station, dedicated phones, fax machines and radios, which link industrial and governmental authorities, are valuable. This redundancy will allow parties to communicate even if some channels fail.

Because the emergency response manager acts as the central focus, gathering and disseminating risk information, it is essential to strengthen 'horizontal' links within the hierarchy of communications to avoid over-centralization. Each local government jurisdiction should be able to communicate with the other jurisdictions without having to channel information through a central manager. These horizontal links enable the communication system to function even if the central manager is inoperative. They also allow flexibility to use alternative channels of communication should several channels to one party become blocked. An essential component of such horizontal communication is a pre-established and pre-distributed format for the information that needs to be exchanged. Such a format serves as a checklist for avoiding errors of omission.

Finally, a computerized graphics capability may be an appropriate way to relay much of the necessary information, such as location of a release, traffic problems and the locations of screening or decontamination stations. Links to local television or radio stations may also facilitate the rapid dissemination of information to the public.

In any emergency, people get information from sources other than industry and government officials. They talk to others at home, in the neighbourhood and at work. Emergency planners, decision makers and emergency workers should recognize this propensity and encourage people to talk to each other. Their goal is to provide clear, comprehensive information in a timely fashion, and thereby to minimize the generation and circulation of false and erroneous information. Rumours abound during emergencies. Once in motion, they are virtually uncontrollable, but their extent and impact can be minimized by providing a consistent and comprehensive flow of information from the beginning and throughout the duration of the emergency.

EVALUATING RISK COMMUNICATION PROGRAMMES

Effective risk communication that takes account of the social amplification of risk requires a sensitive balance among providing factual information on risk, enhancing protective actions by publics and avoiding undue anxieties. Evaluation provides a central means for assuring appropriate goals, content and outcomes of risk communication programmes. Such evaluation has the potential for both good and harm, and requires clear criteria by which to conceptualize and measure success, maximize public safety, and avoid human and ecological harm. Evaluation needs to be a central part of any effective risk communication programme, and not merely an activity to conduct if sufficient funds are left when the programme is ended. The following criteria are proposed for evaluating the effectiveness of risk communication.

Appraising communication needs

Risk communication should not be based solely on assumptions by the manager of what those at risk need to know about risks. Rather, a careful appraisal should be made of their needs and how they might best be met. Such judgements should be based on information provided by both experts and publics. It should also include the identification of publics who are especially affected by the risks and how communication can best be tailored to reach them. An explicit formulation of concrete objectives of risk communication is an essential prerequisite for evaluating the results.

Complex risks, diverse publics

Despite the propensity to convey risk in one-dimensional terms (reduced life expectancy, lifetime fatality risk, etc), risk, as we know, is multidimensional. Technologies have a broad range of consequences, and defining the particular consequence to be assessed is an important decision. The qualitative attributes of risk – voluntariness, catastrophic potential and degree of familiarity – affect public responses to them. Then, too, cultural groups define risks differently, attach different values to them and incorporate them into differing sociopolitical agenda. A primary challenge in risk communication is making complex phenomena understandable to non-technical people while simultaneously capturing the major attributes of concern to a highly variegated public. In such situations, it is important to err on the side of multiple perspectives, differing characterizations of risk and a richness of communication approaches.

Risk in context

Accident risks are a complex phenomenon, at once technical, uncertain, probabilistic and value laden. Provision of information needs to be accompanied by efforts to assist individuals in comprehending the risk. Types of contextual information include comparisons with other relevant risks (which need to be done with intelligence and sensitivity); comparisons with benefits of the activity or technology; comparisons with regulatory standards or natural background levels, etc; and comparisons of ways in which the risk can be reduced. Invariably, individuals also desire, and may demand, full information on the industrial installations and processes that generated the risk – what accidents may occur, what materials may be released, what is being done to prevent or reduce accident risks and how publics may protect themselves from accidents.

A management prospectus

As suggested by Baruch Fischhoff (1985), risk managers should develop a protocol that ensures that all relevant information concerning the risk management programme is communicated to the public. Such a prospectus would include how the manager sees the facts, what options the manager is legally empowered to consider, what the manager considers to be the public interest, how risk decisions are (or will be) made, and with what envisioned results. A well-thought-out treatment and presentation by the managers is greatly preferable to speculation on such matters by the mass media or piecemeal construction of the picture over time. Prompt provision of such information and openness to public scrutiny may head off fears that the manager is withholding relevant facts or has hidden motivations.

Timeliness

Risk communication should be timely, meaning that it should occur early enough in any accident situation to alert the individual to the risk so that protective actions can be taken to avoid it or to minimize adverse consequences. A common error is for risk managers to withhold information until late in the process, when information and evidence are more complete and control strategies and supporting rationales more fully developed. It is possible, however, for communication to be premature, thereby eliciting unwarranted fear or unnecessary protective actions. Repeated overreactive warnings to evacuate in the face of a predicted natural hazard (e.g. hurricane) or industrial accident (e.g. a chemical release) may result in decreased credibility and, thus, increased risk.

Iterative interaction

Although there may be special circumstances in which risk communication involves only a single transaction or message, multiple or continuous interaction is nearly always necessary to ensure a flow of relevant risk information. Interaction implies the two-way flow of information, with learning by all those participating in the process. Too few risk communication programmes build in the means for risk managers to listen to or to initiate public response, which should be a requisite to developing the communication programme and gauging its effectiveness. There are many good lessons to be gained here from the background paper by Knowles (1995) on the Kanawha Valley experience.

Empowerment

Risk information unaccompanied by appropriate means to use and to act on the expanded knowledge is ultimately frustrating. Clearly, it reduces the incentive to acquire risk information and causes publics to ask: 'If I can't do anything about it, why are you telling me?' Wherever possible, risk communication should be embedded in a broader approach that empowers those at risk to act in the interests of their own protection or to influence those who are managing risks and accidents. The effectiveness of trade union information programmes on workplace hazards, as described by Aro (1988) in the background document for the OECD meeting in Sweden, is connected in no small part to worker participation in risk management programmes.

Credibility

Success in risk communication depends heavily on the confidence individuals place in the sources of information. Credibility is multidimensional, involving how publics view managerial competence, commitment to public health and safety, and caring about those who bear the risks (and social distrust, as Chapter 2 makes clear, poses formidable barriers to risk communication).

Ethical issues

The risk communication initiatives of the OECD and others assure that a great many campaigns will continue to develop and that experience will grow rapidly. Safeguards are needed that reflect thoughtful deliberations on the potential ethical issues involved, including:

- the identification of unintended adverse consequences in programmes and of structured means for avoiding them;
- respect for the autonomy of the individual and avoidance of paternalism;
- recognition of potential self-interest or bias in the institution acting as risk communicator;
- respect for the rights of those bearing the risks so that programmes will be responsive to them;
- means to ensure that risk communication will be compassionate and respectful of those addressed by the communication;
- avoidance of undue worry and fear;
- assurance that managerial personnel will have the right to refuse to engage in unethical conduct.

To assure that these ethical issues (and others; see Chapters 12 and 13) are addressed, the creation of codes of conduct for risk communicators would be helpful.

Resiliency

Since we can claim only limited understanding of how best to accomplish the goals of risk communication, false steps and faulty approaches are virtually certain. A well-designed risk communication programme should therefore expect and plan to accommodate surprises and failures. The designers and implementers of such programmes should take in their stride the inevitable conflict (noise) among different sources of information; the occurrence of unforeseen events; the potential roadblocks in some channels of communication; deficiencies in identifying all citizens and groups at risk; the existence of unidentified value structures and community agenda; the prevalence of higher levels of distrust than previously assumed; and the wide divergence in the risk judgements of experts and publics. Anticipating problems will go a long way toward achieving a resilient process that permits the flow and delivery of information, promotes requisite interactions with publics, and enhances credibility in the face of adversity and of the unexpected, which, after all, always happens.

5 Risk and the Stakeholder Express

Roger E. Kasperson

The risk field has gone through episodic infatuations with alternative 'fixes' to the formidable challenges presented by assessing diverse risks and reaching wise decisions in messy situations. Alternatively, we have, over time, pursued the metric that would provide a consistent approach to 'how safe is safe enough?', looked to risk comparisons as the proper analytic frame for decision making, and, for a period before reality set in, elevated risk communication to the holy grail of risk management. Currently, we are on the stakeholder involvement express, barrelling down the rails of well-intentioned but often naive efforts to address growing public concerns over risks, changed public expectations over the functioning of democratic institutions, and historic declines in social trust in those responsible for protecting public safety.

This journey abounds with allusion to democratic ideals and principles and the good things assumed to follow. Implicit throughout is the notion that broad public involvement, if achieved, is the principal route to improved decision making, especially where the risks are controversial and disputed. Other outcomes that can be expected, it is claimed, are increased trust in experts and decision makers, greater consensus among publics, reductions in conflict and opposition, greater acceptance of the project or proffered solution, and ease in implementation. The list is, of course, revealing as to whose interest is really at stake in many stakeholder processes.

The notion of stakeholder itself is a misnomer, of course. Typically, the person who holds the stakes in a wager is the neutral party who has no particular interest in the outcome and can be counted upon to act fairly. Stakeholders in current practice are customarily local activists who have a clearly defined role in the process or a material interest (or 'stake') in the outcome. Left out, meanwhile, are those who do not yet know that their interests are at stake, whose interests are diffuse or associated broadly with citizenship, who lack the skills and resources to compete, or who have simply lost confidence in the political process. Some would call them 'spectators' of American politics – they make up the mainstream of

Note: Reprinted from *Risk Newsletter*, 4th quarter, Kasperson, R. E., 'Riding the stakeholder express', © (2003), with permission from the Society for Risk Analysis

communities and how to draw them into deliberative processes has been the enduring project of democratic theorists over the past century.

The long tradition of democratic theorizing provides some cautions concerning our current infatuation with the stakeholder express. Two principal justifications, both apparent since Aristotle, show up in writings over time for more democratic processes and institutions – that they are the means for (1) developing the full capabilities and dignity of the individual and/or (2) creating the 'good' political society and governance system (and not, it should be noted, for improving individual decisions). These writings have also consistently noted how formidable such goals are and how numerous the pitfalls along the ways – participatory effectiveness is a learned skill that requires resources, it is cumulative and long term in nature, it is cultural in that it requires participatory domains in the various spheres of one's life (family, community, social networks, work, etc). Similarly, social trust is a phenomenon built through socialization over many years into society and polity and further developed or modified as the result of unfolding encounters with authority, political processes and outcomes of participatory experience. Developing effective participation, building trust and orchestrating 'good' decisions, these theories suggest, is not a 'one time' thing but emerges through participatory cultures and supporting structures over long periods of time.

Currently, despite countless books, articles and reports on public participation, we know relatively little about which participatory interventions are likely to be successful, or even what success means, in different communities and social settings. Clearly, success is not smoothing the way for experts or proponents to achieve agency or project goals but entails deeper questions as to what the process does for a community's or individual's capabilities to deal with the next issue that comes along, the scope of the outcomes (positive and negative) achieved, the extent to which those stakeholders involved communicate with constituents, and how these stakeholder efforts support, rather than usurp, the established political process and elected officials. Properly viewed, stakeholder programmes are all experiments aimed at addressing deficiencies in the existing political process (or they would not be needed), and some consideration and protection should be provided to those on whose behalf experiments in democracy are being conducted. This is not to say that we should reduce in any way our commitment to improved democratic processes; that commitment should be strengthened and deepened.

But perhaps it is time to put the brakes on the current stakeholder express, or to switch to the local, so that these processes become much more reflective and self-critical, that they are goal – not technique – driven, that they are rigorously evaluated by independent parties, that potential abuses (e.g. kicking controversial issues to publics) are controlled, and that they are accountable to and collaborative with those in whose name the experiments are mounted.

Part 2

The Social Amplification of Risk

6 The Social Amplification of Risk: A Conceptual Framework

Roger E. Kasperson, Ortwin Renn, Paul Slovic,
Halina S. Brown, Jacque Emel, Robert Goble,
Jeanne X. Kasperson and Samuel Ratick

INTRODUCTION

One of the most perplexing problems in risk analysis is why some relatively minor risks or risk events, as assessed by technical experts, often elicit strong public concerns and result in substantial impacts upon society and economy. This chapter sets forth a conceptual framework that seeks to link systematically the technical assessment of risk with psychological, sociological and cultural perspectives of risk perception and risk-related behaviour. The main thesis is that hazards interact with psychological, social, institutional and cultural processes in ways that may amplify or attenuate public responses to the risk or risk event. A structural description of the social amplification of risk is now possible. Amplification occurs at two stages: in the transfer of information about the risk, and in the response mechanisms of society. Signals about risk are processed by individual and social amplification stations, including the scientist who communicates the risk assessment, the news media, cultural groups, interpersonal networks and others. The key steps of amplifications can be identified at each stage. The amplified risk leads to behavioural responses, which, in turn, result in secondary impacts. Models are presented that portray the elements and linkages in the proposed conceptual framework.

RISK IN MODERN SOCIETY

The investigation of risks is at once a scientific activity and an expression of culture. During the twentieth century, massive government programmes and bureaucracies aimed at assessing and managing risk have emerged in

Note: Reprinted from *Risk Analysis*, vol 8, Kasperson, R. E., Renn, O., Slovic, P., Brown, H., Emel, J., Goble, R., Kasperson, J. X. and Ratick, S., 'The social amplification of risk: A conceptual framework', pp177–187, © (1988), with permission from Blackwell Publishing

advanced industrial societies. Despite the expenditure of billions of dollars and steady improvements in health, safety and longevity of life, people view themselves as more rather than less vulnerable to the dangers posed by technology. Particularly perplexing is the fact that even risk events with minor physical consequences often elicit strong public concern and produce extraordinarily severe social impacts, at levels unanticipated by conventional risk analysis.

Several difficult issues require attention:

- The technical concept of risk focuses narrowly on the probability of events and the magnitude of specific consequences. Risk is usually defined by a multiplication of the two terms, assuming that society should be indifferent toward a low-consequence/high-probability risk and a high-consequence/low-probability risk with identical expected values. Studies of risk perception have revealed clearly, however, that most persons have a much more comprehensive conception of risk. Clearly, other aspects of the risk such as voluntariness, personal ability to influence the risk, familiarity with the hazard, and the catastrophic potential shape public response (Renn, 1986; Slovic et al, 1982b). As a result, whereas the technical assessment of risk is essential to decisions about competing designs or materials, it often fails to inform societal choices regarding technology (Rayner and Cantor, 1987).
- Cognitive psychologists and decision researchers have investigated the underlying patterns of individual perception of risk and identified a series of heuristics and biases that govern risk perception (Slovic, 1987b; Vlek and Stallen, 1981). Whereas some of these patterns of perception contrast with the results of formal reasoning, others involve legitimate concerns about risk characteristics that are omitted, neglected, or underestimated by the technical concept of risk. In addition, equity issues, the circumstances surrounding the process of generating risk, and the timeliness of management response are considerations, important to people, that are insufficiently addressed by formal probabilistic risk analysis (Doderlein, 1983; Kasperson, 1983a).
- Risk is a bellwether in social decisions about technologies. Since the resolution of social conflict requires the use of factual evidence for assessing the validity and fairness of rival claims, the quantity and quality of risk are major points of contention among participating social groups. As risk analysis incorporates a variety of methods to identify and evaluate risks, various groups present competing evidence based upon their own perceptions and social agenda. The scientific aura surrounding risk analysis promotes the allocation of substantial effort to convincing official decision makers, and the public, that the risk assessment performed by one group is superior in quality and scientific validity to that of others. Controversy and debate exacerbate divergences between expert and public assessment and often erode confidence in the risk decision process (Otway and von Winterfeldt, 1982; Wynne, 1984).

In short, the technical concept of risk is too narrow and ambiguous to serve as the crucial yardstick for policy making.

Public perceptions, however, are the product of intuitive biases and economic interests and reflect cultural values more generally. The overriding dilemma for society is, therefore, the need to use risk analysis to design public policies on the one hand, and the inability of the current risk concepts to anticipate and explain the nature of public response to risk on the other. After a decade of research on the public experience of risk, no comprehensive theory exists to explain why apparently minor risk or risk events,[1] as assessed by technical experts, sometimes produce massive public reactions, accompanied by substantial social and economic impacts and sometimes even by subsequently increased physical risks. Explaining this phenomenon, and making the practice of risk analysis more sensitive to it, is one of the most challenging tasks confronting the societal management of risk. This chapter takes up that challenge.

The explanations that have emerged, while affording important insights, have been partial and often conflicting. The past decade has witnessed debates between the 'objectivist and subjectivist' schools of thought, between structuralistic and individualistic approaches, between physical/life scientists and social scientists. Even within the social sciences, psychologists see the roots of explanation in individual cognitive behaviour (Fischhoff et al, 1978), a claim extensively qualified by anthropologists, who insist that social context and culture shape perceptions and cognition (Douglas and Wildavsky, 1982; Johnson and Covello, 1987), and by analysts of technological controversies, who see 'stakeholder' interaction and competing values as the keys (von Winterfeldt and Edwards, 1984). The assumption underlying these debates is that the interpretations are mutually invalidating. In fact, we shall argue, the competing perspectives illuminate different facets of the public experience of risk. A comprehensive theory is needed that is capable of integrating the technical analysis of risk and the cultural, social and individual response structures that shape the public experience of risk. The main thesis of this article is that risk events interact with psychological, social and cultural processes in ways that can heighten or attenuate public perceptions of risk and related risk behaviour. Behavioural patterns, in turn, generate secondary social or economic consequences but may act also to increase or decrease the physical risk itself. Secondary effects trigger demands for additional institutional responses and protective actions, or, conversely (in the case of risk attenuation), impede the necessary protective actions. The social structures and processes of risk experience, the resulting repercussions on individual and group perceptions, and the effects of these responses on community, society and economy compose a general phenomenon that we term the social amplification of risk. This chapter sets forth an initial conceptualization of the elements, structure and processes that make up this phenomenon.

BACKGROUND

The technical assessment of risk typically models the impacts of an event or human activity in terms of direct harms, including death, injuries, disease and environmental damages. Over time, the practice of characterizing risk by probability and magnitude of harm has drawn fire for neglecting equity issues in relation to time (future generations), space (the so-called LULU (locally unwanted land uses) or NIMBY (not in my backyard) issues), or social groups (the proletariat, the highly vulnerable, the exporting of hazard to developing countries). It also has become apparent that the consequences of risk events extend far beyond direct harms to include significant indirect impacts (e.g. liability, insurance costs, loss of confidence in institutions or alienation from community affairs) (Katzman, 1985). The situation becomes even more complex when the analysis also addresses the decision making and risk management process. Frequently, indirect impacts appear to be dependent less on the direct outcomes (i.e. injury or death) of the risk event than on judgements of the adequacy of institutional arrangements to control or manage the risk, the possibility of assigning blame to one of the major participants, and the perceived fairness of the risk management process.

The accident at the Three Mile Island (TMI) nuclear reactor in 1979 demonstrated dramatically that factors besides injury, death and property damage can impose serious costs and social repercussions. No one is likely to die from the release of radioactivity at TMI, but few accidents in US history have wrought such costly societal impacts. The accident devastated the utility that owned and operated the plant and imposed enormous costs – in the form of stricter regulations, reduced operation of reactors worldwide, greater public opposition to nuclear power, and a less viable role for one of the major long-term energy sources – on the entire nuclear industry and on society as a whole (Heising and George, 1986). This mishap at a nuclear power plant may even have increased public concerns about other complex technologies, such as chemical manufacturing and genetic engineering.

The point is that traditional cost–benefit and risk analyses neglect these higher-order impacts and thus greatly underestimate the variety of adverse effects attendant on certain risk events (and thereby underestimate the overall risk from the event). In this sense, social amplification provides a corrective mechanism by which society acts to bring the technical assessment of risk more in line with a fuller determination of risk. At the other end of the spectrum, the relatively low levels of interest by the public in the risks presented by such well-documented and significant hazards as indoor radon, smoking, driving without seat belts or highly carcinogenic aflatoxins in peanut butter serve as examples of the social attenuation of risk. Whereas attenuation of risk is indispensable in that it allows individuals to cope with the multitude of risks and risk events encountered daily, it also may lead to potentially serious adverse consequences from underestimation and underresponse. Thus, both social amplification and attenuation, through serious disjunctures between expert and public assessments of risk and varying responses among different publics, confound conventional risk analysis. In some cases, the societal context may, through its effects on the risk assessor, alter the focus and scope of the risk assessment. A case in point is the series of actions taken in 1984 by the Environmental Protection Agency (EPA) with regard to a soil and grain fumigant, ethylene dibromide (EDB) (Sharlin, 1985). An atmosphere charged with intense societal concern about protecting the nation's food and groundwater supplies from chemical contaminants prompted the Agency to focus primarily on these two pathways of population exposure to EDB, although it was well aware that emissions of EDB from leaded gasoline were a significant source of population exposure. Consequently, the first-line receivers of the risk information – the risk managers, the mass media, the politicians and the general public – heard from the start about cancer risks from tainted water and food, but not from ambient air. This example illustrates how the filtering of information about hazards may start as early as in the risk assessment itself and may profoundly alter the form and content of the risk information produced and conveyed by technical experts (Sharlin, 1985).

Other researchers have noted that risk sources create a complex network of direct and indirect effects that are susceptible to change through social responses (Hoos, 1980; Wynne, 1984). But because of the complexity and the transdisciplinary nature of the problem, an adequate conceptual framework for a theoretically based and empirically operational analysis is still missing. The lack of an integrative theory that provides guidelines on how to model and measure the complex relationships among risk, risk analysis, social response and socioeconomic effects has resulted in a reaffirmation of technical risk assessment, which at least provides definite answers (however narrow or misleading) to urgent risk problems.

The concept of the social amplification of risk can, in principle, provide the necessary theoretical base for a more comprehensive and powerful analysis of risk and risk management in modern societies. At this point, we do not offer a fully developed theory of social amplification of risk, but we do propose a fledgling conceptual framework that may serve to guide ongoing efforts to develop, test, and apply such a theory to a broad array of pressing risk problems. Since the metaphor of amplification draws upon notions in communications theory, we begin with a brief examination of its use in that context.

SIGNAL AMPLIFICATION IN COMMUNICATIONS THEORY

In communications theory, amplification denotes the process of intensifying or attenuating signals during the transmission of information from an information source, to intermediate transmitters, and finally to a receiver (DeFleur, 1966). An information source sends out a cluster of signals (which form a message) to a transmitter, or directly to the receiver. The signals are decoded by the transmitter or receiver so that the message can be understood. Each transmitter alters the original message by intensifying or attenuating some incoming signals, adding or deleting others, and sending a new cluster of signals on to the next transmitter or the final receiver where the next stage of decoding occurs.

The process of transmitting is more complex than the electronic metaphor implies. Messages have a meaning for the receiver only within a sociocultural context. Sources and signals are not independent entities but are perceived as a unit by the receiver who links the signal to the sources or transmitters and draws inferences about the relationship between the two. In spite of the problems of the source–receiver model, the metaphor is still powerful enough to serve as a heuristic framework for analysing communication processes. In a recent literature review of 31 mass communication textbooks, the source–receiver metaphor was, along with the concept of symbolic meaning, the predominant theoretical framework (Shoemaker, 1987).

Each message may contain factual, inferential, value-related and symbolic meanings (Lasswell, 1948). The factual information refers to the content of the message (e.g. the emission of an air pollutant is X mg per day) as well as the source of the message (e.g. EPA conducted the measurement). The inferential message refers to the conclusions that can be drawn from the presented evidence (e.g. the emission poses a serious health threat). Then those conclusions may undergo evaluation according to specific criteria (e.g. the emission exceeds the allowable level). In addition, cultural symbols may be attached that evoke specific images (e.g. 'big business', 'the military–industrial complex', 'high technology', etc) that carry strong value implications.

Communication studies have demonstrated that the symbols present in messages are key factors in triggering the attention of potential receivers and in shaping their decoding processes (Hovland, 1948). If, for example, the communication source is described as an independent scientist, or a group of Nobel laureates, the content of the message may well command public attention. Messages from such sources may successfully pass through the selection filters of the transmitters or receivers and be viewed as credible. A press release by the nuclear industry, by contrast, may command much less credibility unless other aspects of the message compensate for doubts about the impartiality of the source.

Transmitters of signals may detect amplification arising from each message component (Sorensen and Mileti, 1987). A factual statement repeated several times, especially if by different sources, tends to elicit greater belief in the accuracy of the information. An elaborate description of the inference process may distract attention from the accuracy of the underlying assumptions. Reference to a highly appreciated social value may increase the receiver's tolerance for weak evidence. And, of course, a prestigious communication source can (at least in the short run) compensate for trivial factual messages. But adding or deleting symbols may well be the most powerful single means to amplify or attenuate the original message. Amplification of signals occurs during both transmission and reception. The transmitter structures the messages that go to a receiver. The receiver, in turn, interprets, assimilates, and evaluates the messages. But a transmitter, it should be noted, is also a new information source – one that transcribes the original message from the source into a new message and sends it on to the receiver, according to institutional rules, role requirements, and anticipated receiver interests. Signals passing through a transmitter may therefore, be amplified twice – during the reception of information and in recoding. Signal amplification in communications, therefore, occupies a useful niche in the overall structure of the social amplification of risk. A discussion of the proposed conceptional framework takes up the next section of this paper.

A STRUCTURAL DESCRIPTION OF THE SOCIAL AMPLIFICATION OF RISK

Social amplification of risk denotes the phenomenon by which information processes, institutional structures, social group behaviour and individual responses shape the social experience of risk, thereby contributing to risk consequences (see Figure 6.1). The interaction between risk events and social processes makes it clear that, as used in this framework, risk has meaning only to the extent that it treats how people think about the world and its relationships. Thus there is no such thing as 'true' (absolute) and 'distorted' (socially determined) risk. Rather the information system and characteristics of the public response that compose social amplification are essential elements in determining the nature and magnitude of risk. We begin with the information system. Like a stereo receiver, the information system may amplify risk events in two ways:

1   by intensifying or weakening signals that are part of the information that individuals and social groups receive about the risk;
2   by filtering the multitude of signals with respect to the attributes of the risk and their importance.

Signals arise through direct personal experience with a risk object or through the receipt of information about the risk object (DeFleur, 1966). These signals are processed by social, as well as individual, amplification 'stations', which include the following:

- the scientist who conducts and communicates the technical assessment of risk;
- the risk management institution;

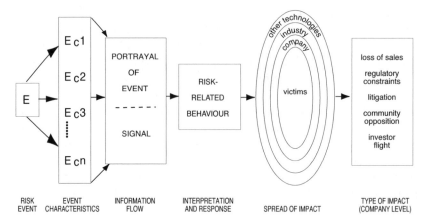

Figure 6.1 *Highly simplified representation of the social amplification of risk and potential impacts on a corporation*

- the news media;
- activist social organizations;
- opinion leaders within social groups;
- personal networks of peer and reference groups;
- public agencies.

Social amplification stations generate and transmit information via communications channels (media, letters, telephones, direct conversations). In addition, each recipient also engages in amplification (and attenuation) processes, thereby acting as an amplification station for risk-related information. We hypothesize that the key amplification steps consist of the following:

- filtering of signals (e.g. only a fraction of all incoming information is actually processed);
- decoding of the signal;
- processing of risk information (e.g. the use of cognitive heuristics for drawing inferences);
- attaching social values to the information in order to draw implications for management and policy;
- interacting with one's cultural and peer groups to interpret and validate signals;
- formulating behavioural intentions to tolerate the risk or to take actions against the risk or risk manager;
- engaging in group or individual actions to accept, ignore, tolerate or change the risk.

A full-fledged theory of the social amplification of risk should ultimately explain why specific risks and risk events undergo more or less amplification or attenuation. Whether such a theory will carry the power to predict the specific kinds of public responses and the anatomy of social controversy that will follow the introduction of new risks must await the test of time. It may prove possible to identify and classify attributes of the risk source and of the social arena that heighten or attenuate the public response to risk. Social amplifications of risk will spawn behavioural responses, which, in turn, will result in secondary impacts. Secondary impacts include such effects as the following:

- enduring mental perceptions, images and attitudes (e.g. anti-technology attitudes, alienation from the physical environment, social apathy, stigmatization of an environment or risk manager);
- local impacts on business sales, residential property values and economic activity;
- political and social pressure (e.g. political demands, changes in political climate and culture);
- changes in the physical nature of the risk (e.g. feedback mechanisms that enlarge or lower the risk);
- changes in training, education or required qualifications of operating and emergency-response personnel;
- social disorder (e.g. protesting, rioting, sabotage, terrorism);
- changes in risk monitoring and regulation;
- increased liability and insurance costs;
- repercussions on other technologies (e.g. lower levels of public acceptance) and on social institutions (e.g. erosion of public trust).

Secondary impacts are, in turn, perceived by social groups and individuals so that another stage of amplification may occur to produce third-order impacts. The impacts thereby may spread, or 'ripple', to other parties, distant locations or future generations. Each order of impact will not only disseminate social and political impacts but may also trigger (in risk amplification) or hinder (in risk attenuation) positive changes for risk reduction. The concept of the social amplification of risk is, therefore, dynamic, taking into account the learning and social interactions resulting from experience with risk.

The analogy of dropping a stone into a pond (see Figure 6.1) serves to illustrate the spread of the higher-order impacts associated with the social amplification of risk. The ripples spread outward, first encompassing the directly affected victims or the first group to be notified, then touching the next higher institutional level (a company or an agency) and, in more extreme cases, reaching other parts of the industry or other social arenas with similar problems. This rippling of impacts is an important element of risk amplification since it suggests that amplification can introduce substantial temporal and geographical extension of impacts. The same graphic representation demonstrates the possibility that social amplification may, quantitatively and qualitatively, increase the direct

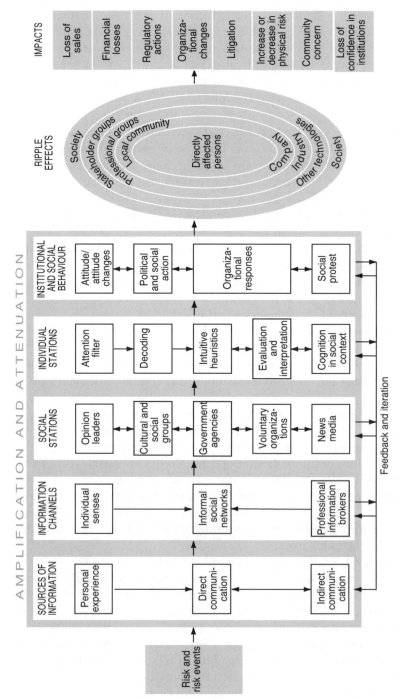

Figure 6.2 *Detailed conceptual framework of social amplification of risk*

impacts. In this case, the inner circle changes it shape with each new round of ripples. Figure 6.2 depicts in greater detail the hypothesized stages of social amplification of risk and its associated impacts for a hypothetical corporation. Several examples illustrate the ripple effect of risk events. Following the Three Mile Island accident, nuclear plants worldwide were shut down and restarted more frequently for safety checks, although these phases of operations (as with aircraft take-offs and landings) are by far the riskiest operational stages. In a more recent case of risk amplification, Switzerland recalled and ordered the incineration of 200 tons of its prestigious Vacherin Mont d'Or cheese because of bacterial contamination. Rival French cheesemakers at first celebrated their good fortune until it became apparent that public concern over the event had caused worldwide consumption of the cheese, from all producers, to plummet by over 25 per cent. An entire industry, in short, suffered economic reversal from a specific risk event (Grunhouse, 1988). The social amplification of risk, in our current conceptualization, involves two major stages (or amplifiers): the transfer of information about the risk or risk event, and the response mechanisms of society.

INFORMATIONAL MECHANISMS OF SOCIAL AMPLIFICATION

The roots of social amplification lie in the social experience of risk, both in direct personal experience and in indirect, or secondary, experience, through information received about the risk, risk events and management systems. Direct experience with risky activities or events can be either reassuring (as with automobile driving) or alarming (as with tornadoes or floods). Generally, experience with dramatic accidents or risk events increases the memorability and imaginability of the hazard, thereby heightening the perception of risk (Slovic, 1986). But direct experience can also provide feedback on the nature, extent and manageability of the hazard, affording a better perspective and an enhanced capability for avoiding risks. Thus, whereas direct personal experience can serve as a risk amplifier, it can also act to attenuate risk. Understanding this interaction for different risks, for different social experiences and for different cultural groups is an important research need.

But many risks are not experienced directly. When direct personal experience is lacking or minimal, individuals learn about risk from other persons and from the media. Information flow becomes a key ingredient in public response and acts as a major agent of amplification. Attributes of information that may influence the social amplification are *volume*, the degree to which information is *disputed*, the extent of *dramatization*, and the *symbolic connotations* of the information.

Independent of the accuracy and particular content of the information, a large volume of information may serve as a risk amplifier. In an analysis of media coverage of Love Canal and Three Mile Island, Mazur argued that the massive quantity of media coverage not only reported the events but defined and shaped the issues (Mazur, 1984). Repeated stories, of course, direct public attention toward particular risk problems and away from competing sources of attention. Moreover, the news media tend to become battlegrounds where various participants vie for advantage. However balanced the coverage, it is unclear that reassuring claims can effectively counter the effects of fear-arousing messages (Sorensen et al, 1987). In Alvin Weinberg's metaphor, it is much harder to 'unscare' people than to scare them (Weinberg, 1977). High volumes of information also mobilize latent fears about a particular risk and enhance the recollection of previous accidents or management failures or enlarge the extent to which particular failures, events or consequences can be imagined. In this way, technologies or activities may come to be viewed as more dangerous (Kahneman et al, 1982; Renn, 1986).

The second attribute of information is the degree to which individuals or groups dispute factual information or inferences regarded as credible by interested members of the public. Debates among experts are apt to heighten public uncertainty about what the facts really are, increase doubts about whether the hazards are really understood, and decrease the credibility of official spokespersons (Mazur, 1981). If the risks are already feared by the public, then increased concern is the likely result.

Dramatization, a third attribute, is undoubtedly a powerful source of risk amplification. The report during the Three Mile Island accident that a hydrogen bubble inside the reactor could explode within the next two days, blow the head off the reactor and release radioactive material into the atmosphere certainly increased public fears near the nuclear plant (and around the world). Sensational headlines ('Thousands Dead!') following the Chernobyl accident increased the memorability of that accident and the perceived catastrophic potential of nuclear power. If erroneous information sources find ready access to the mass media without effective antidotes, then large social impacts, even for minor events, become entirely possible.

The channels of information are also important. Information about risks and risk events flows through two major communication networks – the news media and more informal personal networks. The news media as risk articulators have received the bulk of scientific attention for their critical role in public opinion formation and community agenda setting (Mazur, 1981; USNRC, 1980). Since the media tend to accord disproportionate coverage to rare or dramatic risks, or risk events, it is not surprising that people's estimates of the principal causes of death are related to the amount of media coverage they receive (Combs and Slovic, 1978).

Informal communication networks involve the linkages that exist among friends, neighbours, and co-workers, and within social groups more generally. Although relatively little is known about such networks, it is undoubtedly the case that people do not consider risk issues in isolation from other social issues or from the views of their peers. Since one's friends or co-workers provide reference points for validating perceptions but are also likely to share a more general cultural view or bias, the potential exists for both amplifying and attenuating information. If the risk is feared, rumour may be a significant element in the formation of public perceptions and attitudes. Within social group interaction, these interpretations of risks will tend to be integrated into larger frames of values and analysis and to become resistant to new, conflicting information. It should be expected, therefore, that interpersonal networks will lead to divergent risk perceptions, management preferences and levels of concern. Since experts also exhibit cultural biases in their selections of theories, methods and data, these variable public perceptions will also often differ as a group from those of experts.

Finally, specific terms or concepts used in risk information may have quite different meanings for varying social and cultural groups. They may also trigger associations independent of those intended (Blumer, 1969). Such symbolic connotations may entail 'mushroom clouds' for nuclear energy, 'dumps' for waste disposal facilities, or feelings of 'warmth and comfort' for solar power technologies.

RESPONSE MECHANISMS OF SOCIAL AMPLIFICATION

The interpretation and response to information flow form the second major stage of the social amplification of risk. These mechanisms involve the social, institutional and cultural contexts in which the risk information is interpreted, its meaning diagnosed and values attached. We hypothesize four major pathways to initiate response mechanisms:

1 *Heuristics and values.* Individuals cannot deal with the full complexity of risk and the multitude of risks involved in daily life. Thus people use simplifying mechanisms to evaluate risk and to shape responses. These processes, while permitting individuals to cope with a risky world, may sometimes introduce biases that cause distortions and errors (Kahneman et al, 1982). Similarly, the application of individual and group values will also determine which risks are deemed important or minor and what actions, if any, should be taken.

2 *Social group relationships.* Risk issues enter into the political agenda of social and political groups. The nature of these groups will influence member responses and the types of rationality brought to risk issues (Rayner and Cantor, 1987). To the extent that risk becomes a central issue in a political campaign or in a conflict among social groups, it will be vigorously brought to more general public attention, often coupled with ideological interpretations of technology or the risk management

process (Douglas and Wildavsky, 1982; Johnson and Covello, 1987). A polarization of views and an escalation of rhetoric by partisans typically occur and new recruits are drawn into the conflicts (Mazur, 1981). These social alignments tend to become anchors for subsequent interpretations of risk management and may become quite firm in the face of conflicting information.

3   *Signal value*. An important concept that has emerged from research on risk perception is that the seriousness and higher-order impacts of a risk event are determined, in part, by what that event signals or portends (Slovic, 1987b). The informativeness or 'signal value' of an event appears to be systematically related to the characteristics of the event and the hazard it reflects. High-signal events suggest that a new risk has appeared or that the risk is different and more serious than previously understood (see Table 6.1). Thus an accident that takes many lives may produce relatively little social disturbance (beyond that experienced by the victims' families and friends) if it occurs as part of a familiar and well-understood system (such as a train wreck). A small accident in an unfamiliar system (or one perceived as poorly understood), such as a nuclear reactor or a recombinant-DNA laboratory, however, may elicit great public concern if it is interpreted to mean that the risk is not well understood, not controllable or not competently managed, thus implying that further (and possibly worse) mishaps are likely. In sum, signals about a risk event initiate a process whereby the significance of the event is examined. If found to be ominous, these implications are likely to trigger higher-order social and economic impacts.

4   *Stigmatization*. Stigma refers to the negative imagery associated with undesirable social groups or individuals (Goffman, 1963). But environments with heavy pollution, waste accumulation or hazardous technology may also come to be associated with negative images. Love Canal, the Valley of the Thousand Drums, Times Beach and the Nevada Test Site evoke vivid images of waste and pollution. Since the typical response to stigmatized persons or environments is avoidance, it is reasonable to assume that risk-induced stigma may have significant social and policy consequences (Slovic, 1987a). Research is needed to define the role of risk in creating stigma, the extent of aversion that results, and how durable such stigma become.

In addition to these four mechanisms, *positive feedback to the physical risk itself* can occur due to social processes. If a transportation accident with hazardous materials were to occur close to a waste disposal site, for example, protests and attempted blockage of the transportation route could result. Such actions could themselves become initiating or co-accident events, thereby increasing the probabilities of future accidents or enlarging the consequences should an accident occur. Or, alternatively, an

Table 6.1 *Risk events with potentially high signal value*

Events	Messages
Report that chlorofluorocarbon releases are depleting the ozone layer.	A new and possibly catastrophic risk has emerged.
Resignation of regulators or corporate officials in 'conscience'.	The managers are concealing the risks: they cannot be trusted.
News report of off-site migration at a hazardous waste site.	The risk managers are not in control of the hazard.
Scientific dispute over the validity of an epidemiological study.	The experts do not understand the risks.
Statement by regulators that the levels of a particular contaminant in the water supply involve only very low risks as compared with other risks.	The managers do not care about the people who will be harmed; they do not understand long-term cumulative effects of chemicals.

accident in waste handling at the facility could lead opponents, or a disgruntled worker, to replicate the event through sabotage. Especially where strong public concern exists over a technology or facility, a wide variety of mechanisms is present by which health and safety risks may be enlarged through social processes (Kasperson et al, 1987).

NEXT STEPS

Only partial models or paradigms exist for characterizing the phenomenon we describe as the social amplification of risk. Understanding this phenomenon is a prerequisite essential for assessing the potential impacts of projects and technologies, for establishing priorities in risk management, and for setting health and environmental standards. We put forth this conceptual framework to begin the building of a comprehensive theory that explains why seemingly minor risks or risk events often produce extraordinary public concern and social and economic impacts, with rippling effects across time, space and social institutions. The conceptualization needs elaboration, and competing views. Empirical studies, now beginning, should provide important tests and insights for the next stage of theory construction.

ACKNOWLEDGEMENT

This work was supported by the Nevada Nuclear Waste Project Office and by NSF grant No SES 8796182 to Decision Research. We wish to thank Brian Cook, Christoph Hohenemser, Nancy Kraus, Sarah Lichtenstein, Steve Rayner and three anonymous reviewers for their constructive comments on earlier drafts of the manuscript.

NOTE

1   In this chapter, the term 'risk event' refers to occurrences that are manifestations
    of the risk and that initiate signals pertaining to the risk. Risk events therefore
    include routine or unexpected releases, accidents (large and small), discoveries of
    pollution incidents, reports of exposures or adverse consequences. Usually such
    risk events are specific to particular times and locations.

7 Hidden Hazards

Roger E. Kasperson and Jeanne X. Kasperson

INTRODUCTION

At the end of the 20th century, hazards have become a part of everyday life to an extent that they have never been before. It is not that life, at least in advanced industrial societies, is more dangerous. Indeed, by any measure, the average person is safer and is likely to live longer and with greater leisure and well-being than at earlier times. Nevertheless, the external world seems replete with toxic wastes, building collapses, industrial accidents, groundwater contamination and airplane crashes and near collisions. The newspapers and television news daily depict specific hazard events, and a parade of newly discovered or newly assessed threats – the 'hazard-of-the-week' syndrome – occupies the attention of a host of congressional committees, federal regulatory agencies, and state and local governments. Seemingly any potential threat, however esoteric or remote, has its day in the sun.

How is it, then, that certain hazards pass unnoticed or unattended, growing in size until they have taken a serious toll? How is it that asbestos pervaded the American workplace and schools when its respiratory dangers had been known for decades? How is it that after years of worry about nuclear war, the threat of a 'nuclear winter' did not become apparent until the 1980s? How is it that the Sahel famine of 1983–1984 passed unnoticed in the hazard-filled newspapers of the world press, until we could no longer ignore the spectre of millions starving? How is it that America 'rediscovered' poverty only with Michael Harrington's vivid account of the 'other Americans' and acknowledged the accumulating hazards of chemical pesticides only with Rachel Carson's *Silent Spring*? How is it that, during the 20th century, a society with a Delaney amendment and a US$10 billion Superfund programme has allowed smoking to become the killer of millions of Americans? And why is it that the potential long-term

Note: Reprinted from *Acceptable Evidence: Science and Values in Hazard Management*, Mayo, D. C. and Hollander, R. (eds), 'Hidden hazards', Kasperson, R. E. and Kasperson, J. X., pp9–28, © (1991), by Oxford University Press, Inc. Used by permission from Oxford University Press, Inc

ecological catastrophes associated with burning coal command so much less concern than do the hazards of nuclear power?

These oversights or neglects, it might be argued, are simply the random hazards or events that elude our alerting and monitoring systems. After all, each society has its 'worry beads', particular hazards that we choose to rub and polish assiduously (Kates, 1985b). Because our assessment and management resources are finite, certain hazards inevitably slip through and surface as surprises or outbreaks. Or are hazards simply part of the overall allocation of goods and bads in a global political economy, so that the epidemiology of hazard events is only one of many expressions of underlying social and economic forces? Alternatively, are the 'hidden hazards' simply those that occur in distant times, distant places or distant (i.e. not proximate) social groups?

The following discussion explores the phenomenon of hidden hazards, arguing that neither randomness nor any single structural hypothesis adequately explains the diversity of their causes and manifestations. Like the world of hazards of which they are part, hidden hazards have to do with both the nature of the hazards themselves and the nature of the societies and cultures in which they occur. The 'hiding' of hazards is at once purposeful and unintentional, life threatening and institution sustaining, systematic and incidental. We see five distinct aspects of hidden hazards – global elusive, marginal, ideological, amplified and value threatening – associated with differing causal agents and processes. As Table 7.1 indicates, some multiple hazards defy pigeon-holing and span one or more categories.

GLOBAL ELUSIVE HAZARDS

Some hazards remain hidden from society's close scrutiny and management efforts because of the nature of the hazards themselves. Writing in 1985, Robert Kates noted a series of significant changes in society's management agenda (Kates, 1985b). Government concern has traditionally focused on the visible issues of automobile smog and raw sewage and only recently on the less visible problems posed by low concentrations of toxic pollutants. Corporations have historically allocated most of their hazard management budgets to ensuring industrial safety; only now are the more subtle long-term effects to health receiving much attention. Meanwhile, a shift has begun in the temporal perspective, from the commonplace accidents of everyday existence, for which experience and actuarial data exist, to the possibility of rare but catastrophic accidents that may occur in the future, for which simulation and scenarios must substitute for experience.

Similarly, most of the hazards commanding our attention have been those that can be pinpointed to places and localities, where cause and effect can often be closely linked. The newer, more elusive hazards involve problems (e.g. acid rain) associated with complex regional interactions

Table 7.1 *Dimensions of hidden hazards*

	Global Elusive	Ideological	Marginal	Amplified	Value threatening
Abortion					X
AIDS (early stages)			X		
Asbestos in manufacturing		X	X		
Assembly lines		X	X		X
Automation/unemployment		X	X		X
Botulism				X	
Climatic change	X				
Computers					X
Deforestation	X				
Desertification	X				
Export of hazardous technologies			X		
Famines			X		
Gene-pool reduction	X				
Genetic engineering				X	X
Global poverty		X	X		
Handguns		X			
Hazardous wastes				X	
Indoor air pollution			X		
Information banks					X
Nuclear power				X	X
Nuclear winter	X				
Occupational hazards		X			
Oral contraceptives			X		X
Ozone depletion	X				
Pesticides	X			X	
Sickle-cell anaemia			X		
Soil erosion	X				
Televised violence		X			X
Terrorism				X	X
Toxic material				X	
VDTs			X		X

Note: VDT = visual display terminal

and, most troublesome, global sources, distribution and effects (stratospheric ozone depletion, climatic change, global warming). Lengthy lag times between activities and alterations in global fluxes of energy and materials, geographical separation in source regions and the regions where the effects are manifested, complex interactions of human and physical systems, and the slowly developing accumulation of materials in environmental sinks characterize this class of elusive hazards.

It is these global elusive hazards that promise to be particularly troublesome in the years ahead. With the exception of long-term climatic change, it is only recently that such hazards have attracted substantial scientific and political attention. Soil degradation and erosion, global deforestation, desertification and the accumulation of trace pollutants in the oceans and the stratosphere have all received only limited scientific scrutiny and yet have the capacity to undermine the long-term sustainability of the earth. For the first time in history, the unintended consequences of human actions and social processes approximate the scale of the processes of nature in terms of their potential effects on the Earth as a life-support system (ICSU, 1986, p2). Despite the belated and limited attention, the warning signs of what the Brundtland report (WCED, 1987) has characterized as 'interlocking environmental crises' show up in (1) fossil fuel burning linked to widespread acid deposition in North America, Europe and China; (2) the recently discovered hole in the stratospheric ozone layer over Antarctica; (3) the extensive tropical deforestation implicated in species extinction and the flooding of lowland farms; and (4) large-scale air and water pollution threatening human health in the emerging megacities of developing countries.

The potential severity of global elusive hazards tends to be hidden, not only because of their diffuseness and complexity but also because their management challenges a politically compartmentalized world, one in which there is a significant North–South conflict. These hazards typify the archetypal global-commons problems in which individual nations have incentives to allow others to undertake ameliorative initiatives and expend scarce resources. Lacking a global environmental ethic or a coherent international legal or regulatory regime, it is – despite the recent success of the Montreal Protocol (1987) concerning ozone depletion – unclear whether international initiatives to deal with such hazards will be successful.

Encouraging in this regard is the newly formed International Geosphere-Biosphere Program, a massive undertaking of the International Council of Scientific Unions (ICSU), whose aim is 'to describe and understand the interactive physical, chemical, and biological processes that regulate the total earth system, the unique environment that it provides for life, the changes that are occurring in that system, and the manner by which these changes are influenced by human actions' (Malone, 1986, p8). Even here, however, although the programme salutes the importance of human actions in global environmental transformations, it currently includes only a modest effort to forge the links between human causes and environmental transformations. (New initiatives, we should note, are currently under way by the Human Dimensions of Global Change Programme [Toronto] and the International Social Sciences Council, as well as by the National Science Foundation, the National Research Council and the Social Science Research Council in the United States to begin to fill this void (see also Volume II, Chapter 14)). Similarly, there is no provision for mobilizing the results into international policies or management programmes.

The chance of these elusive hazards becoming visible and high-priority concerns depends on whether (1) the potential changes can be expressed in terms that indicate vividly the long-term risks associated with particular human activities; (2) an international constituency of public concern over these hazards can be built and sustained; and (3) the serious equity problems between developed and developing countries referred to in Chapter 13 can be overcome. Global elusive hazards could become the major environmental challenge of the 1990s and might well revise long-held notions of national and international security (Mathews, 1989).

IDEOLOGICAL HAZARDS

Some hazards remain hidden or unattended because they lie embedded in a societal web of values and assumptions that either denigrates the consequences or deems them acceptable, elevates associated benefits, and idealizes certain notions or beliefs. Since the advent of television, violence has been an intrinsic part of news and programme content, including Saturday morning cartoons aimed at children. The effort of several decades to regulate televised violence has run aground on the twin shores of the political power of the networks and the belief that violence is a part of American reality and that the protection of free speech should override the need to prevent antisocial behaviour.

Handguns are a similar matter. Despite an extraordinary annual national toll from handgun-related violence and the assassination or attempted assassination of a succession of the nation's political leaders, control efforts have failed to overcome the credo that the right to bear arms is one of the most inalienable of American rights. Or to take a different case, the notion that unemployment is primarily a failure of individuals rather than economic systems accords this social hazard a status very different from that prevailing in socialist societies. In the latter, social programmes are enacted to correct the structural imperfections in the economy and to ensure that the victims of these imperfections can provide for their basic needs.

Ideological hazards are present no less, of course, in Marxist and socialist societies. There the growth of bureaucracy and extensive controls over the economy have produced widespread concerns over the lack of incentives for personal initiative and means for career fulfilment. The emphasis on economic growth over other societal goals has often led to widespread air and water pollution. The resulting environmental damage has played a significant role in the independence movements in Eastern Europe and the autonomous Soviet republics, as the centralized control of information has eroded the recognition of hazards by those who bear the risks.

A striking illustration of ideological hazards at work in the American context is the little-noticed differential in prevailing standards for the protection of workers and publics discussed in Chapter 12. This discrepancy in protection is rooted in the idealization of private enterprise and the assumption that it should enjoy wide latitude of freedom from government interference. In the US hazard management system, the Occupational Safety and Health Administration (OSHA) is the primary regulator of occupational hazards, whereas the US Environmental Protection Agency (EPA) is the primary regulator of hazards to the general public. Other agencies' regulations govern special groups of workers (e.g. miners), particular classes of hazards (consumer products) or special types of hazards (such as radiation), but OSHA and EPA have the principal responsibility for most occupational and general environmental hazards.

Typically, OSHA's standards regulating the exposure of workers to hazardous substances involve limitations on the concentration of a substance in the air (typically averaged over an eight-hour shift), as respiration is the most likely pathway for the hazard and as, at least in principle, it is not too difficult to monitor exposure levels. The EPA's regulations for most substances, on the other hand, limit emissions (the rate at which the substance may be discharged into the air or water). Hazard management through emission control is natural, as the population at risk and the environment in which exposure to the substance occurs are likely to be difficult to characterize. Thus direct comparison with OSHA's regulations is no easy task.

To overcome this problem, Derr et al (1981, 1986, see Chapter 12) examined a small but important class of substances that are emitted in sufficiently large volume and by sufficiently dispersed sources that the EPA has found it practical to establish standards for ambient concentrations. Even for these substances, the comparison with OSHA's standards has its problems: the time periods over which the concentrations are to be averaged are frequently different, and uncertainties in dose–response information make it difficult to determine whether a short exposure to high concentrations is better or worse than is a long exposure to lower concentrations.

Despite these difficulties, a comparison is possible. Figure 7.1 shows, for ten substances for which it is possible to compare limits on concentration, the current EPA and OSHA standards information on medical effects and background level, and the ratio of the environmental standard to the occupational standard. Except for ozone and carbon monoxide, for which there are only short-term standards and for which the primary health concerns are short-term stresses, the comparison is based on the limits that the standard imposes on the cumulative annual dose. The figure also shows two quantities useful in characterizing each hazard: the natural background level for the hazard and the lowest level of concentration at which adverse human health effects have been observed.

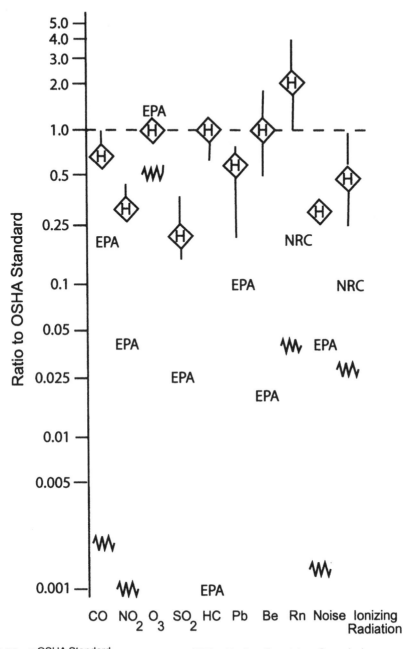

Source: Derr et al, 1981, p14

Figure 7.1 *Public (EPA) and worker (OSHA) standards, levels of observed harm, and normal background levels for ten hazards*

Table 7.2 International comparison of occupational standards (all standards in milligrams per cubic metre mg/m³)

Countries	Benzene	Cadmium oxides	Carbon monoxide	DDT	Heptachlor	Lead	Berylium	Mercury	Nickel	NOx	Ozone	Parathion
Belgium	30	0.05	55	1	0.5	0.15	0.002	0.05	0.1	9	0.2	0.1
Finland	32	0.01	55	1	0.5	0.15	0.002	0.005	–	9	0.2	0.1
German Democratic Republic	50	–	35	1	–	0.15	0.002	0.1	–	10	0.2	–
Federal Republic of Germany	50	0.1	55	1	0.5	0.2	–	0.1	–	9	0.2	0.1
Italy	20	0.01	55	1	–	0.15	0.002	–	1	5	0.2	0.1
Japan	80	0.1	55	1	–	0.15	0.002	0.05	1	9	0.2	0.1
The Netherlands	30	0.05	55	1	0.5	0.15	0.002	0.05	0.1	9	0.2	0.1
Romania	50 (max)	0.2 (max)	30	0.7	0.3	0.1	0.001 (max)	0.05	–	10 (max)	0.1	0.05
Sweden	30	0.02	40	1	–	0.1	0.002	0.05	0.01	9	0.2	–
Switzerland	32	0.1	55	1	0.5	0.15	0.002	0.05	–	9	0.2	0.1
USSR	5	0.1	20	0.1	0.01	0.01	0.001	0.01	0.5	5	0.1	0.05
Poland	30	0.1	30	0.1	–	0.05	0.001	0.01	–	5	0.1	–
US	30	0.1	55	1	0.5	0.2	0.002	0.05	1	9	0.2	0.11

It is apparent that regulators afford a greater measure of protection to members of the general public than to workers. Although one might reasonably expect that the standards for both groups would be set at or below the point at which measured harm occurs, this is not the case. General environmental standards are set below levels of measured harm, but workplace standards tend to be set above that level. In fact, the OSHA's standards are set at about the level of observed harm in four cases, at two times higher in two cases, and at four times higher in three cases. In only one case, radon, is the standard below the level of observed harm, and given recent advisories by the surgeon general and the EPA (Hilts, 1988), that is a wise decision. The standards generally reflect a belief that US workers may be appropriately exposed to hazards between 10 and 100 times the level considered to be unsafe for the US public.

The double standard, of course, reflects a long-term societal reluctance to intervene in the operation of private industry in the US. It is not surprising that OSHA was an early target of the Reagan Administration's efforts to weaken regulatory efforts and enforcement capabilities (Simon, 1983). Not infrequently, workplace hazards have grown into serious occupational health problems as their presence has remained obscure because of corporate concerns over the release of 'proprietary information'.

Despite its affluence and leadership in health research, the US does not possess the most stringent standards for the protection of workers. Table 7.2 shows comparative occupational standards for some 12 airborne toxic substances in 13 industrialized countries. There is a general East–West dichotomy, with the Soviet Union and the East Europeon countries exhibiting the greatest stringency in standards and the US the greatest permissiveness. Although most of the differences are within an order of magnitude, factors of 20 or more appear for heptachlor, lead and parathion. A transnational analysis of some 169 workplace standards found that only 19 were most stringent in the US, whereas some 147 (87 per cent) were most stringent in the Soviet Union (Winell, 1975; Kates, 1978). The reasons for the differences between US and USSR standards are historical but also clearly ideological. Equally notable, it should be added, is the tendency in Marxist societies to set rigorous workplace standards (which are often not met in practice) while permitting widespread degradation of the general environment (Jancar, 1987).

Ideological mechanisms exist, of course, to explain and justify the tolerance of high workplace risks. Workers, it is argued, are accustomed to dealing with hazards, are generally well informed and able to protect themselves, and are, in any case, compensated in workers' wages. A lengthy refutation of these myths is beyond the scope of this discussion. Suffice it to note that the available evidence shows that:

- Few workers are given information about risks at the time of employment and only unevenly after employment (Melville, 1981a;

Nelkin and Brown, 1984), although the hazard communication standard of the OSHA (1983) has upgraded most practices.

- Few workers arc genuinely free to accept or reject a job, or to move to a different job, on the basis of risk information (Melville, 1981a).
- Some workers in the major unionized manufacturing sectors receive a small risk premium in wages, but most workers in secondary labour sectors receive no risk premium, despite frequent high risks (Graham and Shakow, 1981).

Despite the evidence, claims are nonetheless commonplace in US political discourse that the American workplace is safe, that workers are knowledgeable about hazards and well equipped to protect themselves, and that they receive compensation for any damage to their health and safety (Viscusi, 1983).

MARGINAL HAZARDS

Those who occupy the margins of human populations, cultures, societies and economies are often exposed to hazards hidden from or concealed by those at the centre or in the mainstream. Marginal existence in itself heightens vulnerability because many of those who live in this way are already weakened from malnutrition, and access to societal resources and alternative means of coping are few (Kates et al, 1988, 1989). Then, too, the effects themselves are often quite literally invisible and unrecognized, such as the chronic hunger of many rural populations throughout the Third World or the malnutrition of many of the elderly in the US. In some cases, the imposition and concealment of the hazard can be quite purposeful, as in the periodic actions in Ethiopia and Sudan to withhold food relief from political opponents and to hide the results from the world's view (Harrison and Palmer, 1986). Although the social sciences have devoted much attention to marginality as a social and political phenomenon and have made some effort to assess its role in the experience of hazards and disasters, it is a concept that remains imperfectly understood and lacking an adequate theory.

Marginality can arise from position in age or gender. Young children, who are highly susceptible to neurological damage from lead exposure, have also often been exposed to particular sources of lead (e.g. eating lead paint) at higher levels than adults have (Chisolm and O'Hara, 1982; Kane, 1985). Although the hazards of lead have long been known and documented (Nriagu, 1983), the hazards for children were allowed to exist and even to grow for decades before effective action was taken. Both children and women have traditionally spent much more time in the home than have adult men, but only recently has indoor pollution been recognized as a serious source of contaminants. The household, not officially recognized as a workplace in the US, does not come under

OSHA's jurisdiction. It has received little attention from the EPA as an element of a public environment to be protected, although recent warnings on radon may signal a change. Because women tend to receive the highest exposures to a wide variety of contaminants (including benzopyrene, suspended particles and nitrogen oxides) in working over the stove or cooker, they are the major group at risk. Recent evidence has laid bare the extraordinary level of this as a global hazard, with a conservatively estimated 300 million to 400 million people (mostly women in developing countries) being at risk (UNEP, 1986, p33). Despite these figures, Bowonder (1981a) specifically describes how this large hazard has remained hidden in developing countries.

Managing marginal hazards poses its own dangers because societal interventions may actually exacerbate existing social problems or even spawn new ones. It is already worrisome, for example, that so much attention to the management of high susceptibility to reproductive and occupational hazards has been devoted to women when so few data exist indicating significant sex differences in susceptibility (Bingham, 1985, p80). Much of the current concern, for example, is about the possible effects of a variety of chemicals in the workplace on female reproductive ability or on the foetus (USOTA, 1985b). The temptation in such cases is to identify all those who are capable of becoming pregnant (whether or not they plan to do so) so as to deny them employment (thereby reducing both adverse health effects and potential liability). Such actions pose the danger that science will be used to secure safety by altering the workforce rather than by reducing exposure in the workplace. Meanwhile, there may be abuses centred on the equality of opportunity in the workplace.

Marginality may also have its genesis in social class and political economy, as particular groups are pushed out to the edge. A body of radical social theory has emerged that seeks to explain this phenomenon. Wisner (1976) sees marginality as the social allocation of space, shaped by the forces of colonialism and capitalism. Dominant classes gain control over more fertile lands and resources, forcing others into more marginal areas. Blaikie and Brookfield (1987) regard what ensues as a series of changes leading to marginalization. The more marginal lands have a high sensitivity und a low resilience to environmental change (e.g. droughts) or management (e.g. overuse). Such environmental degradation may be irreversible as areas lose their capacity to sustain life (Texler, 1986). Not infrequently, a vicious circle sets in of increasing impoverishment and further marginalization of land and land managers. Thus, land degradation becomes both a result and cause of social marginalization (Blaikie and Brookfield, 1987, p23), a situation that, in O'Keefe and Wisner's (1975) terms, requires only 'trigger' events (e.g. drought, smallpox, locusts or civil war) to produce a disaster. Through marginalization, therefore, famine becomes a 'normal' event.

This concept of marginalization has also been used to explain the occurrence of environmental and social disasters. Susman et al (1983) see

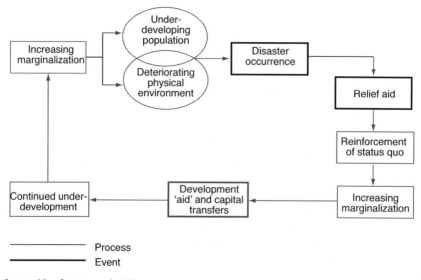

Source: After Susman et al, 1983

Figure 7.2 *Diagram hypothesizing the relationship of marginalization to disaster*

an international retrogressive trend from a state of *undevelopment to underdevelopment*, in which marginalization is a central ingredient (see Figure 7.2). Underdevelopment, in their view, causes the peasants to make their livelihood in more hazardous environments or to change their uses of resources in ways that exacerbate their vulnerability (Sewell and Foster, 1976). Witness, for example, the plight of Bangladesh, as three-quarters of the nation lay under floodwaters in the summer of 1988. Ironically, provision of relief usually reinforces the *status quo ante*, that is, the process of underdevelopment that produced the vulnerability in the first place.

Much remains to be done before we can have a comprehensive and accepted theory of marginalization and its role in hazard experience. But whatever the contribution of marginalization to explaining the occurrence of hazards and disasters, there can be little doubt that hazards concentrated in the margin are often hidden and neglected. Such was the case with the Sahel drought of 1983–84 which, despite its eventual toll as one of the great environmental disasters of the 20th century, passed largely unnoticed by the world press, international organizations and national development agencies until the famine reached its height during 1984 (Harrison and Palmer, 1986). Yet experts had predicted the potential for continuing famine in the Sahel for some time. As early as 1982, for example, the United Nation's Food and Agriculture Organization (FAO) had issued alarming reports (partly contradicted by other sources) on the situation in Ethiopia (Harrison and Palmer, 1986; Downing et al 1987). The Reagan Administration was clearly reluctant to deal with Marxist-Leninist regimes with whom its diplomatic relations were strained. The instability of governments, the diplomatic strains and the remoteness of the affected areas also made accurate food-related information difficult to obtain. Within the US government, policy makers debated whether the appropriate response should be humanitarian or political (Downing et al 1987). Not until the NBC evening news aired a BBC special about Ethiopia in October 1984 did the spectre of emaciated, fly-ridden bodies dying of starvation illuminate the scale of the tragedy (Li, 1987, p415).

Although this was a dramatic case of a disaster's remaining invisible and growing in scale and severity until the world belatedly responded, it is not surprising that marginal hazards are often hidden. Logically, the same forces that produced the marginality may be expected to shroud the associated consequences. Then, too, the margins are not a high priority with the centre; information flow and interaction are characteristically weak; ideological and political differences often cause separations; and the margins lack the power and resources to project the hazard event into the worldview. So it should be expected that hazards occurring among native peoples, ethnic and tribal minorities, isolated regions and locales, and secondary labour forces and peasants will often pass unheeded or remain obscure to those in the mainstream of power and society.

AMPLIFIED HAZARDS

Hidden hazards arise not only from social opaqueness but also because of limitations in the practice of science and the place of science in politics. The passage of the 1970 National Environmental Policy Act (NEPA) in the US established a precedent – that the assessment of the major environmental and social effects on projects must precede their implementation – that has been emulated worldwide. Indeed, it is instructive to see China coping with this innovation in the late 1980s (Ross, 1987). A host of procedural requirements has emerged regarding the environmental impact statement, and a variety of assessment methodologies have been nourished. More recently the field of risk analysis has arisen to supplement and extend earlier modes of analysis. These new techniques, concepts and methods are currently germinating in corporate and governmental programmes designed to protect human health, the environment and individual well-being.

Innovations in assessment practices have demonstrated an extraordinary power to evaluate and compare many of the environmental prices of new and existing technologies and major projects. But, ironically, as these innovative techniques illuminate some hazards, they obscure others. One reason for this is that the technical approach to hazards (usually labelled risk analysis) often focuses narrowly on the probability of certain events and the magnitude of specific consequences (often fatalities, morbidity or environmental damage). Yet studies of risk perception and cultural-group response reveal that most people experience hazards much more broadly; they are concerned, to be sure, about health and environmental effects but they also want to know how the risk came about in the first place, whether it is imposed or voluntary, how 'fair' the distribution of benefits and risks associated with a particular technology is, and whether catastrophes are possible (Rayner and Cantor, 1987; Slovic 1987b). It is increasingly clear that technology conveys a variety of impacts, of great concern to the public, that cannot be gauged, or sometimes not even identified, by conventional assessment methodologies. Thus, some hazards are 'hidden' to the professional assessors of technology impacts. These hazards interact with social structures and social groups, individuals, society and the economy in ways unanticipated by technical conceptions of risk, thereby creating *amplified hazards*.

We have conceptualized the structure and processes that compose the social amplification of risk (see Figure 7.3). People experience risks through personal experience or the depiction of the event in communication sources. Risk-related information is processed by social and individual amplification 'stations', including the scientist who communicates the risk assessment, the news media, activist social organizations, informal networks of friends and neighbours, and public agencies. These information systems amplify risk events in two ways, by intensifying or weakening signals of the risk and by filtering the signals with respect to the attributes of risk and their importance. The informational amplification of risk both generates and reacts to behavioural responses in social groups and individuals. These, in turn, result in such secondary impacts as mental imagery and anti-technology attitudes, impacts on business sales and property values, and political and social pressures. Through such secondary effects, the impacts of the risk event may 'ripple' to other parties, distant locations or future generations. Such was the case with the Three Mile Island accident of 1979 which, although probably resulting in no fatalities, shut down nuclear plants worldwide, cost billions of dollars, and eroded public confidence in nuclear power and (perhaps) other high technologies, industry and regulatory institutions.

Not all technologies or projects, of course, involve amplified hazards. For these, conventional assessment techniques suffice to make visible the hazards of concern. But the most controversial technologies and projects are those with amplified hazards and for which the existing assessment and management approaches miss the mark. An example is hazardous-facility siting in the US. After decades of siting industrial facilities in rural areas, the intense public opposition to a variety of such facilities – prisons, refineries, hazardous-waste incinerators, power plants and genetic-engineering laboratories – has perplexed decision makers and confounded existing institutional processes (Lindell and Earle 1983; Greenberg et al, 1984; von Winterfeldt and Edwards, 1984; USOTA, 1987).

Social scientists have abetted the concern among public officials over the 'irrational' public and 'hysterical' media, by resorting to overly

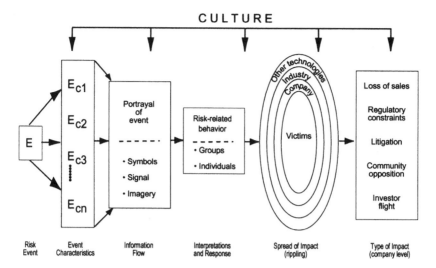

Source: Kasperson et al 1988e

Figure 7.3 *Highly simplified representation of the social amplification of risk and potential impacts on a corporation*

simplistic characterizations of public responses as so-called LULU (locally unwanted land use) or NIMBY (not in my back yard) syndromes (Popper 1983; Freudenberg, 1984). What is in fact occurring is a set of complex but rational public reactions to both the risk and the social circumstances involving the social amplification of risk.

Instead of laying bare and addressing the hidden hazards, policy makers have fashioned siting processes addressed to misconceptions (see Chapters 14 and 15). When the public has sought assurance of the safety of hazardous facilities, developers and siters have offered compensation (not infrequently construed by the public as bribery) for risk. When fairness in site selection has been demanded, poor communities with high unemployment levels have been the siting targets. When institutional trust has been lacking, developers have engaged in public relations to improve their image, rather than in sharing power. Thus, the national effort to site such facilities has stumbled on the rocks of ungauged hazards amplified through public concern, community conflict and institutional distrust. The effects have been quite dramatic. By 1987, 22 states in the US still, despite various federal and state efforts, had no commercial hazardous-waste facilities, and 35 states had no commercial land disposal facilities. Of 81 siting applications over the 50 states for hazardous-waste disposal facilities between 1980 and 1987, 31 have been withdrawn or denied permits. Meanwhile, only 6 of the 81 have resulted in operational facilities; 2 have permits to operate; 2 are under judicial review; and 4 failed to become operational owing to market factors (Condron and Sipher, 1987). Yet the need for facilities persists.

Amplified hazards are hidden, then, in a more specialized sense than are the three preceding classes of hidden hazards. They remain hidden to the professional assessors until the consequences are upon us, at which point they become highly visible to society generally. Improved methods of assessment are needed to pinpoint hazards whose nature and magnitude are defined substantially by their interaction with social structures and processes. But even improved assessment will have difficulty securing acceptance for its findings, because making such hazards visible threatens the established regulatory and siting processes and alters the ground rules of whose values will prevail, which impacts are legitimate, and what evidence will count.

VALUE-THREATENING HAZARDS

Every technology, as Edward Wenk (1986) vividly recounted, plays Jekyll and Hyde. Among the most pervasive and resistant to formal assessment of the Hydeian effects are those that alter human institutions, lifestyles and basic values. Because the pace of technology outstrips the social institutions that husband it, disharmony occurs in purpose, economy and social stability. Technology has promoted the growth and power of industrial enterprises, thereby necessitating a growth in governmental policies to regulate their potential hazards. While nurturing technical complexity, technological growth hinders public understanding and engenders feelings of anxiety. In trying to cope, some people seek spiritual explanation; others look to cults for the comfort of simplistic explanations (Wenk, 1986, p8).

Hazards that threaten basic human values are as amorphous as they are profoundly troubling. Such values continually shape the directions of science, the unfolding of technological applications, and the institutions that manage both. Equally certain is that technology is a major driving force in shaping social values. Consider the impacts of the automobile on families, contraceptives on sexual mores, life-extending technologies on religious beliefs, and computers and informational banks on privacy. Like amplified hazards, value-threatening hazards are often not hidden, as the noisy conflicts over abortion, smoking and motorcycle helmets make clear. Yet some technologies pose uncertain and dimly perceived threats to values, intermingled with substantial benefits. Others involve subtle effects, that in themselves are not dramatic but that add to the long-term erosions already in progress. Somehow, the wariness that often greets a new technology seldom includes an acknowledgement that threats to values have been instrumental to its innovation.

Why is it that nuclear power and genetic engineering appear to evoke such public apprehension and so confound formal analysis? Both were born amid great promise for their benefits to humanity and the global environment. Nuclear power promised enough energy to bring electricity to the world's population without damaging the environment. Genetic engineering promises a new revolution in agriculture for the world's hungry and the eradication of diseases that have been the scourge of health and well-being for centuries. Yet both technologies generate great unease amid the optimism. Is it that the power of nuclear energy may ultimately fuel destruction rather than progress? And for genetic engineering, have humans usurped the gods by intervening in the fundamental matter of our existence? The means to bring to the surface and debate these issues seem lacking in our institutional processes, in which the social conflicts over risk may be, at heart, projected worries over technologies that touch the wellsprings of our existence.

Then there are the more subtle cumulative effects on values that may already be deteriorating. Privacy, under constant assault from technologies ranging from computerized information banks to electronic eavesdropping, may be disappearing as a basic social value in America. The proliferation of video display terminals, with their far-reaching potential for social isolation and the routinization of labour, may in the future be categorized with piecework, factory assembly lines and 'sweatshops' as socially harmful innovations. Meanwhile, biological and genetic screening, with its potential for selecting among peoples in a host of institutional settings, threatens the basic notions of equity and equality of opportunity. The unrelenting portrayal of violence on television and videotapes erodes our sensitivity to the use of force in human relations and the settlement of arguments. Frequently, ideological trappings colour our perceptions of such hazards.

How do these hazards make their way onto the public agenda? Hazards that threaten human values and that are incremental, uncertain and cumulative appear esoteric and unsubstantiated in a world of scientific evidence and discourse. Hazards that pose issues that transcend the capability of existing institutions to confront and debate them remain unarticulated, are expressed as emotional outcries in a cost–benefit and risk-reduction optimizing world, or find their arena of debate outside established institutions. The means to incorporate these murky hazards into deliberative public policy and decision making continue to elude us.

MULTIPLE HIDDEN HAZARDS

This exploration of hidden hazards has concentrated on the archetypal hazards of each class. But it is surely the case that many hazards have multiple attributes or dimensions that, especially in their interaction, obscure hazards to experts or publics. Thus, occupational hazards involving reproductive effects may simultaneously be ideological (involving notions of the workplace in a market economy), marginal (particularly if construed as gender specific), and value threatening (if affecting beliefs about contraception and abortion). Nuclear power and genetic engineering elicit such strong concerns because they are both amplified and value-threatening hazards. Global poverty surely involves ideological interpretations of the causes and effects of poverty as well as its marginality to the more affluent advanced industrial societies. In short, probably few hazards are hidden purely because of a single attribute; rather, their multi-attribute character conceals them from expert assessment or from more general societal recognition.

CONCLUSIONS

What can one conclude about this perplexing genus of hidden hazards? What is the prospect that such hazards will be better integrated over time into our overall knowledge of the epidemiology of natural and technological hazards?

There are few reasons to be optimistic, for such hidden hazards are deeply embedded in our belief systems, scientific practices, and social relations. Uncovering them will not only require new departures in the sciences and social sciences but will also constitute a political act and challenge. Because these hazards vary in their genesis and impacts, any observations must be specific to particular classes:

- *Global elusive* hazards will certainly command determined scientific efforts in the coming decade to delineate their causes, distribution and global implications. In this sense, these hazards should increasingly assume their place on society's strand of worry beads. At the same time, it is unclear whether our understanding of their human causes will progress equally or whether such hazards will overcome the global political conflicts that their amelioration will certainly provoke. Disjunctures in assessment and global management could well flourish.
- *Ideological and marginal* hazards lie deeply embedded in the belief systems and social structures of different societies. They are not likely to become more visible with advances in science and assessment capabilities. Because they have the same roots as do society's institutions and values, they are not 'manageable'. Rather, they are likely to linger as sources of continuing social and technological controversies.
- *Amplified and value-threatening* hazards will continue their dichotomous opaqueness to anticipatory assessments of technology and overt stimulus to social clashes over technology deployment and governmental decisions. Through these encounters, both the assessment and the operation of the political economy will continue to discover, and define, their limits.
- *Multiple* hazards will continue to be a changing domain, as hazards ebb and flow in their social meaning in differing societies and cultural groups. But they will continue to furnish society with hazard surprises as well as deep challenges to assessment practices.

8 Media Risk Signals and the Proposed Yucca Mountain Nuclear Waste Repository, 1985–1989

Jeanne X. Kasperson, Roger E. Kasperson,
Betty Jean Perkins, Ortwin Renn and Allen L. White

People experience risks in a wide variety of ways – through direct experience, media, reports in time, conversations with friends and neighbours, and grass-roots groups and organizations. With an issue such as the proposed nuclear waste repository at Yucca Mountain, Nevada, in the US, for most people, including those of the nearby community of Caliente and Lincoln County, this experience will be largely indirect, through the depiction and interpretation of unfolding events associated with the repository. The amount, duration and character of media coverage may, in particular situations, influence public perceptions of the repository, the types of concerns that arise, and the extent to which interested people who will be affected by the repository are informed.

But in addition to providing an ongoing flow of information about issues and events, the media also act as interpreters about the larger social meaning of what is occurring. So the media in a wide variety of subtle ways provide *messages* that shape the perceptions of readers and viewers about what has occurred. Such messages appear explicitly in the editorializing about the facility, the process by which it is being created, and its implications for people and their well-being. But such messages are also embedded in the choice of headlines, the location of stories, pictures used for depiction, and symbols and metaphors that are evoked to assist interpretation. The 'flows' or 'streams' of such messages certainly affect, but in ways that are yet unknown, people's views of proposed

Note: Excerpted from *Final Report* to the city of Caliente and Joint City/County Impact Alleviation Committee, Kasperson, J. X., Kasperson, R. E., Perkins, B. J, Renn, O. and White, A. L., 'Information content, signals and sources concerning the proposed repository at Yucca Mountain: An analysis of newspaper coverage and social group activities in Lincoln County, Nevada', © (1992) with permission from Center for Technology, Environment and Development (CENTED), Clark University

developments and prospective risks. Systematic treatment of risk signals has yet to arise in studies of public perceptions of or public responses to risk. Analyses of mass media coverage of risk have also yet to delve into the notion of 'risk signals' and their potential effects.

The study reported in this chapter explores the flow of risk-related signals relating to the proposed Yucca Mountain repository. Since we were interested in the flow of mass media information to the people of Caliente, we selected for study reporting in the *Las Vegas Review-Journal.* The study period covers the time-span between January 1985 and December 1989, a period in which the proposed repository became a possible reality and public perceptions of its significance were in formation. The basic objective of the study is to answer the following question. *If a person were a regular reader of the Las Vegas Review-Journal and interested in the proposed repository, what is the flow of messages interpreting the meaning of the repository that this person would have encountered?*

Before attempting to answer this question, we begin with a necessary discussion of definitions and methodological approach.

DEFINITIONS AND METHODOLOGY

To begin, we define a *signal* as a message about a hazard or hazard event that affects people's perceptions about the seriousness and/or manageability of the risk. Analysing signals, then, is necessarily a complex matter, that entails operationalization of the definition and development of detailed guidelines for identifying, classifying and evaluating such signals. Appendix 8.1 provides full details of the guidelines and rules developed for this exploratory study. Appendix 8.2, meanwhile, delineates the scoring categories used to analyse various qualitative and inferential aspects of the signals examined. Here we set forth some of the core distinctions and rules that evolved for studying signals. Principal among these were that:

- To be a signal, a statement must satisfy our definition of a signal, which means that the statement must meet three criteria: (1) looking for *messages* (as we define them); (2) the messages must be about *hazards or hazard events*; and (3) they must potentially affect people's perceptions of the *seriousness and/or manageability of the risk in question.*
- To be a signal, a statement, must go *beyond the provision of factual information.* For example, an inference, interpretation, generalization or abstraction would satisfy this guideline. This is the overriding, all-encompassing criterion that all signals must meet.
- Signals may include statements that *ascribe qualitative characteristics to a hazard or hazard event* such as purporting that it is catastrophic, unfamiliar inevitable...; statements that *ascribe qualitative characteristics to the decision and management process as well as to the management style of risk*

managers, such as competence, trustworthiness, fairness...; statements that *assign blame or responsibility* for a hazard or hazard event to some general source such as nature, technology, people, institutions; statements that *address the moral or value implications of the hazard event* such as whether it is liable to harm children or future generations, is inequitable, unethical or immoral.

- Signals include statements that contain *images or symbols* (e.g. of disaster) or terms that conjure up such images or symbols in people's minds.
- Signals include statements containing *metaphors and other figures of speech* if they are about a hazard or hazard event that affects people's perceptions about the seriousness, manageability, or both, of the risk.

Identification of signals

To identify signals, we used the following basic procedure:

1 The compilation of a database:
   - selection of material (see Appendix 8.1 for selection procedure);
   - sorting by type – editorials, news stories, cartoons, letters – and year.
2 We began with editorials, then headlines, cartoons and letters to the editor;
3 The 'physical' process: careful reading (this was particularly true of the editorials, which required at least two or three readings), then highlighting possible signals and relevant contextual material, underlining of significant words, phrases and expressions, and developing a rationale for those choices in a concise, albeit rudimentary, manner.
4 The application of our two-part test:
   - Does it satisfy our definition of a signal?
   - Does it satisfy at least one of the guidelines for identifying signals? (See the preceding pages and Appendix 8.1 for an elaboration of the definition and guidelines.) To be a signal, a message must pass the test!
5 Checking for accuracy and consistency.

In the process of identifying signals, we encountered a series of hurdles:

1 Some signals are very clear, straightforward, pointed or just jump out; others are more subtle (perhaps hidden), abstract and complex.
2 Not all messages, no matter how powerful, are signals. It is necessary to keep in mind our definition of a signal and the objective of the study at hand. There may be messages about other risks – which may indeed be signals but not for this exercise – or about the nature of local politics (which may be unrelated to the Yucca Mountain repository deliberation process).

3   A signal to one person may not be a signal to another person. This problem may well lessen as our knowledge of and research into risk signals increases, but will persist nonetheless due to a kind of built-in ambiguity attendant on the nature of communication and language and the workings of the human brain.

4   A single sentence may contain more than one signal and thus confound identification and analysis. At the same time, a whole paragraph may be one signal. It may well be that even an editorial can be a single signal, although our evaluation has not yet achieved that level of sophistication. And, of course, it is possible to entertain any number of variations in between! In short, a signal can be a word, a phrase, a sentence, a couple of sentences, a paragraph, a cartoon.

5   Context is important, particularly when dealing with editorials and with letters to the editor. Context is relative. Some words or phrases such as *radioactive grave or dump* can stand alone. In other cases, the signal value of a word, phrase, sentence, etc, may be lost if detached from what comes before or after – if it is taken out of context. (As a practical matter, we established guideline #13 – see Appendix 8.1). When copying down signals, include full sentences. Do not use only a part of a sentence as a signal. Context is important in understanding a signal's significance. In some cases, it may be necessary to include a whole paragraph. And, in some cases, a whole paragraph may be a signal. In other cases, a single sentence may be adequate.

6   Each type of material has its own idiosyncrasies. For example:
   * *Headlines*: Context is irrelevant in dealing with headlines. Since the point of a headline is to seduce a reader into reading the whole article, one needs to read a headline as if it stood alone – as if divorced from the text below – for purposes of signal identification.
   * *Cartoons*: Instead of words, we are dealing primarily with pictures or graphic representations. It is important to determine how to incorporate them effectively into our present scheme of identification and analysis.

Once the identification of signals was complete, it was time to move on to the anlaysis.

ANALYSIS OF SIGNALS

To conduct the analysis, we developed a taxonomy of risk signals as well as the use of symbols, images and metaphors as signals.

Taxonomy

The development of a taxonomy of signals occurred over several months through a group process that elicited a universe of possible risk signals, the classification of those signals separately by each group member, and the eventual formulation of a consensual classification based on dominant themes or messages (Appendix 8.2).

Villains/victims

Although our taxonomy of signals includes villains to blame and unfair/innocent victims as two of its themes, we established classes for each because of the extensive presence of villain and victim signals. It is important and interesting to know not just that there is a villain and/or victim but also who or what that villain and/or victim is or is claimed, purported or perceived to be (by the media). Unlike our taxonomic categories which are general or universal, our villain and victim classes are specific to the risk under discussion (i.e. the Yucca Mountain repository). We, therefore, envision these categories as varying for each new project.

We tried to develop lists of villains and victims that were inclusive and complete but not unwieldy based on our knowledge of the Yucca Mountain repository issue and our 'impressions', gained through the signal identification process, of who the villains and victims were. Prime candidates for villainhood included the US Department of Energy (DOE), Congress and the federal government in general, whereas our list of victims includes the people of Nevada, the state of Nevada, future generations and children. (See Appendix 8.2 for a complete list.)

Symbols, images, and metaphors

We did not initially include separate categories for symbols, images and metaphors. Although we intuitively thought they would be important, we also assumed that our other categories would incorporate them. It rapidly became apparent that we would be missing a lot without a more explicit recognition of the existence of symbols.

Our initial classification of symbols, images and metaphors was based on general concepts relating to allusions from mythology and other literature. Some of those concepts, such as 'Doomsday' and the so-called 'Faustian bargain' of selling one's soul to the devil, proved relevant in this case of a proposed repository for radioactive waste. Others were not so useful. In the process of signal identification, we found that certain symbols, images and metaphors directly related to the repository issue kept popping up, such as the 'screwing' or rape of Nevada and nuclear garbage, which we subsequently added to our categories of symbols, images and metaphors (see Appendix 8.2).

This class of elusive signals is particularly complex, and we recognize the need for more precise definitions of symbols, images and metaphors. Such definitions will come more easily with the evolution of a systematic classification scheme and the advance of the concept of risk signals.

Global categories

Our global categories reflect broad, universal themes, such as Risk, Fairness, Ethics, Morality and Trust, which did not seem to be addressed at this level anywhere else in our analytical scheme. They provide a big-picture look, an overview (see Appendix 8.2).

In order to conduct the analysis, we:

1   assigned a number to each signal (remember a single sentence can contain multiple signals);
2   analysed every fifth signal:
    •   recorded each selected signal on a coding sheet (including as much contextual material as deemed necessary by the coder; at least the full sentence in which the signal appeared);
    •   scored each signal sampled by going through categories – obviously, some signals proved more complicated than others to score, one signal can fit into a single category, all categories or any variation in between;
    •   conducted computer analyses of scoring sheets and produced graphs and tables.

Editorials

Editorials, we discovered, were the largest source of signals in repository coverage by the *Las Vegas Review-Journal*. Indeed, some editorials contained as many as 10–15 different signals. A sampling strategy of selecting every fifth signal yielded some 219 signals for the five years from 1985 to 1989. The results provide a telling portrait of this newspaper's flow of messages to its readers.

Placing signals into broad categories indicates immediately that although the risks, benefits and impacts associated with the repository are important, the flow of messages accords them a relatively minor role (Table 8.1). Indeed, after the first year (1985), they never occupy more than 15 per cent of all signals. Instead, as Table 8.1 makes abundantly clear, a nexus of issues associated with fairness, power and trust completely dominates the signal stream associated with the proposed Yucca Mountain repository.

The classification of signals is revealing in this regard. One view of repository development is that some trade-off of assumed risk and adverse impact is necessary for progress in resolving an important national problem. And such signals do appear in the *Las Vegas Review-Journal*, as indicated by the following:

•   He also raised a valid point that some have overlooked, in that we can't always have our cake and eat it too: 'We cannot push to have space reactors tested at the Test Site and on the other hand say no to the dump site,' he said. 'That's a little inconsistent.' (24 February, 1985)

Table 8.1 *Classification of signals into global categories*

| Global categories | Number of signals | | | | |
	1985	1986	1987	1988	1989
Risks (health, environmental, etc)	3	1	3	3	7
Social/economic impacts (adverse)	1	0	1	0	0
Benefits	0	2	1	2	3
Fairness/ethics/morality	7	13	30	10	21
Trust	0	0	7	5	21
Future generations	1	0	1	0	0
Vulnerable groups/people	1	0	1	0	0
Power and powerlessness	3	9	24	11	18

- Mercenary as it may seem, the key question becomes, 'what can we squeeze out of the federal government in exchange for acceptance of the site?' (23 July, 1986)
- The rational course of action, then, is not to continue dancing a jig to the tune of 'The Sky is Falling' but to make sure that Nevada benefits from the situation. (25 June, 1989)

Yet, this signal stream is minor compared with the increasing dominance of three interrelated types of signals – villains exist in the repository development process, innocent victims are unfairly affected, and individuals are powerless to affect the situation. Table 8.2 depicts the 'victim status' that the pool of signals accords to the state of Nevada, its inhabitants and its government. Interestingly, 'future generations' do not significantly make their way into the victim category. The signals are very clear as to who the villains are – they are the federal government, the Congress and the US Department of Energy (Figure 8.1). Figure 8.1 also shows the rapid increase of villain-related signals between 1986 and 1987, and especially the dominance of villain signals focused on Congress and Senator Bennett Johnston, particularly as related to the so-called 'screw Nevada' bill passed in 1987, which designated Yucca Mountain as the

Table 8.2 *Victims in signals on Yucca Mountain*

| Victims | Number of times cited as victim | | | | |
	1985	1986	1987	1988	1989
People of Nevada/Nevada State/Nevada Government	9	12	34	17	23
Future generations	0	0	0	0	0
Poor people	1	0	1	0	1
Others	1	1	1	1	3

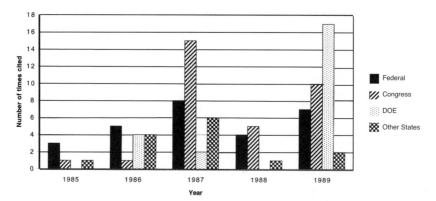

Figure 8.1 *Villains cited in signals on Yucca Mountain*

preferred site, prior to the completion of technical studies. The signals are quite pointed as to the nature of these villains:

- The wording of the Screw Nevada Bill is designed not only to speed up the search for a high-level nuclear waste site, but also virtually to guarantee that the search will end at Yucca Mountain, north of here. (16 November, 1987)
- Johnston, a masterful legislator, patronized Hecht in the committee for his reasonable attitude by suggesting reprocessing as an alternative when all the cagey Louisianan cared about was sticking the dump in Nevada. (20 December, 1987)
- It was 'On Johnston, On Dingell, On Udall and Sharp.' They dumped on Nevada, a quick fix with no heart. (24 December, 1987)
- Johnston, a Shreveport Baptist and Democrat, known in his home state as an incurable moderate, has emerged as Nevada's worst enemy in the US Senate. (12 June, 1988)
- But Bryan warns against a false sense of security. Congress, he says, may fiddle with the Screw Nevada Bill for the following reason: the present federal law makes it illegal to put a temporary high-level waste site in Nevada because the state is slated to receive the permanent underground facility. With the deadline for opening the permanent Yucca Mountain burial site pushed back to 2110, Congress might 'fix' that law to allow a temporary facility in Nevada. (19 December, 1989)

The intensity of villain signals falls back in 1988 but re-emerges in 1989, this time focused on the US Department of Energy and the role of the Secretary of Energy, James Watkins. Again, the language of the signals is highly suggestive as to the nature of the villains:

- All of which makes it look like Nevada is the DOE's promised land. (13 July, 1986)
- Here are some examples of how the DOE's performance has been evaluated recently: 'Some (nuclear plants) should never have been undertaken and some failed for what appears to be incompetence that borders on wrongdoing,' House Energy and Commerce Committee Chairman John Dingell told the New York Times on December 12. (15 January, 1989)
- Can our elected officials see through the masterful public relations disguise that the sheepish-appearing Watkins has donned especially for them? (24 May, 1989)
- Energy Secretary James Watkins has all but admitted his department has mishandled the project. (2 November, 1989)

Along the way, the collusion of the 'more powerful Eastern states' with these other villains comes in for some attention, as suggested by the following signals:

- Commercial power plants in the East generate the bulk of the radioactive waste, but the West gets to bury it because it has fewer votes in Congress. (3 August, 1986)
- It looks like Herrington – in the DOE's apparent rush to placate politicians in the populous and politically powerful East – jumped the gun. (14 September, 1986)

Just as the villains are quite apparent in these signals, so are the victims. They are the people of Nevada and the state as a whole. The following signals suggest the nature and extent of this victimization. The related message that individuals are powerless and/or that fate is responsible is also evident, although less dominant than the villain or victim signal streams.

- You don't even have to squint to see the handwriting on the wall – that big R.I.P. already scrawled on the crags of Yucca Mountain. (13 July, 1986)
- Somehow, one gets the feeling that an ill wind is blowing Nevada's way. (17 August, 1987)
- And as a powerful footnote to all of this, Nevadans will have to face the depressing reality that no matter who wins in November, the next administration is likely to carry on the policies that appear inexorably to be bringing the dump to the state. (16 October, 1988)
- Of those polled, 53 per cent said they agree with that pronouncement which shows that a majority of Nevadans still buy into the theory of inevitability – that is, that the dump is coming no matter how much politicians protest. (24 December, 1989)

Table 8.3 *Dominant symbols/images in signals on Yucca Mountain*

Symbols/images[a]	Number of times cited				
	1985	1986	1987	1988	1989
Doomsday	2	1	1	1	1
Trojan Horse	0	0	1	0	1
Faustian bargain	0	3	1	2	5
Mephisto	0	0	4	1	2
'Screwing' of Nevada/rape	0	0	6	0	3
Nuclear junk, radioactive garbage, nuclear refuse, etc	0	0	4	2	1
Nevada as 'target' or 'bulls-eye'	0	3	10	1	4
Nuclear train/nuke train	0	0	0	1	1
Burial ground/graveyard/tombs	1	1	1	0	2
Nevada as a 'colony'	0	2	0	1	1

Note: a For a description of symbols/images, refer to 'Guidelines for entering data onto coding sheet' (Appendix 8.2).

Interestingly, although much discussion in the radioactive waste controversy has focused on risk exported to future generations or the location of hazardous facilities in poor communities, signals relating to these themes are largely absent in our sample from the *Las Vegas Review-Journal*.

Turning to the symbols, imagery and metaphors emerging in signals relating to Yucca Mountain, the messages are highly suggestive of the repository and its effects (Tables 8.3 and 8.4). Thus, one stream of signals focuses on nuclear *junk, garbage or refuse*:

- If we must get the dump, let's make sure *the junk* is safely wrapped. (6 January 1987)
- One cannot shake the distinct feeling that the national media spotlight has become focused on Nevada as the place most likely to become home to the *nation's radioactive gunk*. (2 September, 1987)

Table 8.4 *Metaphors in signals on Yucca Mountain*

Metaphor[a]	Number of times cited				
	1985	1986	1987	1988	1989
Nuclear mafia	0	0	0	0	1
Smoke-filled-room politics	2	4	10	2	9
Dump	9	6	32	18	25
David and Goliath	0	0	2	0	0
Uncertain gamble or wager	0	1	1	1	1

Note: a For a description of metaphor, refer to 'Guidelines for entering data onto coding sheet' (Appendix 8.2).

- The debate over how safe is safe enough when it comes to transporting *the nation's radioactive garbage* to the proposed dump at Yucca Mountain sounds like duelling consultants bashing each other with conflicting actuarial tables and shouting: Yes it can. No it can't. (19 November, 1989)

Other signals evoke *graveyards* and *tombs* as the outcome of radioactive waste:

- Yet the drumbeat of opposition to the *radioactive grave* at Yucca Mountain rumbles on. (23 July, 1986)
- In editorials where 'pejorative' is not a no-no, we'll call it a dump or *a tomb* or a shaft full of gunk or anything else that comes to mind. (29 July, 1987)
- Potential sites in Texas and Washington state were dropped from consideration, and Nevada's Yucca Mountain stood alone: It was the only place Congress was willing to consider as a *burial ground* for 70,000 metric tons of radioactive waste from commercial power plants and other sources around the country. (19 December, 1989)

Still others foresee a *doomsday* future:

- To this, Sawyer told the committee in Carson City: 'The average voter needs no further tests or deliberations. He knows the effects of deadly radiation. He knows what would happen if there were just one accident on the roads or railroads, the deadly effect of pollution of the underground waters, the seepage which might be caused by an earthquake or major earth movement. In my view this is one of the most, if not the most, significant matters to face our state and its future in this century. There should be no equivocation, none, about where we stand.' (21 March, 1985)
- If we are going down the road to nuclear ruin, slopping the swill from roadside to roadside, then let's get started. (12 February, 1989)

With such imagery, the best interpretation that can be placed on the repository is that of the *Faustian bargain*:

- It is possible, he argues, that some poor country, down on its luck and saddled with debt, might gladly accept American atomic garbage, for a price. (14 July, 1987)
- Should we take the package of goodies because we will get the repository regardless? (25 May, 1988)
- In probably any other circumstance, Nevada politicians would welcome with open arms millions of federal dollars earmarked for scientific research at the University of Nevada system. Politicians, being politicians would jump to have their names somehow associated

with such federal largesse. But when the term 'nuclear waste' [sic] is attached to those dollars, the politicians recoil as if the money itself were radioactive. (29 August, 1989)

- Is it finally time to surrender to the imperious federal forces, accept the inevitable and unleash a full-fledged greed grab for the millions of dollars in grants associated with the work at Yucca Mountain? (14 September, 1989)

But, again, many of the images and symbols focus upon the nature of the repository process. They provide texture to the villain-and-victim theme, as in the '*screwing*' or '*rape*' of Nevada:

- With Congress already leaning toward passing Senator Bennett Johnston's 'Screw Nevada Bill,' which limits the selection process to one site, the addition of one of the country's more influential newspapers to the 'Dump on Nevada' forces is not a good sign. (14 October, 1987)
- It is a nuclear suppository department: The Wall Street Journal and other lackies of the Western Establishment fail to grasp soon-to-be-ex-Senator Chic Hecht's careful use of metaphor and alliteration in commenting on federal plans for Yucca Mountain. (1 January, 1989)

and Nevada as a *US colony*:

- Nevada is a state, not a colony administered from Washington, DC. But there are powerful political and technocratic forces in the Capital who apparently view us in that imperious manner. (29 May, 1986)
- Because the federal government – the Congress, federal agencies – have never really trusted Nevada, we have been viewed on occasion more as a colony than as a full-blown state. (24 January, 1988)

The dominant imagery of the process, however, is that of Nevada as a *target* or *bull's eye* for the Congress or other states:

- All in all, it looks like we're 'it,' as the kids who play hide 'n' seek say. (15 June, 1986)
- Still, Lloyd's proposal was the worst example we've yet seen based on the mistaken assumption that 'Nevada will take it. Nevada takes anything.' (29 March, 1987)
- Johnston and friends figured Nevada for a politically soft target in the past, and they can be trusted to do so again. (19 December, 1989)

Meanwhile, the inevitability of the repository and the assembling of irresistible forces and momentum is suggested by the image of a '*nuclear train*' coming down the tracks:

- If the toxic truck convoy winds up dumping all that yuck at Yucca Mountain, then the state should grab everything it can. (30 March, 1988)
- And the nuclear train pulled out of the station long ago. Like an Amtrak express, it is headed this way. It is impossible to say when but it will arrive sooner or later. (12 February, 1989)

'Dump' metaphors that appear in the signals, meanwhile, dominate the signals surrounding the repository itself and are highly suggestive, of course, as to what management and isolation from the biosphere will be. The two other pervasive messages are the extent to which fairness and technical integrity in site selection have disappeared in favour of '*smoke-filled-room politics*':

- Indeed, top Nevada officials and others have charged that the dump selection process has become so politically charged that scientific considerations have fallen by the wayside. (2 June, 1987)
- What we have objected to in terms of the waste site is the politicized siting process and the efforts by bureaucrats and Eastern elected officials to 'dump' the repository on politically feeble Nevada. (29 July, 1987)
- The fact is that the United States Congress and the Department of Energy selected Yucca Mountain as the one and only burial site in the United States not for purely scientific reasons but rather because it was the easiest thing to do politically. (26 February, 1989)
- Watkins, unlike his predecessors, realizes and is willing to admit that the DOE moved 'too aggressively' in its zeal to place the high-level nuclear waste repository in Nevada. That seems to be tacit recognition that the whole process by which Yucca Mountain was singled out was about 90 per cent political and 10 per cent scientific. (30 April, 1989)

Given the prevalence of such dump and political-expediency themes, it is not surprising, especially in view of the gaming setting of Las Vegas, that the repository comes across as an uncertain gamble:

- Let's strike some bargains. (13 July, 1986)
- We have no idea whether, from a scientific point of view, the site will be safe – that won't be known for years. (15 March, 1989)

NEWS HEADLINES

The second major data set in our sample includes headlines for news stories on the repository between 1985 and 1989. The news stories themselves, we discovered, are largely factual, and editorial inferences and interpretations are quite minimal. Headlines are another matter and we found them to be another important source of signals. Again, we used a 20 per cent sample, using every fifth news story headline.

Table 8.5 *Classification of headline signals into global categories*

Global categories	1985	1986	1987	1988	1989
			Number of headlines		
Risks (health, environmental, etc)	2	3	2	1	1
Benefits	0	0	3	0	0
Fairness/ethics/morality	10	10	8	3	9
Trust	3	2	0	2	3
Future generations	0	0	0	0	0
Vulnerable groups/people	0	0	0	1	0
Power and powerlessness	3	5	8	0	7

Table 8.6 *News headlines on Yucca Mountain classified by signal taxonomy and by year*

Taxonomic class	1985	1986	1987	1988	1989
			Number of headlines		
No one to blame	0	0	0	0	0
Trade-offs necessary	0	0	2	0	0
Villain to blame	7	3	4	2	7
Unfair/innocent victims	2	7	6	2	5
Fragility/vulnerability	0	1	0	1	0
Individual is powerless/fate	0	0	1	0	1
Other category	0	0	0	0	0

The results are largely confirmatory of the signal patterns emerging in editorials. Signals that convey messages about risk and benefit and impact on future generations are again largely absent, particularly in the more recent years (see Table 8.5). Again, fairness, ethics, trust and power dominate the signal stream in news headlines. In terms of our taxonomy, villains and victims are once more the dominant signals (see Table 8.6).

As with the editorials, villains lurk in the federal government:

- Feds 'overstated' nuke dump job rate (15 December, 1986)
- Locals doubt fed candor on nuke site (16 May, 1986)
- County cautioned on federal nuclear waste tricks (9 March, 1988)

the Congress:

- Nuke waste bill hit by Nevadans (24 April, 1986)
- Nevada nuke dump target: [Congressional] panel's proposal OKs drilling at Yucca Mountain (26 March, 1987)

the Department of Energy:

- Reid labels DOE 'globe-rotters' (11 August, 1988)
- DOE wants credibility in Nevada (4 April, 1989)

and the other states (and especially eastern states) of the US:

- NJ communities don't want radioactive dirt either (31 July, 1986)
- Search for Eastern nuke dump possible (21 February, 1987).

Corresponding to the editorials, news headlines carry recurring symbols of the victimization of Nevada and its people at the hands of these villains. Again, the signals are suggestive:

- Bryan blasts deceit in nuke dump choice (2 August, 1986)
- Nuke dump moves closer to Nevada (22 December, 1987)
- Most Nevadans see no escape from nuke dump, survey says (14 March, 1989)
- Nevada lawmakers foiled in bid for nuke dump talk (13 May, 1989)

And, as with the editorials, future generations and the poor do not appear (indeed, there is not a single signal for these two groups in our sample).

Turning to our assessment of symbols, images and metaphors, several interesting observations emerge. Not surprisingly, the use of the term 'dump' in news headlines overwhelms all other images and, indeed, is the dominant way of referring to the proposed waste repository. Fully 40–70 per cent of news headlines in our sample over the five years have used the dump imagery. Nuclear *junk*, *garbage* or *refuse* also occasionally appear, but much less frequently. And the *nuclear train* image surfaces again:

- Suit targeting nuke trains expected (30 July, 1985)
- Radioactive dirt to bypass Las Vegas (4 July, 1987)

As does *Nevada as a target*

- Senator: Nevada may be focus of search for dump (15 April, 1987)
- Nuclear waste dump targeted for Nevada (15 December, 1987)

A signal not widely apparent in the editorials but quite frequent in the news headlines is the image of the siting process as a *battle*, *struggle* or *war*:

- Senator: Nevadans can make a difference in waste dump battle (13 September, 1986)
- Nevada faces nuclear waste bill showdown (15 October, 1987)
- State set for fight with US over nuclear dump (29 September, 1989)

Cartoons

It became apparent in looking through our cartoons that they are a rich source of signals – a kaleidoscope of images and messages. This is not surprising since the aim of a cartoon, particularly a political cartoon, is to convey a pointed message. Because they are visual representations, cartoons can express meaning in a way that words alone cannot. The old adage, a picture is worth a thousand words, is very appropriate here! The unique characteristics of cartoons render them wonderful vehicles for purveying signals. Cartoons are fun and interesting, but they do challenge evaluation and analysis.

Indeed, it is no easy task to identify and evaluate, without enlisting the proverbial thousand words, the multitude of signals that inhabit cartoons. Yet we chose to conduct an experiment in order to test the relevance and adequacy of our tentative classification scheme. We used the scheme to classify the 14 cartoons that addressed the proposed repository at Yucca Mountain that appeared in the *Las Vegas Review-Journal* between January 1985 and December 1989. This exploratory exercise highlighted some of the unique qualities of cartoons, produced some interesting results, and illuminated some difficulties in applying our methodology to cartoons – a frustrating as well as a rewarding endeavour. Although we lose some of the richness – 'the essence' of the cartoon – in the process, we gain some ability to identify, evaluate and analyse, which we cannot do merely by looking at a cartoon and commenting on its meaning.

We used essentially the same definition, guidelines and classification scheme to identify and code signals in cartoons. A few adjustments were necessary, however, to incorporate the unique nature of cartoons. For example:

1   One cartoon may 'emit' – in most cases, *did* emit – more than one signal. This dilemma presented two major options: treat each cartoon as a whole and therefore code a cartoon rather than a signal; or attempt to transfer the various signals conveyed by a cartoon into words. In the first instance, each cartoon would be 'a signal' for numbering and coding purposes, whereas in the second instance, one cartoon may account for one, two, three, four or more signals. Editorials and headlines lend themselves easily to the second mode since a paragraph, a sentence or a phrase can easily be dissected from the whole and considered a signal. In this case, however, we chose the first option. Why? It poses fewer problems of interpretation and provides a solid (or semi-solid) basis for analysis. Cartoons brim with subjectivity, implication and veiled references. Cartoons convey different messages to different people. They mean different things to different people. What one person sees in a cartoon is not necessarily what another person sees. Therefore, the process of one, two, three or more people transforming a cartoon into their own interpretation of what it means, into their own words seems somewhat counterproductive to our goal of increasing clarity and decreasing ambiguity and subjectivity. A picture really is worth a thousand words.

2   Our scoring/coding system generally allowed for two, sometimes three, entries per category (taxonomic, global, etc), which worked well for the editorials and headlines. Yet because cartoons are so full/powerful and often emit more than one signal, it is difficult, maybe even impossible and undesirable, to limit the number of entries per category. This was particularly the case with villains, symbols and, to a lesser extent, with the global categories. The decision as to what to retain and what to discard may be too arbitrary here. The instances where it was necessary to make such a decision, to prioritize when coding editorials and headlines, were not fraught with the level of arbitrariness and subjectivity that we find with cartoons. Essentially, much the same reasoning as above applies to this difficulty as well.

The 14 cartoons provided a wealth of symbols, images and metaphors evidenced by the wide distribution over our symbol, image and metaphor classes. Not surprisingly, one cartoon often conjures up four or five symbols or images. As with the editorials and headlines, the risk-related symbols or images of doomsday, nuclear train, radioactive junk or garbage, and graveyards each appear a few times as do the more process-oriented images of the 'raping' or 'screwing' of Nevada and of Nevada as a target. Battle/war/struggle imagery that appeared in the headlines was also captured in one entry here. Interestingly, some categories that were not particularly significant in the editorials or headlines receive considerable attention in the cartoon analysis. Mephisto (Devil, Lucifer, personification of evil, anti-Christ) receives seven mentions, Trojan Horse (deliberate strategy of deception) receives three mentions, and *hubris* (overweening pride) receives one mention.

These negative portrayals in the cartoons point an accusing finger at DOE. A 1987 cartoon of Congress bombing Nevada with nuclear waste received a Mephisto vote and the federal government in general received a few. Another image of DOE, and to a lesser extent the federal government, emerged during this exercise. A new image class may be more appropriate than Mephisto. The image is peopled by incompetent buffoons, bumbling cartoon characters, lazy slobs, amiable boobs. Among the words that the cartoons conjure up to describe DOE and its employees are incompetents, buffoons, fools, misfits, know-nothings, screw-ups, slovenly, lazy slobs, ignorant, not up to the job, irresponsible, insensitive, lacking respect, arrogant, technically unaware and inept, deceitful, dishonest, immoral, unethical. It (DOE) and they (DOE employees) are also portrayed as deceitful, dishonest, even 'criminal' – that's where the Trojan Horse comes in – but again in a buffoonish sort of way. Unfortunately, the issue at hand is deadly serious. Incompetence, ignorance and deception were apparent in the editorials and headlines, but the buffoon image is very striking in the cartoons.

The dump metaphor receives some attention, but not nearly to the extent that it did in the editorials and headlines. Smoke-filled-room politics – the notion that science has taken a back seat to politics and the whole issue and process has been (unfairly) politicized – is quite apparent. The metaphor of a nuclear mafia receives a certain degree of prominence. This relates to the portrayal of DOE and its employees as deceitful, dishonest and criminal, as discussed previously. The process as an uncertain wager or gamble also receives a mention – the whole process is a crap shoot!

CONCLUSIONS

This exploratory analysis of signals related to the Yucca Mountain repository appearing in editorials, news headlines and cartoons in the *Las Vegas Review-Journal* suggests three major conclusions:

1   the overwhelming stream of messages, symbols and imagery concerning the nuclear waste repository focuses on the unfairness and exploitation of the siting process and the view that political expediency reigns over objective science;
2   the federal government, Congress, and the DOE are powerfully depicted as villains who are victimizing the state of Nevada and its people; and
3   facility risks, benefits and impacts occupy a relatively minor role in the stream of risk signals but even there the references are overwhelmingly negative ('dump', 'nuclear garbage', 'nuclear graveyard'). This is consistent with the findings of many other studies of the public images of a nuclear waste disposal facility.

APPENDIX 8.1

RISK SIGNALS: GUIDELINES AND DEFINITIONS

A Definitional guidelines

Definition: Signals are messages about hazards or hazard events that affect people's perceptions about the seriousness and/or manageability of the risk.

1 Defining messages
   a Messages: inferences, interpretations, generalizations that go beyond concrete factual information and that display some level of abstraction.
   b Messages are not simply factual information.
   c Standard dictionary definitions are similar and not very useful for our purposes. Example: A message is a communication transmitted by spoken or written words, by signals, or by other means from one person or group to another. (*The American Heritage Dictionary of the English Language, New College Edition*)
   d We will complete our review of the risk, communication, and semiotics literature to see if they help in validating, clarifying, and/or refining our definition of messages, signals, and any other terms we feel need further elucidation.
2 Before proceeding to other guidelines, make sure the candidate statement satisfies our definition of a signal:
   a Look for *messages* as we define them.
   b The messages must be about *hazards* or *hazard events*.
   c They must potentially affect people's perceptions of the *seriousness and/or manageability of the risk in question*.
   Remember: All three criteria (a–c) must be met for a statement to be a signal as we define it. Always keep the definition in mind; otherwise, it is easy to be diverted from the task at hand.
3 In the media analysis, we are searching for signals (messages, inferences) made, sent, or conveyed by the media (or particular paper, editor or writer).
   (We are interested both in signals generated by the public and signals inferred by the public *but* the latter is a different issue.)
   This media analysis, then, is concerned with signals conveyed by the media that may or may not affect people's perceptions, as opposed to: actual public perception as influenced by media signals and other stimuli, and measured by questionnaires, etc.
4 Bounding the risk
   a For each signals project (radioactive waste, global warming, pesticides, etc), we need to define and delimit the risk.
   b In this case, the risk is radioactive waste.

- *The Problem*: Do we include only those messages that directly relate to or explicitly mention the Yucca Mountain repository or all and any messages about radioactive waste in general?
- *The Solution*: Include all radioactive waste messages even if they are not directly related to the Yucca Mountain repository.
- *Why?* In Nevada, and especially in the Yucca Mountain area, the issues of radioactive waste and the Yucca Mountain repository are apt to be inextricably linked in people's minds even if a direct, explicit connection between the two is not made. A message about radioactive waste in general is most likely meant to be a message about the Yucca Mountain repository as well – a message conveyed by the media (editor, writer or cartoonist).
- *Caveat*: A message can have signal value even if it does not address the radioactive waste issue or does not contain the words 'radioactive waste', as long as the article, editorial, letter or cartoon within which it is contained does address the issue. As we shall see in some of the guidelines to follow, writers often use devices such as comparison or reference to other incidents and stories to make a point (convey a signal) about radioactive waste. However, the connection to the radioactive waste issue must be made somewhere in the article, editorial, letter or cartoon in which the signal is contained.

c   Examples of some (certainly not all) radioactive waste/Yucca Mountain repository issues: radioactive waste in general, transportation of radioactive waste, health concerns, mismanagement and managerial incompetence/competence, equity, future generations, political process and decision making, institutional relationships and problems, blame, sabotage/ terrorism, suitability of Yucca Mountain site, trust, transportation of radioactive soil from New Jersey to Nevada.

d   To be a signal, a statement must not be *only* a directive or command, policy prescription, advice...

However, a statement may contain one of the above and still be a signal if it satisfies another guideline (contains other language that validates it as a signal).

5   Signals do not include messages whose main or only discernible aim is to enhance/tarnish a politician's/party's/organization's/institution's reputation or make a political statement unrelated to the risk at issue. This clearly does not meet our three-point definition of a signal in Section A since it is a message about a politician/political party/organization/institution and not a hazard or hazard event that affects people's perceptions about the seriousness and/or manageability of the risk.

However, a message can tarnish/enhance a politician's/party's/organization's/institution's reputation or make an unrelated political statement and still be a signal if it satisfies another guideline in Section B.

6   Signals include statements that ascribe *qualitative characteristics* to a hazard or hazard event such as purporting that it is catastrophic, unfamiliar, new, irreversible, unpredictable, uncontrollable, dreaded, inevitable... (and the opposites – e.g. reversibility/irreversibility).

7   Signals include statements that ascribe *qualitative characteristics to the decision and management process as well as to the management style of risk managers*, such as competence, trustworthiness, corruptibility, credibility, fallibility, fairness, ability, accountability, reliability, openness, allowance of public participation, sensitivity, concern, respect for others/other points of view... (and the opposites – e.g. competence/incompetence).

8   Signals include statements that *assign blame or responsibility* for a hazard or hazard event to some general source such as nature, technology, people, institutions. They must be a generalization and not a single incident or factual case. For example: if a truck driver hauling radioactive waste causes an accident whereby radioactive waste leaks onto a highway by not keeping his truck in repair, it *is not* a signal (if the account of the incident stops there).

But if an abstraction or generalization is made assigning blame or responsibility to haulers of radioactive waste in general, it is a signal.

This guideline is closely related to 4 and 5 above, but it didn't seem to fit neatly into either of those guidelines.

•   For example: Nature is to blame because it is unpredictable (relating it to Guideline 4).
•   The federal government is to blame because it is corrupt (relating it to Guideline 5).

The assignment of blame seemed to warrant a guideline of its own, since it tends to be a very common human 'instinct' to want to blame some person, group or thing (nature, technology) for our ills, however great or small they are.

9   Signals include statements that *address the moral or value implications* of the hazard or hazard event such as whether it is liable to harm children or future generations, is inequitable, unethical or immoral, deprives people of a choice and a voice, renders people powerless and vulnerable...

The question of morality, ethics, and value judgements also impacts on Guideline 5, although in a slightly different context. The concern there is with fairness in the management and decision-making process.

Commentary on Guidelines 6, 7, 8 and 9:
- a Are there other characteristics that should be included, characteristics that should be omitted, or characteristics that should be moved from one guideline to another?
- b Guidelines 6, 7, 8 and 9 are linked as 'Qualitative Characteristics'. Should they be considered separate guidelines as they are currently denoted or as subguidelines?
- c It was suggested by some group members that these guidelines assume some knowledge of the risk perception field. Therefore, a paper reviewing risk perception characteristics, etc should be read for background by those who need and/or want it.

10 Signals include statements that appear as quotations and satisfy one of the other guidelines.
11 Signals include statements that contain *images or symbols* (e.g. of disaster) or terms that conjure up such images or symbols in people's minds.

Commentary on Guideline 11:
Examples are:
- a References to Chernobyl, Love Canal, Three Mile Island, Bhopal, Rocky Flats, Hanford, local incidents...
- b Terms such as dumps, radioactive graveyard, radioactive tomb.
- c Writers and cartoonists often make *analogues, comparisons and associations* with events such as those mentioned above as the basis of an editorial, article, or cartoon which is certainly meant to conjure up images, symbolize an idea, or stigmatize a person, place or thing. Therefore, this kind of analogue, comparison, or association would be included under this guideline.
- d We need over time to develop a better, more complete definition of symbols and images. A literature review is under way to seek possible useful definitions.

12 Signals include statements containing *metaphors and other figures of speech* if they are about a hazard or hazard event that affects people's perceptions about the seriousness and/or manageability of the risk.
13 Juxtaposition of signal and radioactive waste issue. Signals can include statements that occur before a hazard or hazard event is mentioned or a connection to a hazard or hazard event is actually made if the statement is about a hazard or hazard event that affects people's perceptions about the seriousness and/or manageability of the risk.

Many editorials begin with 'messages' – homilies, stories, philosophies of life or worldviews – which the writers do not relate specifically to the hazard event until later in the editorial and maybe never explicitly connect to the hazard or hazard event. *But* obviously, the beginning of the editorial is meant to tie into the middle and the end where the hazard or hazard event is mentioned and the writer intends to make some point about the hazard event or the risk by the editorial.

14 Signals include statements addressing the *beliefs, values, philosophy, worldview* (whichever word(s) seems most appropriate) of the media (or particular paper, writer or cartoonist) about hazards or hazard events that affect people's perceptions about the seriousness and/or manageability of the risk.

Commentary on Guideline 14:

    a   It seems that the subject of beliefs, values, philosophy about the world, society, human beings, nature, technology, etc, or one's worldview of how things are or should be needs to be addressed somewhere in our guidelines. (Philosophy and worldview are addressed in Guideline 13 above, but in a different context.)

15 When copying down signals, include full sentences. Do not use only a part of a sentence as a signal. *Context* is important in understanding the significance of a signal. In some cases, it may be necessary to include a whole paragraph. And, in some cases, a whole paragraph may be a signal! In other cases, a single sentence may be adequate.

16 Signals can be either *positive*, *negative* or *neutral*.

17 Since this will be an ongoing, continually evolving process, any ambiguities or uncertainties encountered in signal selection and/or coding should be discussed with a senior group member or the group as a whole. In this way, we can continue to develop these guidelines.

18 We may want eventually to add a modest *glossary* to define some crucial terms. It is very important that we all speak the same language in order to maintain as high a degree of consistency as possible.

    a   standard dictionary definitions (probably not very useful for our purposes in most instances);

    b   group definition or informal working definition;

    c   literature review.

B. Selection guidelines

Guidelines for selecting articles, editorials, letters and cartoons

1 *Include* those articles, editorials, letters and cartoons concerning:

    a   the Yucca Mountain repository;

    b   radioactive/nuclear waste in general;

    c   disposal, transportation, clean-up, etc of radioactive/nuclear waste;

    d   disposal of radioactive/nuclear waste in other places in Nevada (e.g. Beatty Dump);

    e   disposal of radioactive/nuclear waste in other states;

    f   controversies and compacts in, between, and/or among states concerning radioactive/nuclear waste;

    g   nuclear, high-level radioactive and low-level radioactive waste;

h   transportation of 'radioactive dirt' from New Jersey to Nevada;

i   WIPP (Waste Isolation Pilot Plant);

j   nuclear waste accident insurance;

k   Bullfrog County;

l   the Nevada Test Site, if the article is about radioactive/nuclear waste disposal, transportation, management, clean-up, etc at the site;

m   the nuclear weapons plants/complex, if as above the article concerns nuclear waste disposal, transportation, management, clean-up, etc.

However, in the case of nuclear weapons plants, include *anything about cleaning up 'the waste mess'* even if the words, 'radioactive and/or nuclear', are not specifically used or hazardous waste clean-up is the main thrust of the article. This seemingly excessive inclusivity stems from the assumption that due to the problem of 'mixed waste' and the general image of nuclear weapons plants, the distinction between hazardous and radioactive/nuclear waste is often a difficult one to make. For example, articles, etc discussing problems with hazardous and mixed waste at Rocky Flats.

n   nuclear power, if the article *addresses* the nuclear waste issue;

o   the controversy over nuclear study grants from DOE to the University of Nevada, Las Vegas (UNLV), if connected to ethical issues/conflict of interest in DOE giving it money to study Yucca Mountain;

p   the supercomputer at UNLV, if the article, etc addresses the issue of getting the supercomputer as a prize for taking the nuclear repository or not getting the supercomputer as punishment for opposing the nuclear repository;

q   a politician's stand on the nuclear waste/nuclear dump issue.

Include even if the article covers the politician's stand on a number of issues besides the nuclear waste dump as long as the nuclear waste/nuclear dump issue is captured in more than one word, phrase, or inconsequential sentence. From a *coverage perspective*, it is important to include articles where the issue is covered, although briefly.

2   *Do not include* those articles, editorials, letters, and cartoons concerning:

a   hazardous waste *only*;

b   Superfund *only*;

c   hazardous material transportation *only*;

d   legislative summaries *only*;

e   the Nevada Test Site, if the article, etc is about atomic testing, radiation exposure to workers, protests, etc and has nothing to do with the radioactive/nuclear waste issue;

f   'atomic veterans', radiation exposure from atomic testing at other locations;

g   the nuclear weapons plants/complexes that do not address 'the waste issue' – for example, articles, etc that discuss the selection of a nuclear weapons chief or restarting a reactor;

h   nuclear power with no discussion of the nuclear waste issue – for example, articles, etc that discuss nuclear power as an energy alternative or the licensing of commercial nuclear power plants.

3   *Judgement calls*

This category will include, for example, articles, editorials, letters and cartoons in which the radioactive/nuclear waste issue is just one of many issues discussed, maybe in a paragraph or two.

In these cases, context (and intuition) will be important!

APPENDIX 8.2

GUIDELINES FOR ENTERING DATA ONTO CODING SHEET

A Taxonomic classification of signals

1 Making a mountain out of a molehill
2 No one to blame
3 Just desserts
4 Trade-offs necessary
5 Progress
6 Resilience
7 Predictability of events
8 Faith in the system
9 Reliance on oneself
10 Tip of the iceberg
11 Villain to blame
12 Unfair/innocent victims
13 No compromise
14 Overstepping boundaries
15 Fragility/vulnerability
16 Unpredictability of events
17 Failure-prone, overcomplex system
18 Individual is powerless/fate
19 Other category (specify _____)

Indicate by number (1–19) on the coding sheet. It is not necessary to indicate three choices for every signal – just note the category/categories that apply to the particular signal.

B Villain

If a villain is present, is the villain:

1 Politicians generally
2 Federal government generally
3 Congress
4 DOE
5 State government/politicians (Nevada)
6 Nuclear industry/technology
7 Media
8 Environmental/public interest groups
9 Other states
10 East/Eastern states/Eastern establishment
11 Universities/scientists
12 NRC
13 Special interest groups/lobbyists
14 Other (specify _____)

Indicate by number(s) under column entitled 'villain'.

C Victim

If a victim is present, is the victim:
1 People of Nevada

2   People of the Yucca Mountain area
3   Children
4   Future generations
5   Poor
6   Media
7   Environmental/public interest groups
8   State government/politicians (Nevada)
9   Universities/scientists
10 Other (specify _____)

Indicate by number(s) under column entitled 'victim'.

The villains and victims will be specific to the particular risk at issue – in this case, Yucca Mountain Repository/radioactive waste. For global warming, pesticides, etc, we would select other appropriate lists of villains and victims.

D Classification of symbols/images and metaphors

1   Symbols/Images
    a   Doomsday (destruction, inferno, holocaust, terror)
    b   Cornucopia (golden age, abundance, paradise, endless progress)
    c   Sisyphus (permanent frustration despite effort; also Don Quixote)
    d   Hubris (leads to overestimating one's abilities and thus causing disaster; pride, arrogance, feeling greater than God; also Babylon)
    e   Trojan Horse (deliberate strategy of deception)
    f   Faustian Bargain (short-term expectations in exchange for long-term disaster; contract with the Devil; revenge of nature)
    g   Sirens (luring people into disaster; sounds good in the beginning but ends in tragedy; also Lorelei)
    h   Pandora's Box (opening the forbidden box of alleged 'goodies' brings disaster; fall of Adam and Eve)
    i   Multi-headed Hydra (if you cut one head, she has another, solving one problem creates an even bigger problem)
    j   Mephisto (Devil, Lucifer, personification of evil; Anti-Christ)
    k   Wolf in 'sheep's' clothing
    l   'Screwing' or 'raping' of Nevada
    m   Monster/monstrosity
    n   Nuclear junk, radioactive garbage, nuclear refuse, etc
    o   Nevada as a 'target' or 'bulls-eye'
    p   Nuclear train, nuke train
    q   Burial ground/graveyard/tomb
    r   Nevada as a 'colony'
    s   Battle/struggle/war

Indicate by number(s) under column entitled 'Classification of Symbols and Images' – if applicable.

2   Metaphors
    a   Mother Earth (personification of nature; nurture)
    b   Virgin forests (metaphors of innocence)
    c   Sins against Nature (metaphor of guilt and evil with respect to human intervention into ecosystems)
    d   Nuclear mafia (criminalization of groups of institutions)
    e   Smoke-filled-room politics (metaphors of secrecy, covert operations, old boy networks)
    f   Dump
    g   David and Goliath
    h   Uncertain gamble or wager

Indicate by number(s) under column entitled 'Classification of Metaphors' – if applicable.

E Global categories (themes)

Can the signal be assigned to any of the following general categories?

1   Risks (includes health, environment, etc)
2   Social/economic impacts (adverse)
3   Benefits
4   Fairness/ethics/morality
5   Trust
6   Future generations
7   Vulnerable groups, people – poor, elderly, young, ill, ethnic/racial, etc
8   Power and powerlessness

Indicate by number which category (categories) the signal can be assigned to under the column(s) entitled 'Global Categories'.

9 Stigma and the Social Amplification of Risk: Towards a Framework of Analysis

*Roger E. Kasperson, Nayna Jhaveri and
Jeanne X. Kasperson*

INTRODUCTION

In March 1996, the British government announced the possibility of a link between a serious cattle disease, bovine spongiform encephalopathy (BSE), and a rare and fatal human neurodegenerative disease, Creutzfeldt–Jakob disease (CJD). The announcement was prompted by the discovery of 10 atypical cases of the disease, which usually afflicts people over 65, in patients under the age of 42. The government's announcement provided scant details of the relevant scientific data but noted that they were 'cause for great concern' (O'Brien, 1996). The great concern did indeed quickly materialize in the form of an avalanche of press coverage, much of it highly dramatized and speculative. Following on the heels of a decade of ministerial denials, reassurances and belittling of this potential hazard, the sudden about-face produced an instant crisis and a collapse of public confidence in the safety managers of the US$3-billion British beef industry, symbolized by the 21 March, 1996, headline in the *Daily Express*: 'Can We Still Trust Them?' (O'Brien, 1996).

The results were speedy. Within days, the European Union imposed an export ban on all British beef and beef by-products. Sales within Britain plummeted before rebounding partially. Meanwhile, the effects 'rippled' to other countries, as consumption of beef from other source countries fell by fully 40 per cent in France and Germany. The impacts also spread to other industry sectors, such as slaughterhouse workers, auctioneers, truckers and beef export firms (Johnson and Vogt, 1996, p4). The long-term effects of the event remain unclear and it is uncertain whether the stigma affecting British beef will persist in the face of remediation efforts

Note: Reprinted from *Risk, Media and Stigma: Unerstanding Public Challenges to Modern Science and Technology*, Flynn, J., Slovic, P. and Kunreuther, H. (eds), 'Stigma and the social amplification of risk: Toward a framework of analysis', Kasperson, R. E., Jhaveri, N. and Kasperson, J. X., pp9–27, © (2001), with permission from Earthscan

to reduce the hazard and to restore consumer confidence in Britain and on the continent.

The 'mad cow disease' case typifies a special class of hazards, those that trigger intense media coverage and strong public concerns, high institutional attention and large secondary or higher-order consequences, what we have termed elsewhere 'socially amplified' hazards (see Chapter 6). In such hazard cases, the connection of biophysical hazards to social processes can generate powerful signals to society either that a new hazard has appeared on the scene or that an existing hazard is more severe or difficult to manage than previously understood. The secondary or indirect effects may assume proportions that eclipse the direct, and more apparent, biophysical and health consequences, elude anticipatory assessments, and take by surprise those charged with managing the hazards as well as society at large. An important property of these socially amplified hazards is their potential for generating stigma-related effects for places, technologies or products (Gregory et al, 1995). In such cases, some critical hazard event, accident or report sends a strong signal of an abnormal risk, and the ensuing negative imagery and attendant publicity become closely linked with the place, product or technology, resulting in its stigmatization. The stigmatization, in turn, generates a series of adverse effects, greatly enlarging any negative consequences that would have occurred in the absence of such stigma.

Beginning with the seminal work of Goffman (1963), a substantial literature has emerged concerning the sources, types and effects of social stigma. This work is primarily associated with the stigmatization of people arising from social interactions surrounding race and ethnicity, disease, mental illness or handicaps (see the references, for example, in Jones et al, 1984). More recently, Paul Slovic and his colleagues at Decision Research (Slovic et al, 1991c; Slovic et al, 1994; Gregory et al, 1995) as well as other researchers (Edelstein 1987, 1988; Vyner 1988) have focused attention on the relationships among toxic materials, pollution, potential contamination, and the stigmatization of places, products and technologies. In particular, the Decision Research group, through its empirical studies of public perceptions surrounding the proposed siting of a high-level nuclear waste repository at Yucca Mountain, has explored important aspects or components of a more general theoretical framework or model of risk and stigmatization. Building explicitly upon this previous work, this discussion seeks further progress toward a general analytic framework.

Towards that end, we enlist the general conceptual base offered by the social amplification of risk approach. The question addressed is: can that framework structure the stigmatization arising from risk in ways that clarify and integrate the factors and processes that affect the emergence, effects and durability of such stigma? This discussion highlights the stigmatization of places arising from the presence of hazardous activities or facilities in these locations, but the approach is relevant to technologies, products and industrial facilities. We begin by examining a broader and older literature – one that treats people's perceptions and images of places – and what it may suggest about the potential stigmatization of places.

IMAGES OF PLACES AND REGIONS

A long tradition exists of geographic studies of environmental perception focused on people's experience and images of places (Hewitt and Burton, 1971; Burgess, 1978; Tuan, 1979). The meaning of 'place' is often evoked through a discussion of 'image', 'environmental image', or 'mental maps'. Typically, this can involve the meaning of a place for individuals, the group or outside people. When people communicate their experience of place, they often convey information about a locale and their feelings about it through images or verbal pictures. This is a combination of ideas and emotions evoked in the individual stemming from direct environmental experience of the place and from secondary and often media-based information garnered from diverse sources, transmitted images and notable previous events.

Conceptualizations and terminology associated with analyses of the images of places cover a range of approaches. Even a frequently used term – 'mental maps' – has quite varied usage. For Beck and Wood (1976), for example, mental maps are 'personal views of the geographic structure of the world expressed in map form'. 'Image' is another commonly used term used to convey the totality of verbal descriptions of individual experiences, feelings, and attitudes towards a place or region (Burgess, 1978). Downs and Stea (1973) offer a more formal definition for the more universal term 'cognitive mapping', which they view as a process composed of a series of psychological transformations by which individuals acquire, code, store, recall and decode information about the relative locations and attributes of phenomena in their everyday spatial environments. They argue that cognitive maps are the base by which individuals develop a strategy of environmental behaviour; they are cognitive representations that have the *functions* of familiar cartographic maps but not necessarily the physical properties of graphic models. Cognitive mapping expands upon the basic road map to capture a level of symbolism, including images, cognitions and mental maps. Throughout, an 'environmental image' or 'image of place', whether held by the individual or a group, is viewed essentially as a process – a dynamic ongoing development. Measurement techniques largely convey the content of an image frozen at a moment in time (Stallings, 1975).

A 'co-orientational approach' to analysing the perception of different social groups (Uzzell, 1982) may bear upon place stigmatization. Here the environment becomes meaningful not only through physical confirmation but through social interpretation. Group communication and negotiation are essential to social processes. Thus, it is argued, one needs to study not only an individual's cognitive map of the environment but also how other members of the social group conceive of the situation and how agreement among different individuals and larger groups may be achieved.

The relationship between attitudes and environmental perception has also received attention. Downs and Stea (1973), for example, have distinguished among attitudes, preferences and traits. Preferences, in their view, are less global and pertain to a specific object rather than a class of objects. They are also less enduring in time as compared with more stable and durable attitudes. Traits, on the other hand, develop when a given attitude has come to embrace a wide variety of objects over a considerable period of time. Craik (1970) regards an environmental trait as one that seeks to identify an individual's self-conception in reference to the natural and human-made physical environment. This idea of trait reverberates in the work of Golledge and Stimson (1987), who view cognitive maps as semantic long-term memory structures. Cognitive maps, they argue, should not be interpreted as a one-to-one 'mapping' of an object or reality. Rather, as Garling et al (1982) have suggested, these semantic long-term memory structures occur as holistic images, semantic networks, or chunks and strings of information organized in a fashion akin to that assumed by various network models of memory. This idea resonates with information processing theory in psychology and recent work in artificial intelligence.

Places, this research suggests, have connotative meanings that possess emotional, metaphorical and symbolic value (Burgess, 1978). It is the 'appraisal' aspects of image construction concerned with feelings, value and meaning that give meaning to the informational aspect of perception (Downs and Stea, 1973; Pocock, 1974). Studies in general show that appraisal varies with the type and depth of personal involvement with a place.

Popular culture, rather than formal education, often extensively shapes images of faraway places (Beyer and Hicks, 1968). Goodey (1973) has noted, for example, that misguided and inaccurate images of immigrant concentrations in the city emerge from interpersonal conversations and selective acceptance of media reports. Once popular maps and images of places emerge, they are slow to change in the face of new and contrary evidence (Thompson, 1969).

A last theme of this research tradition refers to *preferential perceptions*, preferences for movement towards or avoidance of particular places (Goodey, 1974). Two types of preferential perception studies (Goodey, 1973) exist – one pioneered by Peter Gould and concerned with mental maps of residential preferences for sets of locations, the other concerned with preferred areas rather than specific locations. One overall finding is that mental maps of local areas are often very detailed, whereas those for distant places are scanty, rely on sparse information and are easily transformed into stereotypes (and presumably prone to stigmatization). In a study of student preferences for residential locations in the US, Europe and Africa, stereotypes of places and personal experiences played a highly influential role (Gould, 1966). Apparently, stereotyped traits of particular regions, locales and cities may be ready fodder for the creation of place-based stigma.

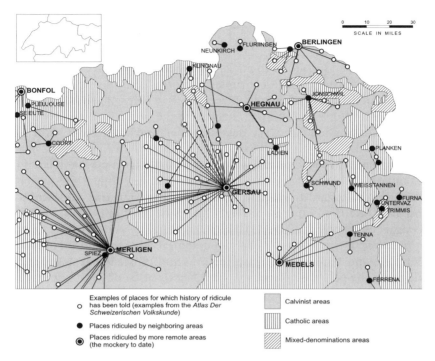

Figure 9.1 *Derogatory images – Canton of Zurich, Switzerland. How extensive is the reputation as a 'stupid-bourgeois place'?*

One such example (see Figure 9.1) came to our attention more than 25 years ago when one of us (REK) was preparing a collection of readings on political geography (Kasperson and Minghi, 1969). This interesting map of derogatory images of places in the Canton of Zurich, Switzerland, provides an early example of empirical work documenting place-related stigma, one in which the importance of ethnic and religious groupings as well as distance relationships was amply apparent. And the stigma itself was quite compelling, for how many of us would want to live in a community regarded as a 'stupid-bourgeois place'?

This previous body of work on environmental perception and mental maps has several implications for our current effort to build an analytic framework for risk-induced stigma. Unfamiliar or distant places may easily fall prey to distorted or stereotypical perceptions. Secondary accounts or media coverage will often be principal sources of image formation. Once perceptions of unfamiliar places are formed, they may become resistant to new or 'corrective' information. The connotative meanings associated with places are not only cognitive but include emotional, metaphorical and symbolic properties. Finally, such mental maps may resemble long-term memory structures involving holistic images, semantic networks and information 'strings'.

With this as background, we now turn to the issue of stigma and its relationship to risk.

RISK AND STIGMA

The term *stigma*, as Goffman (1963) notes, originated with the ancient Greeks who used it to refer to marks placed on a person to denote infamy or disgrace. Current usage continues the original meaning but usually refers to an attribute of people, places, technologies or products that is deeply discrediting or devaluing. Instead of the possessor's being viewed as normal or commonplace, the possessor is viewed as different, with this difference involving important qualities that set the possessor off as deviant, flawed, spoiled or undesirable. Whereas stigma may be related to hazards and involve fear on the part of the beholder, stigma goes beyond the notion of hazard to refer to something that overturns or destroys a positive condition, and, accordingly blemishes or taints the possessor (Gregory et al, 1995, p220).

Marking of the possessor plays an essential role in stigma. The mark identifies and signifies the deviant status and typically has devastating effects on the person or place. The mark need not be physical but may be embedded in, and identifiable from, particular behaviour, features, biography, ancestry or location. It signifies some attribute of the possessor that is associated with the imperfect, or devalued, or dishonoured status. Such marks come to arouse in outside observers strong feelings of repugnance, fear and disdain. Also, the mark may become linked through attributional processes to responsibility, which is also seen as deviant and reprehensible. If these deviant dispositions come to be viewed as central and intrinsic to the person or place, they can become an essential part of identity (Jones et al, 1984), as we argue below.

Following Goffman (1963), *stigmatization* in our usage refers to the process by which persons select an attribute of a person, place, technology or product and denigrate the possessors of the attribute, discriminate against the possessor and may even construct a stigma 'theory' or 'story' to explain the inferiority and its roots. Important to this process are (1) the selection of a negative attribute; (2) perceptions by others of the negative attribute; and (3) the resultant widespread devaluation of the possessor, frequently including labelling and communication of the labels.

Obviously, the context in which stigma arises and the dimensions of the marking process can greatly influence the vividness of the stigma and its effects. Jones et al (1984, p24) identify six major dimensions that are particularly influential, as documented in a wide variety of empirical studies:

1   *Concealability.* Is the condition hidden or obvious? To what extent is its visibility controllable?
2   *Course.* What pattern of change over time is usually shown by the condition? What is its ultimate outcome?
3   *Disruptiveness.* Does it block or hamper interaction and communication?
4   *Aesthetic qualities.* To what extent does the mark make the possessor repellent, ugly or upsetting?

5   *Origin.* Under what circumstances did the condition originate? Was anyone responsible for it and what was he or she trying to do?
6   *Peril.* What kind of danger is posed by the mark and how imminent and serious is it?

Edelstein (1988, p14), drawing on these dimensions and supplementing some of them by adding 'level of fear', 'responsibility', and 'prognosis', analyses what he terms 'environmental stigma'.

Since risk-induced stigma are at the centre of this discussion, some comments on fear are appropriate. Fear, it has been argued, is a highly salient feature of stigma. Normally, studies of stigmatization of people have focused on those with mental illness or handicap, contagious diseases, or racial differences. Susan Sontag, for example, in examining personal experience of cancer, analyses the ways by which Americans symbolically construct and respond to this disease: 'Any disease that is treated as a mystery and acutely enough feared will be felt to be morally, if not literally, contagious... Contact with someone afflicted with a disease regarded as a mysterious malevolency inevitably feels a trespass; worse, like the violation of a taboo' (Sontag, 1978, p6). AIDS is universally characterized as both mysterious and malevolent (Quam, 1990). For environmental problems, Mushkatel and Pijawka (1994) argue that the public stigmatizes environmental features that it views as repellent, upsetting or disruptive. The source of the stigma may be a hazard with characteristics, such as dreaded consequences and involuntary exposure, that typically contribute to high perceptions of risk. Stigmatization can also occur due to a newly discovered or anticipated change in exposure to a toxic substance (Edelstein, 1987; Gregory et al, 1995). The sources of stigma can be direct, as with an increased incidence of cancer or declining market price of properties, or more indirect, as in an exodus of residents from a contaminated area or a decline in sales of a product manufactured in an 'unhealthy' environmental area (Mushkatel and Pijawka, 1994).

The level of uncertainty associated with the hazard generally or events arising from one of the hazard stages may contribute to the stigmatization of a place or technology. Pollution and contamination events are often associated with high levels of uncertainty. The contamination is often indiscernible to direct sensory confirmation and carries the threat that it may exist but be 'invisible'. Many contamination events involve substances or synergistic interactions whose dose–response relationships are poorly understood. Some involve threats to particularly sensitive receptors, such as human reproductive systems, future generations or hypersusceptible individuals or groups. Some involve ill-defined threats to the life-support systems of the local environment, as in contamination of groundwater. Finally, as Kai Erikson (1994) has noted, threats of toxic substances seemingly never end, as some level of residual effects remain, new outbreaks or dimensions of the hazard surface, and the debate and anxiety continue well after the cases are formally settled.

The stigmatization of places due to hazard events typically involves various characteristic properties, including the strong social amplification of the hazard or hazard event (Gregory et al, 1995, pp220–221). An initial event somewhere along the hazard chain emits a 'signal' that a major threat has occurred or is imminent. Extensive media coverage interprets the meaning and projects risk signals, imputing blame, trustworthiness, vulnerability and victimization. The events and media coverage mark the place and propagate its visibility to other places, so that the very identity of the place becomes tightly linked with the hazard and the associated negative and threatening imagery that arise. This change in identity is an essential property of risk-induced stigma and, as we shall see below, is the stage of stigmatization to which indicators and measurement are most appropriately directed. The emerging stigma changes behaviour related to the place, as in avoidance of the place by outsiders, and flight, self-deprecation or anger by residents of the locale.

Because of the critical role that social amplification of the hazard plays in the stigmatization of place, we next turn to a brief description of this approach to hazard analysis and then probe more deeply into the application of this framework to stigma and its effects.

THE SOCIAL AMPLIFICATION OF RISK

As conceived in this framework (Figure 9.2), the social amplification of risk begins with a risk event, such as an industrial accident or a chemical release. It may also emerge from the release of a government report that provides new information on the risk. Since most of society learns about the parade of risks and risk events through information systems rather than through direct personal experience, risk communicators, and especially the mass media, are major agents, or what we term 'social stations', of risk amplification, and by inference, marking. Particularly important in shaping group and individual views of risk are the extent of media coverage, the information conveyed, the 'framing' of the risk, the presence of risk 'signals' in the media, and the symbols, metaphors and discourse used in depicting and characterizing the risk.

The channels of communication are also important. Information about risk flows through multiple communication networks – the mass media represented by television, radio and print media, the more specialized media of particular professions and interests, and, finally, the more informal personal networks of friends and neighbours. Of these, most is known about the mass media, and particularly their multiple and often conflicting roles as entertainers, watchdogs, gatekeepers and agenda setters. In the context of stigma, they play an essential role in maintaining the visibility of the mark. It is also apparent that the mass media cover risks selectively, according those that are rare or dramatic – that is, that have 'story value' – disproportionate coverage while downplaying, or attenuating, more commonplace but often more serious risks.

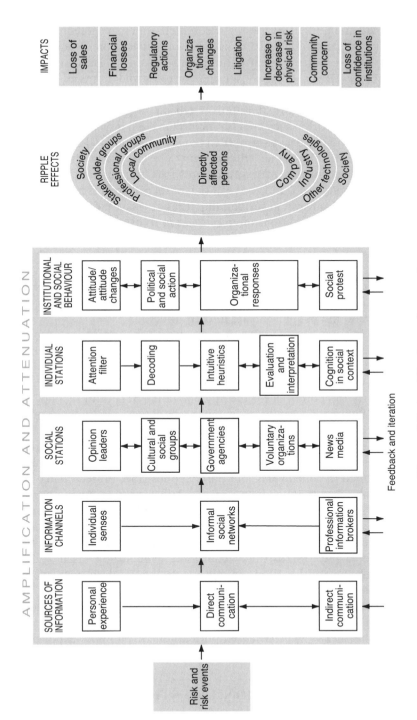

Figure 9.2 *Amplification and attenuation*

Social institutions and organizations take on prominent roles in society's handling of risk, for it is in these contexts that the conceptualization, identification, measurement and management of most risks proceed (Short, 1992, p4). In post-industrial democracies, large organizations – multinational corporations, business associations and government agencies – largely set the contexts and terms of society's debate about risks. Institutions and organizations are major 'nodes' of risk amplification and require detailed attention in gauging how society responds to risk. Risk issues are also important elements in the agenda of various social and political groups, such as non-governmental organizations with environmental and health concerns. The nature of these groups figures in the definition of risk problems, the type of rationality that underlies interpretation, and the selection of management strategies.

The information system surrounding risk questions and the processing of risk by the various stations of amplification transmit signals to society about the seriousness of the risk, the performance of risk management institutions, and, in this context, the hazardousness of place. The degree of amplification will affect the extent to which *risk ripples* and the stigmatization of place accompany a risk or risk event. Where social concern and debate are intense, secondary and tertiary impacts may extend beyond the people who are directly affected.

The consequences of risk and risk events, then, often exceed the direct physical harm to human beings and ecosystems to include more indirect effects on the economy, social institutions, and well-being associated with amplification-driven impacts. Risk ripples and secondary impacts carry the potential for the stigmatization of certain technologies or places. The mere thought of certain technologies, products or places can conjure up enough negative imagery and emotion to render them tainted objects to be shunned and avoided. Nuclear energy and hazardous waste facilities are prime examples of stigmatized technologies or places now embroiled in controversy and public opposition. Biotechnology and chemicals also face some elements of such stigmatization. At the heart of such effects are the ingredients of the social amplification of risk – public perceptions of great risk, intense media coverage of even the most minor incidents or failures, distrust of the managers involved, social group mobilization and opposition, conflicts over value issues, and disappointments with failed promises. In the modern risk society, amplification-driven impacts, such as stigma-related effects, may mar, compromise and diminish the potential benefits to society from economic growth and technological change.

With this overview of social amplification, we can now explore the application and focusing of the framework on stigmatization.

RISK AMPLIFICATION AND STIGMATIZATION

Risk-induced stigma, particularly those that come to characterize particular places or areas, were not central to Goffman's (1963) original thinking. With the recent enhanced knowledge of risk, and the social amplification of such risks, it is opportune to explore alternative ways of structuring the processes by which risk generates social stigma, if only to conceptualize and clarify the contributing elements and how they interact. Here we draw upon our previous collaborative work with colleagues at Decision Research on the social amplification of risk to explore how a risk stigmatization framework might reflect current understanding. The intent, it cannot be overemphasized, is not to set forth *the* way of conceptualizing such complex relationships but to offer one view intended to contribute to the formulation of a robust framework of analysis. Our current conception appears in Figure 9.3 and the discussion that follows is geared to that schematic diagram.

Definitions and measurement

As suggested above, we define *stigma as a mark placed on a person, place, technology, or product, associated with a particular attribute that identifies it as different and deviant, flawed or undesirable.* Here we are interested in stigma arising from risk-related attributes. In our conception, such stigmatization involves three stages:

1   the risk-related attributes receive high visibility, particularly through communication processes, leading to perception and imagery of high riskiness, a process that we refer to as the social amplification of risk;
2   marks are placed upon the person, place, technology or product to identify it as risky and therefore undesirable;
3   the social amplification of risk and marking alter the identity of the person, place, technology or product, thereby producing behavioural changes in those encountering the imagery and marking as well as those to whom they are directed.

Accompanying this process will often be a story or narrative that interprets the evolution of the stigma and assigns responsibility or blame for its presence.

The attributes of risk, as we describe below, may emerge from any stage of the causal chain of hazard, whether it be risk events, exposures or consequences. Since the emergence of stigma follows a similar process of attribute selection, visibility, marking and changed identity, all these stages are relevant to identifying and measuring the stigma. Since the process is cumulative and registers its full impact when a change in identity occurs, as Goffman (1963) notes in his classic statement, identification and measurement are most reliable at that stage of stigma evolution. This parallels risk analysis thinking where the risk is not actualized until risk consequences actually occur. But just as risk analysis has recently given much attention to risk characterization, which includes profiling the various stages in the evolution or development stage, so

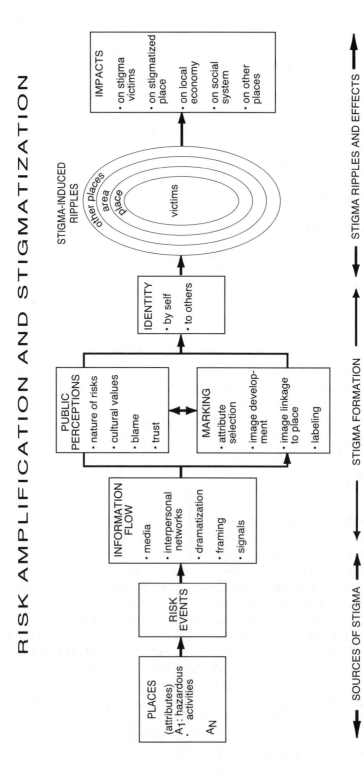

Figure 9.3 *Risk amplification and stigmatization*

something like *stigma characterization* might chart the evolution of the stigma from risk events and experiences, the social amplification and marking, the change in identity, and the ensuing behavioural consequences. Each stage of the characterization would be subject to an assessment of intensity as well as an evaluation of potential contributors to the next stage of stigma formation. The development of indicators for each stage should also be an achievable goal.

Sources of risk-induced stigma

Much of the literature on stigma addresses sources of stigma that lie in interpersonal or social relationships. Here we focus on places that are sites for risky facilities or activities that have the potential to produce risk events that command attention from the various 'social stations' that process such threats. Risk events can occur anywhere across the 'hazard chain'...

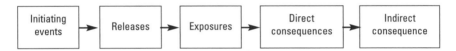

They may be actual risk events or consequences but may also constitute new information, reports or allegations concerning the hazard as a whole or a particular hazard stage. Some such risk events are socially rather than technologically induced. For example, a local environmental group that continually monitors experience in a community for 'targets of opportunity' relevant to its political agenda may seize upon an event occurring elsewhere to sound an 'alert' that a new risk has appeared locally.

The place involved will typically host a conglomerate of social and economic activities or *attributes* that define the nature of life at that site as well as the source of various beneficial and potentially risky activities. As noted above, most places accommodate a rather inconspicuous mix of such activities or attributes, none of which comes to dominate the image of the place or its identity. In some cases, of course, an activity or attribute of the place, such as gambling in Las Vegas or automobile manufacture in Detroit, assumes such prominence as to shape extensively the identity of the place. With regard to hazards, a brew of environmental, technological and social hazards typically defines a diffuse 'hazardousness of place' (Hewitt and Burton, 1971) or 'cartography of danger' (Monmonier, 1997) and no dominant image of a specific hazard emerges as linked to the place. Notable exceptions exist, however, as the very names 'Three Mile Island', 'Love Canal', 'Times Beach', 'Seveso' or 'Bhopal' suggest, often associated with a catastrophic hazard or accident. Socially amplified hazards, such as the murder of foreign tourists in Miami, can provide a powerful source for the stigmatization of a place. Beirut, Lebanon, once the 'Paris of the Middle East', suggests how dramatically a positive image of a place can be transformed into a stigma through a succession of risk events. And New Jersey may struggle forever to live down its 'cancer alley' image and pass itself off as a genuine 'garden state'.

Information flow

The emergence of broadly based stigmatization of places, technologies and products depends upon extensive coverage of the risk and risk events at a place. As noted widely in the stigma literature, the *visibility* and *salience* of the offending or denigrated attribute is essential to the marking of the place, product or technology. From past hazards research, it is known that the mass media exercise considerable selectivity in their coverage of hazards (Singer and Endreny, 1993). Risk and risk events compete for scarce space in media coverage, and the outcome of this competition is a major determinant of (1) whether a risk will undergo social amplification or attenuation in society's processing and disposition of the risk, and (2) whether the risk becomes central to the stigmatization of the place.

The mass media can also play a critical role in dramatizing and framing the risk problem or threat. Particularly important are both the extent of coverage and the particular 'facts' selected and the language used to characterize the risk. Here the radioactive accident in Goiânia, Brazil, in which radioactive material obtained at a junkyard contaminated portions of the city in 1987 (Roberts, 1987; IAEA, 1988; Petterson, 1988), is particularly instructive. Initially, the accident received only minor attention in a casual report in a local newspaper, but on 1 October, 1987, a highly sensational and lengthy São Paulo television broadcast initiated an intense period of dramatic and often exaggerated media coverage of the unfolding incidents and discoveries in the aftermath of the accident. Overnight, an army of reporters and camera crews descended on Goiânia to cover the tragedy. North American headlines spread the news of 'deadly glitter', 'a carnival of glittering poison', and 'playing with radiation', thereby 'marking' Goiânia. This media blitz generated extraordinary public concerns, with perceptions of enormous risk apparent even among people who had no contact with contaminated persons or materials. Similar observations obtain concerning the coverage of Love Canal, the Chernobyl and Bhopal accidents, and the mad cow disease episode.

The mass media also play an important role in interpreting the meaning of the risk event. Such interpretation can provide the base for the subsequent stigmatization of a place or product. Elsewhere we have examined the flow of risk *signals* in the print news media in the area of the proposed Yucca Mountain nuclear waste disposal facility. Defining risk signals as 'messages about risk or risk events that affect people's perceptions about the seriousness and/or manageability of the risk', we analysed the appearance of such signals in five years of coverage in the *Las Vegas Review-Journal* (see Chapter 8). A few examples, chosen more or less at random, may suggest the potential of such signalling for altering risk perceptions, imagery and place identity:

- Yet the drumbeat of opposition to the *radioactive* grave at Yucca Mountain rumbles on. (23 July, 1986)
- In editorials where 'pejorative' is not a no-no, we'll call it a *dump* or a *tomb* or a shaft full of *gunk* or anything else that comes to mind. (29 July, 1987)
- If we are going down the road to nuclear *ruin, slopping the swill* from roadside to roadside, then let's get started. (12 February, 1989)
- It is possible, he argues, that some poor country, down on its luck and saddled with debt, might gladly accept American *atomic garbage*, for a price. (14 July, 1987)
- You don't even have to squint to see the handwriting on the wall – that *big* R.I.P. already scrawled on the crags of Yucca Mountain. (13 July, 1986)

From such examples of risk signals, it is apparent that, in addition to providing an ongoing flow of information about issues and events, the mass media also interpret the larger social meaning of what is occurring. So the media in a wide variety of subtle ways provide messages that shape the perceptions of readers and viewers about what has occurred. Such messages appeared explicitly in this case in the editorializing about the proposed nuclear waste facility in Nevada, the siting process under way, and the implication for people and their well-being. Such messages were embedded in the choice of headlines, the positioning of stories, and the selection and use of pictures, symbols and metaphors to assist interpretation. The 'flows' or 'streams' of signals certainly affect, albeit in ways that are yet unknown, people's views of risks and the marking of places in which the risks occur.

Public perceptions

Risk perception is a critical part of risk amplification and stigmatization. Much is known from past risk research about the characteristics of risks and risk events that are likely to generate strong public concerns and elicit high media coverage. Risks that are new, involuntary, potentially catastrophic and that involve dread all tend to elicit strong concerns and reactions. If the risks connect to a group agenda concerned with the technology, activity or product, additional media scrutiny and social conflict may easily result. Some risks pose threats to deeply held values or social institutions; these, too, often evoke strong public reactions.

The responsibility of the managers of the facility or technology for the occurrence of the risk event, the extent to which they are viewed as blameworthy, and the character of their early response to the event are important compounding factors. It is sometimes the case that a rapid and effective accident response combined with action to protect nearby residents and the community can minimize damage to public confidence in the managers. Much may also depend upon the history of relationships between managers of the facility and members of the host community. On the other hand, if the managers are clearly to blame, betray a history of failures, or seek to conceal their responsibility, then the risk event is likely to be strongly amplified through media revelations and intensified public concerns.

Lack of trust can be another compounding factor. If high levels of trust exist in those responsible for risk management, risk events may undergo only limited social amplification in media coverage and public perceptions. But if reservoirs of social trust have been drawn down, or, worse still, if active distrust prevails, then even small events may generate high levels of public concern, particularly if the risk is one that publics fear. Certain hazards, such as hazardous wastes or radioactive materials, have broader contexts and histories of mismanagement that may contribute to social distrust.

Contending social groups and watchdog organizations, especially those based at the place in question, also can influence risk amplification and stigmatization. To the extent that risk becomes a volatile issue in a community or a source of contention among social groups, it may be vigorously brought to greater public attention and subjected to value-based interpretations. Polarization of community views and escalation of rhetoric often occur. New community members may be drawn into the conflict. These social conflicts outlive the particular risk event and can become anchors for subsequent risk debates, contributing to an image of the place and the emergence of risk-based stigma.

Finally, it is important to note that places do not exist in isolation. Rather, they are often linked in the mental maps of publics with the areas of which they are part or other places possessing similar attributes, including prominent risks. So in the amplification of risk and potential place stigmatization, geographical associations with societal experiences with risk may be a contributing element. Thus, the Yucca Mountain site's proximity to the Nevada Nuclear Test Site and linkages made with unsuccessful nuclear waste disposal facilities at other places, such as West Valley in New York State or the Hanford Reservation in Washington State, can fuel emerging perceptions, images and interpretations. An interesting question is whether a stigma becomes associated with other nearby places or the broader geographic areas of which they are part. And does a 'distance decay' attenuate stigma as one moves away from the stigmatized place or facility?

Marking

Risk events, as major accidents and pollution/contamination cases demonstrate, wield a powerful potential to *mark* the places (and their inhabitants) in which they occur. Edelstein (1988, p14) argues, for example, that 'stigma routinely accompanies the announcement of contamination and the identification of its boundaries'. This marking occurs in many ways and does not require the Scarlet Letter A or a yellow star to identify the outcast. Mitchell et al (1988, p98), for example, note that outsiders make wide use of an imaginary physical sign 'glowing in the dark' to brand Richland (host community for the Hanford Reservation) residents. Richland people, in response, 'celebrate' their imagery, or stigma, by adopting the term Richland High School 'Bombers' and displaying a mushroom cloud insignia on their sports uniforms.

Marking involves the selection of a particular attribute of a facility or place and the deselection of other attributes. Accordingly, the risk event or series of events directs attention to the hazardous facility or activity at a place. Extensive media scrutiny, social debate and conflict, and public concerns – in short, the amplification process – raises to prominence a single attribute of place. Other attributes that otherwise characterize the place are pushed into the background. In the most intense situations, amplification dynamics reconstruct the image of a place around the risk attribute.

Telling evidence of such risk-based image formation is provided by the work of Slovic et al (1991c) on the proposed nuclear waste repository and the nuclear test site in Nevada. Using a method of 'continued associations', images were elicited through telephone interviews. The results, as suggested by Table 9.1, indicate the extraordinarily negative imagery that such facilities or sites can come to have. The research also found that the nuclear weapons test site had led to a 'modest amount of nuclear imagery becoming associated with the state of Nevada' (Slovic et al, 1991c, p693).

Further evidence of the marking of places from hazardous facilities can be found in focus group studies conducted by Mitchell et al (1988) in Richland, Washington. Testimony of the experience of Richland residents speaks of marking, imagery, and stigmatization:

> Female: Even my own people who live in Indiana won't come to visit me because they think they're going to be contaminated. I've lived here since 1944 and they're scared to come here. We can't even convince them, you know, that it's safe to come here. Now that's ridiculous. (p100)
>
> We had a gentleman call yesterday. He was considering a job here and he said: 'I've got to convince my family it's safe. What can I tell them? They all think the plant's right here in town and the people glow in the dark.' (p100)
>
> Female: Well, when our daughter graduated from college, she, of course, had a teaching certificate, had a job in Portland. And right away the people started to turn her against Richland including the principal of the high school. It was just terrible and they were brainwashing her about, you know, your father is crazy for working there, you know. They expected us all to have cancer and all these things. They really did a job on her to convince her that don't go there; don't go there. (p99)

Table 9.1 *Images associated with an underground nuclear waste storage facility*[a]

Category	Frequency	Images included in category
1 Dangerous	179	Dangerous, danger, hazardous, toxic, unsafe, harmful, disaster
2 Death/sickness	107	Death, dying, sickness, cancer
3 Negative	99	Negative, wrong, bad, unpleasant, terrible, gross, undesirable, awful, dislike, ugly, horrible
4 Pollution	97	Pollution, contamination, leakage, spills, Love Canal
5 War	62	War, bombs, nuclear war, holocaust
6 Radiation	59	Radiation, nuclear, radioactive, glowing
7 Scary	55	Scary, frightening, concern, worried, fear, horror
8 Somewhere else	49	Wouldn't want to live near one, not where I live, far away as possible
9 Unnecessary	44	Unnecessary, bad idea, waste of land
10 Problems	39	Problems, trouble
11 Desert	37	Desert, barren, desolate
12 Non-Nevada locations	35	Utah, Arizona, Denver
13 Nevada/Las Vegas	34	Nevada (25), Las Vegas (9)
14 Storage location	32	Caverns, underground salt mine
15 Government/industry	23	Government, politics, big business

Note: a Basis: N = 402 respondents in Phoenix, Arizona

Source: Slovic et al 1991c, p689

Labelling is another means of marking places. Perhaps no example is clearer than the label 'dump' to refer to hazardous waste disposal facilities in the US. Indeed, this is a case where opponents of such facilities have won the battle over language. A dump, in common parlance, is an open hole in the ground to which you back your car or pick-up truck and literally dump rubbish or refuse into the hole. It certainly has nothing in common with the highly engineered, multiple-barrier encapsulation and monitored facilities now being proposed for the disposal of radioactive and toxic chemical waste. Yet in our study of print media coverage of the proposed nuclear waste facility in Nevada, we found that the label 'dump' dominated all other images and descriptors and had become the customary way to refer to the project. Indeed, nearly one of two news headlines during a five-year period used the label 'dump' as the project referent (Chapter 8).

Identity

The net effect of the amplification dynamics, imagery development and labelling can be to alter fundamentally the identity of the place. As a place comes to be dominated by a single negative attribute while other attributes characterizing the place recede into the background or insignificance, identity is altered and stigmatized. And this altered identity is one that is highly tainted and discredited. The various dimensions of imagery blend into a holistic sense of the altered identity. Goffman (1963, pp2–3) refers to the emergence of a *virtual social identity* as opposed to an *actual social identity*; the former dominated by a single negative attribute, the latter composed of the various attributes that the place actually possesses. This altered identity is held not only by others who exist beyond the place but by the victims of stigmatization themselves, the residents of the now tainted and discredited place.

Ripples and effects

As we described above in the general social amplification framework, the consequences of a risk or risk event can, if amplified, ripple to other places, facilities, technologies and society as a whole, or even to future points in time. Risk-induced stigma greatly enlarge the potential for rippling. Such rippling has been apparent in a number of well-publicized accidents. The Bhopal accident not only affected the victims of that city but produced significant changes in hazard management at chemical and other industrial facilities throughout India. Subsequently, widespread changes occurred in Europe and North America in industry management practices concerning inventories of hazardous materials, risk communication and community preparedness. Similarly, the accident at Seveso, Italy, resulted in the Seveso Directive in the European community, with far-reaching changes in many countries concerning emergency preparedness, response and information dissemination.

But certainly the accident at Goiânia, Brazil, offers a perhaps unsurpassed case of stigma-induced ripples and secondary consequences. The first weeks of the media coverage following the accident found more than 100,000 persons voluntarily standing in line for radiation monitoring. Within two weeks of the event, consumer concerns over possible contamination fuelled a drop of some 50 per cent in the wholesale value of agricultural production within Goiâs, the Brazilian state in which Goiânia is located. Although no contamination was ever found in the products, a significant adverse impact was still apparent some eight months later. Meanwhile, the number and prices of homes sold or rented within the immediate vicinity of the accident plummeted; hotel occupancy in Goiânia, normally near capacity at that time of year, experienced vacancy levels averaging about 40 per cent in the six weeks following the São Paulo television broadcast. One of the largest hotels lost an estimated 1000 reservations as a direct consequence of risk perceptions and stigmatization. And even a hot-springs tourist attraction, situated a full one-hour drive from Goiânia, experienced a 30–40 per cent drop in occupancy rates immediately following the São Paulo television broadcast. Hotels in other parts of Brazil turned away Goiânia residents. Some airline pilots refused to fly airplanes carrying Goiânia residents. Elsewhere in Brazil cars bearing Goiâs licence plates were stoned. Even nuclear energy as a whole in Brazil was affected, as several political parties used the accident to mobilize against 'nuclear weapons, power, or waste' and to introduce legislation designed to split the National Nuclear Energy Commission into separate divisions.

RISK AND STIGMA IN MODERN SOCIETY

Remarkable as the Goiânia and 'mad cow' cases are, where modern society has publics that are often risk averse to certain hazards (e.g. radiation, toxic chemicals) where suspicions about technology have mounted and where information systems are highly developed, it may be expected that stigma-induced hazard disasters may assume greater prominence in risk management. The stigmatization of one of the world's major sources of renewable energy due to the accidents at Three Mile Island and Chernobyl and the subsequent paralysis in many countries in building new nuclear energy plants are telling evidence. The worldwide effects on the chemical industry of the Bhopal accident suggest the potential for rippling from one to many other countries. The 'mad cow' case in England demonstrates not only how powerfully an entire industry can be affected by an amplified risk, followed by stigmatization, but how foreign producers in other countries can be undeservedly tainted as well. The lesson seems clear – some places and technologies may experience enormous indirect consequences that far exceed the direct consequences and define the societal experience of the risk or the event. We need to understand much better than we currently do this process of amplification, stigma-induced ripples and the propagation of more indirect secondary and tertiary consequences. And we may anticipate that risk events followed by intense social amplification of the risks and associated stigmatization of technology, industry or places may be recurring surprises that will exact high societal prices and will increasingly intrude upon the societal experience with risk.

10 Risk, Trust and Democratic Theory

Roger E. Kasperson, Dominic Golding and Jeanne X. Kasperson

INTRODUCTION

Recent practice in managing environmental risks in the US demonstrates how firmly the principles of democratic values and procedures have intruded on the previously sheltered world of scientifically defined risk. Recurrent failures in risk management, it is now widely argued, stem from a failure to recognize the more general requirements of democratic society, and especially the need for social trust. Accordingly, risk control strategies have gone awry due, alternatively, to a lack of openness and 'transparency', the failure to consult or involve so-called 'stakeholders' (usually a poorly defined misnomer), a loss of social trust in managers, inadequacies in due process, a lack of responsiveness to public concerns, or an insensitivity to questions of environmental justice.

Such interpretations abound across a wide spectrum of environmental debates: global warming, biodiversity, genetic engineering, clean-up of defence and other hazardous wastes, lead in the environment, the siting of hazardous waste facilities and the protection of wetlands. Ruckelshaus has recently warned that:

> Mistrust engenders a vicious descending spiral. The more mistrust by the public, the less effective government becomes at delivering what people want and need; the more government bureaucrats in turn respond with enmity towards the citizens they serve, the more ineffective government becomes, the more people mistrust it, and so on, down and down (Ruckelshaus, 1996, p2).

Ruckelshaus's dread spiral is reminiscent of Supreme Court Justice Stephen Breyer's tripartite 'vicious circle – public perception, Congressional reaction, and the uncertainties of the regulatory process'

Note: Reprinted from *Social Trust and the Management of Risk*, Cvetkovich, G. and Löfstedt, R. (eds), 'Risk, trust and democratic theory', Kasperson, R. E., Golding, D. and Kasperson, J. X., pp22–44, © (1999), with permission from Earthscan

(Breyer, 1993, p50) that thwarts effective regulation of risk. Clearly, obligations to democratic procedures and attention to issues of trust have become essential elements of any successful regime's addressing environmental risks that command public concerns and place claims on limited societal resources.

A noteworthy marker of this recognition of democratic requirements is the US National Research Council (NRC) report *Understanding Risk* (Stern and Fineberg, 1996). This report is the most recent in a series of NRC efforts to define and rationalize the risk assessment function in government and, by inference, the relationship between the nation's assessment and management of environmental threats and the functioning of democratic society. Indeed, a striking change of social ethics and democratic expectations has attended the handling of environmental and health threats in American society. The progression of ethics is what Kates (1985b, p53) would characterize as 'third-generation ethics' bursting on American society in the twilight of the 20th century, ethics bearing on how risks will be allocated and managed with strong attention to the 'fairness of the process as well as the outcome'. (The two earlier generations of ethics involved, respectively, a time of non-maleficence that called for avoiding unnecessary harm and informing those at risk, and a period of maximizing the aggregate societal utility of balancing risks and benefits.) Similarly, it is clear that those affected by risk must be informed and provided ample opportunity to participate in decisions and that managers must be publicly accountable for their actions.

These social re-anchorings have found their way progressively, but often painfully slowly, into recognitions by government and corporations that the game has changed. The so-called 'Red Book', *Risk Assessment in the Federal Government* (USNRC, 1983), was predicated on the need to distinguish, and clarify, the technically based assessment process from the value-laden decision process. The first was, it was argued, the domain of science; the second that of politics. Beyond that, the book allotted little attention to the complications of reconciling the scientific process of risk assessment with the needs of democratic procedure; rather, noting the potential tensions and ambiguities, that volume, as well as subsequent NRC reports, concentrated on ways to improve the scientific bases of risk assessment. *Understanding Risk* (Stern and Fineberg, 1996), therefore, is a striking departure: the book explores in depth the bases of public response, enumerates contributions of public assessment to risk characterization, demarcates the myriad entrances of value questions into both assessment and policy, and investigates means for integrating expert assessment and democratic process. In short, the report symbolizes, and recognizes, that the new requirements of third-generation risk ethics and democratic procedure have invaded the main corridors of policy discourse.

Salutary as this is, the discussion of how to reconcile risk assessment, trust and democratic procedure has thus far proceeded largely from the insights gained from the experience of those charged with the

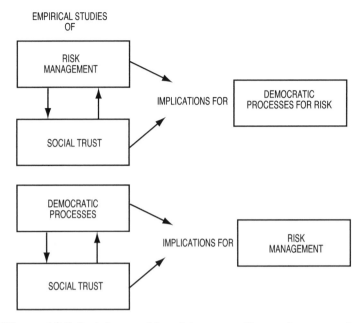

Figure 10.1 *Social trust, risk and democracy: Contrasting approaches*

responsibility of managing risk or from those social scientists who analyse societal encounters with environmental and health threats. Meanwhile, a literature of democratic theorizing has emerged addressing the social conditions necessary for democracy and the relationships between democratic institutions and economic and social well-being. As yet, these discussions have remained quite separate.

We seek to join these disparate inquiries, but we do so by reversing the perspective that has thus far guided much of the discussion among risk analysts, whom we would characterize as seeking to answer a difficult question: what does our experience concerning the interaction of risk management and social trust suggest about how better to bring democratic procedures into risk management to improve the process? Rather, our approach is to examine recent theorizing about democracy and its relation to social trust for insights on how to bring risk assessment and management into greater conformity with democratic regimes (Figure 10.1). This exploration is heuristic in the best sense: we are uncertain whether this shift in perspective will afford new insights and leave it to the reader to judge.

APPROACHES TO DEMOCRATIC THEORY

After considering several examples of democratic theorizing, we turn to what various public surveys and opinion polls may suggest about trust in American democracy. We also inquire into how trust is lost and regained, the levels of social trust that enter into democratic processes, how we may think about social distrust, and finally we note some promising avenues of future inquiry. Discussions of democratic theory, and the role that trust plays in democratic society, are as rich and diverse as the examples of democracy found in different corners of the globe, Not only is there little consensus as to what democratic values are once one moves beyond the veneer of rhetoric but, more significantly, the underlying notions of democracy itself are so fundamentally different as to be frequently in direct conflict. Some approaches begin with the societal conditions or basic values necessary for the emergence of democratic institutions and processes; others stress the normative goals or outcomes that democracy should achieve. Pennock (1979, p161) distinguishes between *justificatory democratic theory*, treating how power ought to be distributed and exercised in democratic government, and *operational democratic theory*, focused on how people actually organize for the conduct of democratic institutions. Opting for the better, Pennock classifies approaches to democratic theory according to their conceptualization of power relationships and whether they are descriptive theory, prescriptive theory or models.

Here, in centring upon what appear to be the principal approaches in the literature over the past several decades, our intent is to distinguish among types of theorizing that are empirically based. Accordingly, we recognize five major approaches: institutional (or constitutional) designs, socioeconomic development, cultural perspectives, dialogic models and civil society/civic engagement. Since the last, as represented particularly by the influential work of Robert Putnam (1993, 1995a, 1995b, 1996) has attracted much discussion and builds upon several of the other approaches, we examine it at greater length. For each approach, we characterize essentials of the theory and then explore what role, if any, social trust plays in the construct of democracy.

Institutional (constitutional) designs

This approach centres upon the design of institutions that maximize democratic values and processes. Implicit is the distribution of power over branches of government and institutions as well as means for limiting the exercise of power. Often this is coupled with notions of the rational political actor who, operating through rational choice, maximizes individual utility, as suggested by the work of Buchanan and Tullock (1962). Thus, Elinor Ostrom in *Governing the Commons* (1990) emphasizes the constitutional arrangement of rules and institutions that underlie the operation of successful common property systems. Given the strong role of rational individualism in such approaches, social trust is seen as implicit in that institutions function akin to markets, delivering outcomes associated with rational political choices according to the requirements of the political regime.

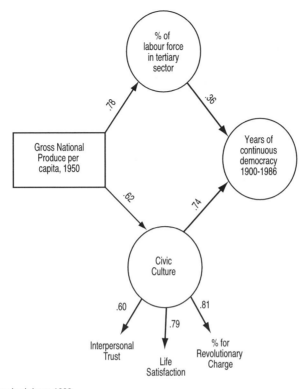

Source: After Inglehart, 1988

Figure 10.2 *Economic and cultural prerequisites of stable democracy*

Economic development

Economic development, or 'modernization', sees the emergence of democracy as an outcome of economic growth and progress. Development promotes democracy by contributing to higher levels of legitimacy of political authority, decreased propensity for political radicalism and increased stability of the political system. It is not economic development or growth per se, however, that is important to the emergence of democratic institutions and procedures, but a dense cluster of social changes and improvements that are broadly distributed over the population, such as the minimization of environmental risks (air pollution, groundwater depletion, etc), improved health care, lowered infant mortality, and increased literacy and education of the population. Such outcomes encourage, and provide enabling conditions for, political participation while also serving to increase social trust and to reduce class tension and political radicalism. Broad support for this theory is available in a wide array of empirical studies; Figure 10.2 suggests a general relationship between economic development and the emergence of high levels of social trust across a spectrum of developed societies.

The structure of causality between economic development and democracy remains opaque in much of this theorizing. The argument generally claims that economic development facilitates the emergence of democratic values and institutions through key intervening variables, such as more democratic political culture, less polarized class structure, a broadening of civil society and more integrated state–society relations. But the exact causal mechanisms by which these linkages come into being are not precisely defined nor do they enjoy the support of incontrovertible empirical evidence.

Cultural approaches

Analysts who take cultural approaches argue that a consistent syndrome of interrelated attitudes toward life satisfaction, political satisfaction, interpersonal trust and support for the existing social order is apparent across a wide variety of societies (Inglehart, 1988, 1997). This syndrome is the essential mediating link between economic and social development and the persistence of democratic institutions. Indeed, broad empirical evidence suggests that more than half the variance in such persistence can be attributed to this syndrome (Inglehart, 1988).

In revisiting their classic 1963 work on political culture, Almond and Verba (1980) tapped the work of David Easton (1965) on the political system to distinguish among three attributes or components of political culture. *System culture* involves the distribution of public attitudes toward national community, regime and political authorities, including different levels of political trust. *Process culture* includes attitudes towards oneself and toward other political actors, and, thus, levels of interpersonal trust. Such attitudes are cognitive, affective and evaluative. *Policy culture* reflects the relatedness or internal consistency of the various components or attributes of the political system. Below, we also pick up this notion of multiple levels in the political system.

Figure 10.2 suggests the critical role of political culture in the persistence of democracy across a wide variety of societies. Using linear structural relationships (LISREL) to help delineate the causal links among conditions leading to democracy, the analysis shows the importance of the syndrome of attitudes in the evolution of 'civic culture', a type of political culture conceptualized by Almond and Verba (1963) as particularly amenable to democratic regimes. The importance of the syndrome for this culture is quite apparent, as is the correlation between civic culture and years of continuous democracy.

From Almond and Verba's cross-national study of five political cultures, it is possible to glean a number of propositions concerning how social trust may contribute to democratic institutions and processes. In summary, social trust:

- increases individual propensity to join with others in political activity;
- tends to translate into politically relevant trust;

- leads to a closer fusion between the primary group structures or society and the secondary structures of politics;
- mediates, and ameliorates, the extent to which commitments to political subgroups lead to political fragmentations;
- makes citizens more willing to turn power over to political elites, who tend also to be viewed as part of the political community rather than as an alien force;
- leads to a more integrated and stable political system. (see Almond and Verba, 1963, pp284–288, 494–495)

Through such propositions, cultural studies elevate social trust to a key role in democratic theory.

Dialogic models

Dialogic models of democracy proceed from several critical assumptions. First, democracy, in this view, depends upon the presence or creation of an enlightened citizenry that has broad-based opportunities for participating in public decisions and that is part of an ongoing, meaningful public dialogue. But such dialogue is greatly impeded by the fact that the various contending parties operate within the logic of alternative discourses. Such dialogue, according to Williams and Matheny (1995, pp3–10) includes such markedly different discourses as *managerial, pluralist* and *communitarian languages*. Overcoming these impediments is essential to fulfilling the requisites for democracy: namely, the clarification of comforting assumptions, the identification and narrowing of grounds of disagreement, and the capability of citizens to determine for themselves the adequacy of competing conceptions of public policy and the public interest (Williams and Matheny, 1995, p61).

Barber (1984, p261) also maintains that a 'strong' democracy requires institutions that involve individuals at both the neighbourhood and national level in common 'talk', common decision making and political judgement, and common action:

> To talk where one votes and to vote where one debates, to debate where one learns ... and to learn in a civic fashion where one talks is to integrate the several civic functions in a way that nurtures public seeing and strengthens political judgment (Barber, 1984, p271).

An enlightened citizenry emerges only in a context of broad-based opportunities for participation, policy-making institutions capable of accommodating ambiguity and tentativeness, and a political community capable of transforming partial and private interests into public goods.

Democratic talk, then, is a powerful mechanism for building social trust and democratic institutions, what Inglehart (1997, p163) refers to as a 'culture of trust'. But several societal conditions must be met. Individual disputes need to be placed in the context of the full range of decisions that affect public life and not be viewed as idiosyncratic. Similarly, public discourse needs to be continuous and ongoing and not, as often happens, occur only sporadically or episodically. For discourse to be continuous, citizens require not only the opportunities but the means and resources to acquire and evaluate information. Finally, people must be empowered to enter into decisions and to see the results actually implemented.

Some see in dialogue and narrative the potential for a new democratic order and a new basis for social trust. Earle and Cvetkovich (1995, p10), who observe that 'social trust [is] based on cultural values that are communicated in narrative form within society by elites', favour a movement away from divisive pluralism and toward what they term *cosmopolitanism*. Cosmopolitans work to free themselves from the past and to seek new community-based futures. All local narratives become open to 'continuing reconstruction based on unconstrained persuasion' by cosmopolitan leaders (Earle and Cvetkovich, 1995, p152). Cosmopolitan social trust bridges the gap between the past and the unknown future, and people enlist imagination and dialogue to fashion their own, and a new, future.

Across these different approaches to democratic theory, social trust is a central ingredient, viewed as providing important bases for democratic society. High levels of social trust ease the functioning of institutions and governance by facilitating greater cooperation in society. Indeed, as Etzioni (1990, p8) affirms: 'It is hard to conceive a modern economy without a strong element of trust running through it.' Trust creates and sustains solidarity in social relationships and systems. It also, as Luhmann (1979, 1993) maintains, functions 'to comprehend and reduce' social complexity and enlarges individual and societal benefits through the taking of risks. This enlargement of benefits accrues in no small part to the greater efficiency of economic and political transactions. And many theorists also see trust as indispensable to political stability – in values that underlie the political community, in the functioning of the regime and institutions, and in vesting requisite authority in those who govern. It is not surprising in this context that many risk-management analysts proceed from an underlying assumption that social trust is indispensable to institutional effectiveness and thus the more the better.

Civil society/civic engagement

The fifth approach to democratic theory builds on all of the four approaches discussed above. Over the past several decades, few works in the social sciences have evoked more attention and debate than Robert Putnam's publications on civic engagement and civil society (Putnam, 1993, 1995a, 1995b, 1996). Although portrayal of Americans' 'bowling alone' (Putnam, 1995a) has garnered much public attention, the major theoretical structure for his ideas is presented in his book *Making Democracy Work* (Putnam, 1993).

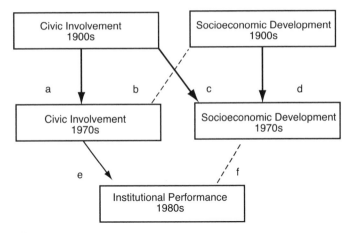

Source: After Putnam, 1993

Figure 10.3 *Actual effects among civic involvement, socioeconomic development and institutional performance: Italy, 1900–1980*

Putnam identifies the conditions necessary for the creation and maintenance of strong and responsive democratic institutions. He characterizes the regionalization of government in Italy during the 1970s as a 'natural experiment' to explore the impact of civic engagement on economic development and institutional performance in particular. Tapping three of the four approaches outlined above, especially sociocultural explanations, he invokes Alexis de Tocqueville's (1969) Democracy in America:

> As depicted in Tocqueville's classic interpretation of American democracy and other accounts of civic virtue, the civic community is marked by an active, public-spirited citizenry, by egalitarian political relations, by a social fabric of trust and cooperation. Some regions of Italy, we discover, are cursed with vertically structured politics, a social life of fragmentation and isolation, and a culture of distrust. These differences in civic life turn out to play a key role in explaining institutional success (Putnam, 1993, p15).

Putnam develops an elaborate set of indicators of institutional performance (e.g. cabinet stability, budget promptness, legislative innovation, expenditures), socioeconomic development (e.g. infant mortality, agricultural workforce, industrial workforce), and civic involvement (e.g. membership in cooperatives and mutual aid associations) based on extensive interviews and historical data. Multiple-regression analyses of these data reveal some startling associations. Most notably, as Figure 10.3 shows, civic involvement is the prime driver of development and the major factor shaping institutional performance. Civic traditions between 1860 and 1920 are the most powerful predictor of contemporary civic community (arrow a), whereas historical socioeconomic development has little independent impact on contemporary socioeconomic conditions (d) and absolutely no impact on the contemporary civic community (b). Thus, the 'uncivic' south of Italy is socioeconomically blighted, whereas the civic north, with its dense network of civic engagement, experiences an economic prosperity comparable with the most developed regions and nations of the world.

Putnam develops an elegant theory to explain how civic involvement, such as membership in mutual aid associations, creates this phenomenal difference in socioeconomic development. He begins by noting that all societies face 'dilemmas of collective action' where short-term individual interests, such as overgrazing of common lands and pollution of drinking water and other common property resources, may result in collective harm (Putnam, 1993, p162). Putnam asserts that third-party enforcement by government agencies has failed to overcome these kinds of dilemmas in the past, and that mutual trust and cooperation offer the only solution. Indeed, the many rotating credit associations, mutual aid societies and farming cooperatives that exist in the world attest to the ability of communities to overcome such predicaments, but that entails the generation, through civic engagement, of a significant reservoir of social capital.

Social capital comprises stocks of trust, norms or reciprocity and networks of civic engagement that make voluntary cooperation easier to attain. These stocks are 'moral resources' that may be created or destroyed through 'virtuous' and 'vicious' circles. Successful cooperation breeds economic prosperity by promoting civic ends that would otherwise be impossible. For example, a group of farmers may get together to help each other harvest crops or to raise barns, activities that they would not be able to do alone – in effect, putting the social capital of the community to work. Such successful cooperation not only leads to greater economic prosperity but also tends to be mutually reinforcing, so that the stock of social capital increases with each rewarding application.

Networks of civic engagement generate social capital by encouraging robust norms of reciprocity, reducing incentives to cheat, fostering communication (and thus reducing uncertainty about the trustworthiness of others), and building models of cooperation for use in the future. Norms of reciprocity evolve because they lower transaction costs, and cooperating individuals soon learn to trade off between long-term altruism and short-term self-interest. Horizontal networks typical of community associations, where individuals have equivalent status and power, facilitate communication among members. This reduces the uncertainty about the trustworthiness of new members and allows for rapid and effective application of sanctions should any member act opportunistically. By contrast, vertical networks involve hierarchies with asymmetric power relations that tend to discourage the flow of information and cannot sustain social trust and cooperation (Putnam, 1993, p172).

Trust is an essential component of social capital generated by civic engagement. Trust lubricates cooperation and cooperation breeds trust (Putnam, 1993, p171). Trust entails an expectation about the behaviour of individuals:

> You do not trust a person to do something merely because he says he will do it. You trust him because, knowing what you know of his disposition, his information, his ability, his available options and their consequences, you expect that he will choose to do it (Dasgupta, 1988, pp55–56).

Such predictions are based on the intimate, interpersonal, 'thick trust' (Williams, 1988, p8) generated in small, closely knit communities. The more indirect, impersonal, and 'thin trust' is typical of large, complex societies. With thin trust, the structure of the situation is more important than personal character.

Putnam (1993, p162) concludes that all societies face the 'dilemma of collective action' and evolve toward one of two social equilibria to avoid a Hobbesian war of all against all. The 'uncivic' south of Italy, with its patron–client relationships and extra-legal enforcers, epitomizes a social equilibrium of dependency and exploitation that harbours high social distrust and little cooperation beyond the limits of the family. This is the same lack of civic virtue that Banfield (1958) found in Montegrano, which he described as 'amoral familialism'. The second equilibrium, characteristic of the north of Italy with its dense network of civic engagement and high levels of social trust, Putnam (1993) calls 'brave reciprocity'. Each of these equilibria is self-reinforcing and represents a polar extreme of what is possible.

Turning to the US, Putnam (1995b) is troubled by the declining levels of social trust and group membership observed in the 'general social survey' (GSS) conducted by the National Opinion Research Center (NORC). In *Tuning In, Tuning Out*, Putnam (1995b) explores several plausible but ultimately inadequate explanations, including levels of education, longer working hours and the increasing participation of women in the workplace. Rising levels of education and increasing leisure time should have resulted in an increase in group membership, and although the increased number of women in the workplace might be expected to reduce civic engagement, working women tend to participate in group activities more than other women. But Putnam (1995b) concludes that generational effects best explain the downturn in social trust and group membership. Those people born in the earlier part of this century were always, and remain, more trusting and engaged than those born more recently. As the population ages and dies, overall levels of trust and engagement decline. But what accounts for this generational change?

Putnam believes television is the prime culprit. Those individuals born in the 1940s and 1950s came of age at about the time television became a major influence in day-to-day life. Several possible mechanisms explain the association between television viewing and declining trust and group membership. Watching television is invariably a solitary activity that takes up time and displaces group activities. Television also changes the outlook of viewers, especially children, so that they are less trusting of institutions and individuals around them. In sum, watching television destroys the social capital generated by civic engagement.

Some researchers have proposed that variations in trust and confidence are related to structural factors, such as the state of the economy, whereas others see specific events, such as the Vietnam War and Watergate, as the culprits (Lipset and Schneider, 1987). In the next section we examine some of these arguments and take a closer look at some of the empirical evidence, especially that available in public surveys and opinion polls.

SURVEYS/OPINION POLLS

Given the recent litany of political scandals in the US, it is scarcely surprising that the public appears to have little trust or confidence in Congress. It may surprise some, however, that numerous opinion polls appear to show that public confidence in many of the other major social institutions in the US is also quite low and has declined precipitously from levels apparent three decades ago. For example, Lipset and Schneider (1983) found a rapid decline in confidence in ten major institutions during the late 1960s and early 1970s. In 'this era of political distrust' (Breyer, 1993) since that time, public confidence has oscillated in response to important events but has remained at relatively low levels. Several factors have been proposed to explain this decline. Some see events such as the Vietnam War, the Watergate scandal, social protests and the clergy crisis as particularly important. Others point to structural changes in society and economy, such as unemployment and inflation, as altering the levels of social trust and explaining why business and government bear the brunt of public disaffection.

In their revised edition of *The Confidence Gap*, Lipset and Schneider (1987) offer a glint of optimism in noting that the average percentage of the public expressing 'a great deal of confidence' in the leadership of ten institutions rose from a low of 23 per cent in 1982 to an average of 31 per cent in 1984. Observing this trend back in 1985, it would have been difficult to say whether it would continue upwards or very soon collapse. Using poll data from Louis Harris and NORC, we have extended the graphs of Lipset and Schneider (Figure 10.4). Clearly the upswing evident in the most recent edition of *The Confidence Gap* (Lipset and Schneider, 1987) was only short-lived and ended with the revelations emerging from the Iran-Contra affair. More importantly, however, the graph in Figure 10.4 illustrates two major points. On the one hand, public confidence in institutions appears to be quite sensitive (at least in the short run) to

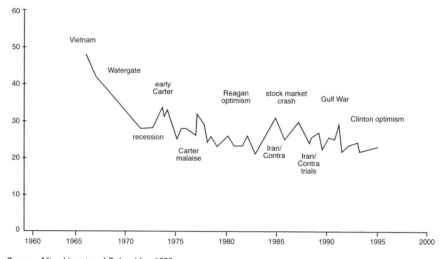

Source: After Lipset and Schneider, 1983

Figure 10.4 *Average percentage of respondents expressing 'a great deal of confidence' in the leadership of ten institutions, 1966–1995*

events, and rises and falls rather steeply over relatively short periods. On the other hand, although public confidence varies noticeably from month to month according to events, the overall trend has remained relatively stable since the mid-1970s and betrays no dramatic decline comparable with that during the 1960s and early 1970s. Hibbing and Theiss-Morse (1995, pp35–36), noting that 'data are the sparsest right where we need them to be the most dense', suggest that high levels of support may be 'fleeting' and 'atypical'. One might be tempted, therefore, to conclude that the high levels of confidence during the 1950s and 1960s were aberrations, and that the lower levels of confidence since 1970 are more 'normal' for American society (see Rosa and Clark, 1999, for support for this view). Below, we take up the question of whether social distrust has positive social functions.

In Figure 10.4, the use of an average value of confidence in ten major institutions masks much of the inter-institutional variation in public confidence. Figure 10.5 breaks down levels of confidence for seven of the ten institutions and demonstrates how particular events may affect the confidence levels in particular institutions (three others are excluded for clarity and for comparability with the Gallup data), and how these are then reflected in the overall average confidence levels. Most notably, Figure 10.5 illustrates that the Gulf War boosted public confidence in the military beginning in late 1990 and that this accounts for the peak observed in Figure 10.4. Coincident with this peak in public confidence in the military, the apparent declining levels of confidence in the other institutions may reflect the worsening economic situation at the end of George Bush's presidency. The decline in confidence in the Supreme Court may also

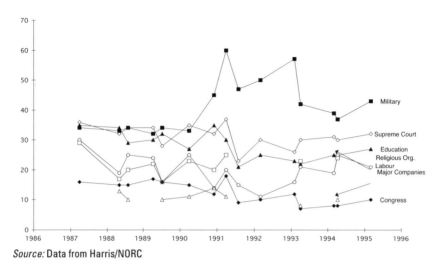

Source: Data from Harris/NORC

Figure 10.5 *Average percentage of respondents expressing 'a great deal of confidence' in the leadership of seven institutions, 1987–1995*

reflect public concern over the nomination of Judge Clarence Thomas in the summer of 1991. Without trying to explain every peak and valley, we note that Figure 10.5 gives credence to two important points made by Lipset and Schneider (1987, p8): confidence *trends* tend to be parallel for different institutions and may well, therefore, have the same general causes, whereas *patterns* of trust in different institutions tend to be more specific and may well have disparate causes (see also Hibbing and Theiss-Morse, 1995).

When we compare the results from different polling organizations, we see that the general trends and patterns are similar (compare Figure 10.5 showing the Harris/NORC data with Figure 10.6 showing the Gallup data). Generally, the public appears to have relatively high levels of confidence in the military and organized religion and relatively low levels of confidence in Congress, big business and organized labour. At the same time, however, a surprising 15-point difference separates the levels of confidence expressed to the different pollsters (Figure 10.7), with much higher levels of confidence being reported by Gallup than by Harris/NORC.

Subtle differences in wording and response categories may account for this discrepancy. The Harris/NORC survey asks:

> I am going to name some institutions in this country. As far as the people running these institutions are concerned, would you say you have a great deal of confidence, only some confidence, or hardly any confidence at all in them?

The Gallup organization asks:

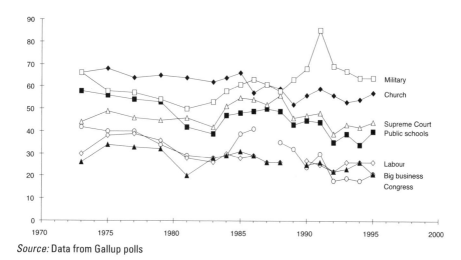

Source: Data from Gallup polls

Figure 10.6 *Percentage of respondents expressing 'a great deal' and 'quite a lot' of confidence in the seven institutions, 1973–1995*

> I am going to read you a list of institutions in American society, would you tell me how much confidence you, yourself, have in each one – a great deal, quite a lot, some, or very little?

In 1980, Civic Service Inc conducted a national survey to examine the impact of the different wording and response categories (Lipset and Schneider, 1983, pp91–96). Surprisingly, perhaps, they found that the emphasis on *leaders* in the Harris/NORC polls had little impact on the expressed levels of confidence. The major influence is the choice of response categories. Whereas the Harris/NORC polls allow only one positive response ('a great deal' of confidence) and two negative ones ('only some' and 'hardly any'), the Gallup polls allow two positive responses ('a great deal' and 'quite a lot'), one neutral response ('some'), and one negative response ('very little').

The point here is not that survey results must be viewed with great caution, but rather that the purported decline in public trust and confidence over the past two decades may not be so severe as some analysts have claimed. Whereas the Harris/NORC polls are more commonly cited to demonstrate declining levels of public trust and confidence, the Gallup polls are the preferred evidence base for those more optimistic about US politics. Indeed, we do not know, as we shall argue later, what is an 'appropriate' level of confidence. So, although the survey and poll evidence is persuasive, at least for the period between the 1950s and 1970s, as to the relative decline of social trust, it has little to say concerning different types of trust or the roots of apparent variations in levels of trust and confidence.

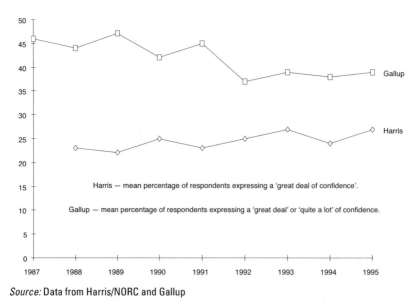

Source: Data from Harris/NORC and Gallup

Figure 10.7 *Mean percentage of respondents expressing confidence in seven institutions, Harris versus Gallup, 1987–1995*

TYPES OF TRUST: EMERGENCE AND EROSION

For all the work on social trust, our understanding of it remains limited and incomplete. Our examination of the various approaches to democratic theory has yielded only partial explanations for the creation and loss of trust. Drawing on recent experience in radioactive waste management, Slovic (1999) has observed that trust is asymmetrical – it is easy to lose and difficult to regain. As another author puts it: 'Trust takes a painfully long time to build. It can be destroyed in a heartbeat' (Carnevale, 1995, p199). Unfortunately, social and political scientists can only speculate about the steps necessary to regain social trust, and little firm empirical evidence exists to support these views.

Elsewhere we define social trust as a person's expectation that other persons and institutions in a social relationship can be relied upon to act in ways that are competent, predictable and caring (see Chapter 2). Social trust presumably is built slowly and incrementally in our socialization processes, especially when we are young, and in our day-to-day interactions with each other and the institutions around us. Since social trust is probably never completely or permanently attained or attainable, and, we will argue, probably should not be, it must be continuously maintained and reinforced through networks of civic engagement and norms of reciprocity (to use Putnam's terminology). Such networks and norms encourage the development of and bolster different types of trust, among them: *cognitive*, *emotional* and *behavioural* (see Lewis and Weigert, 1985; Koller, 1988; and Chapter 2).

Cognitive trust is based on the degree of knowledge one has about others in a relationship. We are better able to judge the trustworthiness of those we know than those we do not. Close social networks promote familiarity, either directly or vicariously, and thereby increase cognitive trust. Trusting someone we do not know requires a cognitive leap of faith. *Emotional trust* may provide a basis for this cognitive leap of faith. *Behavioural trust* is to act as if the uncertain future actions of others were certain and predictable. For example, an Amish farmer may choose to cooperate in raising a neighbour's barn with the expectation that the neighbour may one day reciprocate. This is what Putnam calls 'brave' reciprocity because it implies some level of risk (the neighbour may never reciprocate) Behavioural acts such as this within a social network tend to bolster both cognitive and emotional trust, reduce uncertainty about individuals, and provide positive models for future cooperation.

The mix of cognitive, emotional and behavioural trust may well vary according to the nature of the social relationship in question. In primary group relationships, such as between family and friends, emotional trust may be high and relatively resistant to contrary behaviour, especially since strong incentives or sanctions may effectively limit such behaviour (Lewis and Weigert, 1985, p972). By contrast, behavioural and cognitive trust may be most important in secondary group relationships (e.g. between community members and a government agency) where emotional trust is limited. Thus, Luhmann (1979) distinguishes between the *interpersonal trust* that prevails in small, relatively undifferentiated societies and the *systemic trust* that prevails in the bureaucratic institutions of modern, complex societies, a distinction relevant to the 'thick' and 'thin' trust discussed above. This differentiation is also consistent with Putnam's distinction between personal and social trust. Both authors view the shift from personal to social trust as one of the important transformations of modern times.

But perhaps the most important feature of social trust for democratic society is its multi-layered structure. Trust in the political system is onion-like, with the deepest level, the core of the onion, being trust in the basic *political community* that underlies the constitutional structure of politics and democratic institutions. Next is a layer of trust in the political regime, the norms and rules of the game that provide the context for democratic processes. Then comes trust in governmental and other *political institutions*. And finally there is the most superficial level of trust – that in the *particular representatives* of the institutions.

Among these layers, trust at the core is most essential for the continued functioning and effectiveness of democratic society. As long as high levels of trust prevail at the political community and regime levels, distrust at the institutional and representative levels, particularly if strongly anchored in the rational assessment of institutional performance, may stimulate the reforms and changes that protect more basic levels of trust. This is where much writing on the 'trust crisis' in the US and elsewhere misses the mark. As we have seen above, the survey data that are invariably cited are those depicting trust at the most superficial levels of the political system. It is informative that surveys and opinion polls soliciting attitudes toward whether there are better societies or democracies than the US, or whether the economic system should undergo major changes, invariably return very high levels of regard and support. Particularly problematic is that erroneous inferences concerning trust in the core of democratic society are made from data that pertain to the most variable and transitory levels of the political system. Thus, it is the arrangement or layering of trust and the interrelationships among these layers that deserve close attention in assessing the 'system dynamics' of trust.

Whereas Putnam attributes much of the erosion of social trust to the decline in social networks, including the influence of television on the post-war generations, major social events that shape the general social climate may also play a significant role. The high levels of social trust evident during the 1950s and 1960s may have reflected the general social optimism associated with the end of World War II and the phenomenal economic growth of the post-war period. In such a positive social and economic climate, the public may have been more inclined to invest more trust in social institutions and to have been more forgiving when this trust was abused. Such extreme optimism, on the other hand, may be the exception rather than the rule.

The debacle of the Vietnam War, the protracted period of social unrest in the 1960s and 1970s, revelations about environmental problems and scandals such as Watergate have likely sown seeds of scepticism among the American public. In this more negative social climate, people may well have been more cautious about investing trust in any social institution, and indeed this scepticism may have been self-reinforcing, since new scandals always came along to stoke the fires. In spite of the apparent lack of confidence in the major institutions in the US, Lipset and Schneider (1987, p8) argue:

> A striking characteristic of the decline of confidence is that it is almost entirely related to events beyond people's own personal experience: conflicts, scandals, protests, and failures that affect their own lives indirectly, if at all. Americans repeatedly express optimism and confidence about their own lives and their personal futures, even while decrying the terrible mess the country is in.

Hence *The Confidence Gap* is an apt title.

THE POSITIVE FUNCTIONS OF RATIONAL DISTRUST

In light of this mixture of personal and social trust, the widespread view that high levels of social trust are indispensable to democratic societies and that such trust should be maximized so that institutions work smoothly, public mandates are available to authorities, and social conflict is minimized, is somewhat surprising. Many apparently agree with Ruckelshaus (1996, p2) that we 'must generate a renaissance of trust, so that government, at all levels, is no longer *them* but *us*, as it ought to be in a democracy'.

There is another view. Social distrust may well arise from rational and realistic public assessments of government failures or breaches in fiduciary responsibility. As Breyer repeatedly emphasizes, public respect hinges on government's 'successful accomplishment of a mission that satisfies an important societal need' (Breyer, 1993, p65). Public trust in government during the conduct of the Vietnam War or confidence in the government's management of environmental protection at the nation's nuclear weapons facilities was undoubtedly misplaced, and the decline in trust over these issues helped to stimulate policy changes.

The changing structural conditions that underlie conditions of American democracy may carry even more far-reaching implications. The 20th century has witnessed a dramatic growth of power and its increasing concentration in American society. Yankelovich (1991) argues persuasively that 'culture and technical control' are undermining the ability for agreement between publics and experts on the serious problems that beset US society. He echoes noted political scholar V. O. Key in arguing that when the 'proper balance' exists between the public and the nation's elites, US democracy works beautifully. When that balance becomes badly skewed, however, the system malfunctions, and a chief symptom of imbalance is a lack of national consensus on how to cope with the most urgent problems (Yankelovich, 1991, p8). The growing dependence of policy decisions on highly specialized knowledge and technical expertise presents a major challenge to this balance.

In such a context, social distrust holds in check the growing power of economic elites and technical expertise. Distrust also generates alternative control mechanisms that enable democratic institutions to maintain social order as well as fragile political balances. In particular, social distrust encourages realistic appraisal of the operation of elites and the imperfections of democratic institutions without fostering the withdrawal of social mandates or the development of radical political movements aimed at regime-level change. Indeed, the absence of full trust in governmental institutions and representatives and the presence of distrust seem entirely consistent with the Madisonian conception of democracy, in which any one economic interest is prevented from achieving dominance through the emergence of coalitions of other interests to hold it in check and to prescribe and limit the power of centralized authority.

So the pressing need is not to maximize trust but to concoct the appropriate mixtures of trust and distrust that should prevail within the political system. Different societies and political cultures presumably will function best with different mixture systems. And the appropriateness of the social control mechanisms that arise out of distrust and how they function in the democratic system warrant greater attention. At the same time, levels of distrust cannot grow so high as to dissipate the reservoirs of social trust imperative for effective governance, thereby producing undue political transaction costs or threatening the stability of the political system, particularly at the regime or political community levels.

INSIGHTS AND PROMISING AVENUES FOR EXPLORATION

The foregoing examination of recent writings on democratic theory, supplemented by our review of survey and poll data, suggests several insights about how social trust and risk issues may interact in a setting of democratic institutions and processes. It is clear, on the other hand, that a wide gap separates formal democratic theorizing and empirical studies of the role of social trust in risk controversies.

Trust comes in different types, relates to different levels of the political system, and characterizes different relationships between people and aspects of democratic systems. These are often muddled in empirical research. In particular, social trust may relate to different levels of the political system – to institutions, the political regime, or, more basically, the political community itself. Survey results reveal that trust or confidence in the representatives of institutions is more transitory and superficial than trust in the institutions themselves. It is also apparent from studies of political culture that trust exists in some graduated or hierarchical form, with the deepest and most resilient forms associated with the more basic levels of the political system (i.e. the regime and the political community). This suggests that losses of trust in institutional representatives or even institutions may be less dire than analysts often surmise, *provided* that trust in the more foundational levels of the political system remains strong. But what are the relationships among these different trust relationships? How do losses or gains in trust at one level affect trust patterns at other levels? Obviously we need a better understanding of those linkages and inter-level effects and the dynamics that shape change and stability. But in the meantime, making inferences from particular trust patterns to the functioning of democratic societies needs to proceed with the utmost caution and restraint.

Although our understanding of how social trust emerges and is lost in different societies is incomplete, it seems clear that trust is the result of cumulative processes and protracted political socialization, attachment to culture and continuing encounters with social institutions and political authority. Some democratic theorists would also point to structure characteristics of society and economy as well as the flow of major events shaping and anchoring public perceptions and assessments. These interpretations are at odds with the oft-proclaimed objective of building trust around a particular risk management effort or a particular sector of society. Risk decisions and management processes sit in a fabric of social trust that has emerged historically and that is stitched to other parts of the social system and political culture. How changes in trust occur in the context of this 'embedding' in social and cultural fabric, how durable such changes are, and what causal factors produce the greatest departures are clearly important to understand. In the meantime, expectations of the degree to which trust 'leverage' will contribute to virtue and good decisions, such as suggested in the 'cardinal rules of risk communication' (Covello and Allen, 1988), may need tempering if not outright revision.

At least one conception of democracy regards social trust as one of the more important ingredients of social capital. Social capital refers to features of societies – such as social networks, norms and trust – that increase their productive potentials. The presence of social capital is a major asset for effective and efficient governance, for widely based civic engagement and public participation, for conflict resolution, for political stability, and ultimately for enhanced economic growth and social well-being. How trust functions as social capital and how large stocks of such social capital may enhance the functioning of democratic institutions, including how matters of risk are addressed and negotiated, rather than contribute to elitism and more authoritarian systems, needs more careful empirical investigation.

Finally, conceptual and empirical studies have yet to grapple fully with social distrust, let alone prepare frameworks that open up new questions concerning its role in social and political processes. Discussions of the need for more trust generally proceed from a set of assumptions concerning the disutility and dysfunctional effects of distrust and, not uncommonly, reflect where the author sits. Yet it seems apparent that complete trust in political institutions and authority would be highly dangerous to democratic processes. Why, then, should we assume that greater levels of trust are necessarily advantageous to democratic societies? Indeed, the architecture of US constitutional authority reflects a high degree of distrust of any concentrations of elite power and political dominance. Greater attention, in our view, should centre on the positive functions of distrust rooted in rational assessments and on the mix of trust and distrust that serves different political systems and cultures.

11 The Social Amplification of Risk: Assessing 15 Years of Research and Theory

*Jeanne X. Kasperson, Roger E. Kasperson,
Nick Pidgeon and Paul Slovic*

THE SOCIAL AMPLIFICATION OF RISK FRAMEWORK IN BRIEF

More than 15 years has elapsed since the introduction in 1988 of the social amplification of risk framework (SARF) by researchers from Clark University (Kasperson, Renn, Slovic and colleagues) and Decision Research (Slovic and colleagues). During that time, various researchers have enlisted the framework to complete a substantial number of empirical studies. All the while, the emergence of a much larger body of relevant knowledge has spawned a lively debate on aspects of the framework. In this chapter, we consider these developments, inquiring into refinements, critiques and extensions of the approach, the emergence of new issues, and the findings and hypothesis growing out of 15 years of empirical research.

The theoretical foundations of SARF are developed in five principal publications (Burns et al, 1993; Kasperson, 1992; Kasperson and Kasperson, 1996; Kasperson et al, 1988e; Renn, 1991), several of which (Chapters 6–9 in this volume, and Chapter 13 in Volume II) we have included in this work. The idea arose out of an attempt to overcome the fragmented nature of risk perception and risk communication research by developing an integrative theoretical framework capable of accounting for findings from a wide range of studies, including: from media research; from the psychometric and cultural schools of risk perception research; and from studies of organizational responses to risk. The framework also serves, more narrowly, to describe the various *dynamic* social processes underlying risk perception and response. In particular, those processes by which certain hazards and events that experts assess as relatively low in risk can

Note: Reprinted from *The Social Amplification of Risk*, Pidgeon, N., Kasperson, R. E. and Slovic, P. (eds), 'The social amplification of risk: Assessing 15 years of research and theory', Kasperson, J. X., Kasperson, R. E., Pidgeon, N. and Slovic, P., © (2003), with permission from Cambridge University Press

become a particular focus of concern and sociopolitical activity within a society (risk amplification), while other hazards that experts judge to be more serious receive comparatively less attention from society (risk attenuation). Examples of significant hazards subject to social attenuation of risk perceptions might include naturally occurring radon gas, automobile accidents or smoking. On the other hand, social amplification of risk perceptions appears to have been one result of events such as the King's Cross and Lockerbie tragedies in the UK, the Bhopal (Wilkins, 1987), Chernobyl (Otway et al, 1988), and Three Mile Island accidents, as well as the recent concerns precipitated by 'mad cow' disease (Phillips et al, 2000) and by the future of genetically modified food in Europe (Anand, 1997; Marris et al, 2001).

The theoretical starting point is the assumption that 'risk events', which might include actual or hypothesized accidents and incidents (or even new reports on existing risks), will be largely irrelevant or localized in their impact unless human beings observe and communicate them to others (Luhmann, 1979). SARF holds that, as a key part of that communication process, risk, risk events and the characteristics of both become portrayed through various risk signals (images, signs and symbols), which in turn interact with a wide range of psychological, social, institutional or cultural processes in ways that intensify or attenuate perceptions of risk and its manageability (see the figures in Chapters 9 of this volume and Chapter 5 of Volume II). The experience of risk, therefore, is not only an experience of *physical* harm but the result of processes by which groups and individuals learn to acquire or create *interpretations of risk*. These interpretations provide rules of how to select, order and explain signals emanating from the physical world (Renn et al, 1992, p140). With this framework, risk experience can be properly assessed only through the interaction among the physical harms attached to a risk event and the social and cultural processes that shape interpretations of that event, secondary and tertiary consequences that emerge, and the actions taken by managers and publics.

The authors adopt the metaphor of amplification from classical communications theory and use it to analyse the ways in which various social agents generate, receive, interpret and pass on risk signals. Kasperson et al (1988e) argue that such signals are subject to predictable transformations as they filter through various social and individual *amplification stations*. Such transformations can increase or decrease the volume of information about an event, heighten the salience of certain aspects of a message, or reinterpret and elaborate the available symbols and images, thereby leading to particular interpretations and responses by other participants in the social system. Amplification stations can include individuals, social groups, and institutions, for example, scientists or scientific institutions, reporters and the mass media, politicians and government agencies, or other social groups and their members.

For *social stations of amplification*, the likes of institutional structure, functions and culture influence the amplification or attenuation of risk signals. Even the individuals in institutions do not simply pursue their personal values and social interpretations; they also perceive the risks, those who manage the risks, and the risk 'problem' according to cultural biases and the values of their organization or group (Johnson and Covello, 1987; Dake, 1991; Rayner, 1992; Peters and Slovic, 1996; Marris et al, 1998).

Individual stations of amplification are affected by such considerations, well documented in the psychometric tradition, as risk heuristics, qualitative aspects of the risks, prior attitudes, blame and trust. These same individuals are also members of cultural groups (e.g. Vaughan, 1995; Palmer et al, 2001) and other social units that codetermine the dynamics and social processing of risk.

In a second stage of the framework, directed primarily at risk intensification processes, Kasperson et al (1988e) argue that social amplification can also account for the observation that some events will produce 'ripples' of secondary and tertiary consequences that may spread far beyond the initial impact of the event and may even eventually impinge upon previously unrelated technologies or institutions. Such secondary impacts include market impacts (perhaps through consumer avoidance of a product or related products), demands for regulatory constraints, litigation, community opposition, loss of credibility and trust, stigmatization of a product, facility, or community and investor flight. The terrorist attacks of 11 September 2001 in the US and their ensuing consequences (spanning a range of behavioural, economic and social impacts) provide perhaps the most dramatic recent example of such secondary social amplification effects (Slovic, 2002).

The analogy of dropping a stone into a pond is apt here, as it illustrates the spread of these higher-order impacts associated with the social amplification of risk. The ripples spread outward, first encompassing the directly affected victims, or the first group to be notified, then touching the next higher institutional level (a company or an agency), and, in more extreme cases, reaching other parts of the industry or other social arenas with similar problems. This rippling of impacts is an important element of risk amplification, since it suggests that the processes can extend (in risk amplification) or constrain (in risk attenuation) the temporal, sectoral and geographical scales of impacts. It also points up that each order of impact, or ripple, may not only allocate social and political effects but may also trigger (in risk amplification) or hinder (in risk attenuation) managerial interventions for risk reduction.

THE RECORD OF EMPIRICAL RESEARCH

Since SARF is by design inclusive and integrative, the literature of relevant empirical work accomplished over the past 15 years is potentially very large indeed. We begin by addressing the studies that apply the general

Table 11.1 *Risk events with potentially high signal value*

Events	Messages
Report that chlorofluorocarbon releases are depleting the ozone layer	A new and possibly catastrophic risk has emerged
Resignation of regulators or corporate officials in 'conscience'	The managers are concealing the risks: they cannot be trusted
News report of off-site migration at a hazardous waste site	The risk managers are not in control of the hazard
Scientific dispute over the validity of an epidemiological study	The experts do not understand the risks
Statement by regulators that the levels of a particular contaminant in the water supply involve only very low risks as compared with other risks	The managers do not care about the people who will be harmed; they do not understand long-term cumulative effects of chemicals

Source: Kasperson et al, 1988e, p186

framework or core ideas and then proceed to more specialized applications and extensions of the framework.

The concept of 'signal'

Slovic et al (1984; also Slovic 1987b, 1992) first proposed that hazardous events might hold a 'signal value'. They reported that risks in the upper right-hand sector of the classic dread/knowledge psychometric factor space have high signal value in terms of serving as a warning signal for society, providing new information about the probability that similar or even more destructive mishaps might occur with this type of activity. They also suggest that high signal value might be linked to the potential for second-order effects, and hence may provide a rationale in specific cases for stricter regulation of such risks. Risk events, it is clear, can have high signal value (see Table 11.1).

Building upon Slovic's work on risk signals, the research group at Clark University has developed a detailed methodology for identifying, classifying and assessing risk signals in the print media pertaining to the proposed nuclear waste repository at Yucca Mountain in the US, as described at length in Chapter 8. Risk signals were defined as 'messages about a hazard or hazard event that affect people's perceptions about the seriousness or manageability of the risk'. They analysed the 'signal stream' as it appeared in the *Las Vegas Review-Journal* between 1985 and 1989, including the symbols, metaphors and images in news headlines, editorials, letters to the editor and cartoons. The results reveal a dramatic shift in the discourse, symbols and imagery, in which risk-related matters recede in importance in the face of a growing depiction of victimization, distrust, unfairness and villainy.

In an individual difference analysis based upon the psychometric work of Slovic and colleagues, Trumbo (1996) uses people's judgements along the dread/knowledge dimensions to categorize individuals into risk 'amplifiers' and 'attenuators'. He concludes that perceived individual risk (for amplifiers) and satisfaction in institutional response (for attenuators) are the important differences between the two groups in their interpretation of risk signals (see also Vlek and Stallen, 1981). Interestingly, he also finds that, among amplifiers, concern over risk is driven more by interpersonal communication than by mediated communication (as in the mass media).

The 128 hazard event study

This collaborative study between Clark University and Decision Research involved a large comparative statistical analysis of 128 hazard events, including biocidal hazards, persistent/delayed hazards, rare catastrophes, deaths from common causes, global diffuse hazards and natural hazard events that had occurred in the US. Researchers used the news file of the Nexis database to collect data on the actual volume of media coverage that each event received and then related the data to judgements made by experts and student panels of the physical consequences, risk perceptions, public response, potential for social group mobilization and the potential for second-order societal impacts of each event. Findings indicated particularly that social amplification processes are as important as direct physical consequences in determining the full array of potential risk consequences. Hence, a risk assessment that is based solely upon direct physical consequences might seriously underestimate the full range of consequences of an event. Among the conclusions from this work (see Chapter 2 and Renn et al, 1992) are the following:

- A high degree of 'rationality' is evident in how society responds to hazards (e.g. the volume of press coverage is roughly proportional to first-order physical consequences; risk perceptions incorporate aspects of human exposure and management performance).
- The extent of exposure to the direct consequences of a hazard has more effect on risk perceptions and potential social group mobilization than do injuries and fatalities.
- The contention that public perception mirrors media coverage needs further careful empirical study (no perceptual variable – except the ubiquitous dread – correlated with the extent of media coverage once the extent of damage was controlled for).
- The role of risk signals and blame attributable to incompetent risk management seemed particularly important to public concerns (see also Burns et al, 1993). Situations involving the blaming of corporations or government agencies after the event appear particularly worthy of further study.

Two limitations of this quantitative study bear noting. The outcome variable for the magnitude of secondary consequences was a judgement by experts rather than a direct measure of actual societal impact. Hence, the analysis neither demonstrates, nor concludes, that heightened perceptions as a result of media coverage will *necessarily* lead to secondary impacts and rippling, a point to which we return below. Secondly, the indices of media coverage used were primarily quantitative (volume) rather than qualitative (the content of what is presented in media reports), so did not allow a test of whether the media significantly alter risk representations (a question taken up by Freudenburg et al, 1996).

Qualitative field studies

The qualitative study by Kasperson and colleagues (reported in Kasperson, 1992) yielded complementary findings to the quantitative cross-risk work. Six risk events (four in the US, one in Brazil, and one in Germany) – all but one involving some form of nuclear hazard – were studied in depth. The cases were: a transportation accident involving low-level radioactive material in Queens, New York; a serious 1982 nuclear plant accident in Ginna, New York; a brine seepage controversy at a planned nuclear waste facility in Carlsbad, New Mexico; the closure of a hazardous waste site on Long Island (Glen Cove, New York); a construction accident at a planned nuclear waste disposal facility in Gorleben, Germany; and a radioactive accident in Goiânia, Brazil (Petterson, 1988). Components of the amplification framework explored included physical impacts, information flow, social-group mobilization and rippling effects. Interviews with key participants were conducted in each case. This set of in-depth case studies yielded the following conclusions:

- Even heavy and sustained media coverage does not by itself ensure risk amplification or significant secondary effects. In some cases, the secondary effects expected by the researchers failed to materialize. Trust (see also Chapter 2 and Slovic, 1993) appears to be a relevant critical issue, as are perceptions of the managerial handling of the accident and emergency response.
- The cases pointed to layering of attenuation/intensification effects across different groups and at different scales. Specifically, amplification at the national or regional scale accompanied by attenuation at the local scale may not be uncommon.
- Following on from the first point, it may be that several factors need to be present in combination (e.g. media coverage plus the focused attention of a local interest group, or an accident plus suspicions of incompetence) to generate what Kasperson (1992) terms the 'take-off' (see also Gerlach, 1987; Cvetkovich and Earle, 1991) of an issue. Other examples of this can be found. Referring to the 1911 Triangle Shirtwaist Company fire in New York, Behrens (1983, p373) concluded

that 'a disaster only prepares the groundwork for change... The potential for reform created by a disaster can be fulfilled only if the appropriate interest groups recognize and successfully use the opportunities available to them.' With respect to nuclear power, Slovic et al (2000) found much higher levels of trust in experts, government and science to manage the risks in France (where until quite recently this technology has not been a source of significant social conflict) as compared with the US.

- The economic benefits associated with risks appear to be a significant source of attenuation at the local level (see also Metz, 1996). As a result of both these quantitative and qualitative studies, further research might usefully focus upon the following: case studies giving insight into full social context; cultural studies (particularly those exploring the cultural prototypes drawn upon to interpret risk communications); and investigations of how different communities experience similar risks.

Desired risk

Arguing that studies of hazards and risks have virtually overlooked a range of human activity (e.g. hang-gliding, rock-climbing, dirt-biking, etc) involving the deliberate seeking of risk, Machlis and Rosa (1990) have explored whether SARF can be extended to this domain of risk (also Rosa, 1998). Evaluating key propositions and current knowledge about desired risks, the authors reach several conclusions. First, they find the social amplification concept quite suitable for incorporating desired risk, although some terminology (e.g. 'victims') may need to be recast. Secondly, the key variables defined in the framework are appropriate but may need to be broadened to treat such issues as benefits as part of consequences and mass culture (as subsequently incorporated in the framework). Thirdly, individual processing of risk can lead to increased risk taking, an outcome not addressed in the early conceptual statements or empirical studies. Generally, their application of the social amplification conception led the authors to conclude that 'the framework has promise, since it generally performed well against the evidence examined' (Machlis and Rosa, 1990, p167).

Communications and the mass media

In one of the earliest studies of mass media coverage of risks and public perceptions, Combs and Slovic (1978) analysed two US newspapers for their reporting of various causes of death. They found that homicides, accidents and some natural disasters systematically received heavy coverage, whereas death from diseases received only light treatment. Whereas the authors noted that these patterns of coverage correlated with lay public judgements of the frequency of these causes of death, they also pointed out that substantial further research would be needed to define the relationships between mass media coverage and the formation of opinion concerning risk.

Subsequent research suggests how complicated these relations are. Allan Mazur (1984) has examined media coverage of Love Canal and the Three Mile Island accidents and argues that the massive quantity of media coverage, independent of the specific content, influenced public perceptions of the seriousness of the events and the political agenda of social groups and institutions. In a subsequent examination of mass media coverage of nuclear power and chemical hazards, Mazur (1990, p295) found evidence that 'extensive reporting of a controversial technological or environmental project not only arouses public attention, but also pushes it toward opposition'. This may occur, Mazur argues, even when the treatment in the news is balanced. He proposes a theory with four interrelated propositions: (1) a few national news organizations are very influential in selecting which hazards receive most attention each year; (2) public actions to alleviate a hazard or oppose a particular technology rise and fall with the amount of media reporting; (3) public concerns over a risk or technology rise as press and television coverage increases; and (4) it is important to distinguish between the substantive content of a news story about risk and the simple image that the story conveys.

Not all agree. Renn (1991) argues that the pure volume effect is only one of many influences of the media on public perceptions of risk. Filtering effects, deleting and adding information, mixing effects (changing the order of information in messages), equalizing effects (changing the context), and what he calls 'stereo effects' (multi-channel effects) can all be important. Some analyses (e.g. Singer and Endreny, 1993, p163) argue that the media report on risk events and not risk issues, and on harms rather than risks. Others see the media, whether providing warning or reassuring messages, as extensively framing discourse and perceptions in which the social processing of risk occurs (Wilkins, 1987; Wilkins and Patterson, 1991; Bohölm 1998). Lichtenberg and MacLean (1991) have pointed out that cross-cultural media research is difficult to conduct because the news media are so diverse and are influenced by the political cultures in which they operate.

Using the 128 hazard events from the Clark University–Decision Research study, Freudenburg et al (1996) examined the amount of media coverage, public demand for further information, estimates of damage, dread, 'outrage' and anger, and recreancy (the misuse of authority or failure to merit public trust). As part of their analysis, the researchers read not only the Nexis abstracts but the entire original articles, complete with headlines and accompanying photography and artwork. The authors conclude, despite common beliefs to the contrary, that media coverage overall did not exaggerate risks or display an 'anti-technology' bias. Indeed, among the factors examined, only those involving the 'objective' severity of the event showed any significant predictive power for the amount of coverage devoted to risk events (Freudenburg et al, 1996, p40). Indeed, if anything, the general pattern was for full news articles to de-emphasize the severity of the risks and to provide reassurance. On the other hand, an analysis of television coverage of environmental biotechnology revealed a tendency to focus on extremes, and unknown risks, and to be superficial and incomplete (McCabe and Fitzgerald, 1991).

Although the dramatization of risks and risk events in the media has received much attention, the circularity and tight interrelations between the media and other components of social amplification processes (e.g. contextual effects, historical settings, interest group activity, public beliefs) render it difficult to determine the specific effects of the volume and content of media coverage. There can be no doubt that the mass media are an important element in communication systems, the processing of risk in amplification stations, and, as Vaughan and Seifert (1992) have persuasively argued, how risk problems are framed and socially constructed. And Renn's (1991) recommended attention to coding, decoding, filtering and stereo processes remains a highly promising avenue of research. From a social amplification perspective, other interesting questions centre upon how the mass media interact with other elements of social amplification processes to construct, intensify, dampen and modify signals concerning risk and its manageability. In addition to analyses aimed at the discerning of media-specific influence components of amplification, the search for patterns, syndromes, or dynamics of interrelationship and the conditions under which they take particular forms is a promising avenue of amplification research.

Hidden hazards

Risk events, when they undergo substantial amplification and result in unexpected public alarms or what some would call 'social shocks' (Lawless, 1977), often surprise managers and others. No less remarkable is the extreme attenuation of certain risk events so that, despite serious consequences for the risk bearers and society more generally, they pass virtually unnoticed and untended, often continuing to grow in effects until reaching disaster proportions. In Chapter 7, we described such highly attenuated risks as 'hidden hazards' and offer a theoretical explanation for their existence. Hidden hazards, in our view, have to do with both the nature of the hazards themselves and the nature of the societies and cultures in which they occur. The 'hiding' of hazards is at once purposeful and unintentional, life threatening and institution sustaining, systematic and incidental.

We described in Chapter 7, five aspects of such hazards that drive attenuation, each associated with differing causal agents and processes. *Global elusive hazards* involve a series of complex problems (regional interactions, slow accumulation, lengthy time lags, diffuse effects). Their incidence in a politically fragmented and unequal world tends to mute their signal power in many societies. *Ideological hazards* remain hidden principally because they lie embedded in a societal web of values and assumptions that attenuates consequences, elevates associated benefits, or idealizes certain beliefs. *Marginal hazards* befall people who occupy the edges of cultures, societies or economies where they are exposed to hazards that are remote from or concealed by those at the centre or in the mainstream. Many in such marginal situations are already weakened or highly vulnerable while they enjoy limited access to entitlements and few alternative means of coping. *Amplification-driven hazards* have effects that elude conventional types of risk assessment and environmental impact analysis and are often, therefore, allowed to grow in their secondary consequences before societal intervention occurs. And, finally, *value-threatening hazards* alter human institutions, lifestyles and basic values, but because the pace of technological change so outstrips the capacity of social institutions to respond and adapt, disharmony in purpose, political will and directed effort impede effective responses and the hazards grow. The presence of some of these 'hidden hazards' has been documented in subsequent analyses of environmental degradation and delayed societal responses in nine regions around the world (as treated in Chapter 11, Volume II).

Organizational amplification and attenuation

As yet, limited attention has addressed the role of organizations and institutions in the social processing of risk. Pidgeon (1997) has suggested that linking risk amplification to the considerable empirical base of knowledge concerning organizational processes intended to prevent large-scale failures and disasters would be an important extension of the framework. Most contemporary risks originate in sociotechnical systems (see Turner, 1978; Perrow, 1984; Short, 1992) rather than natural phenomena, so that risk management and internal regulatory processes governing the behaviour of institutions in identifying, diagnosing, prioritizing and responding to risks are key parts of the broader amplification process. As Short (1992) points out, large organizations increasingly set the context and terms of debate for society's consideration of risk. Understanding amplification dynamics, then, requires insight into how risk-related decisions relate to organizational self-interest, messy inter- and intra-organizational relationships, economically related rationalizations, and 'rule of thumb' considerations that often conflict with the view of risk analysis as a scientific enterprise (Short, 1992, p8). Since major accidents are often preceded by smaller incidents and risk warnings, how signals of incubating hazards are processed within institutions and communicated to others outside the institution do much to structure society's experience with technological and industrial risks.

Noting the relative void of work on organizational risk processing, Freudenburg (1992) has examined characteristics of organizations that serve to attenuate risk signals and ultimately to increase the risks posed by technological systems. These include such attributes as the lack of organizational commitment to the risk management function, the bureaucratic attenuation of information flow within the organization (and particularly on a 'bad news' context), specialized divisions of labour that create 'corporate gaps' in responsibility, amplified risk taking by workers, the atrophy of organizational vigilance to risk as a result of a myriad of factors (e.g. boredom, routinization), and imbalances and mismatches in institutional resources. Freudenburg concludes that these factors often work in concert to lead even well-meaning and honest scientists and managers to underestimate risks. In turn, such organizational attenuation of risk serves systematically and repeatedly to amplify the health and environmental risks that the organization is entrusted to anticipate and to control.

Other studies of organizational handling of risk confirm Freudenburg's analysis and provide further considerations. In an analysis of safety management at Volvo, Svenson (1988a) found that patterns of access by various parties to reliable information about hazards, understanding of the relation between changes in the product and changes in safety levels, attributes of the information network that informs various interested parties about changes in safety (either positive or negative), and the presence of organizational structures for negotiating about risk between the producer and other social institutions were all important. In her analysis of the *Challenger* accident in the US, Diane Vaughan (1992, 1996) also found communication and information issues to be critical, but argued that structural factors, such as pressures from a competitive environment, resource scarcity in the organization, vulnerability of important subunits, and characteristics of the internal safety regulation system were equally important. In counterpoint to these assessments, the well-known DuPont safety culture has sought to identify characteristics that *amplify* even minor risks at the corporation so as to achieve high attentiveness to risk reduction throughout the organization (as we discuss in Chapter 7, Volume II). La Porte and colleagues have examined similar amplification mechanisms in high-reliability organizations that drive performance to error minimization (Weick 1987; Roberts 1989; La Porte 1996), as have Pidgeon and O'Leary (1994, 2000) in their analysis of safety cultures and the use of incident reporting in aviation contexts.

Several theoretical perspectives on the organizational processing of risk can be drawn upon within the amplification/attenuation framework. When considering individual responses to hazards within organizations, the idea of psychological denial of threatening information has had a particularly long history (see, for example, Leventhal, 1970). Perhaps surprisingly, however, this topic has only rarely been investigated in contemporary psychological risk research, where the current 'cold' cognitive paradigm for understanding responses to hazard and environmental threat, based upon the two traditions of cognitive psychology and decision-making research, has long undervalued the role of 'hot' motivational variables upon behaviour and choice. Notable exceptions are the studies by Janis and Mann (1977) on decision making under stress, the related threat coping model of Stallen and Tomas (1988), and the treatment of worry by MacGregor (1991). More recent work has now begun to explore the relationship between affective variables and risk perceptions (Finucane et al, 2000; Langford, 2002; Slovic et al, 2002).

Evidence of a range of broad social and organizational preconditions to large-scale accidents is available in the work of Turner (1978; see also Turner and Pidgeon, 1997). As a result of a detailed analysis of 84 major accidents in the UK, Turner concluded that such events rarely come about for any single reason. Rather, it is typical to find that a number of undesirable events accumulate, unnoticed or not fully understood, often over a considerable number of years, which he defines as the *disaster incubation period*. Preventive action to remove one or more of the dangerous conditions or a *trigger event*, which might be a final critical error or a slightly abnormal operating condition, brings this period to an end. Turner focuses in particular upon the information difficulties, which are typically associated with the attempts of individuals and organizations to deal with uncertain and ill-structured safety problems, during the hazard incubation period.

Finally, in a series of persuasive case studies of foreign and domestic policy decisions, Janis (1982) describes the small group syndrome of *groupthink*, marked primarily by a strong concurrence-seeking tendency in highly cohesive policy-making groups. Particular symptoms of groupthink include an overestimation by members of the group's inherent morality as well as of its power to influence events, a collective closed-mindedness (or mindset) to new information, and pressures within the group towards conformity to the majority view. Janis argues that the groupthink syndrome is responsible for a range of observable decision-making defects, including incomplete searches for new information, biased appraisal of available information, and a failure to work out contingency plans to cope with uncertainties.

Despite these valuable explorations, our knowledge of risk amplification and attenuation in different types of institutions remains thin and eclectic. Systematic application of the amplification framework in a comparative study of organizations, issues and institutions (see for example the work comparing regulation of radon, chemicals, and BSE by Rothstein, 2003) might well yield highly useful results, particularly demonstrating how signals are denied, de-emphasized or misinterpreted.

Imagery and stigma

The 1988 article that set forth SARF identified stigmatization as one of four major response mechanisms of amplification processes. Research on

risk stigmatization was only beginning at that time, both in the path-
breaking work of Edelstein (1987) and as part of the Decision Research
studies on public perceptions of the proposed Yucca Mountain nuclear
waste repository (Flynn et al, 1998; Slovic et al, 1994; Slovic et al, 1991a;
Slovic et al, 1991c). Subsequent work has underscored the importance of
stigmatization as a principal route by which risk amplification can generate
ripples and secondary consequences (Flynn et al, 2001).

It is clear from this work that stigma-induced effects associated with
risky technologies, products or places may be substantial. Nuclear energy,
for example, once so highly regarded for its promise of cheap, safe power,
is today subject to severe stigmatization, reflecting public perceptions of
abnormally great risk, distrust of management and the disappointment of
failed promises. Certain products of biotechnology also have been rejected
in part because of perceptions of risk. Milk produced with the aid of bovine
growth hormone (BGH, or bovine somatotrophin, BST) is one example,
with many supermarket chains refusing to buy milk products from BGH-
treated cows. Startling evidence of stigmatization of one of the modern
world's most important classes of technology comes from studies by Slovic
and others. Asking people to indicate what comes to mind when they hear
or read the word 'chemicals', researchers find that the most frequent
response tends to be 'dangerous' or some closely related term such as
'toxic', 'hazardous', 'poison', or 'deadly' (see Chapters 14 and 15).

The ancient Greeks used the word 'stigma' to refer to a mark placed
on an individual to signify infamy or disgrace. A person thus marked was
perceived to pose a risk to society. An extensive literature, much
stimulated by the seminal work of Goffman (1963), exists on the topic of
stigma as it applies to people. By means of its association with risk, the
concept of stigma has recently been generalized to technologies, places
and products that are perceived to be unduly dangerous.

Stigmatized places, products and technologies tend to share several
features (Gregory et al, 1995, p221). The source of the stigma is a hazard
with characteristics, such as dread consequences and involuntary exposure,
that typically contributes to high public perceptions of risk. Its impacts
are often perceived to be inequitably distributed across groups (for
example, children and pregnant women are affected disproportionately) or
geographical areas (one city bears the risks of hazardous waste storage for
an entire state). Often the impacts are unbounded, in the sense that their
magnitude or persistence over time is not well known. A critical aspect of
stigma is that a standard of what is right and natural has been violated or
overturned because of the abnormal nature of the precipitating event
(crude oil on pristine beaches and the destruction of valued wildlife) or
the discrediting nature of the consequences (innocent people are injured
or killed). As a result, management of the hazard is brought into question
as concerns surface regarding competence, conflicts of interest or a failure
to apply needed safeguards and controls. Stigmatization of places has

resulted from the extensive media coverage of contamination at sites such as Times Beach, Missouri, and Love Canal, New York. Other well-known examples of environmental stigmatization include Seveso, Italy, where dioxin contamination following an industrial accident at a chemical plant resulted in local economic disruptions estimated to be in excess of US$100 million, and portions of the French Riviera and Alaskan coastline in the aftermath of the *Amoco Cadiz* and *Exxon Valdez* oil spills.

Stigmatization of products can also occur and result in severe losses. A dramatic example is that of the pain reliever Tylenol, where, despite quick action on the part of the manufacturer, Johnson and Johnson, seven tampering-induced poisonings that occurred in 1982 cost the company more than US$1.4 billion. Another well-known case of product stigmatization occurred in the Spring of 1989, when millions of US consumers stopped buying apples and apple products because of their fears that the chemical Alar (used then as a growth regulator by apple growers) could cause cancer. Apple farmers saw wholesale prices drop by about one-third and annual revenues decline by more than US$100 million. More recently, the BSE (bovine spongiform encephalopathy) affair stigmatized the European beef industry resulting in billions of dollars in losses and a crisis in trust and confidence in risk management in the UK (Phillips et al, 2000), while the perceptions of the Spring 2001 foot and mouth epidemic in the UK led to large losses to the rural economy as people cancelled trips to the UK countryside and Britain (see Harvey, 2001).

In Chapter 9, we extend the social amplification model, to enhance its applicability to analysing stigmatization processes. In this adaptation, the early part of the amplification framework remains the same, with risk events generating information flow and social communication treating the risk. Not only do public perceptions and imagery emerge or become modified, but the associated technologies, products, or places become *marked*. Marking involves the selection of a particular attribute of a place or technology and focuses on some symbol or physical representation of the place. In Hawthorne's *The Scarlet Letter*, it was the letter A; in Nazi Germany, it was the yellow star. At Richland, the host community of the Hanford Reservation in the US, it is the mushroom cloud insignia worn on school sport uniforms. Research by Mitchell et al (1988) has provided extensive evidence of such marking, imagery and stigmatization. Labelling, such as the use of the term 'dump site', is an essential part of such marking. Eventually, amplification dynamics and imagery formation can fundamentally alter the *identity* of the place or technology, so that it is viewed as tainted and discredited by residents of the place, workers in the technology and by outsiders. And, as a result, stigma-induced ripple effects and secondary consequences follow.

Extending the current knowledge base of risk-induced stigma and their effects is, in our opinion, a high-priority area for research on social amplification. Such stigma effects currently raise the spectre of gridlock for important avenues of technology development and for public policy initiatives. Can we anticipate which new technologies may become stigmatized through amplification processes? Can, and should, stigma effects be counteracted? How can responsible authorities act to ameliorate stigma-induced gridlock and the associated fallout on trust and confidence? What are the broad implications for risk management and risk communication?

Trust and confidence

The original framework article (Kasperson et al, 1988e) hypothesized four major pathways or mechanisms – heuristics and values, social group relationships, signal value and stigmatization – in the second stage of amplification. High or growing social distrust of responsible institutions and their managers is certainly a fifth. A broad literature now indicates that recurrent failures in risk management stem in no small part from a failure to recognize the more general requirements of democratic society, and especially the need for *social trust* (see for example, contributions to Cvetkovich and Löfstedt, 1999). Accordingly, risk control efforts have frequently gone awry due to a lack of openness and 'transparency', a failure to consult or involve so-called 'interested' and 'affected' persons, a loss of social trust in managers, inadequacies in due process, a lack of responsiveness to public concerns, or an insensitivity to questions of environmental justice. Such interpretations abound across a wide spectrum of environmental and risk debates: global warming, biodiversity, genetic engineering, clean-up of defence and other hazardous wastes, the siting of hazardous waste facilities and the protection of wetlands. As Ruckelshaus warned:

> Mistrust engenders a vicious descending spiral. The more mistrust by the public, the less effective government becomes at delivering what people want and need; the more government bureaucrats in turn respond with enmity towards the citizens they serve, the more ineffective government becomes, the more people mistrust it, and so on, down and down (Ruckelshaus, 1996, p2).

Ruckelshaus's dread spiral is reminiscent of US Supreme Court Justice Stephen Breyer's tripartite 'vicious circle – public perception, Congressional reaction, and the uncertainties of the regulatory process' (Breyer, 1993, p50) – that thwarts effective risk management.

Slovic (1993, 2000) has argued that trust emerges slowly, is fragile, and is easily destroyed. And once lost, it may prove to be extremely difficult to recover. He posits an 'asymmetry principle' to explain why it is easier to destroy than to create trust: negative (trust-destroying) events are more visible or noticeable than positive (trust-building) events (see Chapter

15). Negative events often take the form of specific, well-defined incidents such as accidents, lies, discoveries of errors or other mismanagement. Positive events, although sometimes visible, are often fuzzy or indistinct. Events that are invisible or poorly defined carry little weight in shaping our attitudes and opinions. And even when events do come to our attention, negative (trust-destroying) events carry much greater weight than positive events (see Cvetkovich et al, 2002; also Slovic, 1993).

Trust is typically discussed in terms of an implicit relationship between two or more parties. It has long been discussed as a facet of political culture that facilitates the working of the political system (Almond and Verba, 1980; Inglehart, 1988), and more recently as an important dimension of social capital (Coleman, 1990, pp300–321; Putnam, 1993, 1995b). It also functions to reduce complexity in our social environment (Barber, 1984), hence making life more predictable. Renn and Levine (1991) list five attributes of trust:

1   *competence* (do you have the appropriate technical expertise?)
2   *objectivity* (are your messages free from bias?)
3   *fairness* (are all points of view acknowledged?)
4   *consistency* (of your statements and behaviour over time?)
5   *faith* (a perception of your good will?)

They argue that trust underlies confidence, and, where this is shared across a community, one has credibility. A somewhat different view of social trust is provided by Earle and Cvetkovich (1995; also Siegrist and Cvetkovich 2000; Siegrist et al, 2000), who argue that it is similarity in our basic values, rather than attributes of technical competence, that underlies whom we trust or distrust. Hunt et al (1999) have recently shown that both perceived 'truthfulness' and 'expertise' are important but perhaps superficial factors as well. One public policy implication of the trust research is that we need to frame the principal goals of risk communication around building trust through participation (Royal Society, 1992; Stern and Fineberg, 1996; UK Interdepartmental Liaison Group on Risk Assessment, 1998b). The candid communication by an agency of risk uncertainties to people, however, can signal honesty for some while invoking greater distrust in others. Moreover, given that conflict is endemic to many risk controversies, effective risk communication may follow only if a resolution of conflict is obtained first, perhaps by searching for decision options that address all of the stakeholder's principal values and concerns (Edwards and von Winterfeldt 1987; Renn et al, 1995; Arvai et al, 2001), or by identifying superordinate goals to which all parties can agree. Despite these difficulties, broad 'stakeholder' participation is also increasingly seen, often alas uncritically, as essential to the wider processes of risk assessment and management and a route to success (see, in particular, Stern and Fineberg, 1996).

Issues of social trust are clearly important components of the dynamics of social amplification. We know that distrust acts to heighten risk perceptions, to intensify public reactions to risk signals, to contribute to the perceived unacceptability of risk, and to stimulate political activism to reduce risk (Jenkins-Smith, 1991; English, 1992; Flynn et al, 1993; Löfstedt and Horlick-Jones, 1999, and Chapter 2 of this volume). But a host of questions surrounds the interpretation of trust and its effects: there are many types of trust, the processes that create and destroy trust are not well understood, trust (or distrust) exists at multiple levels of the political system, complex attribution issues prevail, and policy responses and their effectiveness are opaque (see Cvetkovich and Löfstedt, 1999). From a social amplification perspective, trust is highly interrelated with other components and mechanisms in what we think of as 'amplification dynamics'. Understanding how trust is shaped, altered, lost or rebuilt in the processing of risk by social and individual stations of risk is a priority need in social amplification research.

Ripple effects

Since the 1988 framework article, the systematic, cross-hazard study of ripple effects and secondary/tertiary consequences has also been a priority research need. It has yet to occur. The 128 hazard event study did elicit expert estimates, informed by documentary evidence, of event consequences. The results were highly suggestive. The societal processing of risk by media, social groups, institutions and individuals played a critical role in the overall magnitude and scope of societal impacts. For risk events that were highly amplified, the amplification-driven impacts frequently exceeded the primary (i.e. health, environmental and direct economic) effects. We also know that ripple effects can be charted and measured along temporal, geographical and sectoral dimensions. Such a broad-based and systematic empirical study could provide invaluable new information for understanding how social amplification processes affect the rippling of effects, the durability of such effects, possible contagion effects on other risks, and overall impacts of rippling upon social capital, such as trust.

What we now have is some suggestive cases. In Goiânia in Brazil, a strongly amplified radiological accident produced dramatic rippling of secondary risk consequences. As reported elsewhere (Petterson, 1988), within the first weeks of the media coverage, more than 100,000 persons, of their own volition, stood in line to be monitored with Geiger counters for indication of external radiation. Within two weeks of the event, the wholesale value of agricultural production within Goiâs, the Brazilian state in which Goiânia is located, had fallen by 50 per cent, owing to consumer concerns over possible contamination, even though no contamination was ever found in the products. Even eight months after the event, when prices had rebounded by about 90 per cent, a significant adverse impact was still apparent. During the three months following the accident, the number and prices of homes sold or rented within the immediate vicinity of the accident plummeted. Hotel occupancy in Goiânia, normally near capacity at this time of year, had vacancy levels averaging about 40 per cent in the six weeks following the São Paulo television broadcast, while the Hotel Castros, one of the largest in Goiânia, lost an estimated 1000 reservations as a direct consequence of risk perceptions and stigma. Meanwhile, Caldas Novas, a hot-springs tourist attraction located a full one-hour drive from Goiânia, experienced a 30–40 per cent drop in occupancy rates immediately following the São Paulo television broadcast. Hotels in other parts of Brazil refused to allow Goiânia residents to register. Some airline pilots refused to fly airplanes that had Goiânia residents aboard. Cars with Goiás licence plates were stoned in other parts of Brazil. Even nuclear energy as a whole in Brazil was affected, as several political parties used the accident to mobilize against 'nuclear weapons, power, or waste' and to introduce legislation designed to split the National Nuclear Energy Commission into separate divisions. Increased public opposition to nuclear energy was apparent throughout Brazil. International ripples of the accident became apparent as Goiânia became a frequent benchmark and rallying cry in anti-nuclear publications throughout the world.

Arvind Susarla (2003) at Clark University compared two risk events in India, one of which was highly amplified and the other attenuated. The amplified event was the discovery of bacterium *Yersinia Pestis* in the city of Surat, which led to a plague scare in India. With media reports of increasing evidence of pneumonic plague, rumours about a large number of deaths due to the disease spread in the city. Despite assurances of safety and mitigative measures from local authorities, the rumours triggered widespread public concern and an extreme public response within hours of the initial reports of the plague. At its peak, over 200,000 persons are believed to have deserted the city of Surat, and hundreds of others reported to public and private hospitals. Authorities in several nearby cities, meanwhile, were alerted to the possible arrival of plague patients from Surat. Administrative officials responded by ordering a series of precautionary steps, including the medical screening of persons from Surat at the bus and train stations and the closure of schools, colleges, public gatherings and meetings, and theatres. These initiatives amplified concerns and alarm that the disease might spread to other parts of the country. Media coverage of the episode is complex, as highly exaggerated death tolls were reported in the English-language dailies whereas Hindi-language newspapers insisted there was no plague and accused neighbouring Pakistan of a smear campaign aimed at bringing India's economy to its knees. The combination of public concern, media reporting and the actions of the authorities also resulted in higher-order impacts due to the hazard event, Many countries imposed travel restrictions on people travelling to and from India. Iran's foreign minister postponed his visit to India. Trade embargoes, withdrawal of personnel by multinational firms, and cancellations of many international airline flights reflect the extent of risk ripples produced by the hazard event.

Barnett et al (1992) report a clear decline (albeit temporarily) of one-third in the use of the DC-10 for domestic US flights following a serious and heavily publicized crash at Sioux City, Iowa in 1989. Such secondary consequences may emerge only on a case-by-case basis and may require the presence of several factors in order to emerge fully (in this case, the DC-10 had a historically untrustworthy image following a spate of crashes in the 1970s). However, the effects were very temporary (fewer than two months). In a very different social 'risk' domain, that of the impacts of media violence, Hill (2001) argues that it is the politics of social-group mobilization (around campaigns against particularly violent videos or movies) which is the key driver of secondary amplification effects such as increased censorship and regulation.

Metz (1996) has conducted a historical impact analysis of stigma (stage 2) effects around US weapons sites. His claim is that, although anticipated stigma or other second-order amplification consequences might be a common response when individuals are asked to *imagine* the future, few of the anticipated negative consequences of siting a hazard in a community (loss of business, decline in land values, etc) were actually manifest in his research *over the longer term*. This is a controversial conclusion, given the central place that stigma and secondary consequences hold in discussions of risk perceptions, and his general argument has drawn vigorous critique (Slovic et al, 1994).

The one theoretical contribution that we know of linking stage 1 processes causally with stage 2 ripple effects is work by Slovic et al (1991c) on stigma effects at the Yucca Mountain nuclear repository site. They designed a series of empirical studies to: (1) demonstrate the concept of environmental imagery and show how it can be measured; (2) assess the relationship between imagery and choice behaviour; and (3) describe economic impacts that might occur as a result of altered images and choices. The research tested three specific propositions: (1) images associated with environments have diverse positive and negative affective meanings that influence preferences (e.g. preference for sites in which to vacation, retire, find a job or start a new business); (2) a nuclear waste repository evokes a wide variety of strongly negative images, consistent with extreme perceptions of risk and stigmatization; and (3) the repository at Yucca Mountain and the negative images it evokes will, over time, become increasingly salient in the images of Nevada and of Las Vegas.

Substantial empirical support was found for these propositions, demonstrating a set of causal mechanisms by which social amplification processes could adversely affect the attractiveness of the area to tourists, job seekers, retirees, convention planners and business developers and produce adverse social and economic effects.

Despite these cases and the Decision Research theoretical work, it is clear that stage 1 relationships in the SARF have been more studied and are better understood than are those of stage 2. Stage 1 posits that signals from risk events become transformed to influence perceptions of risk and first-order behavioural responses. A relatively extensive set of findings from the risk perceptions literature now exists to suggest this is the case, although much remains to be done to pinpoint the *specific contexts* under which amplification or attenuation occurs. Stage 2 involves a direct link between amplification of risk perceptions and secondary consequences, such as calls for stricter regulation, market impacts, and a generalization of responses to other similar risk events and hazards. In many respects, it is stage 2 that is the most important for policy, given the potential here for large economic and social impacts. Despite prima facie evidence, stage 2 processes remain rather opaque, based largely upon current case-specific and anecdotal evidence rather than on systematic empirical evidence. It is also less clear what the direct secondary consequences of *attenuation* might be compared to the more visible impacts of amplification. Consequences of attenuation might include, however, the otherwise avoidable direct impacts of the hazard, and the impacts upon trust and credibility if degraded risk management is subsequently revealed in a serious unanticipated accident.

Having surveyed the empirical work that has tested, elaborated and extended the original conceptual paper, we next turn to a review of critiques and points of debate that have emerged over the past 15 years.

CRITIQUES AND CONTENTIONS

The framework has prompted general critiques, principally in the set of peer review commentaries that accompanied the original 1988 article in *Risk Analysis*. Although most of these authors welcomed social amplification as a genuine attempt to provide more theoretical coherence to the field, they also highlighted points of issue, as well as avenues for further research. In a subsequent paper Kasperson (1992) sought to respond to many of these critiques. Here we review the various critiques and issues that have been raised, clarifying where we can and identifying unresolved questions where appropriate.

The amplification metaphor

Rayner (1988) has criticized the amplification metaphor itself, concerned that it might be taken to imply that a baseline or 'true' risk exists that is readily attached to risk events, which is then 'distorted' in some way by the social processes of amplification. He argues that the emphasis on signal and electronic imagery may be too passive to capture the complexity of risk behaviour. Rip (1988) worries that the focus of amplification work may be directed to what are regarded as 'exaggerated' risks.

It is quite clear, however, that the framework is not intended to imply that any single true baseline always and/or unproblematically exists, particularly in many of the heavily politicized, transcientific settings (Funtowicz and Ravetz, 1992) where amplification is most likely to occur. The conceptualization of the amplification process in terms of construction and transformation of signs, symbols and images by an array of social and individual 'stations' and actors is compatible with the view that all knowledge about risk entails some elements of judgement and social construction (Johnson and Covello, 1987; Holzheu and Wiedemann, 1993). The observation that experts and public sometimes disagree about risks is compatible with the claim that different groups may filter and attach salience to different aspects of a risk or a risk event. Amplification and attenuation, therefore, refer to the processes of signal interpretation, transformation, intensification and dampening as the dynamics of risk consideration proceed iteratively in society. At the same time, it is clear that risks do have real *consequences* (Renn, 1998; Rosa, 1998), and these may be direct (as are usually treated in technical risk analyses) or indirect results from the social processing of risk (stigmatization, group mobilization, conflict, loss of trust).

The metaphor of amplification does come with some baggage, to be sure. Since the very term amplification, in its more general and common usage, refers to the intensification of signals, the framework nomenclature can be taken to have an implicit semantic bias (Rip, 1988). The architects of SARF have repeatedly emphasized in their writings that this approach is intended to describe both the social processes that attenuate signals about hazards, as well as those involved in intensification. Alleged 'overreactions' of people and organizations should receive the same attention as alleged 'downplaying' of the risk. In his extensive review of the topic Renn (1991) discusses the processes and contexts that might be expected to lead to each.

What is amplified or attenuated are *both* the signals to society about the seriousness and manageability *and*, ultimately, the consequences of the risk through the generation, or constraining, of ripple effects. Indeed, the secondary risk consequences will often be connected causally with the various interactions involved in society's processing of risk signals. It is exactly this potential for signal transformation and amplification-driven social dynamics and consequences that has been so confounding to risk managers in various societies.

Is it a theory?

As emphasized in the 1988 article, SARF is not a theory, properly speaking, but 'a fledgling conceptual framework that may serve to guide ongoing efforts to develop, test, and apply such a theory to a broad array of pressing risk problems' (Kasperson et al, 1988e, p180). A theory, as Machlis and Rosa (1990, p164) have emphasized, would require specification and explication of linked concepts, including the application of correspondence rules for converting abstract or inexact concepts into exact, testable ones. We are now beginning to see the first forays into such theorizing, as in the stigma work of Slovic and colleagues referred to above. Progress is also apparent in the empirical work linking events, trust, perceptions and imagery, also discussed in Volume II, Chapters 2, 9 and 10. Meanwhile, a continuing principal contribution of the framework is its 'net' function for catching a broad range of accumulated empirical research, for organizing and bringing into direct analytic interaction relevant phenomena, for theories concerning risk perception and its communication, and for deriving new hypotheses about the societal processing of risk signals (the latter could then, in principle at least, be tested directly).

One limitation of the risk amplification framework, despite its apparent face validity, is that it may be too general (rather as subjective expected utility theory is) to test empirically and particularly to seek outright falsification. This has led some observers (e.g. Rayner, 1988; Wahlberg, 2001) to doubt whether any genuinely new insights can be achieved beyond those already offered by existing approaches. Clearly, the usefulness of this social amplification approach will ultimately stand or fall upon its ability to achieve insights which can be subject to empirical test. Certainly the framework does, at minimum, help to clarify phenomena, such as the key role of the mass media in risk communication and the influence of culture on risk processing, providing a template for integrating partial theories and research, and to encourage more interactive and holistic interpretations. Kasperson (1992) has previously cited three potential contributions of such an integrative framework: (1) to bring competing theories and hypotheses out of their 'terrain' and into direct conjunction (or confrontation) with each other; (2) to provide an overall framework in which to locate a large array of fragmented empirical findings; and (3) to generate new hypotheses, particularly hypotheses geared to the interconnections and interdependencies among particular concepts or components. These still seem highly relevant.

Communications and the mass media

The concern has been raised (Handmer and Penning-Rowsell, 1990) that the communications model on which the social amplification approach is founded unduly emphasizes too simple a conceptualization of risk communication, as a one-way transfer of information (i.e. from risk events and sources, through transmitters, and then onto receivers). So let us remove any existing doubt that this framework, as we conceive it, recognizes that the development of social risk perceptions is always likely to be the product of diverse interactive processes among the parties to any risk communication. Various reviews (USNRC, 1989; Pidgeon et al, 1992; Stern and Fineberg, 1996) discuss the importance of viewing risk communication as a *two-way process* of dialogue. We would take this even further to note that any risk event generates coverage and signals that proceed through a broad array or fabric of ongoing communication networks. Purposeful risk communication programmes nearly always enter a terrain extensively occupied by existing communication systems. Thus, with the United States National Research Council, we see risk communication as:

> an interactive process of exchange of information and opinion among individuals, groups and institutions. It involves multiple messages about the nature of risk and other messages, not strictly about risk, that express concerns, opinions, or reactions to risk messages or to legal and institutional arrangements for risk management (USNRC, 1989, p21).

Certainly, applications of the framework should not lose sight of this important qualification, and although it is relatively easy to finger the public and media as the originators of risk communication problems, the communicators are also key parts of the process (Kasperson and Stallen, 1991).

In this context, a comment on the role of the mass media is also in order. Some have interpreted the framework to assume that we see high mass media coverage as the principal driver of risk amplification. For example Sjöberg (1999) concludes that the framework predicts that enhanced media coverage should increase perceived risk. This is not the case. Although we find incidents where this has occurred, and some (e.g. Mazur, 1990) have advanced this argument, the conceptual work of Renn (1991) and Pidgeon et al (1999) and our empirical research as well reveal that the relationships among media coverage, public perceptions, and stage 2 amplification processes are complex and highly interactive with other components of the amplification process. Indeed, we have speculated that no single amplification component may be sufficient to ensure 'take-off' of the amplification process. We also believe that layering of amplification and attenuation around scale-specific patterns of media coverage may not be uncommon. Indeed, we see the strength of amplification research as oriented to patterns of interacting amplification mechanisms, the nature of the risks and risk events, and social contextual effects. We have also concluded, surveying empirical work over the past 15 years, that the nature of discourse about risk that characterizes the social processing of the risk is important, including the political competition that occurs to control language, symbols, imagery and definition or framing of the risk problem.

Individual versus social processes

Two commentaries on the 1988 article expressed the concern that too much attention was given to the individual level of amplification and too little to social alignments, the mass media and social networks (Rip, 1988, p195). Svenson (1988b, p200) noted that future development of the framework might well benefit from a more articulated system and a broader social psychological approach that would put amplification processes 'even more firmly in the societal context'. As the foregoing discussion of organizational amplification and attenuation illustrates, the empirical work over the past 15 years has accorded the social 'stations' and processes of amplification as much, and perhaps even more, attention as individual processes have received. Indeed, even the extensions of the psychometric model to notions such as stigma, blame and social trust have emphasized heavily the interactions between social context and individual perceptions and behaviour. And, of course, it is precisely these interactions that are highlighted in the amplification framework.

With this review of empirical studies and extensions of the social amplification framework, as well as areas of critique and debate, in hand, we next turn to consider implications for public policy and future research directions.

POLICY AND RESEARCH PRIORITIES

As yet, there has been no systematic exploration of how SARF and the empirical results of the past 15 years can be applied to various public policy matters. Yet there is an urgent need for social analysts of risk to suggest approaches and processes that have the potential to improve society's ability to anticipate, diagnose, prioritize and respond to the continuing flow of risk issues that confront, and often confound, society's risk processing and management functions. The recommendations calling for substantial overhauls in existing risk assessment and decision making, whether for an 'enlarged concept of risk' and trust building (UK Interdepartmental Liaison Group on Risk Assessment, 1998a) or 'analytic and deliberative process' (Stern and Fineberg, 1996), potentially open the door for more socially informed approaches to risk decision making (e.g. see some of the contributions to Okrent and Pidgeon, 1998). The scope and structuring of the social amplification framework allows it to generate policy suggestions (with the usual caveats as to what is possible). And from the last 15 years of work, we do have several examples of substantial policy analysis that draw upon the amplification framework as well as a considerable body of empirical work to inform risk policy questions and ideas for further departures that may enhance management initiatives.

At the outset, it is important to recognize that any policy suggestions proceed from an underlying normative question: is it possible to develop normative criteria for judging the outcomes of social risk amplification as 'good' or 'bad', rather than merely addressing the pathologies of the most visible manifestations of 'over' and 'under' reaction? There is no research to date, as far as we are aware, on this critical issue. The question of when social amplification or attenuation becomes sufficiently pronounced, or more destructive than positive to the social construction and handling of the risk, is a complex one. Consider, for example, the case of social controversy over the siting of waste disposal facilities in the US, an issue that generated widespread disapproval in the form of such acronyms as NIMBY, LULU, NIMTOF and others, and has often been cited as a classic example of public overreaction. In fact, the resistance to land disposal of wastes has driven extensive waste reduction and recycling at source and, arguably, improved overall waste management.

In practical terms, agencies will still attempt to use the best available scientific knowledge and risk assessments in an attempt to produce estimates of 'risk', although as Rappaport (1988) points out, whereas scientific risk assessment is evaluated by its *accuracy*, one criterion for evaluating people's attention to risk signals is the *adaptiveness* of the information gained, and the two may not always correspond. Also, as Svenson (1988b) notes, we do not know when risk amplification has involved changes to people's basic mental models of a hazard (which may then, in principle, be judged as correct or incorrect with respect to some standard; see Morgan et al, 2001), or whether the modification of relevant values or thresholds of tolerability to the risk has occurred. Clearly a complete set of judgements oriented to the amplification process will likely be involved in any such evaluation process. And we should not lose sight of the desire of many responsible authorities to *suppress* the flow of signals in society so that control over the risk consideration process can be kept in the domain of the managers.

As noted earlier, two areas of policy analysis have drawn extensively on SARF. The first involves the future of radioactive waste management in the US. The social amplification concept had its genesis in an ambitious programme of social and economic research funded by the state of Nevada and conducted between 1985 and 1995. Included was a broad array of research aimed at assessing the future potential impacts of the proposed nuclear waste repository at Yucca Mountain, including studies on perceptions and imagery, risk signals, patterns of media coverage, possible stigma-related and other ripple effects, and social distrust. Drawing upon this extensive body of empirical work, which covered much of the scope of SARF, a team of researchers, assisted by a well-known science writer, set forth a broad policy analysis (summarized in Chapter 14). The analysis argued that given the dismal failure of existing policy, a new approach was sorely needed, one that would be based on such elements as acceptance of the legitimacy of public concerns, an enhanced role for interim storage, a voluntary site selection process, negotiation with risk bearers and actions aimed at restoring credibility (Flynn et al, 1995, pp16–18).

A second policy area, one related to the Yucca Mountain case, is the impasse or gridlock over the siting of hazardous facilities more generically in a number of countries. Here the numerous empirical studies conducted as part of the social amplification approach have been an important part of the foundation for several policy prescriptions. Kunreuther and colleagues wedded the amplification concepts to the prescription and compensation research at the University of Pennsylvania's Wharton School and Lawrence Susskind's extensive experience with conflict resolution to develop a new facility siting credo (see Chapter 15), subsequently tested for its prescriptive power (Kunreuther et al, 1993). Similarly, Kasperson and colleagues (see Chapter 15) have drawn heavily upon social amplification research in arguing for new approaches and procedures in facility siting, including such policy elements as a clear demonstration of societal need, steps to narrow the risk debate, approaches that would remain resilient under conditions of high social distrust, building constituencies of support, and the use of adaptive institutional processes. The scope of issues covered in these policy prescriptions, the attention to interactive effects, and their links to rippling effects are suggestive of the types of policy analyses that might flow from amplification-based research.

One clear policy contribution could be to draw upon social amplification to improve society's capability to anticipate which new or emerging risks are likely to be highly amplified or attenuated. Given the inherent complexity of risk communication and social processes, it is clear that the framework cannot be expected to yield simple or direct predictions regarding which issues are likely to experience amplification/ attenuation effects in advance. A parallel problem – which has in part epistemological and in part practical roots – occurs when researchers attempt to use knowledge of the human and organizational causes of past technological accidents and disasters to predict the likelihood of future failures (see Pidgeon, 1988; Turner and Pidgeon, 1997, especially ch 5). Here some practitioners have adopted more holistic methods, seeking to diagnose vulnerability in large organizational systems through screening against broad classes of risk management factors (see for example, Groeneweg et al, 1994). In a similar way, knowledge of the factors likely to lead to amplification effects, and the sociopolitical contexts in which they might operate, could conceivably serve as a *screening device* for evaluating the potential for such consequences, particularly with respect to synergistic effects found among factors. Developing such a screening procedure and testing it retrospectively to explain past experience or against samples of new risks could be a particularly useful line of investigation.

Turning to the empirical foundations of social science research on risk, the extent to which existing empirical work reflects North American experience is striking. Clearly, we urgently need to conduct basic investigations on the transferability of the existing findings (for example, whether trust, blame and responsibility for risk management play as strong a role in Europe or Asia as is reported in the US), as well as the ways in which different cultural contexts uniquely shape risk communication and risk amplification effects. However, as Renn and Rohrmann (2000) make clear, conducting well-founded cross-cultural risk perceptions research is a formidable task, particularly if we consider the multiple parties present in the amplification/attenuation construct. However, if we start from the standpoint of the key mediators of much risk communication – the mass media – then the framework should be capable of describing and organizing the amplification rules used by media institutions in their role between government and sections of society. How the media interface with the other different institutional players in what Slovic (1998) terms the 'risk game' is a key issue ripe for investigation. There is also the question of whether different institutional arrangements can be characterized as operating with predictable sets of amplification or attenuation rules (see Renn, 1991, p300), and whether evidence exists of causal links between such institutional behaviour and subsequent societal impacts. The influence of regional and national legal and cultural frameworks in setting overarching contexts for amplification processes should be part of this research direction.

Social amplification has provided a useful analytic structure for studying stigma-related policy questions (Flynn et al, 2001), although the existing policy *options* for addressing such amplification-driven processes appear quite limited, as Gregory et al (1995) have demonstrated. Litigating stigma claims under the aegis of tort law in the US does not seem to offer an efficient or satisfactory solution. Project developers can, of course, simply pay whatever is asked for as compensation, but such a pay-and-move-on option fails to distinguish between valid claims for compensation and strategic demands based on greed, or politically motivated attempts to oppose a policy or programme. In addition, claims are often made for economic losses predicted to take place years or even decades into the future, despite the many difficulties inherent in forecasting future economic activities or social responses. Stigma effects might be ameliorated if public fears could be addressed effectively through risk communication efforts, but such a simple solution also seems unlikely. All too often, risk communication efforts have been unsuccessful because they have failed to address the complex interplay of psychological, social and political factors that is at the heart of social amplification and that drives profound mistrust of government and industry, and results in high levels of perceived risk and thus opposition. Accordingly, policy responses geared to the interacting factors contributing to stigma at multiple stages of amplification processes are also required.

More open and participatory decision processes could provide valuable early information about potential sources of stigmatization and amplification drivers and invest the larger community in understanding and managing technological hazards. This approach might even help to remove the basis for the blame and distrust that often occurs in the event of an accident or major risk policy failure, and improvements over time in our ability to identify and access the factors contributing to stigmatization may make it possible to predict the magnitude or timing of expected economic losses. This, in turn, could open the door to the creation of new insurance markets and to efforts for mitigating potentially harmful stigma effects. Finally, the societal institutions responsible for risk management must meet public concerns and conflicts with new norms and methods for addressing stigma issues, and improved arenas for resolving conflicts based on values of equity and fairness.

As a concluding comment, we reiterate that a particular policy strength of the framework is its capacity to mesh emerging findings from different avenues of risk research, to bring various insights and analytic leverage into conjunction, and (particularly) to analyse connections, interrelations and interactions within particular social and cultural contexts. Such strengths suggest that the search for patterns and broader-based interpretations may yield new insights and hypotheses, as research on stigma, social trust and 'take-off' of the amplification process suggests. In Chapter 13, Volume II, assessing risk amplification and attenuation in the particular context of transboundary risks, we have pointed to potential 'mirror' structures in the social processing of such risks, with social attenuation in the risk-source region and linked social amplification in the risk-consequence area. In global change research, German social scientists have provided new insights into vulnerability to environmental degradation by analysing 'syndromes' of change (Schellnhuber et al, 1997). Throughout this chapter, and also in our more theoretical writings on social amplification, we have emphasized the potential research and policy value that a broadly based and integrative framework of risk affords. Such meso-level of theoretical analyses within the amplification framework could potentially open up new research questions and potential policy initiatives.

Part 3

Risk and Ethics

12 Responding to the Double Standard of Worker/Public Protection

Patrick Derr, Robert Goble, Roger E. Kasperson and Robert W. Kates

INTRODUCTION

A general social justice problem entailed in the differential protection of people from hazards is apparent with the cases of three hypothetical individuals: a Connecticut glassblower whose workplace exposure to nitrogen oxides, while deemed 'safe', was nearly 25 times greater than his exposure outside the factory; a neighbour of the Three Mile Island nuclear plant whose work decontaminating the plant will expose him to much higher levels of radiation than those experienced by members of the public during the accident; and a US embassy employee in Moscow whose microwave exposure, while exceeding permissible levels in the Soviet Union, was only 1/500th of that allowed in the US.

The exposure of these and other workers to the hazards of technology is generally much higher than that permitted for the public. Inevitably, one is led to question whether such differential protection is justified. A number of issues must be addressed, as we have discussed elsewhere (Derr et al, 1981):

- A double standard of protection exists for workers and publics, manifested in a significant portion of all technologies and in recently enacted occupational and environmental standards. While public protection is ordinarily set below the level of medically defined hazard, worker protection is customarily set above the hazardous level, thereby exposing workers to known dangers.
- This double standard of protection is not unique to the US but exists across a wide variety of economic, political and ideological systems.

Note: Reprinted from *Environment*, vol 25, Derr, P., Goble, R., Kasperson, R. E. and Kates, R. W., 'Responding to the double standard of worker/public protection', pp6–11, 35–36, © (1983), with permission from Heldref Publications

- Differential protection is a problem in part because of the significant, if poorly understood, health toll that it represents and in part because of the serious questions of justice it raises about parts of our social and economic systems.
- Four major justifications – utility, ability, consent and compensation – have been offered to support this double standard, but each is subject to questions concerning the validity of assumptions, both empirical and moral.

In regard to the last, we recognize four justifications as principles of equity that could support the existence of the double standard. Stated briefly, they are:

- *Utility*: An allocation is just if, and only if, it maximizes the summed welfare of all members of the morally relevant community. If 'summed welfare' is understood collectively, the roots of this principle can be traced to the earliest documents of our civilization. If 'summed welfare' is understood distributively (as simply adding up individual welfares), the principle takes its classical formulation from the work of the Utilitarians, Bentham and Mill.
- *Ability*: An allocation of risks is just if, and only if, it is based upon the ability of persons to bear those risks. Since 'need for protection' mirrors 'ability to bear risk', this principle is simply a special case of the more general claim that allocations are just if, and only if, they treat people according to their needs.
- *Compensation*: An allocation of risks is just if, and only if, those assuming the allocated risks are rewarded (compensated) accordingly. This principle is derived from the somewhat more general concept that an allocation is just if, and only if, it is made according to the actual productive contributions of persons.
- *Consent*: An allocation of risks is just if, and only if, it has the consent of those upon whom the risks are imposed. Typical formulations of the principle are found in the Nuremberg Code and in guidelines for experimentation on human subjects.

At one level, these principles are distillations of common sense and readily appear, consciously or unconsciously, as part of a discussion of the magnitude of occupational risk. At another level, the principles are part of the venerable history of writings in ethics. We have used the principles in two ways: as social theory, potential empirical explanations for the discrepancies we have found between worker and public protection; and as a normative base for evaluating the existing state of affairs.

In both cases, we have inquired into the regulatory mechanisms that affect the allocation of risk to determine whether they explicitly consider the principles, and the actual allocations of risk to determine whether they satisfy the conditions of the principles. This inquiry has revealed that it is often difficult to ascertain when the conditions are, in fact, satisfied and that the four principles are frequently in conflict.

In a series of studies, we have reported on the following detailed work:

- *Three case studies* – lead (Hattis et al, 1982), radiation from power plants (Melville, 1981b) and parathion (Johnson, 1982) in which we examined the allocation of risks between workers and the public, identified the operative regulatory structure, and evaluated the extent to which the four equity principles were applicable.
- *Three cross-hazard studies* treating the screening of sensitive workers (Lavine, 1982), the existence of wage differentials based on risk (Graham et al, 1983), and the informing of workers about risks (Melville, 1981a), studies which have permitted an in-depth examination of the operation of three of our equity principles.
- *One international comparison*, contrasting the protection of workers in Sweden and the US (Kasperson, 1983b).

In this discussion, we have two objectives: first, to summarize what we have learned in the various studies about the existence of the double standard and whether it is justified; and, secondly, to propose how society may respond to this situation. We begin with our surprises.

TWO SURPRISES

Unexpected findings in science are a cause of both dismay and delight – dismay because they may lead to the rejection of a favoured hypothesis and delight because the discovery of the unexpected can lead to new hypotheses and understandings. We found two major surprises over the course of our research.

The worldwide existence of differential protection and the lack of safety margins in standards for workers were features we anticipated. We were surprised, however, by the pervasiveness of that pattern and the apparent absence of societal awareness of its existence. Both in the general literature and in our case studies, we unearthed little if any discussion of the double standard and little or no debate as to its justification.

A second surprise is the degree of inconsistency in the treatment of different groups of workers exposed to similar hazards. We found inequities as great as those that prevail in the differential between publics and workers. Primary workers (those unionized and possessing job skills, employment security and high wages) appear on average to receive a wage increment associated with hazard exposure, yet secondary workers (those non-unionized and possessing few job skills, a lack of employment security and low wages) experience greater danger, have higher death rates and appear to receive no wage increment for hazard exposure. Screening procedures intended to identify and protect those workers more sensitive to the hazards themselves, we found, involved potential abuse and unintended consequences (such as social or sexual discrimination).

THE DOUBLE STANDARD IN LAW AND PRACTICE

The scope of differential protection and its associated health toll is striking and may be characterized as follows.

Scope

There is a universal differential in societal protection for workers and the public embodied in law, administrative standards and current practice. The baseline for the occupational standard is to permit workers to be exposed to deleterious materials or energy at levels at or above the level of observed harm without a significant margin of safety. This contrasts with the public standard, where, characteristically, permissible exposure levels 10 to 1000 times lower than the occupational standard prevail.

Our three case studies, noted above, confirm the discrepancy in mandates in governmental regulatory agencies. The discrepancy operates at three levels: in the statutory authority under which the agencies operate; in the regulatory proceedings of the agencies on specific hazards; and in the results of standards *after* they are imposed.

The regulatory authority of the US Occupational Safety and Health Administration (OSHA) derives from the Occupational Safety and Health Act of 1970, which requires the secretary of labour to:

> set the standard which most adequately assures, to the extent feasible, on the basis of the best available evidence, that no employee will suffer material impairment of health or functional capacity even if such employee has regular exposure to the hazard dealt with by such standard for the period of his working life.

The regulatory authority for the US Environmental Protection Agency (EPA) derives from a number of statutes, including the Clean Air Act, the Clean Water Act, the Safe Drinking Water Act, the Toxic Substances Control Act, and the Federal Insecticide, Fungicide, Rodenticide Act (FIFRA). The Clean Air Act, which covers many of the same substances regulated by OSHA in occupational settings, requires the EPA administrator to set standards that 'in the judgment of the administrator ... [allow] an adequate margin of safety ... to protect the public health'.

There are at least two significant differences between the statutes. OSHA is required to consider the technical and economic feasibility of any control it might impose, whereas EPA must not. OSHA is required to prevent 'material impairment', whereas EPA has the more stringent duty of protecting public health with an adequate margin of safety. See the discussion of lead in Hattis et al (1982) for a more detailed explanation of the statutes.

A double standard functioned in the action of the regulatory agencies in each of the three cases we examined. It was most transparent in the EPA's treatment of occupational and public standards for radiation exposure. There, the public standard was set at one-tenth the occupational standard to 'provide a margin of safety'.

In the case of lead, the occupational standard for lead in the air is 50 micrograms per cubic metre ($\mu g/m^3$), more than 30 times less stringent than the public standard of 1.5 $\mu g/m^3$. (The occupational standard, it should be noted, is relevant only during working hours and is based on a different averaging time.) Both EPA and OSHA set the level of their air standard to achieve certain goals in controlling the amount of lead in blood. EPA set a more stringent upper limit, 30 micrograms per 1/10 litre of blood (30 $\mu g/dl$), than OSHA's 40 $\mu g/dl$ level. EPA further demanded a much stricter observance of the upper limit than OSHA. EPA's public standard aimed to leave a maximally exposed group of 6000 (urban children) with blood levels of 30–40 $\mu g/dl$, while OSHA's occupational standard was expected to leave 35,000 workers above 40 $\mu g/dl$ and 2000 above 60 $\mu g/m^3$.

EPA's decision in 1972 to secure increased protection of the environment by banning DDT and substituting parathion was taken with full awareness that an increased risk to the 400,000 workers exposed to parathion was likely. Moreover, the EPA never addressed the particular problems posed by worker exposure to field residues or the presence of large numbers of Mexican agricultural labourers.

The discrepancy is a matter of fact as well as regulation. In the case of radiation, nuclear power plant worker exposure averages 5 times the natural background, with numerous workers receiving 10–30 times natural levels. 'Normal' releases from nuclear power plants, by contrast, are required to produce exposures no greater than one-half of natural background, and the actual average exposure to the public from nuclear power reactors is negligible.

In the case of lead, although compliance with the occupational limit of 50 $\mu g/m^3$ may not be achieved for many years, blood-lead levels are improving and approaching the OSHA targets (which are much higher than levels of public exposure). Air-lead levels in cities are also improving, principally as a result of controls on lead in gasoline; however, measured blood-lead distributions show more people with high levels than predicted by EPA in its model (Hattis et al, 1982).

The case of parathion shows both worker and public impacts (Johnson, 1982). Along with the occupational poisonings from parathion anticipated by EPA, accidents to the general public (particularly children) as well as mass poisonings due to accidental contamination of food in warehouses and cargo ships have occurred.

Interestingly, highly exposed workers are apparently drawn from both the most skilled and the least skilled segments of labour. Thus, in our case studies we found both highly skilled specialty workers and unskilled temporary workers in nuclear power plants, reproductively active workers in lead, and migrant agricultural workers in areas of parathion use to be highly exposed because of the operation of this double standard.

Health toll

The health toll attributable to the double standard varied widely across our three cases. In the case of radiation, the extra occupational toll is small but not negligible (5–9 premature deaths/year). The use of parathion involved a relatively comparable health toll: some 22 job-related deaths, 71 public fatalities and the accidental exposures of 1300 workers and 300 members of the public between 1966 and 1972. The toll from lead is much more serious: 40,000–50,000 workers with blood levels indicating physiological damage, including life-shortening effects to the neurological system and to organs such as the kidneys. Meanwhile, the substantially lower Swedish mortality rates for workers (as compared with the US rates) hint that a more determined effort to reduce the differential could reduce the toll from occupational hazards.

IS THE DOUBLE STANDARD JUSTIFIED?

The double standard for protecting workers and publics from particular technological hazards is not, in itself, necessarily unjust or inequitable. There can be compelling justifications for such differentials in particular cases. But neither should differential protection, in general, be presumed to be acceptable. Each case requires careful analysis of the moral argument, social context and empirical facts. Some differentials may well prove just; it is likely that others will not.

There are, in our view, four major moral justifications that may apply to particular cases of the double standard: differential protection maximizes benefits to society as a whole; workers are better able than members of the public to cope with hazardous exposures; workers are compensated for the risks they bear; and workers voluntarily consent to higher risk as a condition of employment.

Utility

The principle of utility suggests that the discrepancy in protection may be justified on the grounds that the benefit to society outweighs the cost to workers. This is certainly plausible, since the high concentration of hazardous material in the US occupational setting and the comparatively small number of people exposed suggest that there will be differences in the most efficient management of hazards in the two areas.

The evidence from our case studies, however, shows that the particular existing discrepancies do not in fact maximize social welfare. The 'spreading' of risk to temporary workers in nuclear power plants in preference to more effective exposure reduction management programmes and the broader use of remote-control maintenance have contributed to a growing total radiation burden for society and to a reduced incentive to employ cost-effective measures.

In the case of lead, where we were able to compare directly the imposition of controls based on human health effects, the imposed incremental cost-per-health effect on the margin was significantly lower for occupational standards than for environmental standards. It appears likely that the level of parathion exposures for field workers is not justified by any utility calculus.

Ability
Considerations of differential ability to bear hazards can justify differential protection in particular cases. The differential protection in lead and radiation standards, for example, can be partly justified by a consideration of the specially vulnerable publics (e.g. infants, pregnant women) who are excluded from or receive special protection in employment. But there are other cases – and our work would suggest that they are more typical – in which considerations of ability do not justify current practices and standards.

As discussed in our case studies, the regulatory agencies (EPA and OSHA) took seriously the need to identify sensitive populations. Yet, their treatments of sensitivity in the standard-setting process differed. The discrepancies in differential protection for workers and the public, it should be noted, cannot be accounted for by differential sensitivity. In the case of lead, for example, the public standard was based on the characteristics of children, the most sensitive subgroup; OSHA, by contrast, identified workers of reproductive age (both male and female) as the most sensitive group at risk but concluded that it was not feasible to set standards that would protect their potential offspring (Hattis et al, 1982).

We have also considered a second issue with regard to differential sensitivity within the population of workers. The use of screening programmes to identify and remove from the workforce people who are at greater risk of adverse health effects is increasingly common and carries the potential for abuse and unintended consequences (Lavine, 1982). In some cases, the means by which less risk-tolerant workers are protected are themselves unjust, when all potentially fertile female employees, regardless of family plans, are excluded from workplaces posing possible teratogenic hazards.

In other cases, it is the *differential consideration* of such ability that is unjust, as when blacks with haemoglobin defects are 'protected' from military flight duty while white officers with recessive genes for similar haemoglobin defects receive no such similar 'protection'. In still others, the groups placed at most risk are in fact least able to bear the risks imposed, as in the use of the elderly, children or the malnourished for agricultural work in pesticide-treated fields.

Compensation

Explicit compensation through wages for risk occurs rarely. Although a few jobs do appear to compensate occupational risk through specific increments in wages, these are the same parts of the labour market that are already best-off in other ways (Graham et al, 1983). Thus, policemen, who are at far less occupational risk than cab drivers, are explicitly compensated for risk, whereas cab drivers – already much less well paid than policemen – are not.

Temporary nuclear power plant workers hired for specific tasks in high-radiation environments receive no specific compensation for risk. The protracted legal debate over the 'medical-removal' provision of the occupational lead standard never considered risk premiums in wages. The EPA did not count the increased payments that pesticide applicators and farm workers ought to receive as an additional cost of changing from DDT to parathion.

Of course, compensation for hazard exposure in wages need not be explicit. Our detailed analysis of the factors (including health risks) affecting worker earnings (Graham et al, 1983) concluded that some workers in the major unionized manufacturing sectors, the primary segment, may receive an implicit wage premium for hazard exposure. Most workers in the secondary labour segment, in contrast, do not receive any such increment to their wages even though they experience equal or greater risk and their actuarial mortality is higher.

Consent

An ethically adequate consent to specific occupational risks would require at minimum that it be both *free* and *informed*. Our work suggests that these criteria are rarely met in the workplace. Rather, a consistent pattern emerges that (1) workers are primarily provided information directed toward telling them what they should do to control their exposures once they are on the job; they are not provided information with the expectation that they will choose whether or not to accept the exposure; and (2) workers do not generally feel free to accept or reject exposure; the prospect of losing one's job is considered more serious than even the possibility of quite severe health effects (Graham et al, 1983).

Because of workers' fear that a severe lead poisoning could lead to dismissal, when OSHA established a medical-reproval provision for the lead standard, one-and-a-half years' job security and wages protection were offered so that employees would not refuse to have blood-lead measurements taken. Most temporary workers in nuclear power plants and most agricultural field workers are not in a position to refuse employment in an economy where the unemployment rate is running higher than 10 per cent. It is largely for these reasons that the Swedish approach to occupational health protection assumes that free choice of employment by workers is impossible and that information concerning risk should be geared to risk reduction programmes.

WHY THE DOUBLE STANDARD?

In light of our findings that these four potential justifications are not met, why does the double standard exist at all? The roots of differential protection are complex, and they derive from at least three distinct sources: technological, historical and socioeconomic. By definition, workers are at the source of occupational hazards and many of these hazards are concentrated at their points of production. Thus, if no effort were made to reduce exposures, workers would be exposed to higher levels of hazard simply by their connection to the productive process.

Because of these higher exposures, workers have experienced impairment, disfigurement and death from occupational sources for hundreds of years. Thus, the essential inequality in exposure has become fixed in society's practice and expectations. Indeed, we seem to tolerate the highest hazards in some of the oldest occupations (e.g. farming, forestry and mining). The recognition that the general public may also be seriously affected by similar pollutants is of much more recent origin.

The technological principle of heavy concentrations of deleterious materials at points of origin also leads to differential protection arising from socioeconomic stratification. The lives and interests of workers in the older, dirtier, marginal occupations have always been further from centres of power, influence and concern. Employers, quite naturally, have focused on production first and on health issues only secondarily. Workers, as they have gained collective strength in bargaining for conditions and protection under law, have emphasized economic conditions rather than health and safety.

Public health and environmental protection command the support and attention of the majority of citizens, whereas occupational health issues are generally restricted to a small segment of workers and industry. As pointed out in our review of occupational health protection in Sweden (Kasperson, 1983b), strong worker links to a major social democratic or labour party have wielded considerable influence in shaping national responses to workplace hazards. Thus, as the Swedish example demonstrates, public attitudes and political influence can affect the perpetuation or narrowing of differential protection.

To conclude, our analysis of these relevant principles – consent, compensation, ability and utility – finds that these considerations are rarely publicly discussed and are honoured, at best, in very limited ways. Some workers, but not most, are partly informed of risks and tolerate them, but only with hindsight after they have accepted employment. Only under rare conditions are risk premiums in wages directly paid; when they are, these compensations tend to correspond with social class rather than the level of risk experienced by the individual worker. Some workers demonstrate a greater ability to tolerate hazardous exposure either because the least appropriate among them have been screened out of employment,

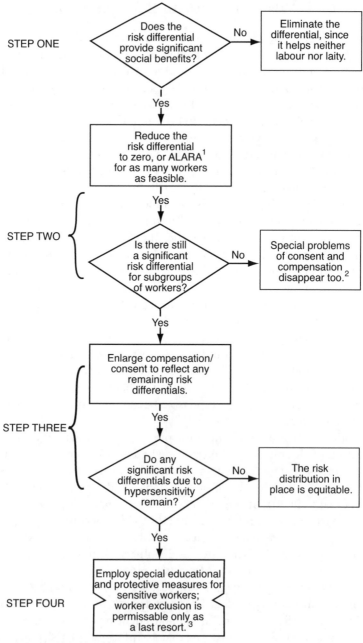

STEP ONE

Does the risk differential provide significant social benefits?

No → Eliminate the differential, since it helps neither labour nor laity.

Yes ↓

Reduce the risk differential to zero, or ALARA[1] for as many workers as feasible.

Yes ↓

STEP TWO

Is there still a significant risk differential for subgroups of workers?

No → Special problems of consent and compensation disappear too.[2]

Yes ↓

Enlarge compensation/consent to reflect any remaining risk differentials.

Yes ↓

STEP THREE

Do any significant risk differentials due to hypersensitivity remain?

No → The risk distribution in place is equitable.

Yes ↓

STEP FOUR

Employ special educational and protective measures for sensitive workers; worker exclusion is permissable only as a last resort.[3]

[1] As low as is reasonably achievable.
[2] Because, of course, there is no excess risk that requires any special consent or compensation.
[3] Because the avoidance of bodily harm in this way carries the potential for substituting other serious harms associated with exclusion and discrimination. Identifying and responding to differential sensitivity to hazards poses a complicated set of scientific and ethical problems, issues which we have begun to explore in a new research effort.

Figure 12.1 *Schematic diagram of guidelines for responding to inequities in risk*

because they are inherently healthier and are thus able to survive as the fittest, or because they have had training and experience to cope with or reduce their exposure. Additionally, there is the widespread belief (to be found both in opinion and law) and some evidence (as in our nuclear and parathion studies) that the overall aggregate social benefit can be increased by selective use of differentials in exposure.

WHAT SHOULD SOCIETY DO?

In light of our findings concerning the broad scope of the double standard, the significant associated health toll, and the intrinsic injustice to workers embodied in differential protection, we believe that society should act to rectify this situation. There are two major responses society can make: it can take measures to decrease differential protection for workers and publics, or it can increase the application of other means of redress to make the differential more morally acceptable. We recommend the following guidelines (see Figure 12.1) for response:

Step 1:   In all cases of differential protection for workers and publics, it should first be determined that the discrepancy carries significant benefits to society as a whole. If such benefits do not exist, the level of risk presented to workers should be reduced to that which prevails for the public.

Step 2:   Even if differential protection carries significant benefits to society, action should be taken to reduce the risk to as many workers as possible and to reduce it to as close to the level of protection afforded to the public as can reasonably be achieved, where 'reasonableness' is determined according to the viability of the industry and net benefits to society as a whole. The argument for such action is not only an equity one; the widely recognized ethical principle of non-maleficence calls for the avoidance of harm wherever possible as a hallmark of decent and responsible behaviour. Care should be taken that the risk is actually reduced and not simply reallocated and that other equivalent new risks are not substituted in its place.

Step 3:   For those workers for whom the risk cannot reasonably be reduced to the level of public protection, action should be taken to increase the degree of consent (through increased information and enlarged choice in employment) and compensation (as through insurance or risk premiums in wages). Increased information will also, of course, better equip workers to enter into negotiation with employers.

Step 4:   As a last step, a determination should be made as to whether there remains residual risk to certain groups of workers due to differential sensitivity to hazards. If so, special educational and protective measures should be undertaken to achieve as much equality in risk as is reasonable. Only as a last resort should exclusion of groups of workers from exposure to the hazard occur, with transfer to equivalent jobs (as measured by various social goods) being the preferred strategy. Since this action carries the danger of abuse and other unintended consequences, it should be particularly avoided where the groups involved are traditional victims of economic or social discrimination.

The potential applicability of these guidelines is suggested by an earlier nuclear power plant case study that we conducted (Kasperson and Lundblad, 1982), where we recommended that:

- the occupational radiation exposure standard should be set at the level of public protection (0.5 whole body roentgen equivalent in man (rem)) except for a small group of specialty workers;
- these high-risk workers should receive special education and training in radiation health risks as well as special hazard compensation (set at US$1000 per person-rem) in their wages;
- annual collective radiation dose limits for individual reactors should be established to reduce the spreading of risk over an expanding workforce, particularly to those workers less able to assess and respond to risk; and
- increased worker participation in risk control should occur, through financial incentives and specially designed programmes.

These guidelines are our preferred approach. But recognizing that they will be employed only by those already committed to narrowing differential protection and that the current anti-regulatory climate in Washington makes a timely response unlikely, we see the need for more direct and pragmatic action.

We recommend, therefore, that the OSHA institute a comprehensive review of its existing standards for the protection of worker health and safety. Where OSHA finds that its standard exceeds (in equivalent terms) the level of protection afforded to members of the public in comparable standards and regulations enacted by other government agencies, we propose that the Secretary of Labor institute procedures to adopt the more protective standard, and thereby eliminate the current discriminatory practices against the American worker.

ACKNOWLEDGEMENT

The authors wish to express their appreciation to their colleagues in the Center for Technology, Environment, and Development of Clark University. The research for this article and for the series was supported by the National Science Foundation under grant number OSS 79-24516. Any opinions, findings or recommendations expressed herein are those of the authors and do not necessarily reflect the views of the National Science Foundation.

13 Developmental and Geographical Equity in Global Environmental Change: A Framework for Analysis

Roger E. Kasperson and Kirstin M. Dow

INTRODUCTION

The past several centuries have been a time of remarkable human progress – in the application of electricity to a host of human tasks, the creation of a chemical industry, the spread of global communications, the eradication of many infectious diseases, and the dramatic increase of longevity and well-being. In the 1980s, however, it became apparent that this progress has been wrought at a high price in global environmental damage. The toll is vivid in China, where forests have now been reduced to only 12 per cent of their original area (as compared with 66 per cent in Japan, 35 per cent in the USSR, and 26 per cent in India), where one-sixth of the total land area is now affected by soil erosion, where floods in 1988 killed 6000 people and inundated 11.3 million hectares of land, where 60 species of wildlife are threatened with extinction, and where only 10 per cent of domestic sewage is treated. And economic growth in China is among the fastest in the world (Forestier, 1989). Although less dramatic in other areas, environmental degradation is clearly global in scope and human activity now threatens, for (arguably) the first time, the planetary environment as a whole (WCED, 1987).

Thus the current call for interventions to begin the task of at least reducing the *rates* of such change has touched wellsprings of human concern. But, despite the initial success of the international response to stratospheric ozone depletion in the Montreal Protocol or to hazardous wastes at the Basel Convention, stabilizing the trends of human impact on the environment will require surmounting a host of difficult equity questions, including who is to blame, why and how much we should care about the future, who will bear the burden of international responses, what institutional procedures or mechanisms are appropriate, and how may conflicts be overcome.

And the reality is that the progress so remarkable in aggregate has been Janus-faced in particular. So whereas gains in human well-being abound in affluent societies, as Gro Harlem Brundtland eloquently pointed out at the 1989 Washington Forum on Global Change and Our Common Future (Defries and Malone, 1989), as far as development is concerned, the 1980s were a lost decade. Living standards have declined by one-fifth in sub-Saharan Africa since 1970; the per capita income of some 50 developing countries has continued to decline over the past few years; and close to a billion people in the Third World now live in poverty and squalor. If a new global ethic such as that espoused by Weiss (1989) is to be had, it must be one that addresses existing inequalities as well as fairness in responding to global environmental challenges.

The complexities and ambiguities surrounding the equity problems embedded in global environmental change are formidable. The causes of environmental destruction are rooted in a variety of basic driving societal forces, such as agriculture, industrial metabolism, population growth and urbanization. And the simple fact of the matter is that nearly all intensive human occupancy and economic activity degrades the environment (albeit in widely differing forms and at differing rates). Beneficiaries and motivations are difficult to discern, and interactions with the physical environment are often poorly understood and highly uncertain. Those likely to be affected in the distant future in far-flung parts of the globe can only be dimly perceived, and we know nothing of their technologies, values, capabilities or living circumstances.

Then, too, there are the complexities and ambiguities attached to the notion of equity itself. Equity means different things to different people. Although it is often conceived of as the 'fairness' of a particular arrangement, the standards and underlying principles of fairness vary. Some see it as a concordance between benefits and burdens; others as an allocation of burdens to those best able to absorb or deal with them. Some view equity as primarily concerned with the substantive outcomes of an activity or project; others as concerned with the procedures used to make the allocations. What is clear is that equity involves both matters of fact and matters of value, and is an expression of culture. So the domain of equity analysis belongs to the scientist, the philosopher, the anthropologist, the public official and the public. And if equity is to be confronted in fashioning global initiatives on environmental change, it will need to capture the diversity of values underlying different perceptions of responsibilities and goals. Whether or not a single principle or set of principles can win endorsement across economies and cultures remains in question.

The discussion that follows does not seek to offer prescriptions as to how these profound equity problems should be resolved or which

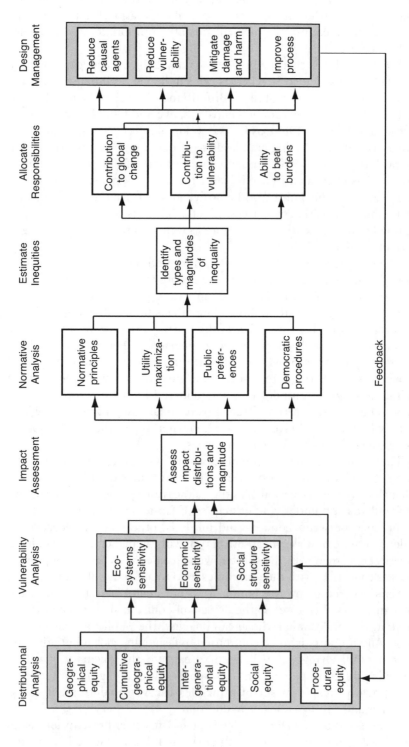

Figure 13.1 *Framework for equity analysis of global change*

conceptions of social justice should prevail. Rather, the intent is to help clarify how we may think about and analyse these problems. The framework we propose is one that we hope will entice others to join us in seeking methodologies and studies that will provide handles for the difficult issues surrounding competing notions of fairness that pervade global policy initiatives.

A FRAMEWORK FOR ANALYSIS

To clarify the equity issues associated with potential climate warming and other types of global environmental change, a structural framework is needed that is comprehensive and that discriminates between questions of fact and questions of value. Such a framework is likely to require development over time and the joint wisdom of physical scientists, social analysts, economists, geographers and philosophers. It should also link equity problems with potential global management policies. Here we propose an initial conception of such a framework (Figure 13.1).

To begin, we define equity as the fairness of both the process by which a particular decision or policy is enacted and the associated outcomes. This suggests that a framework for equity analysis needs to consider two major types of equity studies: distributional equity and procedural equity.

Distributional equity, in our usage, refers to the fairness of the distribution of substantive outcomes, or impacts, arising from a particular project, set of activities, or developmental path. It requires two major types of analyses or information:

1   a statement of the distribution, over some specified population, of benefits and harms that would result from a set of actions undertaken – this requires an empirical analysis that includes (a) a specification of those 'things' – whether social goods, opportunities, harms, or experiences – whose distribution is under investigation, (b) an explicit delineation of the population and relevant subpopulations to be considered in the analysis, and (c) a statement of the actual impact distributions – as defined by (a) and (b) – that would result from alternate proposed solutions to problems associated with global environmental change;

2   a set of standards or principles by which the equity or 'fairness' of particular distributions may be judged and by which the social preferability of one distribution over another may be judged.

It should be noted that both types of information – the specification of relevant populations and the types of impacts to be assessed – involve critical value judgements: (a) the definition of what is regarded as beneficial or harmful; (b) the common denominator for comparing different dimensions of harms and benefits; (c) the normative standards of fairness (for example, the type and amount of compensation appropriate for being exposed to a specific risk); and (d) the structuring of population groups to be used in an equity analysis. These value judgements fundamentally shape the structure and results of the empirical analysis.

Procedural equity refers to the fairness of the particular set of procedures used to arrive at policies and decisions for managing global environmental hazards. Critical to this will be the determination of legitimate interests and the allocation of rights and responsibilities among them. An analysis of procedural equity requires two types of information:

1   criteria by which to gauge the fairness of a particular set of procedures, specifying the roles, rights and responsibilities of various potential interests and the relationships that should prevail among them in reaching decisions;
2   data and information characterizing the procedures and relationships that actually were implemented and to which the normative criteria above can be applied.

As with distributional equity, both elements of this analysis will require the application of values, particularly in the context of assigning and limiting the decision-making power of the affected groups.

Other definitions pertinent to the discussion that follows are:

- *Impact*: a change in the attributes of a nation's or population's resources, social relationships, values or well-being – accordingly, impacts (such as those from climate change) may be either positive or negative, depending on the values of a particular group or society;
- *Hazard*: a threat to people and the things they value;
- *Risk*: a measure of the conditional probability that a particular adverse consequence will follow from a hazardous event or a particular activity;
- *Burden*: an adverse impact that requires additional resource allocation by a group, community or society if it is to be avoided or mitigated;
- *Benefit*: an impact judged as positive by the application of a particular value standard.

It is at once apparent that the assessment of impacts and equity is explicitly value laden – not only of the selection of the principles of fairness to be employed but in the selection of the relevant population groups to be considered and in the attributes of the process or the outcomes to be measured.

DISTRIBUTION ANALYSIS

Depending on how population groups are categorized and processes and outcomes defined, there are many potential types of equity problems. Indeed, the richness of the equity treatment depends heavily on the diversity of theory mobilized for the analysis and the imagination of the analyst. Here we treat five principal equity problems that have each, in different ways, received substantial attention (if not analysis). Four – geographical equity, cumulative geographical equity, intergenerational equity and social equity – involve 'outcome' or 'end state' considerations; the other – procedural equity – focuses on the processes employed.

The primary concern in *geographical equity* is with the geographical pattern of benefits and eventual harms associated with a particular set of activities. Thus the global pattern of CO_2 and other greenhouse gas emissions could, in principle, be compared with the pattern of harmful and beneficial impacts that would ultimately occur. In simple cases, these empirical patterns can then be used as a basis for making inferences about the obligations and responsibility (if any) that beneficiaries have for those harmed and the adequacy of legal structures and institutional mechanisms for meeting these responsibilities. So in hazardous-waste facility siting, for example, it is increasingly common to compensate local host communities through a variety of means for estimated risk and adverse impacts.

Assessing the geographical attributes of impacts associated with global environmental change, alas, is sufficiently complex and uncertain as to erode the feasibility of this type of analysis. Only the broadest types of patterns resulting from climate warming seem to find much evidence: subtropical monsoonal rain belts may be wetter, growing seasons at high latitudes longer, springtimes in high- and mid-latitudes wetter, midsummer conditions in some mid-latitudes drier, and extreme heat waves more common (Schneider, 1989). Even here, the evidentiary base is not likely to suffice as a compelling base for discerning interregional obligations. Generally, there is widespread agreement that, because of the poor spatial resolution of global climate models, the prediction of impacts (and thus the extent of hazard) from global warming at scales smaller than continental regions is unreliable now and is likely to remain so for one or more decades in the future. In short, the empirical capability to provide sufficient geographical information to act as a basis for designation of *future* harmed and benefiting areas from climate change will not exist to guide policies in the near term (although intergenerational distributions may provide other imperatives – see below). This question of who will be the winners and losers is one of the major stumbling blocks to the development of international response (Waterstone, 1985).

What is known quite well, however, is the geographical pattern of past and current *beneficiaries* from fossil fuel burning. Analysis of past growth rates and CO_2 emission levels for developed versus developing countries reveals the large percentage of cumulative CO_2 levels contributed by developed countries. Gross predictions as to how these may change over the next several decades under differing assumptions are also possible. So the past and current beneficiaries driving potential global warming are known at least grossly and they are strongly concentrated in developed countries. This may be useful in allocating responsibilities (see below).

What can be said about future impacts is that substantial economic dislocation (depending on rates of change) is likely to occur from the pattern of global environmental change, so that although the global pattern of harm is unknowable, simulations can suggest the types and magnitudes of potential harms that may occur. The loss of options for potentially impacted regions can also be inferred. So, although future impacts cannot be determined, some indication of future hazard can be estimated (at least grossly). And the most compelling arguments may turn on the need to redress spatially ambiguous future hazards by locatable current beneficiaries.

Equity, it could be argued, cannot be assessed solely within a particular regime or policy area. Climate warming cannot be divorced from other types of environmental change and past inequities involved in the global interaction of peoples, nations and economies. Indeed it can be argued that the type of global environmental change, what we term 'cumulative' global change (Turner et al, 1990b), of greatest impact on the planetary environment and developing societies is exactly that which has received the least attention. We refer to this broader view of inequity as *cumulative geographical equity*. Inequities that correlate with other inequities suffered by disadvantaged societies or marginal groups are particularly pernicious because their effects are likely to be synergistic and not simply additive. Previous inequities are also almost certain to have increased the vulnerability of some groups to global environmental change. Thus it is not surprising that developing countries might object vehemently to admonitions from developed countries to reduce future fossil fuel emissions for the well-being of the global environment. Cumulative geographical inequities, in short, may be expected to form the core of many debates over global environmental policy and are closely related to the suitability of particular policy options, such as tie-in strategies (see below). Also those inequities may be highly relevant to the sequencing of management intervention – particularly, who should clean up their mess first.

For *intergenerational equity*, some empirical dimensions of impact are clearer. There is a widespread opinion, for example, that if present emission trends of greenhouse gases continue, they will cause some degree of warming of the global climate during the next century. Although there is substantial disagreement as to the precise effects that such warming will have on natural ecosystems, water supplies, agriculture and sea level, enough indication of substantial potential global harm (i.e. hazard) exists to spark international efforts to find prospective solutions. Because two-thirds of the world's population lives in low-lying coastal areas, for example, sea level rises of even 0.5 to 1.5 metres will have major effects. In some areas, such as Bangladesh (where half the population lives at elevations below 5 metres), the impact could be catastrophic. The USEPA has projected that a sea level rise of 1 metre would result in a loss of 26–65 per cent of all US wetlands. Although the impacts of global climate change and their precise distribution will remain debated, assigning responsibility for the global impacts is easier, for the causal mechanisms are at least generally understood and can be submitted to the type of matrix analysis suggested by Graedel (1989).

Social equity provides another 'cut' through the world population to contrast with equity analyses focused on the nation-state. It is essential to assess the distribution of impacts according to wealth, social class or stage of development. From previous studies, and as noted below in our discussion of vulnerability, natural disasters continue to take a disproportionate and growing toll in developing countries, a fact that has helped to stimulate the 1987 UN General Assembly designation of the 1990s as the International Decade for Natural Disaster Reduction. Similarly, the links between world poverty and the incidence of famine and hunger have been widely noted. Many other hazards have remained 'hidden' from the public view, eliciting neither media attention nor institutional response (see Chapter 7).

Finally, there is the *procedural equity* of the processes that have created global environmental problems and by which they may be resolved. This differs from the other equity analyses described above, each of which addresses the distributions of problem causation and projected outcomes. Here the concern is with the adequacy and appropriateness of the decision processes leading to stratospheric ozone disruption, CO_2 emissions, global deforestation and to the development of research agenda and other response efforts. The issues appear straightforward – unlike other regimes or policy areas, equity has not been part of the considerations involved in decision making so that self-interest has externalized damage and the burden placed on other places, groups and generations. The adverse impacts on the global environment have only recently been recognized, and the state or the corporation has been the focus of decision. International institutional mechanisms for incorporating equity, meanwhile, have generally been unavailable or undeveloped in any event. So the absence of procedural equity is one of the few unambiguous attributes of global environmental change problems.

Each of these empirical analyses of distributions provides a 'face' of global environmental change. The ultimate risks associated with impact distributions depend not only on the distributional attributes outlined thus far, however, but on the vulnerability and resiliency of the ecosystems and populations. They form that next stage of necessary empirical analysis in our framework.

VULNERABILITY ANALYSIS

The impact of climate change will reflect the distributional considerations discussed above and the sensitivity of the biophysical regions and social groups. The magnitude of the impact depends not only on the extent of the environmental change – increased length of growing season or number of hectares inundated by increased flooding or sea level rise – but on the ongoing processes and existing factors contributing to a group's or region's ability to benefit or capacity to be harmed (i.e. its vulnerability). The serious nature of the threats potentially posed by climate change makes vulnerability a pressing concern, but sensitivity analysis also addresses benefits, given that equity involves both the beneficiaries and those harmed by the change. In this case, the beneficiaries include those who profited from the creation of the problem as well as those who may profit from impacts and responses. We see three broad categories of factors and processes as important to the sensitivity of impacted populations: *ecosystem sensitivity, economic sensitivity*, and *social structure sensitivity*.

The interactions among these categories are complex. Economic and social relations have implications for resource management across scales. Similarly, environmental conditions may affect economic and social decision-making processes. Ecosystem sensitivity may be compensated for by flexibility in social and economic structures. Marginality, the biophysical, social or economic conditions relative to a defined boundary, is often discussed as an aspect of vulnerability. As Blaikie and Brookfield (1987) pointed out, the interaction among different forms of marginality can lead to a downward spiral of increasing land degradation. Land managers can become marginalized through an imposed set of relations, such as taxes or other forms of surplus extraction. The responses to marginalization may then be reflected in land use decisions that degrade the resource base and lead to yet further economic and ecological marginality. Research in climate impact analysis has found marginal regions and groups especially vulnerable to impacts of climate change (Kates, 1985a; Parry, 1985). The sensitivity of the margins may also, however, present opportunities.

Ecosystems sensitivity addresses the spatial shifts as well as the regional changes accompanying climate change. Much of the research on the impacts of climate change has focused heavily on this ecosystem dimension of impact. General circulation models (GCMs) predict different levels of warming across latitudes. In some areas, warming may increase the growing season; in others it may require change in cropping or farming practices. Other analyses focus on the rate of climate change and the ability of species to keep pace with shifts in favourable habitat conditions (Davis, 1988). Predictions of sea level rise note particularly the vulnerability of coastal regions and populations.

Although our approach to equity analysis emphasizes first-order impacts and suggests differential vulnerability within that level of effects, the issues of marginality and higher-order impacts are important and require attention. Depending on the sensitivity of the ecosystem, relatively small environmental changes may have tremendous impacts, a finding now well established in the climate impacts literature (Kates,

1985a; Parry, 1985; Riebsame, 1989). Marginality in ecosystems suggests that the greatest impacts may be associated not necessarily with the areas of greatest quantitative climate change, but with areas on the margin of their successful range. As biophysical changes interact with economic and social factors, the resulting higher-order impacts may change the status of marginal activities.

As Liverman (1990) pointed out, often the most vulnerable people are thought of as those living in the most biophysically vulnerable areas. However, research in natural hazards continues to show natural disasters taking a much higher toll on life in the developing regions (while cost of property damage is higher in developed countries) and to suggest that socioeconomic factors play a critical role in determining the magnitude of the impact of a natural event (Baird et al, 1975; Burton et al, 1978; Susman et al, 1983). The contrast in losses to recent earthquakes in the US, Soviet Armenia and the Philippines offers a tragically vivid illustration of the continuation of this pattern. Recent studies suggest that global warming may be accompanied by an increase in the number of extreme events such as drought and hurricanes (Bolin et al, 1986). Given these past experiences with natural disasters, further research into the social and economic dimensions of vulnerability is required to identify the most vulnerable populations.

Economic sensitivity considers the potential for growth and disruption of economic systems. Maunder and Ausubel (1985) reviewed studies of climate sensitivity, identifying over 20 categories of potentially impacted activities (including construction, manufacturing, transportation, communications, government and taxes, and energy production and consumption). As discussed earlier, the three main aspects of sensitivity we identify are often closely interrelated and interactive. Weather, the length of the growing season, transportation costs and accessibility of natural resources will all affect economic activities, but impacts will be differentially articulated through different economic systems. As various institutions move to respond to the threat of climate change, some sectors of the economy will be well positioned to take advantage of increasing or new activity, whereas others will not be. Climate change-oriented research and design efforts are already under way in some sectors and institutions.

The *vulnerability of the economic system* will also be a key issue in impacts. The economic marginality of an activity in relation to first- and higher-order impacts of change that cascade through the economic system becomes an important consideration. Economic marginality describes a situation in which the returns to an economic activity barely exceed the costs. For example, a small reduction in yield per acre may force a farmer to draw on surpluses or rely on alternative sources of income. These types of impacts may be acute or they may manifest themselves over prolonged periods of stress. A group may have sufficient resources through one or two extreme years, but prolonged stress may reduce those economic reserves and significantly increase vulnerability. The importance of assets and knowledge of the probability and magnitude of events are important to small-scale farmers' strategies for coping with climatic variability in drought-prone areas of Africa (Akong'a and Downing, 1988; Chambers, 1989). Uncertain changes in precipitation patterns such as those accompanying climate change may remove some of the buffering offered by established coping strategies and institutions.

Economic disruption is also possible, of course, in non-marginal systems. Witness the examples of the 1973 oil crisis and Black Monday. Shifts in supply and demand due to biophysical changes may affect trade relationships. As Gleick (1989) has pointed out, shifting patterns of food production and disruption of trade due to climate change can have far-reaching implications for international security. But even in such economic disruption, both winners and losers will still occur.

Social structure sensitivity is broadly concerned with the response capabilities of a particular group. The theoretical research done in this area has identified a number of relevant factors defining sensitivity, ranging from the impact of class and gender on access to societal and natural resources, to the characteristics of formal and informal institutions. Many of these considerations are manifested in terms of economic relationships, but the social processes reproducing patterns of social relations require that they be considered separately.

Social relations are addressed in terms of differences among groups within society. Political economy perspectives stress the importance of social divisions, often by class, in accounting for differential access to resources and assets and differences in the magnitude of the impacts experienced. Differences among nation-states are another critical division in the context of climate change and response. Those with adequate access to resources and information may benefit from investment speculation, whereas others may struggle to survive.

Susman et al (1983, p264) defined vulnerability as, 'the degree to which the different classes in society are differentially at risk, both in terms of an extreme physical event and the degree to which the community absorbs the effects of extreme physical events and helps different classes to recover'. Ali (1984) documented the differential impact of drought according to gender differences in social and economic options. Social marginality as used by Parry (1985), and following Baird et al (1975), refers to situations in which the number of a group's adaptive mechanisms (or in Brooks' (1986) usage, the size and variegation of the response pool) decreases as a result of its separation from its indigenous resource base (and forced movement into another economic system).

Marginality may also refer to an increase in the vulnerability of a group due to reduced access to established institutional response capabilities. The services available to the rural poor are often fewer than those available to more advantaged groups. For instance, whereas two-thirds of the population of Third World countries live in rural areas, only about one-third of the rural population has electricity, and less than 10 per cent of the Third World's energy investment is directed to rural areas (Flavin, 1987). This potential source of support for health clinics, water supply systems and schools is often simply not available.

The types of social institutions and resource management infrastructure pervasively shape the breadth and depth of the response capability. One definition of vulnerability focuses on the growth of technological specialization, homogeneity and centralization and the related loss of diversity, multiplicity and redundancy. Whether institutions are highly adaptive or more narrowly prepared to respond to a set of opportunities, a potential to benefit rests largely with the ability to identify and react to opportunities.

The nature of social and economic institutions is another factor contributing to vulnerability. Increasing the reliance on management to reduce the variability of an ecosystem may erode the overall resilience of the ecosystem and its associated social and economic systems (Holling, 1986). In the context of global climate change and the potential shifts in water resource availability, the ability of the legal system to adjust to changes in the resource base will obviously affect the magnitude of potential disruptions. Similarly, the ability of social institutions to provide insurance, warnings, diagnosis and planning support will be a key element shaping successful coping.

Within the social structure, the ability to meet the needs of special populations is important. The elderly, children and pregnant mothers are often recognized as especially sensitive to environmental degradation. The special nutritional needs of children under the age of five and lactating and pregnant women, for example, are important considerations in assessing vulnerability to famine (Downing, 1988). Hazards research has explored vulnerability or hypersensitivity based on lifestyles and various other factors (Calabrese, 1978; Golding, 1989).

RISK/IMPACT DISTRIBUTIONS

By examining the interaction between potential distributions of effects over regions, generations and social groups, and the respective vulnerabilities of the affected ecosystems and populations, some estimates of the risks and impact distributions that will have to be borne may be made. Currently these effects remain highly uncertain and only very grossly apparent. In many cases, understanding of the impacts will be suggestive only or conditional on particular scenarios. As we have noted above, the incidence of impacts will not be locatable in space or (perhaps) time for many types of global change. Nonetheless, the state of empirical knowledge supporting equity claims and arguments needs to be confronted as clearly as possible. It is also highly likely that equity arguments will need to be framed *in terms of* certain types of ignorance, ambiguities and uncertainties. Funtowicz and Ravetz (1990) argued for a 'second-order science' to address these problems, and O'Riordan and Rayner (1990) explored the relations that exist between types of uncertainty conditions for authority and styles of problem solving.

NORMATIVE ANALYSIS

Armed with these empirical analyses, the next necessary step is to make judgements concerning the major types and magnitudes of inequity that would be associated with particular types of global environmental change. But this is possible only if some normative principle or standard is available that defines fairness. No absolute consensual standard of fairness, in our view, exists, but alternative notions of fairness can be used to show the differing pictures of inequity emerging from the application of different value systems. A precedent for such an approach to equity in the radioactive waste area is available in Kneese et al (1983). Here we identify three major approaches. The first would be identified from the philosophical and legal literature on social justice or from democratic theory normative principles that could serve to define equity. The second approach would use economic procedures of transferring inequities into monetary values and would design compensation programmes in accordance with the results of these 'revealed' inequities. A third approach, public preferences, as defined through empirical studies of public attitudes and values, could be adopted as a de facto normative principle. We explore each of these in turn.

Many candidate principles exist from which fairness in global environment change might proceed. Mill, for example, in his classic statement of utilitarianism ([1863], 1961) calls for 'the greatest good for the greatest number', implying not only the maximization of aggregate utility but also the distribution of utilities in as wide a manner as is feasible. US legislation on radioactive wastes explicitly advocates that the beneficiaries of waste generation should bear the costs of waste disposal, and that such costs should not be exported to future generations. Much the same could be said about coal burning. Aristotle's equality principle – that equals must be treated equally – has sometimes been invoked as a principle of equity. Although originally devised to distinguish between citizens and slaves (non-equals), the basic idea is to provide an even burden to all who share the benefit. Others (e.g. Passmore, 1974) argue for a stewardship principle – that human beings hold the Earth in stewardship and are responsible for passing it on to their descendants without irreversible destruction, and/or having made it more fruitful. A claim might also be made that what would be reprehensible is that we live in luxury while at the same time destining our children to exist at a subsistence level. Some see in John Rawls's *A Theory of Justice* (1971) procedures for developing equitable allocations from underlying principles of justice. The combined use of one or more principles is also possible.

Such an approach has been adopted by Edith Brown Weiss (1989, 1990) who, basing her work on equality principles, has called for a new doctrine on intergenerational equity embodying 'planetary rights and obligations'. Specifically, her notion of intergenerational equity calls for equality among generations and among members of any given generation in their rights to use and benefit from the planet and in their obligation to care for it. To this end, she recognizes three equity principles:

1   each generation should conserve the diversity of the natural and cultural resource base so that it does not unduly restrict the options available to future generations in solving their problems and satisfying their own values, and each generation is entitled to a diversity comparable to those of previous generations;
2   each generation should maintain the quality of the planet so that it is passed on in no worse condition than that generation received it, and each generation is entitled to an environmental quality comparable to that enjoyed by previous generations;
3   each generation should provide its members with equitable rights of access to the planetary legacy of past generations and should conserve this access for future generations (Weiss, 1990, pp9–10).

These egalitarian principles, of course, are highly debatable on grounds of both appropriateness as ethical imperatives and feasibility or lack of realism (Shrader-Frechette, 1985). Indeed, these principles pose many of the same definitional struggles currently preoccupying sustainable development efforts.

The transposition of empirically determined inequities into monetary values has been the focus of economic analyses of income and risk distribution. The classic criterion (Kaldor, 1939) that inequities are tolerable if the beneficiaries are willing to compensate the persons at risk so that they are as 'happy' as they were before the measure was taken, provides a rational basis for procedural equity, but the problem of delineating the correct amount of compensation for all affected individuals has not yet been resolved. Given the high degree of uncertainty surrounding the impacts of global environmental change, the feasibility of identifying those at risk and the level of risk is limited. And, of course, the approach assumes that all harms are compensatable. Although the degree of inequity as expressed in economic terms is certainly a major element for finding a fair procedure, the monetarization of inequities itself is not sufficient to assure fairness in outcomes. Although we question the potential of this particular normative approach, it offers one widely used criterion – utility – that can be explored.

A third alternative in the search for a normative principle is to seek to discover what the world's publics or their representatives prefer. Is there sufficient agreement in global values so that alternative environmental outcomes can be valued, weighted and compared? Is the global ethic called for in the Brundtland Report (WCED, 1987) accessible? A recent analysis of preliminary data on public responses to global change provides few grounds for optimism (Kasperson et al, 1990). Many will argue that sharp cultural divergences are to be expected. Differences in perceptions of the threat and the priority given to global environmental change versus other social and economic problems can also be expected. An abundance of problems will lie in wait for such an effort because public values entering into such equity issues are often labile and ill-understood, even by those who hold them. Also, potential trade-offs among competing values and preferences will need to be understood. Alternatively, public processes may be designed whose purpose is to provide an authoritative statement of such global values or ethic or ethos.

Again, it should be emphasized that the purpose of the normative equity analysis, in our view, is not to choose *the* moral principle or standard that should prevail. Elsewhere, the senior author has argued for a particular set of normative principles to guide policies on radioactive waste management (Kasperson, 1983a). Here our intent is more modest – to clarify how the application of alternative values or principles affects the pictures of inequities that emerge and to provide a useful perspective to those affected or involved in shaping regimes, international initiatives or national policies.

ESTIMATING TYPES AND MAGNITUDES OF INEQUITIES

With the application of one or more normative principle to the estimated risk/impact distributions, major patterns of inequity can be identified. Again, although specification of absolute magnitudes of inequity will certainly elude any calculation, it should be possible to discern some characteristics of types or gross magnitudes of relative inequity. The continued generation of greenhouse gas emissions resulting in the inundation of future populations in coastal areas (who have no recourse to the actions of this generation and who will have to bear enormous coping and adaptation costs) appears to be a clear case of both geographical and intergenerational inequity. Other major patterns should also be identifiable. And the application of alternative normative principles may clarify the presence of inequities across alternative value systems, allowing policy makers to apply different value systems.

ALLOCATION OF RESPONSIBILITY

The next step is to develop some strategy for determining the allocation of responsibility among those who could potentially bear the burden for redressing inequities. This is likely to be a highly contentious part of equity analysis and claims made on behalf of equity. We see three primary bases for allocating such responsibility: a contribution to global environmental degradation, a contribution to vulnerabilities, and an ability to bear the burdens for reducing potential harm.

Because concordance between benefit and risk is a strong equity principle in public policy, there is likely to be significant support for the claim that 'the one who causes the problem should pay for it'. Several dimensions of global problem causation should receive close attention:

- The majority of the increased CO_2 loading to the atmosphere over time is primarily the result of industrialization in the presently developed countries (Kellogg and Schware, 1981). The relative contribution of the developed countries to CO_2 emissions is declining, as developing countries such as China are beginning to increase their fossil fuel consumption.
- Increased NO_2 levels are predominantly the result of increases in fossil fuel combustion, production of mineral fertilizers, biomass burning and increasing areas of cultivated land (Bolle et al, 1986). The sources of methane are also both natural and related to human activity. The major biogenic sources are ruminants, rice paddies, and freshwater swamps and marshes. Human activities that release methane include coal mining, biomass burning and the exploitation of natural gas. Ozone levels are increasing due to photochemical processes involving methane, carbon monoxide and nitrogen oxides (Bolle et al, 1986). These sets of activities are widely dispersed and the degree of uncertainty surrounding estimates of emissions makes it difficult to determine relative contributions.
- Chlorofluorocarbons (CFCs) are industrial products used for solvents, refrigeration coolants and aerosols. They are primarily released from developed countries; however, their use in developing countries is growing. The agreement signed by 80 nations at the UNEP (United Nations Environment Programme) meeting in Helsinki calls for a complete ban of CFCs by 2000. This agreement is conditional, however, on the transfer of technology to developing countries.

A second perspective that has received much less attention in developed societies is the claim that those responsible for creating vulnerabilities among those who will experience the burden of global environmental degradation should bear some, or much, of the responsibility for the harm that occurs. Because the harm that will occur is a joint product of *exposure* to environmental degradation and *vulnerability* to such change, this claim seems no less compelling than the first. But because there is no social science consensus on what vulnerability is, much less its root causes, and because differing interpretations are embedded in conflicting ideologies, clarity or widespread support for these claims is likely to prove elusive. On the other hand, can anyone doubt that this equity claim will underlie much of the upcoming debate at the 1992 Conference on Environment and Development in Brazil?

Finally, there is the argument, especially in view of the ambiguity and uncertainty surrounding distributional causation and effects, that those most able to bear the burdens should have the primary responsibility for alleviating the problem. This is sometimes tempered by the argument that, because the goods and resources needed reside in a global commons, the responsibility should also be *shared*. These claims are not necessarily incompatible. Norway, for example, has recently accepted responsibility for contributing to efforts to respond to global warming despite its heavy reliance on hydroelectric power (and limited contribution to fossil fuel burning). The Netherlands has done the same. Beyond this is the recognition that the worldwide burden of responding to global change will require an ability-to-pay strategy for any viable policy responses that do not threaten developmental futures in the Third World.

DESIGNING MANAGEMENT STRATEGIES

The fact is, if global change is occurring, because of time lags in the biophysical and social systems we are already committed to both prevention and adaptation strategies. Once the inequities have been characterized and responsibilities have been allocated (or at least generally agreed upon), questions inevitably centre on what should be done. Much of the discussion thus far flowing out of the analysis of physical causation and effects has been to specify that emissions should be reduced by X or that technology Y should be phased out by year Z, with scant or no attention to the socioeconomic or political feasibility of such interventions, or to the impact on other socially desired objectives (e.g. the burning of China's coal supplies for energy production). Indeed, for any type of global environmental change, a wide variety of policy responses is available, consisting of some mix of reduction in causal factors, reduction in vulnerability of those impacted, mitigation of the harm, adaptations to change and improvements in the policy process itself. The current sterile discussion of whether prevention or adaptation should be preferred avoids the reality that we are already committed to both and the choice is in fact much larger in any case.

The ethically preferred management option in most cases will be to *avoid or reduce* the risks and adverse impacts that are at the root of the inequity. Avoiding harm and social disruption is almost always morally preferable to compensating for the harm or mitigating its effects, especially because some harms may not be compensatable (the original condition is not reattainable) or we may lack the means to gauge accurately the necessary compensation (because we do not know the future harms or persons). Also, potentially affected persons will surely have a strong preference for avoiding risk as well as receiving compensation, so that additional investments to assure a healthy and diverse environment as well as to transmit accompanying benefits will be necessary in reducing inequities associated with global environmental change. This suggests that strategies linking development assistance with environmental protection may be considerably effective as long as other national interests are respected. As Piddington (1989) pointed out, developing countries do not want 'green conditionality' attached to development resources. National sovereignty and control over decisions affecting the course of development are major areas of policy concern in developing countries. Given equity concerns, it is also probably necessary that:

- developed countries clean up their global legacy first; but
- that this clean-up be tied to progress by developing countries.

But it is also essential to recognize that the environmental degradation associated with growth and development will not end in the near future.

Another example with a strong ethical appeal is to fashion strategies that combine managing the often complicated and politically contentious system of technology control or management of human activities or driving forces with a focus on reducing vulnerabilities. The so-called 'tie-in strategies' that pursue other socially beneficial objectives simultaneously are a good example of this overall approach. This approach recognizes that uncertainties may be difficult to narrow (in many areas they will in fact grow with further scientific work) and that increasing resilience and coping resources may be one of the most effective means of reducing adverse global impacts. Future generations, for example, can be provided with resources and skills that would increase their ability to adapt to future climate change.

A third management option is to compensate for inequities that cannot be avoided. Although compensation can presumably be used to enlarge benefits to potentially harmed regions or future inhabitants of the world, it is unclear whether international law and institutional mechanisms will prove adequate to the challenge or whether new ones can be created. Natural resource severance taxes, such as the 'carbon tax', could provide an incentive both to reduce the problem and to fund greater adaptation capability. Planetary user and trust funds could be another important institutional mechanism.

Finally, investments in improved and more ambitious procedures for global decision making are a distinct, and potentially highly effective, means of inequity management. Especially where the sources of the inequity are procedural and embedded in legal systems as well as associated with the outcomes of human driving forces, an improved process and global institutional structure may greatly reduce the inequities and associated social conflict. The Intergovernmental Panel on Climate Change is a good case in microcosm of the process problems in shaping global consensus to support international initiatives. Expanded efforts in risk communication and public participation, when done well, are resource demanding even at local and regional levels but are potentially very effective management options. Innovative approaches such as an ombudsman for the future (Weiss, 1989, 1990) can also be used.

Final observations

The issues addressed in considering the equity problems in global environmental change are sufficiently complex and our thinking about them sufficiently early that a programme of initiatives is premature. But some key points to guide the next efforts seem clear:

- The primary value of equity analyses associated with global environmental change is to clarify the interaction of empirical and normative questions, thereby to distinguish basic from more superficial or transitory problems.
- A credible equity assessment of global environmental change needs to be sensitive to, and capable of, internalizing history, the broader ebb and flow of societal interactions, and the existence of other accumulated global inequities.
- The creation of global databases and monitoring systems should be structured in such a way as to provide information relevant to delineating equity over space and time and geared to relevant population groupings.
- The equity issues associated with global environmental change are distinctive as compared with most other equity problems in their high degree of uncertainly, ambiguity and unlocatable impacts and hazards (Clark, 1990).
- Competing normative principles or imperatives may be especially useful in a global setting where cultural differences are almost certain to be diverse and where little consensus on moral imperatives or trade-offs between competing social goals may exist in the near term.
- The existing vulnerabilities of ecosystems, economic and social structures may amplify and concentrate impacts and deserve much greater attention in estimating inequities and in fashioning global management schemes than has been thus far recognized.

14 Redirecting the US High-Level Nuclear Waste Programme

James Flynn, Roger E. Kasperson,
Howard Kunreuther and Paul Slovic

INTRODUCTION

The US began producing high-level nuclear wastes (HLNW) more than 50 years ago in the course of developing its first nuclear weapons. Since then, military and civilian uses of reactors have generated a large quantity of such wastes, creating serious management and disposal problems. Even now, after more than 40 years of effort and the expenditure of vast sums of money, the US does not have a technically sound or socially acceptable policy for dealing with its high-level nuclear wastes. Indeed, its current attempt to solve the problem by creating a national repository at Yucca Mountain, Nevada, is mired in conflict and destined for failure.

This chapter takes a fresh look at the problem of disposing of high-level nuclear wastes. After recounting the lessons we have learned during the last four decades, it offers some specific recommendations for moving beyond the present impasse. By way of background, the boxes on pp267 and 270 describe the wastes in question and outline official attempts to deal with them over the years.

AN UNACCEPTABLE APPROACH

A well-designed, effectively managed, and socially acceptable programme for disposing of HLNW would be difficult under the best of circumstances. What makes the current situation so disturbing, however, is that the agency responsible for the programme, the US Department of Energy (DOE), is attempting to develop a repository at Yucca Mountain by unilaterally redefining the rules, standards and procedures that were initially put in place to assure public safety and guide the programme to success.

Note: Reprinted from *Environment*, vol 39, Flynn, J., Kasperson, R. E., Kunreuther, H. and Slovic, P., 'Overcoming tunnel vision: Redirecting the US high-level nuclear water program', pp6–11, 25–30, © (1997), with permission from Heldref Publications

DOE's mandate is to study the Yucca Mountain site and determine if it can safely contain HLNW for thousands of years. What DOE wants to do, however, is build a repository – not just conduct a study. This was signalled earlier when DOE ordered a special machine to dig a 25-foot tunnel as part of a repository design rather than using existing equipment, which could provide a tunnel up to 18 feet and give perfectly satisfactory access to the underground area. The result was a significant additional cost and delay, which added almost nothing to the purpose of what is still called the 'exploratory studies facility' but which symbolically suggests engineering progress on developing a repository at Yucca Mountain.

More recently, DOE proposed new regulations for Yucca Mountain, which would eliminate the current factors for disqualification as well as doing away with socioeconomic, environmental and transportation assessments until after waste storage has taken place (USDOE, 1996). In a letter to energy secretary Hazel O'Leary, Nevada governor Bob Miller complained that the new regulations were contrary to the requirements of the Nuclear Waste Policy Act, but apparently DOE expects Congress to pass legislation endorsing its changes or take on the difficult task of devising a new programme with all the implications of delay and public controversy. The problem of meeting regulatory standards is not just going to disappear, however, and as the General Accounting Office (USGAO, 1997) has recently reported, there are a number of serious impediments to DOE's plans and those plans are unlikely to meet the needs of federal regulatory agencies.

In another recent move, DOE abruptly announced a total revision of its transportation programme under which it plans to contract with private companies to accept spent fuel and transport these wastes to a repository or interim storage facility. This would cancel more than a decade of work on transportation issues, which are of critical interest to 43 states, hundreds of local jurisdictions and more than 50 million citizens residing near shipment routes. The Western Interstate Energy Board, an arm of the Western Governors' Association, called this privatization plan 'an approach that was unacceptable in the 1980s, and it is unacceptable now'. In a letter to DOE, the board said the new plan would 'renege on commitments' and constitutes a 'shirking of responsibilities to states and the public' (Moore and Nix, 1997).

The model that DOE is following, the so-called decide–announce–defend (DAD) approach, failed badly at Lyons, Kansas, 30 years ago. That failure, and the long decade of confusion, delay and frustration that preceded passage of the Nuclear Waste Policy Act (NWPA) in 1982, show clearly that the DAD model does not work. In fact, that model was implicitly rejected with the enactment of NWPA, which provided for regulation by the Nuclear Regulatory Commission and the Environmental Protection Agency, along with oversight by affected states and Indian tribes; created an intricate architecture of provisions for achieving fairness

Box 14.1 High-level nuclear wastes

There are three general categories of nuclear wastes: high-level, transuranic and low-level. High-level nuclear wastes (HLNW) include spent (irradiated) uranium fuel from nuclear reactors and the solidified liquid wastes from reprocessing such fuel to produce plutonium for nuclear weapons. Nuclear fission creates numerous highly radioactive products with half-lives (rates of decay) ranging from seconds to millennia. Strontium-90, for example, has a half-life of 29 years, while plutonium-239 has a half-life of 24,400 years. Spent fuel and other forms of HLNW require careful handling and storage. According to the standard set by the US Environmental Protection Agency, such wastes have to be kept in isolation for at least 10,000 years. This standard is widely accepted throughout the world, although some countries require longer periods of containment.

Transuranic wastes are materials that are not high-level radioactive wastes but contain alpha-emitting radionuclides above the atomic number of 92. Low-level wastes are all other radioactive wastes, which, because of their low radionuclide content, do not require shielding during normal handling and transportation.

Experts expect that by 2035 the total quantity of HLNW produced in the US will be about 110,000 metric tonnes of heavy metal (MTHM), 85,000 MTHM from power generation and 25,000 MTHM from weapons production (USDOE, 1994, p2). There will also be small amounts of spent fuel from navy ships, reactors built by US companies overseas, and research reactors.

Transporting this quantity of HLNW would involve one of the largest shipping efforts ever undertaken. According to one study, transporting all of the US' HLNW to Yucca Mountain from 80 reactors and weapons complex sites located in 36 states would require as many as 79,300 truck-cask shipments and 12,600 rail-cask shipments over 30 years. The average distance travelled would be 2300 miles. Forty-three states would be involved, with major transportation corridors running through Utah, Nebraska, Wyoming, Illinois, Iowa, Kansas, Missouri and Indiana (USDOE, 1994, p2).

(including a requirement that DOE 'consult and cooperate'); and established a process for building public understanding and support. However, DOE has been completely unable to develop alternatives to the DAD approach except in its public relations statements.

A new approach to managing and disposing of HLNW is urgently needed. The current programme should be halted and its unrealistic deadlines abandoned. Claims that a crisis in safe storage of HLNW justifies DOE's rogue programme should be thoroughly evaluated. There appears to be ample time to create a safe HLNW programme and to proceed in a manner that wins public acceptance and support. Two developments over the past decade are encouraging in this regard. First, new technologies such as dry-cask storage will enable the wastes to be stored for a century or more at existing reactor sites or other temporary facilities. Second, attempts to site disposal facilities (including those for low-level and transuranic wastes), along with experience in siting other hazardous facilities, have improved understanding of what is necessary to win public acceptance. Attention to safety, environmental protection, trust and confidence in programme managers and adherence to high standards of public values such as fairness, equity and accountable decision processes are essential.

A DIFFICULT PROBLEM

Before the passage of NWPA in 1982, the prevailing opinion of those managing nuclear power was that disposal of HLNW was not a difficult or serious problem. However, the task turned out to be far more challenging than even the experts could guess. In reflecting on his years as director of the Oak Ridge National Laboratory (ORNL), Alvin Weinberg concluded that he paid 'too little attention to the waste problem. Designing and building reactors, not nuclear waste, was what turned me on.' If he could do it over, he would 'elevate waste disposal to the very top of ORNL's agenda' (Weinberg, 1994, p183). Alas, some experts and technical managers still maintain the old perspective that HLNW is a 'rather trivial technical problem' (Cohen, 1990). Similar opinions have been expressed by Carter (1987).

In response to NWPA, in 1983 DOE embarked on programmes to develop a centralized monitored retrievable storage (MRS) facility in Tennessee; to identify and 'characterize' (study) three first-round sites in the western US for a permanent repository; and to identify a set of potential second-round repository sites in the eastern part of the country. Recognizing that most nuclear power stations were in the East, NWPA called for geographic equity with both a western and an eastern repository site. This ambitious effort failed in many ways, most dramatically in 1986 when DOE abruptly suspended work on an eastern repository site under pressure from congressional representatives in an election year (Carter, 1987).

Lessons from NWPA's early years

A wide range of problems was revealed in the first five years after NWPA was passed. First, obtaining reasonable assurance that a repository would protect human health and the environment was much more complex and uncertain than anticipated, and the public had great concerns about all aspects of handling, transporting and storing HLNW (Jacob 1990; USNRC 1990; Flynn et al 1995). Second, public acceptance was not achieved and the programme ran into vigorous opposition from citizens, communities and states at each potential site (Dunlap et al, 1993). Third, relations between DOE and states and communities were contentious and often bitterly adversarial, as shown by the dozens of legal actions filed against the department in federal court. Fourth, management and administration of the programme were chaotic and inadequate (Nuclear Waste Strategy Coalition, 1994). Schedules slipped and essential programme activities such as quality assurance failed to meet regulatory requirements. Fifth, programme costs soared (USGAO, 1987). Sixth, as information was put together for the environmental reports intended to compare first-round candidate sites, it became increasingly clear that scientific, engineering and management problems would be difficult and contentious (Easterling and Kunreuther, 1995). After five years of effort, the programme was clearly not working (Carter, 1987; Jacob, 1990).

The basic principles of NWPA included a strong emphasis on public health and the environment, with independent regulation and state oversight; fairness and equity in process and outcome; 'consultation and cooperation' with states and affected Indian tribes; and scientific and technical work of high integrity to determine the best sites. Combined with the other failures, DOE's ineffectiveness in putting these principles into effect prompted Representative Morris Udall (Democrat-Arizona), one of the lead authors of NWPA, to call for a programme moratorium and a thorough review in 1987.

An easier alternative was to amend NWPA and reduce the repository programme to something DOE could accomplish. Senator J. Bennett Johnston (Democrat-Louisiana), generally credited as the author of the 1987 Amendments Act, avoided the sort of open policy review that had preceded passage of NWPA and confined the substantive discussions to committees favouring a quick fix at Yucca Mountain. The amendments were steered through a complex and often byzantine process and eventually passed as part of the Omnibus Budget Reconciliation Act of 1987.

The NWPA repository selection process, with all its provisions for technical integrity and its measures to assure fairness, was abandoned. The second-round site selection programme and the Tennessee MRS projects were cancelled. Study of first-round sites, except for Yucca Mountain, was halted. In and out of Congress, the amendments were recognized as an opportunistic choice based on Nevada's weak political position in Congress. (Nevadans called these amendments the 'Screw Nevada' bill.) Equally seriously, the amendments did not address the underlying reasons for the failure of the original programme, perhaps because no real review was conducted to understand why the programme had collapsed (Jacob, 1990; Flynn and Slovic, 1995).

Focus on Yucca Mountain

As a result of the 1987 amendments, a repository at Yucca Mountain became the only option for storing the nation's HLNW. If DOE could not

Box 14.2 A history of high-level nuclear waste disposal efforts

A number of different federal agencies have had a hand in managing the US nuclear programme since the US began producing high-level nuclear wastes (HLNW) in the 1940s. These include the US Army (1942–46), the Atomic Energy Commission (AEC) (1946–74), the Energy Research and Development Agency (ERDA) (1974–78), the Nuclear Regulatory Commission (NRC) (since 1974), the Department of Energy (DOE) (since 1978), and the Office of Civilian Radioactive Waste Management (OCRWM) (since 1983). The following chronology details waste disposal efforts over the years (Carter, 1987; Easterling and Kunreuther, 1995; Flynn and Slovic, 1995):

- **1955–57**: The National Academy of Sciences considers the HLNW problem and recommends consideration of salt formations as a possible geologic medium for disposal (USNRC, 1957).
- **1963–72**: AEC conducts studies at an unused salt mine near Lyons, Kansas. Attempts to site a repository at this location in 1970 fail. The condition of the mine along with opposition by the state of Kansas force abandonment of the site by 1972.
- **1975–82**: ERDA and DOE search for potential repository sites in the states of Michigan, Ohio, New York, Utah, Texas, Louisiana, Mississippi, Washington and Nevada. Various degrees of resistance from state and local representatives combine with geological and technical problems to stall efforts to find a repository site. The federal government establishes an Interagency Review Group to develop a broad-based federal policy. A 1979 report by this group endorsing state participation in the decision-making process influences subsequent congressional legislation. President Gerald Ford orders a halt to the reprocessing of commercial spent fuel in 1976, and President Jimmy Carter reiterates that ban and also stops commercial breeder reactor development in 1977.
- **1979–82**: Congress works to draft the nation's first comprehensive policy on HLNW. The nuclear industry, DOE, environmental and anti-nuclear groups, and potential host states all play key roles in the process.
- **1982**: Congress passes the Nuclear Waste Policy Act, an extraordinarily complex piece of legislation that establishes a Nuclear Waste Fund; requires detailed study ('characterization') of three repository sites from which to make a final choice; imposes a schedule for opening a repository by 1998; and provides for participation by states and Indian tribes. Two repositories are planned, one in the western US (limited to 70,000 metric tonnes of heavy metal) and a second in the eastern part of the country to achieve geographical equity and provide a fair sharing of the disposal burden. The Nuclear Regulatory Commission is assigned the duty of licensing the repository, while the Environmental Protection

Agency is required to establish standards for its safety performance. A fee of one mill per kilowatt hour of electricity produced is imposed on nuclear power plants to provide revenues for the Nuclear Waste Fund, which is to be administered as part of the federal budget.

- **1982–87**: DOE's handling of the study and selection process provokes widespread concern and opposition in both the first- and second-round states. DOE encounters difficulties in implementing the programme. In 1986, DOE selects sites in Nevada, Texas and Washington State for site characterization and, due to opposition from the states in an election year, discontinues study of second-round sites in the Midwest and East. Three sites in Tennessee are recommended for consideration as potential monitored retrievable storage sites as part of the national HLNW disposal programme. Cost estimates for the programme escalate sharply and DOE decisions are widely questioned, with a number of these subjected to litigation and political opposition. Concerns grow that the programme may fail.
- **1987**: The Nuclear Waste Policy Act Amendments of 1987 restructure the programme by selecting Yucca Mountain, Nevada, as the only repository site to be studied, despite the fact that technical studies are only beginning. Further work at Deaf Smith, Texas, and Hanford, Washington, is cancelled. The amendments passed in the last days of December and attached to the 1987 Budget Reconciliation Act discontinue all work on second-round sites and halt DOE's efforts to locate a monitored retrievable storage site in Tennessee. A Nuclear Waste Technical Review Board is established and 'affected local governments' are afforded participation rights and financial assistance.
- **1988–96**: The Yucca Mountain project is hobbled and delayed by unexpected scientific, management, intergovernmental, cost, public opposition, schedule and regulatory compliance problems, leading to expressions of concern by the nuclear industry and Congress. As a result, the National Academy of Sciences Board on Radioactive Waste Management calls for an overall 'rethinking' of the waste disposal programme (USNRC, 1990). DOE executes a series of programme and technical design changes in an attempt to create a programme it can handle while seeking to relax standards for licensing and permitting. Progress is slow, costs continue to rise and deadlines are delayed. In 1996, recognizing that the programme is failing, Congress attempts to revise the HLNW programme via Senate bill 1936, which reduces standards and regulation for Yucca Mountain and mandates an interim storage facility at the Nevada Test Site adjacent to Yucca Mountain. This legislation is abandoned in the weeks before the election under threat of a veto by President Clinton.
- **1997**: Another version of Senate bill 1936 is introduced as Senate bill 104 on January 21.

construct this facility, Congress would have to develop a new programme. Nothing in these amendments effectively addressed public opposition, the lack of trust and confidence in DOE, the scientific uncertainty surrounding the programme, DOE's management problems and the possibilities of other management options, the difficulties presented by intergovernmental conflict, or the rationale and priority of the legislated waste acceptance schedule. The only response to these pressing problems in the amendments was the congressional mandate to look solely at Yucca Mountain.

The prospects for protecting human health and the environment did not improve with the exclusive focus on a single site. The optimistic hunch that Yucca Mountain would prove to be a suitable site, as urged by science writer Luther J. Carter (1987) in his influential book, began to fade along with the idea that DOE could provide the assurances required by regulators and the public. Then, in 1990, the National Academy of Sciences' Board on Radioactive Waste Management (BRWM) reported that the existing programme was 'unlikely to succeed' and that there was a need to 'rethink the program' as a whole (USNRC, 1990).

Despite some advantages of the federal programme, BRWM found one overriding disadvantage: Science cannot '"prove" (in any absolute sense) that a repository will be "safe" as defined by EPA and the USNRC regulations'. The board identified two reasons for this: the 'residual uncertainties' of a repository preclude DOE (or anyone else) from making the required assurances, and 'safety is in part a social judgment, not just a technical one'. The technical problem turned out to be anything but trivial. BRWM suggested an 'alternative approach' that would be more flexible, incremental and adaptive. While the 'ultimate performance' goal could be specified, the alternative approach would enable programme managers to learn as they went along, use expert opinion to address issues of uncertainty, and react to problems rather than trying to anticipate them (USNRC, 1990, pp2–6).

Meanwhile, DOE made little progress in gaining public trust and confidence and in asserting management control over the programme (Secretary of Energy Advisory Board, 1993). The nuclear industry and Congress were greatly concerned by the combined lack of programme progress and escalating costs. Site studies were estimated to cost US$60 to $80 million in 1981; by 1987, the estimates had risen to $2 billion for each of three planned study sites by 1987 and to $6 billion for the single site at Yucca Mountain by 1994. Congressional responses to these figures forced DOE to reduce its efforts and obligations at every turn to maintain some semblance of adequacy in the Nuclear Waste Fund.

The failure to understand and address the problems revealed during the first five years of the HLNW programme and the abrogation of the basic principles in NWPA meant that the programme as it was revised by the 1987 Amendments Act was seriously flawed. DOE's mission, although still cloaked in the terms of site characterization studies and 'reasonable assurance' of safety, became fixated on the transfer of HLNW from the reactor sites to Yucca Mountain. Since 1988, DOE has been struggling to site an HLNW storage facility, churning through a series of programme revisions and strategies, seeking ever-more lenient standards and looser regulations, resisting demands from nuclear power utilities for early removal of their HLNW, fighting states and local communities who are afraid of the transportation and storage risks, striving to reduce programme costs that constantly threaten to outstrip future Nuclear Waste Fund revenues, and attempting to defer licensing accountability for the ultimate safety of a repository at Yucca Mountain into the distant future (USDOE, 1995, section 1–24, I6–I8). DOE's implicit strategy is evident: if it could avoid facing the regulatory, cost, and safety issues long enough, a repository or interim storage facility could be developed at Yucca Mountain as a *fait accompli*.

DOE's evolving, opportunistic approach has presented the nation with two major problems. First, it undercuts important performance goals and leaves the nation with a waste management programme that changes the rules of the game as it goes along. (The department's management of radioactive wastes at the nation's weapons complex, where it set its own environmental and safety standards, suggests the dangers of such a strategy.) Second, if acceptable safety or risk 'is in part a social judgment', then a new social judgement is clearly called for. Widespread lack of public trust, confidence and support for the existing programme make it clear that the 1987 amendments do not entail a societal mandate.

Ultimate goals and social judgements on HLNW

What are the basic terms of a societal judgement? The National Environmental Policy Act of 1969 and subsequent legislation, such as the Clean Air Act and the Safe Drinking Water Act, expanded the standards of health and environmental protection and allocated responsibility for meeting those standards to federal agencies and those in state and local governments. NWPA attempted to structure the HLNW programme so that it would conform with the spirit of the nation's environmental laws (although it also made special provisions to expedite the licensing and permitting process). The EPA determined that a repository should provide containment for at least 10,000 years and that DOE must provide assurances that this ultimate goal would be met. However, these provisions require precise knowledge of future societal and environmental conditions over very long periods of time, thereby posing questions of great complexity and considerable uncertainty.

Much of the research done by DOE has addressed the physical conditions at Yucca Mountain. Preliminary as they are, these studies reveal a number of complex problems. The major radiation pathways from an HLNW repository to the environment are air and water. The geologic structure at Yucca Mountain is so fractured and faulted that it would not meet EPA standards for the release of carbon-14, which as a gas could easily escape to the surface (van Konynenburg, 1991). Congress responded to this disqualifying condition by mandating less stringent methods for calculating the radiation risks for a Yucca Mountain repository in an amendment to the Energy Policy Act of 1992. The recent discovery at repository depths of chlorine-36, an isotope produced by atmospheric nuclear bomb tests, indicates that water migration from the surface has occurred in less than 50 years, contrary to expectations. The existence of this water pathway could compromise protection of HLNW within a repository (Fabryka-Martin et al, 1996). Daniel Dreyfus, the director of the Office of Civilian Radioactive Waste Management (OCRWM), admitted that 'a strict interpretation of the regulations would mean a disqualifying condition "unless you can change the regs"' (Rogers, 1996).

Seismic and volcanic hazards pose further problems (Broad, 1990, p37). On 29 June 29 1992, an earthquake of magnitude 5.6 occurred at Skull Mountain, just 12 miles from the repository site, seriously damaging DOE's project buildings at Yucca Mountain. This was followed on 17 May, 1993 by an earthquake of magnitude 6.0 south of Bishop, California, about 100 miles west of Yucca Mountain. The southern Nevada area is a young, geologically active environment. The Ghost Dance Fault, which cuts directly through Yucca Mountain from south to north, is of particular concern. As government geologists explained in May 1993, they do not know when this fault was last active or whether it is in a zone connected to other faults (Monastersky, 1994, p310; Rogers, 1994).

Yucca Mountain was created from volcanic ash compressed into the rock ('tuff') that is the geologic medium for the repository. The Crater Flat area, which includes one dormant volcano about 7 miles from Yucca Mountain, is a source of potential volcanic activity (USDOE, 1986, section 1.2.3.2). According to Geomatrix Consultants, Inc. and TRW (1996, pp2–14) a DOE contractor, there are 'uncertainties in models that describe the future locations of volcanic events and models that describe the temporal distribution or rate of events'. In early 1995, DOE assembled a panel of experts and elicited their opinions about how likely future volcanic eruptions are. The panel concluded (in a report that was released in June 1996) that 'the probability of a volcano erupting through the repository during the next 10,000 years is about 1 in 10,000' (Kerr, 1996, p913). Eliciting opinions as substitutes for data and predictive models saves DOE money, time and research effort, but how well this use of subjective judgement defines the risks and uncertainties at Yucca Mountain is an open question. According to a report in *Science*, DOE will attempt to address other scientific and engineering uncertainties at Yucca Mountain in the same manner, calling on expert panels that have been put through an extensive training programme and coached to reach a consensus (Kerr, 1996).

In the face of massive technical uncertainty, contractors working for DOE at Yucca Mountain are put in an equivocal position. An example of how one DOE contractor attempted to convert unresolved uncertainty into a benefit is demonstrated by a site suitability study which stated (in somewhat convoluted language) that uncertainty and lack of evidence fail to show that the repository will not meet qualifying conditions (Younker et al, 1992). This curious logic was then endorsed by DOE's Yucca Mountain project director as evidence that the repository programme was on the right track (Shrader-Frechette, 1993).

Responding to complexity and uncertainty and taking into account the surprises that certainly will occur over a 10,000-year period requires a new level of adaptability – that is, the ability to adjust to technological and social change as well as to unforeseen circumstances. Important questions abound in this area. Should DOE, on its own, make the necessary adjustments? Can DOE define what is acceptable to society, or is it too committed to Yucca Mountain to conduct objective studies and achieve real public acceptance?

Another legislative fix

Some people think the government is now too far along with the Yucca Mountain project to back away. Given where we are, they say, lower standards should be adopted so that we can move ahead. Science writer Luther J. Carter recently voiced this view, stating: 'Today the nation simply does not have the political stomach for another search for sites, for either a geologic repository or a surface storage facility.' Besides, Carter says, even if Yucca Mountain has problems, other sites might not be any better (Carter, 1997, p13). However well such casual observations might apply to ordinary government programmes, they seem out of place for a first-of-its-kind HLNW repository that must ensure safe isolation of radioactive wastes for 10,000 years or more.

The problem for proponents of the Yucca Mountain project is that to save it they will have to change the law and the rules. An attempt to 'fix' the Yucca Mountain programme was passed by the Senate in 1996 (Senate bill 1936) but died in the House under the threat of a presidential veto. The terms of that bill – which has been described as a nuclear industry wish-list – have now been incorporated into Senate bill 104, introduced by Senator Frank Murkowski (Republican-Alaska) on 21 January, 1997. The primary strategy is to pass a new law that weakens the standards again and attempts to force acceptance of both an interim storage facility and a repository at Yucca Mountain. Senate bill 104 provides rewards for small, local jurisdictions in Nevada that are viewed as allies of the DOE's programme and completely removes the state of Nevada as a participant.

Special standards for Yucca Mountain would assess radioactive doses to the public for 1000 rather than 10,000 years, even though HLNW will remain hazardous well beyond 10,000 years (USOMB, 1996). An 'average member of the general population in the vicinity of Yucca Mountain' could receive doses of radiation as high as 100 millirems (mrem) per year. The

Canadian standard, by contrast, is less than 1 mrem per year, while the (US) National Academy of Sciences' recommendation is 2–20 mrem per year, similar to the standards in other countries. The New Mexico Waste Isolation Pilot Project (for disposal of less dangerous transuranic wastes) is limited to 15 mrem per year, and the NRC's low-level waste (the least dangerous radioactive wastes) standard is 25 mrem per year (USOMB, 1996, EPA Attachment, 4).

Regulatory concern about human intrusion at a repository would be removed by having NRC *assume* that the engineered barriers and post-closure oversight will prevent human intrusion and exposure. John Cantlon (1996, p7), chairman of the Nuclear Waste Technical Review Board, clearly stated the problem confronting us here: 'There is no scientific basis for predicting the probability of inadvertent human intrusion over the long times of interest for a Yucca Mountain repository.' But rather than suggesting scientific study of this important problem, he concludes that 'intrusion analyses should not be required and should not be used during licensing to determine the acceptability of the candidate repository' (Cantlon, 1996, p7). Inadvertent and deliberate intrusion appear confounded here, but in any case it is curious to hear eminent nuclear experts argue that the current inability to assess a risk is a reason for eliminating it from consideration in the licensing process.

It is not only scientific uncertainty and the possibility of human intrusion that present risks to human health and the environment at Yucca Mountain. Having DOE the manager of the HLNW programme entails risks that are seldom acknowledged but deeply troubling. Some nuclear industry supporters claim that storage of HLNW at nuclear power stations is an urgent problem. They demand that these wastes be transferred from places where they have been managed safely for 40 years or more, and where they can be securely stored for another century, to a federal facility. It is ironic that they wish to hand them over to DOE, which is now struggling to clean up – at a cost that may reach hundreds of billions of dollars – massive radioactive contamination at weapons sites across the US.

WHERE DO WE GO FROM HERE?

A new approach to managing and disposing of HLNW is needed. The first step is to halt the current programme and drop the unrealistic schedule. Flexible and realistic timetables would allow time for adequate research on technical and social problems and comparison of alternative approaches, such as seabed disposal.

We should attend to the experiences of other countries, which have developed much more flexible schedules and research programmes, learning and adapting when faced with public opposition to their HLNW plans. The programmes in Canada, Sweden, the UK and France are certainly not without problems, but the governments of those countries have also been willing to change – often dramatically – to address public concerns (Greber et al, 1994; Flynn et al, 1995, ch 6). The experience of these countries suggests quite strongly that the decide–announce–defend approach and the use of central government authority to override public concerns are not likely to be successful. France used such an approach prior to 1990, when widespread public opposition led to a temporary moratorium on the search for disposal sites. Similarly, the UK scrapped its DAD approach in favour of 'The Way Forward', a more open programme with involvement by a wide range of stakeholders. In Sweden, a low- and intermediate-level waste facility and an interim HLNW storage facility have been opened and a specially designed transport ship put into service. This was accomplished with a programme that listened and responded to critics and host communities to achieve a broad public consensus. The US clings to its rushed schedule and the aim of 'getting the waste into the ground' with a DAD strategy that is now widely discredited across advanced industrial societies. Failure to learn from its problems and restructure its programme, as other societies have done, remains one of the most puzzling attributes of the US experience.

Dry-cask storage could be used at reactor sites or at centralized, perhaps regional, locations. There are some questions about such interim storage, but it provides necessary additional time for research and public consultation and it is considerably less costly than the pursuit of a troubled geologic repository programme.

In looking toward permanent disposal, it will be important to examine more than one site and more than one option. Keeping the available options open until a firm social, political and technical consensus develops is a prudent way to address the issues of uncertainty and intense public opposition. A new process should employ a voluntary site selection programme. Congress should mandate that no community be forced to accept a repository against its will, and potential host communities should be encouraged and empowered to play a genuinely active role in the planning, design and evaluation of any HLNW facility, especially a repository. A voluntary process should be structured to acknowledge the legitimacy of public concerns, provide for public participation, develop agreed-upon procedures, commit to openness and fairness (including mitigation and compensation where appropriate), and empower state and local communities in decisions about safety.

Experience with other noxious facilities has revealed that the siting process is most likely to be successful when trust is established between the developer and the host region. This trust is likely to emerge only if the public has an opportunity to participate fully in the siting process (Kunreuther et al, 1993). The credibility of the US HLNW programme must be established. This requires a new organization to replace DOE, one capable of fulfilling the management and oversight roles required to address this complex and uncertain programme. A new and different approach is needed – one committed to implementing a restructured programme in an open, consultative and cooperative manner, and one that does not seek to deny or avoid the serious social, political and economic problems.

Review, learn, improve

The experience of the past 15 years contains many lessons for restructuring the nation's high-level nuclear waste programme. Understanding the past is a necessary prelude to a better future. Over the past several years, industry groups, state and local governments, public advocacy groups, congressional representatives, the US General Accounting Office, the Western Governors' Association and numerous individuals have recommended a searching, high-level review. To make recommendations and lay the foundation for a successful new programme, this review must address six issues: protection of human health and the environment; public participation; intergovernmental relations and stakeholder participation; programme and project management; costs and funding; and the scientific and technical challenges.

Protection of human health and the environment

The public sees HLNW as one of the most dangerous technological hazards in existence and wants assurances of safe handling, transportation and storage through all steps of the disposal process. The review should do the following: examine and make recommendations about the classification of radioactive wastes, taking into consideration the type and longevity of equivalent hazards for inclusion in an HLNW programme; evaluate the safety of on-site, interim and permanent storage, including the risks of handling and transportation; consider the health and environmental regulations needed for interim and permanent storage; recommend guidelines for making societal judgements about major issues of uncertainty and determining how the burden of proof is shared; define the role of host states and communities in an HLNW programme; review how engineered and geological barriers can be integrated to provide safe storage; investigate the quality of programme management as a risk factor; and provide guidance on ways to determine how safe is safe enough for social acceptability.

Public participation

Public opposition has bedevilled HLNW projects for decades, and public support and acceptance will be required of any new programme. This problem has led to numerous studies on risk perceptions, attitudes and opinions about HLNW, the role of trust and confidence in HLNW managers, and the possibility of cooperation among industry, federal officials, states, communities and citizens. This literature is now extensive and should be carefully reviewed. New standards for meeting public participation goals should be recommended and new programme sponsors should commit to an ambitious effort to this end.

Intergovernmental relations and stakeholder participation

The establishment of guidelines for public participation and accountable project management will go a long way toward solving some of the traditional intergovernmental conflicts. However, additional steps will be needed to ensure that state and local governments, Indian tribes and special stakeholder groups (e.g. environmental, cultural and scientific groups) have an important place in the national HLNW programme. The review commission should therefore recommend which stakeholders (including industry and regulators) should be involved in the national HLNW programme and at what level and stages in the process; assess how their participation can be authorized, maintained over time, funded and guaranteed; determine what interaction and adjudication processes will be needed; and address the intergovernmental legal issues, including the constitutional rights of states in a federal programme that is largely designed to benefit the privately owned nuclear power industry.

Programme and project management

DOE's HLNW programme management has been widely criticized as inefficient, ineffectual, and unresponsive to stakeholder concerns. The review should examine past problems with the HLNW programme; consider alternative management organizations; define personnel, performance and outcome criteria for the HLNW programme organization; and recommend actions to establish a programme that actually has the resources, authority and accountability needed to implement an effective and resilient HLNW effort.

Costs and funding

The Nuclear Waste Fund is seriously underfunded. DOE has attempted to restructure the programme and reduce costs, but the fund simply cannot meet the real costs of a national disposal programme. Under the current programme, even with its cutbacks, an increase in the fee is called for. However, so little progress has resulted from the time and money already spent, that it is difficult for DOE to advocate fee increases to cover shortfalls in the fund.

The review needs to examine the ways by which costs are estimated and provide recommendations to improve their accuracy. The cost impacts of the decision to combine military and civilian wastes should be reviewed and recommendations should be made for ensuring systematic and adequate payments. The administration of civilian waste fees through the federal budget process has led to the use of the fees to balance the federal budget. The review should examine the current federal management of fund revenues and evaluate other options for funding a national HLNW programme. Ultimate cost responsibility for HLNW belongs to those who own the wastes. A major complication is that the time period required for the HLNW programme, which will extend well beyond the operating lifetime of the nuclear power plants producing the wastes, means that at some point in the relatively near future the real costs of spent fuel disposal could become unrecoverable. The review commission should examine the cost and liability implications that would accrue if the federal government were to take title to the wastes under various conditions prior to final disposal. Finally, the commission should re-examine the adequacy of the Nuclear Waste Fund, as well as how changes in fees should be made and how fair cost allocations can be established.

Scientific and technical challenges

Historically, strategies to manage HLNW have been dominated by the idea that a combination of scientific, engineering and technical fixes can be developed to provide acceptable long-term HLNW disposal. The complexity and uncertainty of permanent disposal preclude demonstrations of 'reasonable assurances' with such fixes, however, and major social, economic and political concerns have clearly overwhelmed the HLNW programme. The primary response to this dilemma so far has been to reduce or even eliminate standards for assuring repository performance and to prevent critics and host area people from being part of the process. A review should consider scientific and technical issues within the larger societal framework, not as the dominant solution to pre-empt individual, public and institutional decisions, but as a component in structuring a socially acceptable decision about a national HLNW programme.

SUMMARY

The time is long overdue to recognize publicly that Yucca Mountain is a failed programme. We can learn from this failure, however. We now know, for example, how important public acceptance and trust are to the success of any HLNW programme. We have learned that intergovernmental cooperation must be earned and not simply mandated by Congress; that funding and budgeting will have to be reconceptualized and restructured; that the scientific and engineering challenges of locating, building and operating a geologic repository are complex and will involve significant levels of uncertainty; and that the ultimate goal of protecting human health and the environment can easily be eroded unless continuous societal oversight takes place. The existing programme has demonstrated that it is fundamentally incapable of addressing the problems of HLNW. The next essential step is to pause and explore the proper questions, learn from past mistakes and the experience of other countries, and begin the difficult task of creating a socially acceptable solution in the US.

15 Siting Hazardous Facilities: Searching for Effective Institutions and Processes

Roger E. Kasperson

INTRODUCTION

In the unfolding technological advances and economic growth of advanced industrial societies, few problems have proven more contentious or perplexing than the siting of hazardous facilities. The extent to which these problems have been shared across diverse societies differing in industrial structures, political cultures and social institutions is quite remarkable. As Chapters 2 and 14 make clear, the issues that underlie public concerns and opposition are sufficiently deeply seated to create policy impasses in varying social and political settings. This fact in itself should signal that these challenges are likely to be durable over time and unlikely to be readily resolved without major rethinking and significant redirections in responsible institutions and siting processes.

This chapter considers lessons apparent in siting experience over the past two decades and explores implications for improved institutional approaches. It begins with an assessment of the siting problem – why has it proved to be so difficult? It then reviews major approaches that have been taken to siting hazardous facilities, suggesting constraints and limits that circumscribe each. Lessons from comparative experience are noted. Finally, considerations are set forth for elements that must be addressed in order to achieve greater siting success.

SITING HAZARDOUS FACILITIES: Why is it so difficult?

Although many specific issues can contribute to any given siting situation, comparative experiences suggest a number of key problems that can

Note: Reprinted from *Challenges and Issues in Facility Siting: Conference Proceedings*, Lesberal, S., Hayden and Shaw, D. (eds), 'Siting hazardous facilities: Searching for effective institutions and processes', Kasperson, R. E., © (2000), with permission from Columbia University Press

greatly complicate and impede siting efforts. These experiences, and post-mortems on them, suggest an anatomy of problems that requires careful assessment and exploration.

Unclear need

Although the need for a particular industrial or public facility is usually abundantly apparent to the advocates or sponsors of the facility, it is often not so to the community leaders and publics who are being asked to act as hosts. If the need for the facility is not clearly established, there is often little prospect that local communities will be willing to take on the burdens or risks that such a facility may entail. Establishing need can, of course, be disputed, and sometimes for good reason. So public resistance to siting solid waste landfills in US communities, for example, was eventually successful in forcing greater waste minimization and recycling. Similarly, public concerns over waste disposal have driven substantial gains in waste reduction in nuclear and chemical plants in a variety of countries. In their review of low-level radioactive waste disposal facility siting in six countries, Vari et al (1994) identify four major factors necessary for siting success, of which clarity of programme goals and process – and particularly the need for a repository – is the first. In many cases, however, siting sponsors have simply failed to address adequately the need to create a broad-based understanding among government officials and publics of facility need, and this lack of agreement has then ultimately sabotaged the siting process as a whole.

Lack of a systems approach

Facility siting is typically viewed as a single-case process. Yet facilities are always part of much broader production systems, be they the complex of energy facilities found in the coal production cycle, the nuclear power industry or chemical waste processing and disposal. The deployment of a waste management system, for example, requires a network of processing, storage and disposal facilities, interconnected by waste transportation links. This network may be designed in ways that minimize overall system risk, lower associated costs and reduce potential inequities. Alternatively, a myopic fixation on a single facility in this network can unintentionally exacerbate many of these problems and lead to suboptimal solutions, as with nuclear waste facility siting in the US (Chapter 14). Unfortunately, most siting processes across various countries have yet to recognize facility siting as a system problem, and most parliamentary, agency or policy stipulations have repeated this failure in the institutional structures that have been established.

Risks and risk perceptions

Although considerable consensus may be achieved in the expert community, including informed critics and opponents, that a well-designed and well-managed modern industrial waste disposal facility poses only limited risks to host communities and publics, acceptance of such risks by those who must bear the burdens has proved difficult to achieve across various societies. Often this has to do with public perceptions of high risks – chemicals, radioactive materials and genetically altered materials are known to elicit particular concerns. Incinerators that put waste emissions into the atmosphere or waste disposal plants that threaten groundwater also typically generate fears over the ultimate effects of hazardous materials that disappear from public view into highly valued ecological components (such as groundwater) of the environment. Such risks have qualitative properties, such as newness, dread or involuntary risk, that are known from past psychometric research to result in public perceptions of high risk (Slovic, 1987b).

At a time when societies may be becoming more risk averse, it is apparent that risk avoidance is taking on greater weight in many communities in the balancing of risks and benefits. And, thus far, quantitative risk assessments and risk-communication efforts intended to assure local publics that the risks are minimal and will be well managed have generally not been persuasive. Ironically, the greater flow of information and discussion of risk intended to reassure publics that the risks will be minimal may actually, when taken up by local activists and media, contribute to a strong social amplification of the risk (see Chapters 6 and 11), feeding public opposition and heightening controversy. And even higher knowledge, according to at least one Swedish study (Biel and Dahlstrand, 1991), does not appear to explain risk perception or public resistance to a repository.

Inequities

Exacerbating the risk concerns is the mismatch between the concentration of risk in the host community and the diffuse distribution of benefits. In one of the few thorough empirical analyses of distributional equity at a hazardous waste site, associated with the nuclear waste reprocessing facility at West Valley, New York, Kates and Braine (1983) painted a complex picture of gains and losses over more than a dozen locations stretching across the US and a concentration of losses in the host community and region. The degree of mismatch can reach quite dramatic proportions, as is evident in the distributional pattern of nuclear high-level waste generation in relation to their potential disposal sites across a number of countries. This lack of concordance between benefits and burden is compounded by the opportunism frequently exhibited in the past by those involved in siting facilities in 'down and out' communities where high unemployment rates and limited access to political power undermined and limited community opposition and the ability of local opponents to challenge decisions. These equity problems have been the primary focus of an emergent environmental justice movement in the US.

They have also become an important aspect of siting in many European countries and have been very evident in a number of Asian countries as well (Shaw, 1996). Indeed, Japan has perhaps the most elaborated set of principles for guiding compensation to remove or reduce inequities (Lesbirel, 1998; Tanaka, 1999).

Assessing equity in siting cases, it needs to be appreciated, is a complex matter. Multiple equity problems may exist simultaneously, such as 'geographical or distributional inequity' in the choice of a site, the issues relating to intergenerational equity, the 'cumulative inequity' problem arising from past siting and other actions that have created a legacy of risk bearing in the community and region, trade-offs between protecting workers and protecting publics, and 'procedural inequity' if fairness in the site consideration and selection process has been violated. The analytic framework presented in Chapter 13 seeks a comprehensive approach to assessing such diverse equity problems.

Social distrust

The complexity of the risk and equity problems points to the need for high levels of public trust and confidence in the institutions and people responsible for siting hazardous facilities and managing the risks. It is quite apparent, however, as Chapter 2 explores in some depth, that the requisite social trust often does not exist. Where prospective risk bearers harbour suspicions over the fairness of the siting process and doubt the trustworthiness of those responsible for protecting them, the conditions exist for intense conflict and impasse. Studies in Sweden (Biel and Dahlstrand, 1991; Sjöberg and Drottz-Sjöberg, 1994) have documented the low level of trust in government in nuclear waste decisions and its importance in public attitudes. At the proposed high-level radioactive waste disposal facility at Yucca Mountain, the US Secretary of Energy (1993) saw the need to commission a far-reaching study of the deep-seated distrust in the US Department of Energy. But distrust problems occur widely throughout North America, Europe and Asia. Past inequities, meanwhile, exacerbate the distrust and anchor it more deeply in accumulated negative experiences.

Assessing trust and distrust and the sources responsible for them is no less complicated than equity analysis. Chapter 2 identifies four dimensions that may contribute to or erode social trust:

1   *Commitment.* To trust implies a certain degree of vulnerability of one individual to another or others, to an institution or to the broader social and political system. Thus, trust relies on perceptions of uncompromised commitment to a mission or goal (such as protection of the public health), and fulfilment of fiduciary obligations or other social norms. Perceptions of commitment rest on perceptions of objectivity and fairness in decision processes and the provision of

accurate information. Commitment, however, does not entail blind progress toward predefined goals, nor insufficient awareness of and response to changing circumstances.

2 *Competence.* Trust is gained only when the individual or institution in a social relationship is judged to be reasonably competent in its actions over time. While expectations may not be violated if these individuals or institutions are occasionally wrong, consistent failures and discoveries of unexpected incompetence and inadequacies can lead to a loss of trust. In particular, risk managers and institutions must show that they are technically competent in their mandated area of responsibility.

3 *Caring.* Perceptions that an individual or institution will act in a way that shows concern for and beneficence to trusting individuals are critical. Perceptions of a caring attitude are important where dependent individuals rely upon others with greater control or authority over the situation and the individual's opportunities and well-being.

4 *Predictability.* Trust rests on the fulfilment of expectations and faith. Consistent violations of expectations nearly always result in distrust. It should be noted, however, that predictability does not necessarily require consistency of behaviour. Complete consistency of behaviour would require unchanging actions or beliefs, even in the face of contradictory information, and also more consistency in values and related behaviour than most individuals, groups or institutions possess.

Here, too, a system perspective is important. Trust is a primary property of the social capital that exists in society, as Putnam (1993) has persuasively argued, and it is built over time in the socialization of individuals into the political culture and in their encounters with others and the political system. It is likely, as we argue in Chapter 10, that trust exists at different levels of the political system, including the most basic level of the political community, the regime of norms and basic authority structures, at specific institutions (often doing the siting), and most superficially in the particular representatives of the institutions. Since patterns of trust in institutions and representatives appears to be quite stable over time, changing levels of distrust over the short time frame of most siting encounters may be unrealistic in most cases. Nonetheless, siting institutions and their representatives persist in seeking to enlarge trust as a key part of the siting strategy and are usually destined to disappointment and unpleasant outcomes. And, of course, little is known of the processes by which trust is lost and regained. Such unrealistic goals have the unfortunate effect of diverting siting officials from the search for institutional processes that are *geared to conditions of high social distrust*.

Amplification-driven impacts

When the siting of a facility becomes controversial, opposition groups tend to arise, extant distrust becomes mobilized, prior injustices are revisited and media coverage expands. The result is a process that we describe as the *social amplification of risk* (see Chapters 6 and 11). The social processes for depicting and debating the risk can provide strong signals to society that the risks may be more serious, more inequitable and more difficult to manage than earlier thought, as Chapter 8 shows. These signals, in turn, drive greater concerns about the proposed facility. Eventually, this process of alarm and controversy can contribute to secondary impacts of the risk – and what we term 'risk ripples' – including conflicts within the community, the stigmatization of the facility and the community, the possible out-migration of residents, and a decrease in property values. A telling example of such stigmatization is the negative imagery that has grown up around the proposed Yucca Mountain nuclear waste repository described in Chapters 8–10 and depicted in Table 15.1. What is striking is that, for certain risk problems, the amplification-driven impacts may be the dominant adverse effects, exceeding the direct public health or environmental impacts. This suggests the need for a very different approach to environmental impact assessment than has evolved over the past several decades in nearly all industrialized countries and is now well embedded in established institutional processes. Facility siting appears to be a prominent example of a case where amplification-driven impacts are the primary risk problem and where, accordingly, extraordinary attention to perceptions, inequities, trust and social processes generally is required.

The problems described above constitute a phalanx of issues for assessing siting institutions and processes. To what extent are existing siting approaches well adapted to these problems? How do we best move forward with innovations in siting approaches that will be more effective and robust in addressing these issues? How may new approaches best be adapted to different political cultures? What level of success can realistically be expected?

APPROACHES TO SITING FACILITIES

Various institutional approaches have evolved over time for siting facilities. There is some time dimension to how they have been employed, as contexts have changed and as siting processes have become more contentious. We begin with the earlier approaches and work toward more recent models.

Decide, announce and defend

Historically, facilities have often been sited by a developer who has surveyed the candidate sites and, having once met various substantive

Table 15.1 *Public images of a nuclear waste repository: Totals for four surveys, 1988–1990 (per cent of 10,000 images recorded)*

			% of images
I		Negative consequences	
	(a)	Dangerous/toxic	16.83
	(b)	Death/sickness	7.83
	(c)	Environmental damage	6.92
	(d)	Leakage	2.16
	(e)	Destruction	1.33
	(f)	Pain and suffering	0.18
	(g)	Uninhabitable	0.07
	(h)	Local repository area consequences	0.06
	(i)	Negative consequences – other	0.08
		Subtotal	35.46%
II		Negative concepts	
	(a)	Bad/negative	6.81
	(b)	Scary	4.01
	(c)	Unnecessary/opposed	2.96
	(d)	Not near me	2.73
	(e)	War/annihilation	1.26
	(f)	Societally unpopular	0.41
	(g)	Crime and corruption	0.40
	(h)	Decay/slime/smell	0.39
	(i)	Darkness/emptiness	0.37
	(j)	Negative toward decision makers and process	0.32
	(k)	Commands to not build or to eliminate them	0.24
	(l)	Wrong or bad solution	0.19
	(m)	No nuclear, stop producing	0.15
	(n)	Unjust	0.14
	(o)	Violence	0.10
	(p)	Prohibited	0.05
	(q)	Negative – other	0.15
		Subtotal	20.68%

Source: Flynn et al, 1993, p648

locational needs (available land, accessibility, physical site properties, etc), has sought those places where sites are available, where land and labour are cheap, and where the ability of the targeted community to resist is minimal. These have often been communities that were rural and small and where unemployment was high and income low. Residents of such places were more likely to trade safety or environmental quality for material gain – through jobs, increased tax revenues and improved services. Communities with high standards of living, for whose residents new jobs associated with a waste facility had less appeal, where safety and environmental quality were more highly valued, and where a strong capacity to resist the siting existed, were places to be avoided.

The process utilized for siting typically involved quietly exploring, often through agents, alternative sites until an appropriate one was found. Often there were closed discussions with political officials or business interests within the community. Applications for permits then proceeded, and it was only then that word leaked out or a public announcement of the siting would be made. If controversy or opposition occurred, the strategy was to ride it out, since the site and perhaps even the needed permits were already in hand.

Such a siting process was a creature of its time when siting decisions were private economic matters and expectations for public consultation and involvement were minimal or non-existent. It is apparent that the process is objectionable on both distributive and procedural equity grounds, since burdens are disproportionately allocated either to poor communities that usually share little in the benefits of waste generation or to localities already so contaminated that additional health burdens are viewed passively. The process itself is almost always objectionable: developers tend to withhold information or create intentional ambiguity, the capacity for community participation tends to be minimal, and the means of redress are few. The opportunism involved in such a siting approach carries a large potential for eroding the technical criteria necessary to ensure the safety and the economic efficiency of the system. More fundamentally, this kind of covert approach no longer works in a radically altered political setting where public expectations for consultation and involvement, and capability to force their use, have grown dramatically in many countries (see, for example, experience in Australia, as described by Kellow, 1996).

Technically based site screening and selection

Over the past two decades, the siting of controversial facilities, such as radioactive waste disposal plants, in Europe, North America and Asia has typically employed a technically based process of identifying a large array of prospective sites, evaluating them according to technical criteria, gradually reducing the candidate options, and eventually selecting the one that best meets these criteria. This approach was also the preferred one until recently in most European countries, where it has often been combined with a hierarchical institutional approach that still commands significant public support (Linnerooth-Bayer, 1999). The rationale for such a siting approach is that the general well-being of society requires overriding individual (or local) interests and the principal issues are the technical qualities of the site. Selection may be done with or without compensation arrangements for redressing inequities and with varying degrees of local participation. The actual selection process frequently includes provisions intended to ensure that the decision is analytically sound and unbiased, guided by technical criteria aimed at protecting health and safety.

The key assumptions of site search and selection through technical appraisal by some siting agencies are as follows:

- the siting of controversial facilities is not fundamentally different from siting any other industrial facility in a rural area;
- local concern over risk can be abated through an unbiased, technically oriented siting process, using established means, such as public hearings and information meetings;
- authorities responsible for siting and for the protection of public health possess sufficient legitimacy and credibility to win eventual local acceptance of the siting decision;
- committed opponents will not succeed in generating sufficient political resources to resist the siting decision.

Although special cases may exist in which these assumptions hold, they are generally problematic. The public perception of risk, as we note above, evokes substantial fear of sites, and this cannot be allayed by institutions that command little trust (Rabe, 1994). In the absence of special efforts to achieve fairness, the chosen site almost invariably views itself as victimized. The use of pre-emptive actions to overcome the opposition usually succeeds only in escalating the intensity of the opposition and broadening its scope. For these reasons, as broad experience in Europe, North America and Asia attests, the power of government authority to override local concerns tends to be illusory.

Bartered consent

The evident problems with the two preceding siting approaches produced a search for alternative siting strategies and for institutions capable of dealing with public distrust, value conflicts and local controversy. One siting approach that emerged has aimed at achieving greater local acceptance of siting through the proffering of compensation and bargaining. This is the case in Japan, for example, where compensation, negotiation and local acceptance are all required (Ohkawara, 1996; Lesbirel, 1998). The central problems of siting, as viewed in this approach, are the geographical dissociation of benefits and harms and the inability of the host area to share in the siting decision. This conception of the siting problem has led to a clear solution – provide compensation to the residents of a prospective host site and give them the means to bargain for the appropriate amount. Compensation and incentives, in this approach, have been intended to serve four purposes: (1) to reduce local opposition; (2) to help redress inequities; (3) to increase the overall efficiency of the siting process; and (4) to promote negotiation instead of conflict.

Easterling and Kunreuther (1995) have provided a searching assessment of the potential and limits to compensation-based siting approaches.

Compensation arrangements and negotiation in siting are sophisticated and extensively developed in Japan, growing out of earlier practices in managing common pool resources for agricultural and fishing cooperatives (Lesbirel, 1998, p21). A wide array of legally acceptable means exists for negotiating siting agreements with communities and property owners. Tanaka (1999) identifies four such types of compensation: fishing rights compensation; regional development cooperation funds; 'Dengen Sanpoh' community siting grants; and fixed property taxes. Despite such compensation and incentives, opposition to facility siting in Japan appears to be growing (Tanaka, 1999).

In the US, an innovative market bargaining approach emerged in the state of Massachusetts, which contained a number of key ingredients:

- primary siting roles for the developer and the host community;
- a required negotiated or arbitrated settlement between the two;
- impact mitigation and compensation to the host community as key features of the siting agreement;
- a tightly specified basis on which the community could exclude the facility; and
- impasses between the developer and host community to be submitted to an arbitrator (O'Hare et al, 1983).

In practice, the US approach ran into a number of problems. Communities tended to view the prospect of compensation as a bribe rather than a means for redressing inequity. Also, it was quickly apparent that communities were unwilling to accept compensation as a trade-off for facility risks and burdens. The intense social amplification of risk in communities also undermined the processes of bartering and negotiation, making such activities appear as immoral. While the bargaining process was intended to facilitate the development of community consensus, a spiral of growing polarization and conflict was often the unintended result. But the use of compensation and public responses to it appear to vary significantly with political culture. Sweden and Switzerland, for example, do not permit compensation in siting, whereas its use in Japan and Taiwan in siting contexts is well established.

Voluntary/partnership siting

Over the past 15 years, in the face of determined local resistance to facility siting in many countries, interest has grown in a process capable of achieving greater voluntary acceptance of a facility by a local community. In large part, this has reflected a judgement, based on much contentious experience, that strategies of pre-emption or coercion are unlikely, in the end, to be successful. With changing expectations for high levels of public information, consultation and participation, and with societies apparently growing more risk averse, it seems clear that a viable siting process will need (1) to address public concerns over the risk; (2) to redress inequities to the furthest extent possible; (3) to empower local communities in the siting process; (4) to win broad-based consent or acceptance of the facility by the host community; and (5) to engage in negotiation to win greater local acceptance.

A noteworthy example of such a process has occurred with the siting of a low-level radioactive waste facility in Canada. In 1988, the Canadian federal government appointed a Low-Level Waste Siting Task Force with a mandate to implement a siting process based on voluntarism and partnership (Frech, 1998). This Task Force sent invitations to all municipalities in Ontario to attend regional information meetings, and 400 community representatives turned out. Twenty-six communities discussed the process for volunteering to be a site, and 14 community liaison groups were appointed to examine issues in detail. The process allowed a community to negotiate the terms under which it would be willing to act as a site. In the case of the finalist community, the Town of Deep River, the dormitory community for Atomic Energy of Canada Limited's Chalk River Laboratories, its negotiated agreement included an CAN$8.75 million economic package and employment guarantees for 15 years. In 1995, the community held a referendum in which 72 per cent of those casting ballots voted in favour of the facility. Negotiations eventually broke down, however, during implementation. Another site, the Town of Port Hope, remained a prospective volunteer community until the end of the process and apparently would have accepted the site but for the unnecessary rigidity in the technical solutions mandated by the Task Force (Frech, 1998). Nonetheless, after ten years, CAN$20 million, and extraordinary efforts in public consultation and participation, an ambitious national siting programme failed to deliver an approved site.

The recent experience in the UK considering the use of the Sellafield site for intermediate radioactive waste storage suggests the movement occurring in many countries for greater transparency. Nuclear authorities proceeded with a public inquiry in well-established manner, seeking to build a technical and governmental consensus about the site. The multidimensional controversy that occurred and the ultimate failure of the effort have led to a major turnaround in the UK institutional approach, one emphasizing transparency, extensive information sharing, consultation with publics and efforts at trust building. Similar changes have occurred in the French nuclear waste programme as well.

In the US, various states and regional compacts have initiated siting efforts for low-level radioactive waste and other hazardous wastes. A number of these siting processes have developed extensive mechanisms aimed at partnership arrangements and voluntary acceptance, as indicated by the abortive New Jersey example (Figure 15.1). Generally, these processes have not been successful, although the experience is difficult to judge since this species of siting processes is still very new. But some

Protection of Health, Safety and the Environment

Any proposed site must:

- meet the Board's siting criteria
- protect public health, safety and the environment
- meet state and federal regulations

A community can establish additional measures to satisfy its particular concerns.

Voluntary Participation

- A community's request for information and its participation in the process is entirely voluntary and will not be regarded as a commitment to host a facility.
- An interested community chooses how far to proceed in its consideration and can withdraw from the voluntary siting process at any time; prior to its decision to volunteer.

Shared Decision Making

- Any interested community undertakes careful examination of the merits and impacts of hosting a low-level radioactive waste disposal facility.
- To aid a community in making informed decisions the Siting Board will provide information and assistance.
- The municipal governing body acts as the decision maker of record on matters that are of community interest.
- Community-wide dialogue and citizen involvement is central to the voluntary process throughout the consideration and decision making.
- Municipalities are encouraged to work with neighbours who may be affected by its decision to propose a site.
- The voluntary approach is intended to be truly interactive and cooperative among the interested community, the Siting Board, and the facility operator.
- Ultimately, the municipal governing body must pass a resolution if it wishes to propose a site to the Board.

Compensation/Resources

- The Siting Board will support interested communities with resources so each can develop its own community education programme.
- All out-of-pocket expenses related to examining environmental, health, economic and social impacts can be compensated.

Benefits/Incentives

NJ Siting Law guarantees certain benefits to a host community. In addition, the voluntary siting process allows a community to establish added measures to meet its local needs and to improve quality of life, such as:

- preserving open space
- upgrading recreational and park areas
- tax and monetary incentives

Facility Development Agreement

- The host community, Siting Board, and facility operator agree upon protection, compensation and incentives related to facility design and operation.
- These measure are represented in a Facility Development Agreement.

Source: New Jersey Radioactive Waste Advisory Committee, 1994.

Figure 15.1 *Elements of the New Jersey voluntary siting approach*

elements of the various programmes have been successful, and nearly all have faced the difficult legacy of proceeding in social contexts already highly polarized by earlier siting failures. For example, both the Ontario and New Jersey voluntary siting processes were viewed by their managers as potentially workable if some things had been done differently (in the New Jersey case, for example, by having the compensation package up front in the process). A very advanced siting process in the state of Connecticut found it difficult to surmount the polarization remaining from the legacy of earlier conflicts associated with a technically based siting effort.

The New Jersey experience is instructive for what were and what were not problems. Issues that were not problems in the view of the programme managers included:

- *money*: the programme provided for a generous award of US$2 million per year to a host community;
- *anti-nuclear and environmental groups* were not a dominant opposition;
- *the press*: local coverage was fair and accurate;
- *local leadership*: generally very capable and willing to lead.

Issues that were major obstacles included:

- public fear of radiation;
- public distrust in all levels of government, including local officials;
- a high discomfort with local controversy, especially the 'grief' local leaders experienced 'every time we went out for a quart of milk';
- very few people were willing to invest the time to become knowledgeable about the project; and
- circular arguments: 'you say the facility is safe; then why are you willing to give us so much money?' (Weingart, 1998).

An extensive Canadian assessment of nuclear waste management in 1998 reached a series of conclusions highly instructive to siting efforts generally:

- broad public support is necessary in Canada to ensure the acceptability of a concept for managing nuclear fuel wastes;
- safety is a key part, but only one part, of acceptability. Safety must be viewed from two complementary perspectives: technical and social.

To be considered *acceptable*, a concept for managing nuclear fuel wastes in Canada must:

- have broad support;
- be safe from both a technical and social perspective;
- have been developed within a sound ethical and social framework;
- have the support of aboriginal people;

- be selected after comparisons with the risks, costs, and benefits of other options; and
- be advanced by a stable and trustworthy proponent and overseen by a trustworthy regulator (Nuclear Fuel Waste Management and Disposal Concept Environmental Assessment Panel, 1998).

Obviously, cross-national experience with these more voluntary siting approaches is yet too early to allow an assessment of how their elements may best be developed in different national contexts. But experience suggests that no single voluntary/partnering siting model has yet emerged that incorporates all the elements that would consistently contribute to success. On the other hand, there are indications of the changes and modifications needed, and enough encouraging progress, to suggest how a more resilient and effective voluntary siting model might be designed.

TOWARDS GREATER SITING SUCCESS

A variety of specific institutional and process mechanisms can contribute to more effective siting outcomes, many of which are specific in detail to the situation, historical context or political culture. The 'facility siting credo' (Figure 15.2) authored by Kunreuther et al (nd) provides a good list of more generic considerations. Here we continue this search for what may be considered as 'strategic imperatives' for improved siting approaches, setting aside for this discussion the issue of which tactical or site-specific measures are likely to be most helpful in what specific national or subnational contexts.

Establish need

As noted above, very little can move forward in any siting case of a controversial or risky facility if the societal need for the facility is not apparent. The controversies over low-level radioactive waste facilities in a variety of countries, it must be appreciated, have driven dramatic reductions in waste generation. In doing so, siting conflicts have greatly simplified the siting task, since fewer sites must be found. Assuming that a clear need for the facility can be demonstrated, substantial efforts are needed *in advance of the siting process* to establish a widespread recognition and consensus that the proposed siting is in the general public interest and that non-siting alternatives have been duly considered and rejected for appropriate causes.

Experience from Canada underlines this point (Frech, 1998). In successful voluntary siting experiences of waste facilities in the provinces of Alberta and Manitoba, the need for the facility was an important issue. Extensive discussions were begun over the need question well in advance of initiating the siting processes. And the siting agencies viewed the siting process as a search for willing communities, not for potential technically

When planning and building Locally Unwanted Land Uses (LULUs), every effort ought to be made to meet the following objectives:
1. Seek consensus through a broad-based participatory process
2. Work to develop trust
3. Achieve agreement that the status quo is unacceptable
4. Choose the facility design that best addresses a solution to the problem
5. Fully address all negative aspects of the facility
6. Seek acceptable sites through a volunteer process
7. Consider a competitive siting process
8. Work for geographic fairness
9. Keep multiple options on the table at all times
10. Guarantee that stringent safety standards will be met
11. Fully compensate all negative impacts of a facility
12. Make the host community better off
13. Use contingent agreements
14. Set realistic timetables

Source: Kunreuther et al, nd

Figure 15.2 *The facility siting credo*

qualified sites, and the relationship between the developer and the prospective host community as akin to courtship. The federal process, although ultimately unsuccessful, did address the need part of the process well, allocating a two-year discussion of need to precede actual siting initiatives. A social consensus on facility need, in short, is an essential base on which to build, a recognition supported both by cross-national studies in Europe (Vari et al, 1994) and North America (Gerrard, 1994).

Narrow the risk debate

In most technical or engineered systems, the safety goal is to optimize investment. This is embodied in notions such as ALARA (as low as reasonably achievable) where investments are required to lower the risk so long as the gain registered can be justified economically. In routine risk management, such an approach makes eminent sense in balancing risks and benefits and choosing most cost-effective risk reduction strategies.

But in situations of polarized risk debate over a proposed facility, or what the author would term highly amplified risks, the failure to win a consensus that a high level of safety will be achieved is usually fatal. There is little prospect that the siting process can move forward if local concerns over safety cannot be assuaged. Accordingly, there is much to be said for the approach used in siting nuclear facilities in Sweden to resolve risk controversies wherever possible and to narrow the risk debate where such opportunities exist. This will require, not infrequently, *overbuilding the safety function*. If the vantage point is optimizing the siting process rather than optimizing the cost of technical safety at the facility, then such an approach and the additional marginal investments may be very sensible. Involving the host community leaders in negotiations about the safety level and design of the facility is also a means of local empowerment, and the development of a negotiating climate may encourage public involvement and help to build trust. Additional mechanisms that can be employed include: (1) funding for technical consultants for the community so that they conduct their independent evaluations and participate in negotiations in an informed and effective way; and (2) provision for the host community to monitor facility performance and to have the means, under prescribed procedures, to initiate a review to shut down the facility if standards are violated.

Assume trust does not exist; act to deserve it

As noted earlier, many siting processes are initiated under conditions of high social distrust in the siting agencies. The automatic response by developers in such cases is to resolve to change the trust context, usually by seeking to demonstrate that this particular siting agency, unlike others the community may have encountered, is trustworthy. Currently our knowledge of the conditions under which trust may be recovered or strengthened is very limited. Slovic (1993) has demonstrated that a series of actions or events that might be expected to either build or erode trust do not appear to have equal effects on individuals. Rather an asymmetry principle appears to prevail for trust, as indicated in Figure 15.3, in which trust is more easily lost than it is gained by comparable events and actions. Moreover, we know from siting experience that efforts predicated upon regaining trust within the time frame of siting decisions have generally been unsuccessful (English, 1992). Worse still, they may encourage siting advocates to employ the wrong institutional mechanisms and processes, those predicated on assumptions of trust, consensus and cooperation that may not exist.

By contrast, the siting agency could assess that the reality is that a climate of social distrust exists and is likely, despite the best efforts of the agency, to continue during much of the siting process. Such a determination would encourage institutional approaches that afford prospects of success in the absence of trust or confidence in the siting agency. Strategies of partnership, power sharing, collaboration and negotiation allow a host community to proceed with a siting process that relies less on judgements of the reliability of some external group than upon the host community's own capabilities and evaluation. Specific mechanisms involved in such an approach include community participation in all phases of the siting process, support for independent consultants, community review of facility design and safety systems, monitoring of facility performance, property value protection and the right to initiate shutdown if health and safety standards are violated.

Local board authority to close plant
Evacuation plan exists
On-site government inspector
Rewarded for finding problems
Responsive to any sign of problems
Effective emergency action taken
Local advisory board established
Public encouraged to tour plant
Mandatory drug testing
No problems for five years
Hold regular public hearings
Employees carefully trained
Conduct emergency training
Community has access to records
Serious accident is controlled
Nearby health is good
Monitor radioactive emissions
Employees informed of problems
Neighbors notified of problems
No evidence of withholding information
Contribute to local charities
Employees closely supervised
Try to meet with public
Managers live nearby
Operates according to regulations
No problems in past year
Record keeping is good

TRUST INCREASING

Don't contribute to local charities
No public hearings
Little communication with community
Emergency response plans not rehearsed
Officials live far away
Poor record keeping
Accident occurs in another state
Accused of releasing radiation
Denied access to records
Employees not informed of problems
Delayed inspections
Public tours not permitted
Health nearby worse than average
Official lied to government
Serious accident is not controlled
No adequate emergency response plan
Plant covered up problem
Employees drunk on job
Records were falsified

TRUST DECREASING

60%   40%   20%   0%   20%   40%   60%

Percent very powerful impact

Note: only percentages of Category 7 ratings (very powerful impact) are shown here.
Source: Slovic, 2000, p322

Figure 15.3 *Differential impact of trust-increasing and trust-decreasing events*

Maintain a systems view

There are clear opportunities for taking a broader view of facility siting, in which it is recognized that public agencies and jurisdictions will need to site a multitude of potentially controversial facilities over time. Strategies could be developed that aim at an equitable sharing of the burden among communities within the jurisdiction. So if one area, for example, hosts a waste disposal plant, it might be excepted from (or ineligible in) the next round of siting involving an incinerator. Or the political officials of a jurisdiction could examine the overall pattern and risk implications involved in a network of facilities, treating efficiency, risk reduction and risk sharing, and equity as relevant considerations in making decisions. It is clear that we need to get beyond the myopia associated with single-facility siting processes and to view siting in system terms.

Compensate for irreducible inequities

The preferred ethical base for siting, as we argue more generally in Chapter 13, should be to avoid or reduce risk rather than to compensate for it. Indeed, any approach that does not proceed from this principle may exacerbate problems involving risk perception and trust. The strategy of narrowing the risk debate and erring on the side of safety noted above is consistent with this ethical imperative.

But, of course, residual risks and uncertainty will remain that cannot feasibly be eliminated. A compensation or benefit-sharing package should be available, intended: (1) to restore the original condition before the facility-related risk and burden were introduced; (2) to reward the community for contributing to resolving one of society's difficult problems (finding facility sites) and for allowing a needed industrial sector to operate; and (3) to provide an additional flow of benefits to the host community (and nearby region) as compensation for irreducible uncertainty and potential amplification-driven impacts (Easterling and Kunreuther, 1995). Such a compensation package should be negotiated with the host community and region so as to deliver a package of benefits, usually not a cash award, most relevant to local needs and development goals.

Build a constituency of support

The institutional aspects of a successful siting process will need to address the development of a constituency of support for the facility. A number of major interests must be convinced that they cannot stay out of the fire and in the background if a successful political coalition is to be created. The make-up of such a coalition or concert of support will vary from country to country and with the particular facility involved. In the US, industry must commit to support of the siting process early and assume a visible leadership role. The political head of the jurisdiction, be that a governor of a state or a mayor of a city, will need to be a firm supporter, even when the debate becomes acrimonious. A coalition of local officials who are knowledgeable about and open to the siting process needs to be created. Effective contacts with local media will be essential. And dialogues should be opened with prospective critics and opponents so that they are kept well informed and their concerns, where appropriate, are addressed.

Adaptive institutions and processes

Finally, comparative experience suggests that, because of the strong intermingling of social and technical issues and the high political volatility involved in facility siting, highly adaptive institutions and approaches are needed. Siting facilities, it is clear, is not a highly predictive process that can be mounted in the programmed way that many developmental programmes or projects can. Issues change dramatically, unlikely opponents enter the fray, participants change over the course of the controversy, the debate links to other agenda and concerns in unpredictable ways, the media may frame debates in ways beyond the control of the siting agency, and the routes to conflict resolution are often unclear. Accordingly, the siting agency and process need to be highly flexible, able to respond rapidly to surprise, open and attentive to the external environment, and to have a strong capability to gather and assess diverse information.

In other words, the siting and the siting agency need to be smart. Such an institution needs not only high technical expertise but strong capabilities in political diagnosis, communications, constituency building and political analysis. It must be able to work collaboratively with communities, and the elected officials and informal leaders that may enter the debate. The siting process may need to be reinvented multiple times over the course of achieving a successful site, and, as we have argued elsewhere (Cook et al, 1990), the siting agency should regard the siting and management task as experimental. One need only look at the radioactive waste facility siting experience in countries such as France, the UK, Canada and the US to see how extensively established processes and institutions have changed in the search for siting models and how altered approaches better geared to the challenging problems posed in facility siting have evolved.

CONCLUSIONS

While the facility-siting experience across countries has proven a rocky road over the past two decades, important social learning has occurred which may presage more effective approaches and outcomes in the coming years. There is now a broad recognition in many societies about the nature of the siting challenge and that decide–announce–defend or technically oriented approaches are unlikely to be successful. In particular, it is apparent to most that a set of interlocking social transformations are in process that are shaping the nexus of problems involved in hazardous facility siting. First, the publics in many societies appear to be more preoccupied with, and perhaps more averse to, risks than at earlier times, especially if the risks are involuntary in nature and imposed on concerned communities. Second, it is also clear that hazardous facility siting carries with it an intermingling of difficult intra- and inter-generational equity problems that interact with, and greatly complicate, the prospects for achieving a consensus that procedures and outcomes are fair. Third, many countries have experienced a loss of trust in governmental and social institutions that have placed new demands on, and erected obstacles for, siting institutions. Finally, a wave of democratization is apparent at the close of the century that entails heightened responsibilities for consultation, involvement and more explicit forms of consent from communities and publics hosting hazardous facilities (see Chapter 10).

A full realization of the depth of these changes is yet to come but, increasingly, those responsible for siting facilities are grasping the general outline of changed conditions. This was remarkably in evidence recently at an international symposium on high-level radioactive waste management sponsored by the US National Research Council held in Irvine, California (USNRC, 1999). Representatives from various countries repeatedly acknowledged the centrality of social issues to the siting task and indicated adaptations and innovations under way to address them. Although no single approach is yet to emerge in this siting arena, new departures show some common emphasis in elements of more voluntary and democratic procedures, namely greater transparency, early and sustained involvement with prospective host communities, power sharing and negotiation, a greater burden of proof on the siting authority and its experts, and more open acknowledgement of uncertainties and surprises.

Just as siting processes are in metamorphosis, so are the institutions. A wide range of siting institutions is still apparent, with a continuum from those emerging from military models to those aligned to the new emphasis on power sharing, collaboration and negotiation. But the shifts in process are forcing changes in institutional designs and cultures, with new capabilities required in information gathering and dissemination, conflict resolution, appraisal of value issues and social impact analysis. This path of institutional adaptation will certainly continue to step into potholes and run down cul-de-sacs. But current trends are encouraging that the siting problem is being reconceptualized and approaches are being recentred in better accord with the actual sociopolitical impediments that have thwarted progress until now.

16 Climate Change, Vulnerability and Social Justice

Roger E. Kasperson and Jeanne X. Kasperson

INTRODUCTION

As we enter a new century, it is apparent that people have already altered the climates in which they live and will alter them even more dramatically in the coming decades. We know from the Third Assessment of the Intergovernmental Panel on Climate Change (IPCC, 2001) that over the past century average surface temperatures across the globe have increased by 0.6°C, and we now have stronger evidence that human activities are responsible for most of this warming. We also know that the 1990s were the warmest decade and 1998 was the warmest single year since 1861. These ongoing and future changes in climate will continue to alter nature's life-support systems for human life in many parts of the globe: through an ongoing rise in global average sea level, increases in precipitation over most mid- and high-latitudes of the northern hemisphere, increased intensity and frequency of droughts, floods and severe storms, and as yet unforeseen abrupt changes and extreme climatic events. Meanwhile, decades will pass before the current human efforts to reduce ongoing climate change will register their effects. In short, time is at a premium. The impacts of these human-induced changes in climate, although in their early stages, are showing up in shrinking glaciers, thawing permafrost regions, longer growing seasons in mid- and high-latitude agricultural areas, shifts in plant and animal ranges and declines in some plant and animal populations. But these effects now in progress only suggest the much more far-reaching changes likely to come. Major global warming threats to human security and well-being across the planet include diverse risks and some potential benefits (see Box 16.1).

Unfortunately, it is unrealistic to expect that positive and negative effects will balance out, because they will register their impacts on different regions, ecosystems and people. And many of these regions and peoples will be highly vulnerable and poorly equipped to cope with the

Note: Reprinted from *Climate Change, Vulnerability and Social Justice*, Kasperson, R. E. and Kasperson, J. X., © (2001), with permission from the Stockholm Environment Institute

Box 16.1 Threats and potential benefits of global warming

Threats:

- reduced potential crop yields in some tropical and subtropical regions and many mid-latitude regions;
- decreased water availability for populations in many water-scarce regions, particularly those with inadequate management systems;
- an increase in the number of people exposed to vector-borne diseases (e.g. malaria) and water-borne diseases (e.g. cholera);
- increases in the number of people dying from heat stress, particularly in large cities in developing countries;
- a widespread increase in the risk of flooding for many human settlements throughout the world;
- severe threats to millions of people living on low-lying islands and atolls.

Potential benefits:

- increased potential crop yields in some mid-latitude regions;
- a potential increase in global timber supply from appropriately managed forests;
- increased water availability for populations in some water-scarce regions (e.g. parts of Southeast Asia);
- reduced winter mortality in mid- and high latitudes.

major changes in climate that may occur. Furthermore, many people and places already face severe stress and vulnerability arising from other environmental and socioeconomic forces, including those emanating from globalization processes. The last thing they need is to have to add climate change impacts to the problems of population growth, increasing concentrations of populations in megacities, poverty and poor nutrition, accumulating levels of atmospheric, land and water contamination, a growing dependence upon distant global markets, growing gender and class inequalities, the ravages of the AIDS epidemic, and politically corrupt governments. Climate change will produce varied effects that will interact with these other stresses and multiple vulnerabilities, and they will take their toll particularly among the most exposed and poorest people of the world. As we have stated elsewhere:

> The lesson from climate change is a more general one: risks do not register their effects in the abstract; they occur in particular regions and places, to particular peoples, and to specific ecosystems. Global environmental risks will not be the first insult or perturbation in the various regions and locales of the world; rather, they will be the latest in a series of pressures and stresses that will add to (and interact with) what has come before, what is ongoing, and what will come in the future (Kasperson and Kasperson, 2001b, pp274–275).

Recognizing and understanding this differential vulnerability is a key to understanding the meaning of climate change. And understanding both the nature of the stresses that climate change will exert upon ecological and human systems and the extent of their vulnerabilities to those stresses is essential. Over the past decade, studies of climate change have largely focused on issues of science – how releases of greenhouse gases accumulate in the atmosphere and interact with biogeophysical processes to alter attributes of climate. In-depth analysis of the impacts of climate change, and particularly the impacts on the most vulnerable people and places, is only just beginning. It will be the commanding task for climate-related studies over the next decade. And yet, we do know something about the major types of vulnerability that exist and about where to find the most vulnerable regions and places.

Indeed, it is easy to identify some of the most vulnerable human and ecological systems. One-third to one-half of the world's population already lacks adequate clean water, and climate change – due to increased temperature and droughts in many areas – will add to the severity of these issues. Many developing countries (especially in Africa) are likely to suffer declines in agricultural production and food security, particularly among small farmers and isolated rural populations. Increased flooding from sea-level rises will ravage low-lying coastal areas in many parts of the globe, in both rich and poor countries, leading to loss of life and infrastructure damages from more severe storms as well as the loss of wetlands and mangroves. Small island states in particular face the prospect of such devastating effects that it may prove necessary for some peoples to abandon their island homes and migrate to other locales.

The poor, elderly and sick in the burgeoning megacities of the world face an increased risk of death and illness from more severe heat and humidity. Dense populations in developing countries face increased threats from riverine flooding and its associated impacts on nutrition and disease. These threats only suggest, of course, the broad panoply of effects that will confront the most vulnerable regions of the world. It is the rates and patterns of climate change and their interaction with place-specific vulnerabilities that will drive the realities as to the eventual severities of these effects and the potential effectiveness of mitigation efforts and human adaptation.

WHAT IS VULNERABILITY?

Put simply, vulnerability is the capacity to be wounded from a perturbation or stress, whether environmental or socioeconomic, upon peoples, systems or other receptors. In the case of this discussion, it is the exposure and susceptibility to harm or damage from climate change. The IPCC has adopted the following definitions relevant to assessing vulnerability:

- *Vulnerability.* The extent to which climate change may damage or harm a system; vulnerability is a function of not only the system's sensitivity, but also its ability to adapt to new climatic conditions.
- *Sensitivity.* The degree to which a system will respond to a change in climatic conditions (e.g. the extent of change in ecosystem composition, structure and functioning, including net primary productivity, resulting from a given change in temperature or precipitation).
- *Adaptability.* The degree to which adjustments are possible in practices, processes or structures of systems to projected or actual changes of climate; adaptation can be spontaneous or planned, and can be carried out in response to or in anticipation of changes in conditions.

Assessments of the ecological and human risks from climate change need to take account of both the magnitude of the stresses that may result from alterations in the characteristics of climate – precipitation, temperature, droughts, severe storms – and the degree of vulnerability of human and ecological systems to them. Thus, even modest changes in climate, either in mean temperature change or in the frequency and severity of extreme events, can have large effects if people or ecological systems are highly sensitive to the climate change. Such sensitivity may be very high if exposure to the change is high or if the buffering or coping capacity of people or systems is constrained. Assessing such effects requires an integrated approach, one that examines interactions between ecological and human systems as a particular place or region responds to the change or perturbation.

Ecosystems are important in relation to climate change because they provide the life-support systems that sustain human societies. In doing so, they deliver such essential goods and services as: (1) providing food, fibre, shelter, medicines and energy; (2) processing and storing carbon and nutrients; (3) assimilating and remediating wastes; (4) purifying water; (5) building soils and reducing soil degradation; and (6) housing the planet's store of genetic and species diversity. Climate change will alter these goods and services in complex and uncertain ways – through their geographic location, mixes of species, and array or bundles of services essential to human well-being. Those ecological goods and services themselves are also constantly changing because of ongoing human activities, so that climate change and human activities will interact, often in unknown ways, in modifying patterns of ecological goods and services that support human societies.

Human societies, as discussed in Volume II, Chapter 14, show a wide variability in their sensitivity to environmental change and their abilities to anticipate, cope with and adapt to such change. Many factors shape this variability, including wealth, technology, knowledge, infrastructure, institutional capabilities, preparedness and access to resources. Human endowments in such assets vary widely in a world of mounting inequality.

Developing countries, and particularly the least developed countries, are clearly the most vulnerable regions to climate change. They will experience the greatest loss of life, the most negative effects on economy and development, and the largest diversion of resources from other pressing needs. Since such countries and regions are also under stress from the forces of globalization, including population growth, urbanization, resource depletion, contamination of environments, dependence on global markets and growing poverty, climate change will interact in uncertain ways with other accumulating problems. All peoples and regions have some level of vulnerability, and even the richer countries will not escape future damage and loss of life from climate change. Nevertheless, the vulnerable countries, regions and places of the world will almost certainly bear most of the ongoing and future toll that will occur as a result of climate change.

PEOPLES AND SYSTEMS VULNERABLE TO CLIMATE CHANGE

Food-insecure areas

Climate change will affect agriculture and food security in a variety of ways, bringing benefits to some areas and losses to others. On the one hand, increased carbon dioxide in the atmosphere can enhance plant growth and crop yields; on the other, agricultural pests may thrive under increased CO_2 concentrations while excessive heat and drought may produce widespread adverse effects on agriculture. Much depends upon the rate, magnitude and geographic pattern of climate change. Some regions, particularly in the mid-latitudes, are likely to register modest gains in agricultural yields and food supply, whereas agriculture in food-insecure regions will undergo radical declines or even disappear due to rising sea level or salt-water intrusion.

Geographic shifts in agriculture will certainly pose major challenges for those regions caught in the largest transitions. In some areas, agriculture will encroach on virgin lands and natural ecosystems. A warmer climate regime will generally alter the present distribution and productivity of forests, grasslands, savannahs, wetlands and tundras. For example, the thawing of permafrost regions may dry out tundras, sea-level rises may lead to the flooding of coastal agricultural areas, and the prior adaptation of plants and animals to a particular region may be disrupted. In areas with larger or more abrupt climate changes, farmers will find their accumulated experience a less reliable guide to the future than it has been in the past. Their ability to adapt without making large errors will be severely tested. In many areas, they will be forced to change planting dates, rates of fertilization, uses of irrigation and selection of plant and animal species, and to do so within a changing physical environment and uncertain regional and global markets. Trial and error will have both winners and losers, and the losers are likely to be those with the highest sensitivity and the least adaptive capacity.

Past studies suggest that adverse effects of climate change on agriculture and food security will be concentrated in developing countries. There, these impacts will interact with other environmental and socioeconomic vulnerabilities to exacerbate hunger and to endanger food security (IPCC, 2001). Economic assessments suggest that a climate change of a few degrees centigrade can jeopardize the growth of the global food supply. Much of the adverse impact will be on small agriculturalists and the urban poor in developing countries. The incomes of the most vulnerable people are likely to decline as the numbers of people at risk of hunger increase. Over all, owing to geographic and temporal shifts in agriculture, worsening social and economic situations, and new extremes in temperature and precipitation, food security in areas already insecure, and particularly in Africa, will worsen.

The case of Egypt suggests how far-reaching climate change may be for some developing countries. Historically, Egypt's rich agricultural system has been predicated on favourable temperature conditions, fertile soils and abundant irrigation water from the Nile River. With a rapidly growing population that now numbers some 63 million people (World Bank, 1996, p26), Egypt has expanded its agriculture into desert lands adjoining the Nile basin and reclaimed long-used areas that have become salinized or waterlogged. Nonetheless, Egypt remains totally dependent upon water from the Nile, a situation posing severe challenges to Egypt's economic future, even without climate change. But with climate change, an array of serious threats is apparent. A sea-level rise will jeopardize areas of the Nile delta currently lying below 1 metre in elevation; as much as 12–15 per cent of the existing agricultural land in the Nile delta could be lost (Nicholls and Leatherman, 1994). A sea-level rise is likely to accelerate the intrusion of saline water into surface water sources and the underlying coastal aquifer (Sestini, 1992). Temperature rises are likely to reduce agricultural productivity throughout Egypt. Although the effects of climate change upon the flow of the Nile itself are uncertain, they are likely to increase demand for irrigation water and to exact a toll on heat-sensitive crops. Much can be done to mitigate these effects over the coming decades, including slowing population growth, but widespread and vigorous intervention will be essential to ward off a growing shortage and eventual crisis of food supply in Egypt.

The Philippines are another case of potential food insecurity. Indeed, agriculture is the economic lifeline of this archipelago nation; more than 70 per cent of the foreign exchange earnings of the Philippines come from agricultural exports and 50 per cent of the country's working population is in the agricultural sector (Rosenzweig and Hillel, 1998, p200). Rice, the primary staple crop, is very vulnerable to the pattern of tropical cyclones, floods and to drought-inducing delays in the onset of the rainy season.

Climate change could lead to declines in rice yields in this highly dependent country. Major changes in cropping patterns, with earlier planting dates and choice of cultivars, may be needed. But such changes will also require a major transformation in the farming system of this poor country and farmers may be subject to new and uncertain risks (such as strong winds later in the season) that may arise (Escano and Buendia, 1994).

Water-scarce regions

One-third of the world's population now lives in countries that are water stressed (where more than 20 per cent of the renewable water supply is being used). The world's population living in such circumstances is expected to increase from an estimated 1.5 billion people currently to about 5 billion people in 2025 (IPCC, 2001). One in five of the world's people now lacks access to safe and affordable drinking water. Half of the world's population does not have access to sanitation. Each year 3–4 million people die of water-borne disease, including more than 2 million young children who die of diarrhoea. Half of the world's wetlands have been destroyed in the 20th century. As much as 10 per cent of global annual water consumption may come from depleting groundwater resources that are also undergoing contamination. In most countries, highly fragmented water institutions manage growing water scarcities and block integrated water management approaches (Cosgrove and Rijsberman, 2000). Indeed, the greatest vulnerabilities worldwide in 2001 are in unmanaged or unsustainable water systems in developing countries. Typically, such systems are already at high risk due to other forces – population growth, water contamination, poor pricing systems and growing irrigation uses – pushing the systems further into unsustainability. Climate change threatens to exacerbate problems that are already severe and create further water deficits and shortages.

Climate change, it is generally thought, will produce increases in annual mean stream flow in high-latitude countries but reductions in central Asia, the Mediterranean, southern Africa and Australia. Higher temperatures will mean a general trend toward increases in demands for irrigation water. Higher water temperatures may also degrade water quality in many regions, particularly when taken in conjunction with increased pollutants attendant on growing populations, urbanization and consumption. The frequency and magnitudes of floods will also increase in many regions due to more frequent heavy rainfalls. In some regions, increased precipitation will offset higher temperatures and evaporation; in other regions, greater stress on existing water resources will occur.

These potential effects of future climate change are very apparent in Africa. Currently, approximately two-thirds of Africa's rural population and one-quarter of the urban population lack safe drinking water. Even higher percentages are without proper sanitation (Zinyowera et al, 1998, p49). In

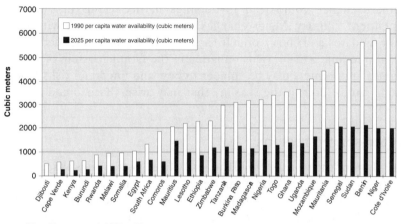

Source: After Sharma et al, 1996, p15

Figure 16.1 *Projected water scarcity in Africa*

1990, eight African countries south of the Sahara were experiencing water stress or scarcity, and the situation has worsened since then. By 2025, it is estimated that the number of countries subjected to water stress will grow from 8 to 18 countries and affect some 600 million to 4 billion people (World Bank 1996; Cosgrove and Rijsberman, 2000, p28). Eight African river basins already face water stress and another four confront water scarcity. Simply taking account of declining water availability due to population growth reveals the grim picture apparent in Figure 16.1.

The effects of ongoing and future climate change on water availability in Africa are still uncertain, but Africa has experienced serious droughts in 1965–66, 1972–74, 1981–84, 1986–87, 1991–92 and 1994–95. These droughts have often been connected to El Niño Southern Oscillation (ENSO) anomalies. But if projections of reduced stream flow from climate change on southern Africa materialize, they will overlay a precarious situation already jeopardizing poor countries beset by a panoply of other environmental and social threats and in a weak position to cope with additional climate-induced threats.

Northern China is another area highly vulnerable to further water scarcity induced by climate change. With a population of 371 million, it is a major economic centre of China. It is a region already at risk from normal climate variability and longer-term climatic shifts. Both surface water and groundwater are quite sensitive to climate variability, especially on the Huang-Hai plain. Already this is a region under water-shortage stress; water resource availability is only 500m³ per capita – one-half the critical value of the UN standard of 1000m³ per capita for maintaining sustainable development. Because of the shortage of surface water, groundwater resources are being depleted, and 'the water table under some of the major grain-producing areas of northern China is falling at a rate of five feet (1.5 metres) per year' (USCIA, 2001, p20). To these immense shortages, add those induced by climate change, which have the potential in dry years to exacerbate a serious situation and hamper socioeconomic development in the region.

Vulnerable marine ecosystems

Climate change will change oceans in important ways: sea ice cover will decrease in the polar regions, salinity and wave conditions will change, sea surface temperatures and mean sea level will rise, and more severe storms and shore erosion must be anticipated. Such changes, interacting with growing population densities and developmental pressures in coastal areas, will impose major ecological and human impacts, principally:

- loss of land and displacement of population;
- flooding of low-lying coastal areas;
- loss of agricultural yields and employment;
- negative impacts on coastal aquaculture;
- erosion of sandy beaches and associated losses in tourism.

But serious impacts will also befall marine ecosystems, such as coral reefs, atolls, salt marshes and mangrove forests, depending on the rate of sea-level rise. The case of coral reefs, which the World Conservation Strategy has identified as one of the ecological life-support systems essential for global food production, health and sustainable development, highlights the magnitude of possible effects. Their future is already in jeopardy due to overexploitation, coastal development and land-based pollution. Coral reefs are, however, highly sensitive to prolonged rises in seawater temperature and increased irradiance. Future sea surface warming associated with global warming could seriously increase the stress on coral reefs. Moreover, experience with severe coral bleaching in Indonesia signals that coral reefs may well fail to recover successfully over the longer term, even after warming events have receded (Brown and Suharsono, 1990).

The mean temperatures of the world's oceans are increasing at an accelerating rate, currently approximately 2°C per century (Souter et al, 2000, p12). When this warming combined with the strongest El Niño ever recorded in 1998, corals throughout the world's tropical islands suffered extensive bleaching and mortality. Along the coasts of East Africa and in Indian Ocean islands, 90–100 per cent of corals exposed to water temperature higher than 32°C died. And 18 months later, the coral reefs showed few signs of recovery (Souter et al, 2000, p14). Global warming poses a serious further threat to coral reefs through increases in sea surface temperature and an increased frequency of marine diseases. Since healthy coral are essential in the Indian Ocean for coastal fisheries and tourism, declines in fish stocks, threats to food security and losses in income from tourism are likely for large portions of coastal populations.

Other human effects of sea-level rise may be widespread and serious. One estimate, for example, suggests that losses of land from a 1-metre rise in sea level would total 30,000 km^2 in Bangladesh, 6000 km^2 in India, 34,000 km^2 in Indonesia, and 7000 km^2 in Malaysia (Nicholls et al, 1995). Vietnam could find 5000 km^2 of land inundated in the Red River delta, while 15,000–20,000 km^2 of land could be threatened in the Mekong delta.

The case of the Ganges–Brahmaputra delta, one of the world's most densely populated regions, speaks to the range of interlocking problems that climate change is likely to produce. With higher sea levels, severe storms and storm surges will affect larger areas of the delta as saline and brackish waters increasingly contaminate inland freshwater lakes and aquifers. Tidal damages will move further upstream and increases in soil and freshwater salinity may cause widespread problems for potable water and irrigation sources. Since these are already under pressure owing to a very large and growing population, the human impacts and obstacles for attempts to control the damage are almost certain to be far-reaching (Alam, 1996; Broadus, 2001).

Awareness of the widespread potential effects on coastal systems already undergoing rapid change has prompted rethinking about whether human societies can effectively adapt. The focus is shifting away from strategies aimed at protecting shorelines with engineered protection systems (e.g. seawalls, groins) to strategies geared to coastal land-use planning, efforts to enhance resilience in biophysical and social systems, and even managed retreat from coastal regions (IPCC, 2001).

Fish-dependent societies

Many societies depend heavily upon fish as a significant part of their food supply. For example, as much as one-third of the protein supply in densely populated Nigeria comes from fish. The vulnerability of fisheries to climate change depends upon the character and rate of the change, the nature of the fishery, and changes in the associated species and habitat. According to Carpenter and colleagues (1992), climate change threatens to affect fisheries through:

- changes in water temperatures;
- the timing and duration of temperature extremes;
- the magnitude and patterns of annual stream flows;
- surface water elevations; and
- the shorelines of lakes, reservoirs and near-shore marine environments.

The Organisation for Economic Co-operation and Development (OECD) has recently flagged overfishing as a 'red light' issue of global significance. Indeed, a recent report indicates that more than one-quarter of the world's marine fisheries are 'already either exhausted, over-fished, or recovering from over-fishing' (OECD, 2001, p8). Climate changes are expected to increase sea surface temperature and mean sea level of the oceans. Associated changes in oceans are now recognized to alter strongly patterns of fish abundance and those population dynamics. If we take just one, but the most important of these changes – elevated temperatures – vulnerable areas dependent upon marine fisheries will face severe stresses:

- a shift in centres of fish production and the composition of species as ecosystems change in their distribution and their internal structure;
- falling economic return until long-term stability in the fisheries is achieved; and
- disproportionate suffering among the subsistence and other small-scale fishermen in Africa (Zinyowera et al, 1998, p63).

The situation in Africa suggests that it is the most vulnerable people and places that will bear most of the costs. Fish make up a significant part of the total food supply of Africa. In the past, economic activities rather than climate variability have been the major stressors on the productivity of freshwater areas and the sea margins. But climate-induced fluctuations could cause significant disruption in the food supply in those African societies that depend heavily upon fisheries and that have limited potential for adaptation to other sources of food supply. Mauritania, Namibia and Somalia are particularly at risk.

The potential impacts of climate change on fisheries in tropical Asia have not been well established. But fisheries are very important throughout the region, including inland areas in which people depend on freshwater fish in the food supply. In the Philippines, fisheries employ nearly 1 million people, 26 per cent of whom are in aquaculture operations and 68 per cent in marine and freshwater fishing (Lim et al, 1995). Throughout much of South and Southeast Asia, overexploitation of inshore and inland fisheries is already endangering fishing livelihoods. Climate change will affect the region's fisheries in uncertain ways, by changing marine conditions that alter the abundance of fish populations, introducing saline waters into inland freshwaters, and inundating regional aquaculture.

The type of fisheries disruption that environmental changes can induce is apparent in the case of the Nile. There the building of the Aswan Dam so regulated the flow of the Nile that the river delta succumbed to thorough ecological degradation. A dramatic change in surges of floodwater and nutrient pulses triggered a collapse of the local sardine population that had long thrived and provided an important source of food for the region.

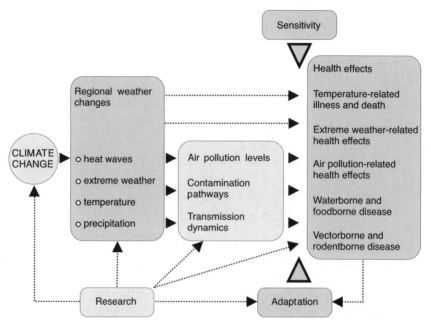

Source: After Patz et al, 2000, p369.

Figure 16.2 *Assessing potential health effects of climate change*

Threats to human health

Climate change may be expected to affect human health and disease patterns in various direct and indirect ways (Figure 16.2). Direct effects will occur in the form of changes in temperature and humidity, heat-stress mortality, flooding, tropical vector-borne diseases and decreases in cold-related illnesses. But climate change will also affect the proportion of the world's population living in cities, through the availability of sanitation and potable water supplies, human migration and living conditions. These all interact to complicate the task of gauging the impacts of climate on human health.

But some things are reasonably clear. The World Health Organization has concluded that climate change is likely to alter the incidence and range of major tropical vector-borne diseases (see Table 16.1). The geographic range of two important infectious diseases – malaria and dengue – is likely to increase. It is estimated that, should a temperature increase in the upper part of the IPCC-projected range (3–5°C by 2100) occur, the proportion of the world's population affected by malaria would increase from the current 45 per cent to about 60 per cent in the second half of the 2100s. This would produce about an additional 50–80 million cases annually (Watson et al, 1998, p7). Malaria is already one of the most serious and complex global diseases and it is the disease most likely to be affected by climate change (Kovats et al, 2000). Currently, around 270 million

Table 16.1 *Climate change and major tropical vector-borne diseases*

Disease	Likelihood of change with climate change	Vector	Present distribution	People at risk (millions)
Malaria	+++	Mosquito	Tropics/subtropics	2020
Schistosomiasis	++	Water snail	Tropics/subtropics	600
Leishmaniasis	++	Phlebotomine sandfly	Asia/Southern Europe/ Africa/Americas	350
American trypanosomiasis (Chagas disease)	+	Triatomine bug	Central and South America	100
African trypanosomiasis (Sleeping sickness)	+	Tsetse fly	Tropical Africa	55
Lymphatic filariasis	+	Mosquito	Tropics/subtropics	1100
Dengue	++	Mosquito	All tropical countries	2500–3000
Onchocerciasis (River blindness)	+	Blackfly	Africa/Latin America	120
Yellow fever	+	Mosquito	Tropical South America and Africa	—
Dracunculiasis (Guinea worm)	?	Crustacean (copepod)	South Asia/Arabian peninsula/Central- West Africa	100

Source: Kovats et al, 2000, p20.

people are infected by malaria at any given time, 1–2 million people die from malaria each year (mostly in Africa), and approximately 2 billion people worldwide are at risk (McGranahan et al, 1999, p176). Climate change will affect the underlying conditions – higher temperatures, increased precipitation and relative humidity, mosquito habitats and access to washing and drinking water – that support the spread of the disease. Recent models of the potential effects of climate change suggest that the global population at risk of malaria would increase significantly, including a widespread increase in the seasonal duration of transmission in new areas (Kovats et al, 2000, p18). At particularly high risk would be the latitudes adjoining the current malarial zones and the high-altitude areas within the zones, particularly the mountainous areas in Eastern Africa where temperatures currently curtail transmission of the disease (McGranahan et al, 1999, p179).

Climate change may be expected to have other health consequences, both positive and negative. Schistosomiasis would be likely to spread beyond its current distribution limits, although it might well also decrease in some areas. Dengue may undergo a latitudinal and altitudinal expansion similar to malaria. Certain other vector-borne diseases, such as onchocerciasis (river blindness), yellow fever and possibly trypanosomiasis (sleeping sickness) might also undergo climate-induced redistribution (McGranahan et al, 1999, p180). Increased frequency of heat waves, often accompanied by increased humidity and urban air pollution, will cause increases in heat-related deaths and illnesses, particularly among the elderly and those in poor health. Finally, increased flooding events, should they occur, could produce serious consequences from flood disasters, particularly in densely populated areas (such as parts of China and Bangladesh).

Extreme vulnerability: small island states

The island states of the world are among the areas most endangered by climate change. They also hold an extraordinary richness in the planet's cultural resources and diversity. Over one-third of all known languages, for example, are spoken in four countries of Melanesia (Papua New Guinea, the Solomons, Vanuatu, New Caledonia). The island states possess distinctive human cultures and traditional knowledge and technologies found nowhere else.

Although these islands are culturally heterogeneous and diverse, they share common features that endanger them. Generally, they have high population densities concentrated in limited land areas, and the largest settlements are typically located no further than 1–2 km from the coast. In nearly all the states, large settlements are found on beaches or sand terraces. Because populations are often concentrated in the few urban centres where most infrastructure is located, sea-level rises could produce widespread disruption to economic and social activities. Indeed a sea-level rise of between 50 cm and one metre could convert many islands to sandbars and substantially reduce remaining drylands on even the larger and more heavily populated islands. Table 16.2 lists the small island states that fall into this category.

Beyond the question of direct inundation resulting from sea-level rise is the vulnerable nature of small island economies. A few activities – agriculture, fisheries, tourism and international transport – typically dominate small island state economies. As a result they are highly sensitive to global market forces beyond their control. The survival of many islands also depends heavily upon remittances from expatriate nationals and development funds from the international donor community. Since primary production plays a large role in the economies, disruptions to agricultural support systems from climate change are likely to produce widespread disruption and economic loss. Meanwhile, island populations are growing at more than 3 per cent per year, and populations are migrating to island cities or emigrating in search of work (Pemetta, 1992).

The physical circumstances of island states leave them highly vulnerable to potential climate-induced changes. Much of the critical infrastructure and economic activities are located close to coastal areas,

Table 16.2 *Small island states (United Nations member states and members of the Alliance of Small Island States (AOSIS))*

Antigua and Barbuda	Malta
The Bahamas	Marshall Islands
Barbados	Mauritius
Cape Verde	Nauru
Comoros	Palau
Cook Islands	Saint Kitts and Nevis
Cuba	Saint Lucia
Cyprus	Saint Vincent and the Grenadines
Dominica	Samoa
Dominican Republic	Sao Tome and Principe
Federated States of Micronesia	Seychelles
Fiji	Solomon Islands
Grenada	Tonga
Haiti	Trinidad and Tobago
Jamaica	Tuvalu
Kirbati	Vanuatu
Maldives	

many of which are at or close to current sea level. Coastal erosion, saline intrusion and sea flooding are already serious problems. Potable water supplies are typically in short supply. Of particular concern is whether climate change will lead to an increase in the frequency and severity of storms that may be experienced by these island states, particularly the effects of hurricanes and typhoons. Adding to the concern over vulnerability is the cumulative and interacting presence of non-climate-related natural disasters, rapidly growing populations and few possibilities for adaptation.

The Republic of the Maldives reveals dramatically the extreme vulnerability of small island states to climate change. The Maldives include 19 major atolls and approximately 1190 islands, of which 202 are populated. No island is more than 3 metres above mean sea level and most are less than 1 metre high. With a tidal range of 1 metre, even distant storms in the Indian Ocean cause severe flooding. The offshore reef system supports a complex coral community that sustains the economy and everyday life of the Maldives. Coral are used for building material, fisheries are the leading economic activity and tourism is the second pillar of the economy. Confronted by an array of economic and development problems and rapid population growth, the Maldives face possibly devastating effects from climate change-driven sea-level rise and severe storms, as indicated in Box 16.2.

It is clear that small island states are among the regions of the world most endangered by climate change and will require extensive

---

Box 16.2 Maldives: Risks associated with global climate change

- Increased rates of coastal erosion and alteration of beaches with increased impacts from high waves.
- Changes in aquifer volume associated with increased saline intrusion.
- Increased energy consumption (e.g. air conditioning).
- Coral deaths as a result of increased seawater temperatures.
- Loss of capital infrastructure on smaller tourist resort islands.
- Changes in reef growth and current patterns.
- Increased vulnerability of human settlements due to aggregation and increasing size.

Sources: Pemetta and Sestini, 1989; May, 2001

---

intervention by the larger international community to ward off long-term disruptions and the loss of the rich cultural heritage of the islands.

Environmental security and environmental refugees

A major concern surrounding climate change is that, owing to the potential effects and disruptions noted above, increased tensions and conflict among nations or cultures may occur in the international system. A case in point, described by Postel (2000, pp46–47), is the prospect for increased international competition for water as populations grow rapidly in a number of water-scarce regions. In what she describes as 'hot-spots of water dispute', the Aral Sea region, the Ganges, the Jordan, the Nile and the Tigris–Euphrates, populations of the nations within these basins are projected to grow by 32–71 per cent by 2025. If water-sharing agreements are not found, she warns, 'competition could lead to regional instability or even conflict' (Postel, 2000, p47).

Homer-Dixon et al (1993), meanwhile, have attempted to explore systematically the relationships between environmental degradation and political conflict, concluding that:

- resource scarcity, per se, does not promote much direct violence, although water may be a partial exception;
- environmental degradation can lead to mass migration, which can spark ethnic conflict; and
- environmental harm can bring about institutional decay and economic deprivation, leading to civil strife.

The tenuous nature of such findings, after more than a decade's research, suggests how limited our knowledge remains of these relationships and how opaque the structure of causal linkages between environmental change and security outcomes is. As Levy (1995, p58) points out, 'by the time one arrives at the end of the logical chain – violent conflict – so many intervening variables have been added that it is difficult to see the independent contribution of environmental degradation'.

A similar situation surrounds the dire warnings concerning a potential future flood of 'environmental refugees'. Norman Myers and Jennifer Kent (1995, p1) have estimated that such refugees, people forced to leave land that can no longer support them, have grown to an all-time high of 25 million. They are concerned particularly over 'environmental discontinuities', events that occur when resources, stocks or ecosystems absorb stresses over long periods of time without much outward sign of damage, until they suddenly reach a disruption level. They see the clear prospect of countries such as the Philippines, Mexico and the Ivory Coast losing most of their forests within the next few decades, while Ethiopia, Nepal and El Salvador will have little of their topsoil remaining. Unless immediate action is taken, they warn, the flow of environmental refugees is likely to become unprecedented in scale. Indeed, their analysis of climate change concludes that 200 million people globally are at risk from global warming and that this is a 'conservative minimal figure' (Myers and Kent, 1995, p149). Earlier Homer-Dixon (1991) had warned that environmental degradation would produce 'waves of environmental refugees that spill across borders with destabilizing effects on domestic political stability and international relations'.

Such arguments remain quite speculative, given the difficulties in defining and identifying 'refugees' and in establishing clear linkages between environmental change and population displacement. Homer-Dixon (1991, p97; 1999, pp93–96) himself notes that environmental disruption will be only one of many interacting physical and social variables that ultimately force people from their homelands. On the other hand, the greatest effect of climate change could be human migration – millions of people displaced due to coastal inundation, shoreline erosion and agricultural disruption. There is, in short, enough indication of potential effects to suggest that linkages among climate change, environmental modification, and security and refugee risks need to be much better established so that vulnerabilities and risks can be better specified (Lonergan and Swain, 1999).

CONSIDERATIONS OF SOCIAL JUSTICE

It is widely appreciated that in fashioning a socially acceptable and viable international regime for climate change, equity issues must play a prominent role. And vulnerability considerations underlie global equity issues in a fundamental way. The authors find that most deliberations about global equity are incomplete and propose the following as key elements of climate change problems that need to be addressed in developing equity or social justice principles upon which global policy may proceed:

- taking into account past and current emissions, the industrialized countries are overwhelmingly responsible for the current legacy of greenhouse gas emissions;
- annual greenhouse gas emissions of developing countries are growing rapidly and will equal those of developed countries around 2037;
- per capita emissions of greenhouse gases are higher in industrialized countries than in developing countries and are likely to remain so for the foreseeable future;
- because of their greater vulnerability, the negative impacts of climate change will be disproportionately concentrated in developing countries and particularly in the poorer regions of such countries;
- similarly, because of their sparser social and economic endowments and their pressing development needs, developing countries are far less able to reduce emissions or mitigate potential impacts without interfering with other development priorities;
- developing countries are at a disadvantage in the processes to develop an international climate regime because of their more limited expertise and access to knowledge bases.

The Kyoto Protocol recognizes the general need for equity, and thus calls upon the industrialized nations to take the lead in reducing their own greenhouse gas emissions and to assist developing countries to fulfil their obligations. But equity is one element of a broader approach in which greenhouse gas emissions reduction is the overriding goal and economic efficiency the primary means of getting there. Various other objectives were involved, including other environmental goals, technology transfer and trade liberalization. And within the Kyoto approach, trade-offs are always a possibility (Jackson et al, 2001, p4). The emphasis upon flexibility mechanisms, joint implementation and the introduction of carbon sinks has significantly enlarged the potential for the rich countries to avoid the basic Protocol objective – reducing greenhouse gas emissions.

This is a situation in which vulnerability-driven considerations have occupied a secondary place as efforts to implement the Protocol have proceeded. Thus it is not surprising that some analysts in developing countries see the Protocol's Clean Development Mechanism as designed 'to get the cheapest and most efficient deal to "assist the industrialized countries avoid their commitments"' in a 'creative carbon accounting game' (Agarwal and Narain, 1999, p18). And so, Agarwal and Narain have called for the adoption of two social justice principles – the *principle of convergence* and the *principle of equitable entitlements*. The principle of entitlement would set emission levels for all nations, either by establishing an overall CO_2 atmospheric-concentration target and sharing the resulting

CO_2 budget equitably, or by accepting a per capita carbon entitlement for all people. The principle of convergence would hold every nation responsible for making efforts to live within its entitlements. Put simply, this approach would require the world's largest emitters (the industrialized countries) to make urgent efforts to reduce their emissions to entitled amounts and the world's growing emitters (the developing countries) to take steps not to exceed their amounts (Agarwal and Narain, 1999, p19), Whether one accepts the Kyoto approach, that suggested by Agarwal and Narain or some other view, an effective climate regime over the longer term needs to be rooted in social justice principles that command support from developed and developing countries alike. Principles that would appear to be useful in fashioning such an ethical base are:

- those who have created the existing environmental problem have the early and primary responsibility to reduce further emissions and to ameliorate harm that past emissions may cause for current and future generations, wherever they may live;
- those with the greatest capability to reduce future emissions and to avert potential climate-related harm have the primary responsibility to undertake mitigative action and to assist those with fewer capabilities; and
- those who are most vulnerable to climate change and who will bear the greatest harm deserve special consideration and protective assistance by those who will be less affected.

Such principles, however, which may be articulated in future climate regimes, point to the responsibility of the industrialized countries to undertake early action and assume burdens on behalf of the greater global community. At the same time, they underscore the need for those who will almost certainly bear the greatest harm – the developing countries – to be among the principal architects of global solutions.

FORGING CONSTRUCTIVE RESPONSES

Under the Kyoto Protocol, despite some significant inroads, progress is well short of the scale and effectiveness of what is needed. Most emphasis has been on emissions reductions and economically efficient ways of securing them. Thus primary attention has been given to no-regrets interventions, co-benefit policies and flexibility mechanisms. No-regrets strategies involve actions with such secure benefits that they involve no regret in the future. Emission-reduction opportunities exist that arise from market failures and other barriers that impede economically efficient solutions. No-regret strategies here will permit emission reductions at negative costs. Co-benefit approaches seek to secure emission reductions while achieving other desired benefits. These involve curbing air pollution, promoting energy efficiency, improving land-use practices and designing better transportation systems. In some cases, the co-benefits of reducing greenhouse gas emissions may be comparable to costs, and thus become part of no-regret measures (IPCC, 2001). Finally, flexibility mechanisms, such as the Clean Development Mechanism and Joint Implementation, are designed to create a broad panoply of emission-reduction options so that interventions can proceed flexibly with many options and choice, high efficiency and low social disruption. Taken together, these efforts aimed at emissions reductions are essential for global efforts for climate stabilization and must be expanded as a matter of urgency.

But as a risk-management strategy for combating global warming, emissions reductions are insufficient in themselves. The stressors and environmental perturbations are only one part of the risk problem. Differential vulnerability and strategies aimed at creating greater resilience are the other part. Such efforts at increased adaptation and resilience have received much less attention and shown fewer signs of progress. To achieve a comprehensive and equitable risk-management approach, one that works on all major components of the climate-change problem, major new efforts are in order.

What is the 'stuff' of such a resilience strategy to complement current efforts at emissions reductions? A full treatment is beyond the scope of this chapter but some primary elements include:

- *Broad transition strategies.* The essential task of ameliorating vulnerabilities to climate change is part of a broader global transition needed for a more sustainable world. Increasing coping resources and adaptive capacity for more vulnerable societies is an essential part of the required transitions from ever-greater vulnerability to increased sustainability. Thus, climate-change mitigation and impact reduction need to be integrated into broader socioeconomic developmental programmes aimed at sustainable futures.
- *Attacking poverty and inequalities.* Efforts aimed at poverty reduction are now under way in a broad set of aid and financial institutions. These initiatives need to be expanded and accelerated, with greater funding commitments from the richer nations, which need to keep centre stage the insight of the Brundtland Commission (WCED, 1987, p8) more than a decade ago, that 'widespread poverty is not inevitable'.
- *Technology flow.* As emphasized in nearly all analyses of climate change and at the Earth Summit in 1992, the transfer of needed technologies to developing countries is an essential part of the transition referred to above. Such broadened technology choices will undoubtedly expand the portfolio of options for these countries but may, on the other hand, require substantial related institutional and social development.

- *Institutions and governance.* The development of civil society and the strengthening of local institutions are an essential part of global transition strategies. Effective means for reducing vulnerability must be built bottom-up, from the places in which vulnerability resides. The articulation of the importance of vulnerability can occur only in governance systems in which such views can be articulated and heard.
- *Knowledge gaps.* Most of the access to knowledge concerning climate change resides in the richer nations. Much can be done to improve the participation of developing countries in the climate-change regime. Unlike the science of climate change, vulnerability is a matter of what happens in particular places to particular people in particular local cultures. The building of the knowledge system needed to reduce vulnerability and to build resilience must proceed bottom-up. And the active participation of those whose well-being and livelihoods are at stake is required. The generation of such vulnerability/resilience knowledge systems calls for new assessment procedures and techniques that, in turn, will be necessary ingredients for global strategies aimed at enhancing resilience and adaptive capacity.

References

Agarwal, A. and S. Narain (1999) Kyoto Protocol in a unique world: The imperative of equity in climate negotiations. In K. Hultcrantz (ed), *Towards Equity and Sustainability in the Kyoto Protocol*. Papers presented at a seminar during the Fourth Conference of the Parties to the United Nations Framework Convention on Climate Change, Buenos Aires, November 8, 1988. Stockholm: Stockholm Environment Institute, pp17–30

Akong'a, J. and T. E. Downing (1988) Smallholder vulnerability and response to drought. In M. L. Parry, T. R. Carter, and N. T. Konijn (eds), *Impact of Climatic Variations on Agriculture: Vol 2: Assessments in Semi-arid Regions*. Dordrecht: Kluwer, pp221–248

Alam, M. (1996) Subsidence of the Ganges-Brahmaputra delta of Bangladesh and associated drainage, sedimentation and salinity problems. In J. D. Milliman and B. V. Haq (eds), *Sea-level Rise and Coastal Subsidence: Causes, Consequences and Strategies*. Dordrecht: Kluwer, pp169–192

Ali, M. (1984) Women in famine. In B. Currey and G. Hugo (eds), *Famine as a Geographical Phenomenon*. Boston: Reidel, pp113–134

Almond, G. A., and S. Verba (1963) *The Civic Culture: Political Attitudes and Democracy in Five Nations*. Princeton, NJ: Princeton University Press.

Almond, G. A. and S. Verba (eds) (1980) *The Civic Culture Revisited*. Boston: Little, Brown

Anand, P. (ed) (1997) Symposium: Economic and social consequences of BSE/CJD. *Risk Analysis*, vol 22, pp401–454

Arnstein, S. R. (1969) A ladder of citizen participation. *Journal of the American Institute of Planners*, vol 35, pp215–224

Aro, P. (1988) Role of workers and their representatives in accident prevention and response. Revised discussion document prepared in conjunction with the Workshop on the Provision of Information to the Public and on the Role of Workers in Accident Prevention and Response, 11–14 September, 1988. Reprinted in OECD, 1990, pp51–76

Arvai, J. L., R. Gregory and T. L. McDaniels (2001) Testing a structured decision approach: Value-focused thinking for deliberative risk communication. *Risk Analysis*, vol 21, pp1065–1076.

Baird, A., P. O'Keefe, K. Westgate and B. Wisner (1975) *Towards an Explanation of Disaster Proneness*. Bradford: University of Bradford, Disaster Research Unit, Occasional Paper no 11

Banfield, E. (1958) *The Moral Basis of a Backward Society*. Chicago: Free Press

Baram, M. (1993) Corporate risk communication: New challenges for makers and users of toxic chemicals. *Pollution Prevention Review*, vol 3, pp167–175

Barber, B. R. (1984) *Strong Democracy: Participatory Politics for a New Age*. Berkeley: University of California Press

Barnett, A., J. Menighetti and M. Prete (1992) The market response to the Sioux City DC-10 crash. *Risk Analysis*, vol 14, pp45–52

Beck, R. J. and D. Wood (1976) Cognitive transformation of information from urban geographic fields to mental maps. *Environment and Behavior*, vol 8, pp199–238

Behrens, E. G. (1983) The Triangle Shirtwaist Company fire of 1911: A lesson in legislative manipulation. *Texas Law Review*, vol 62, pp361–387

Berkes, F. and C. Folke (1998) Linking social and ecological systems for resilience and sustainability. In F. Berkes and C. Folke (eds) with the editorial assistance of J. Colding, *Linking Social and Ecological Systems: Management Practices and Social Mechanisms for Building Resilience*. Cambridge: Cambridge University Press, pp1–25

Beyer, B. K. and E. P. Hicks (1968) *Images of Africa: A Report of What Secondary School Students Know and Believe About Africa South of the Sahara*. Pittsburgh, PA: Carnegie Mellon University, Project Africa

Biel, A. and U. Dahlstrand (1991) *Riskupplevelser I samband med lokalisering av ett slutfövar för använt kärnbränsle*. SKN Rapport No 46, Stockholm, Statens Kärnbränslenämnd

Bingham, E. (1985) Hypersensitivity to occupational hazards. In *Hazards: Technology and Fairness*, National Academy of Engineering. Washington, DC: National Academy Press, pp79–118

Blaikie, P. M. and H. C. Brookfield (1987) *Land Degradation and Society*. London: Methuen

Blakeney, R. N. (1986) A transactional view of the role of trust in organizational communication. *Transactional Analysis Journal*, vol 16, pp95–98

Blumer, H. (1969) *Symbolic Interactionism: Perspective and Method*. Englewood Cliffs, NJ: Prentice Hall

Bohölm, A. (1998) Visual images and risk messages: Commemorating Chernobyl. *Risk Decision and Policy*, vol 3, no 2, pp125–143

Bolin, B., J. Jäger and B. R. Döös (1986) The greenhouse effect, climatic change, and ecosystems. In B. Bolin, D. R. Döös, J. Jäger and R. A. Warrick (eds), *The Greenhouse Effect, Climatic Change, and Ecosystems*, SCOPE 29. Chichester: Wiley, pp1–32

Bolle, H.-J., W. Seiler and B. Bolin (1986) Other greenhouse gases and aerosols: Assessing their role for atmospheric radiative transfer. In B. Bolin, D. R. Döös, J. Jäger and R. A. Warrick (eds), *The Greenhouse Effect, Climatic Change, and Ecosystems*, SCOPE 29. Chichester: Wiley, pp157–205

Bowonder, B. (1981a) Environmental risk assessment issues in the Third World. *Technological Forecasting and Social Change*, vol 19, no 1, pp99–127

Bowonder, B. (1981b) Environmental risk management in the Third World. *International Journal of Environmental Studies*, vol 18, pp223–226

Bradach, J. and R. Eccles (1989) Price, authority, and trust: From ideal types of plural forms. *Annual Review of Sociology*, vol 15, pp97–118

Breyer, S. (1993) *Breaking the Vicious Circle: Toward Effective Risk Regulation*. Cambridge, MA: Harvard University Press

Broad, W. J. (1990) A mountain of trouble. *New York Times Magazine*, November 18, p37

Broadus, J. (2001) Sea-level rise and the Bangladesh and Nile deltas. In J. X. Kasperson and R. E. Kasperson (eds), *Global Environmental Risk*. Tokyo: United Nations University Press (London, Earthscan), pp353–372

Brooks, H. (1986) The typology of surprises in technology, institutions, and development. In W. C. Clark and R. E. Munn (eds), *Sustainable Development of the Biosphere*. Cambridge: Cambridge University Press, pp325–348

Brown, B. E. and Suharsono (1990) Damage and recovery of coral reefs affected by El Niño-related seawater warming in the Thousand Islands, Indonesia. *Coral Reviews*, vol 8, pp163–170

Brundtland, G. H. (1989) Global change and our common future: The Benjamin Franklin Lecture. In R. S. DeFries and T. F. Malone (eds), *Global Change and our Common Future: Papers from a Forum*. Washington DC: National Academy Press, pp10–18

Buchanan, J. and G. Tullock (1962) *The Calculus of Consent: Logical Foundations of Constitutional Democracy*. Ann Arbor: University of Michigan Press

Burgess, J. A. (1978) *Image and Identity: A Study of Urban and Regional Perception with Particular Reference to Kingston upon Hull*. Occasional Papers in Geography, no 23. Kingston upon Hull: University of Hull

Burke, E. M. (1968) Citizen participation strategies. *Journal of the American Institute of Planners*, vol 34, pp287–294

Burns, W. J., P. Slovic, R. E. Kasperson, J. X. Kasperson, O. Renn and S. Emani (1993) Incorporating structural models into research on the social amplification of risk: Implications for theory construction and decision making. *Risk Analysis*, vol 13, no 6, pp611–624

Burton, I., R. W. Kates and G. F. White (1978) *The Environment as Hazard*. New York: Oxford University Press

Butler, J. K. (1983) Reciprocity of trust between professionals and secretaries. *Psychological Reports*, vol 53, pp411–416

Calabrese, E. T. (1978) *Pollutants and High-risk Groups: The Biological Basis of Increased Human Susceptibility to Environmental and Occupational Pollutants*. New York: Wiley

Cambridge Reports (1990) *Window on America: Solid Waste*. Cambridge, MA: Author

Cantlon, J. (1996) *Nuclear Waste Management in the United States: The Board's Perspective*. Arlington, VA: Nuclear Waste Technical Review Board

Carnevale, D. G. (1995) *Trustworthy Government: Leadership and Management Strategies for Building Trust and High Performance*. San Francisco: Jossey-Bass

Carpenter, S. R., S. G. Fisher, N. B. Grimm and J. F. Kitchell (1992) Global change and freshwater systems. *Annual Review of Ecological Systems*, vol 23, pp119–139

Carter, L. J. (1987) *Nuclear Imperatives and Public Trust*. Washington, DC: Resources for the Future

Carter, L. J. (1997) It's time to lay this waste to rest. *The Bulletin of the Atomic Scientists*, vol 53, no 1, pp13–15

Chambers, R. (1989) Editorial introduction: Vulnerability, coping and policy. *IDS Bulletin*, vol 20, no 3, pp1–8

Checkoway, B. (1981) The politics of public hearings. *Journal of Applied Behavioral Science*, vol 17, pp566–582

Chisolm, J. J. and D. J. O'Hara (1982) *Lead Absorption in Children: Management, Clinical and Environmental Aspects*. Baltimore: Urban and Schwarenberg

Clark, W. C. (1990) Towards useful assessments of global environmental risks. In R. E. Kasperson, K. Dow, D. Golding and J. X. Kasperson (eds),*Understanding*

Global Environmental Change: The Contributions of Risk Analysis and Management, Worcester, MA: Clark University, The Earth Transformed Program, pp5–22

Cohen, B. (1990) *The Nuclear Energy Option: An Alternative for the 90s*. New York: Plenum

Coleman, J. S. (1990) *Foundation of Social Theory*. Cambridge, MA: Bellknap Press

Colglazier, E. W. (1991) Evidential, ethical, and policy debates: Admissible evidence in radioactive waste management. In D. G. Mayo and R. Hollander (eds), *Acceptable Evidence: Science and Values in Hazard Management*. Oxford: Oxford University Press, pp137–159

Colglazier, E. W. and R. B. Langum (1988) Policy conflicts in the process for siting nuclear waste repositories. *Annual Review of Energy*, vol 13, pp317–357

Combs, B. and P. Slovic (1978) Newspaper coverage of causes of death. *Journalism Quarterly*, vol 56, pp837–843, 849

Comfort, L. K. (1980) Evaluation as an instrument for educational change. In H. M. Ingram and D. E. Mann (eds), *Why Policies Succeed or Fail*. Beverly Hills, CA: Sage, pp35–57

Condron, M. M. and D. L. Sipher (1987) *Hazardous Waste Facility Siting: A National Survey*. Albany: New York State Legislative Commission on Toxic Substances and Hazardous Wastes

Cook, B. J., J. L. Emel and R. E. Kasperson (1990) Organizing and managing radioactive waste disposal as an experiment. *Journal of Policy Analysis and Management*, vol 9, no 3, pp339–366

Cosgrove, W. J. and F. R. Rijsberman for the World Water Council (2000) *World Water Vision: Making Water Everybody's Business*. London: Earthscan

Covello, V. T. and F. W. Allen (1988) *Seven Cardinal Rules of Risk Communication* (folded sheet). Washington, DC: US Environmental Protection Agency

Craik, K. M. (1970) Environmental psychology. In T. Newcomb (ed), *New Directions in Psychology*. New York: Holt, Rinehart, and Winston, pp1–121

Creighton, J. (1990) Siting means safety first. *Forum for Applied Research and Public Policy*, vol 5, pp97–98

Cvetkovich, G. and T. Earle (eds) (1991) Risk and culture. Special issue of *Journal of Cross-Cultural Psychology*, vol 22, no 1, pp11–149

Cvetkovich, G. and R. Löfstedt (eds) (1999) *Social Trust and the Management of Risk*. London: Earthscan

Cvetkovich, G., M. Siegrist, R. Murray and S. Tragesser (2002) New information and social trust: Asymmetry and perseverance of attributions about hazard managers. *Risk Analysis*, vol 22, pp359–369

Dake, K. (1991) Orienting dispositions in the perception of risk: An analysis of contemporary worldviews and cultural biases. *Journal of Cross-Cultural Psychology*, vol 22, 61–82

Dasgupta, P. (1988) Trust as a commodity. In D. Gambetta (ed), *Trust: Making and Breaking Cooperative Relations*. Oxford: Basil Blackwell, pp49–72

Davis, M. B. (1988) Ecological systems and dynamics. In National Research Council, Committee on Global Change (ed), *Toward an Understanding of Global Change*. Washington, DC: National Academy Press, pp69–106

de Tocqueville, A. (1969) *Democracy in America*, tr. J. P. Mayer, tr. George Lawrence, (2 vols in 1), Garden City, NY: Anchor Books

DeFleur, M. L. (1966) *Theories of Mass Communication*. New York: D. McKay

DeFries, R. S. and T. F. Malone (eds) (1989) *Global Change and Our Common Future: Papers From a Forum*. Washington, DC: National Academy Press

Derr, P., R. Goble, R. E. Kasperson and R. W. Kates (1981) Worker/public protection: The double standard. *Environment*, vol 23, no 7, pp6–15, 31–36

Derr, P., R. Goble, R. E. Kasperson and R. W. Kates (1986) Protecting workers, protecting publics: The ethics of differential protection. In C. Whipple and V. T. Covello (eds), *Risk Analysis in the Private Sector*. New York: Plenum, 257–269

Deutsch, M. (1973) *The Resolution of Conflict*. New Haven, CT: Yale University Press

Doderlein, J. M. (1983) Understanding risk management. *Risk Analysis*, vol 3, pp17–21

Douglas, M. (1985) *Risk Acceptability According to the Social Sciences*. New York: Russell Sage Foundation

Douglas, M. and A. Wildavsky (1982) *Risk and Culture: An Essay on the Selection of Technological and Environmental Dangers*. Berkeley: University of California Press

Downing, J., L. Berry, L. Downing, T. E. Downing and R. Ford (1987) *Drought and Famine in Africa, 1981–1986: The US response*. Worcester, MA: International Development Program, Clark University

Downing, T. E. (1988) Climatic variability, food security and small holder agriculturalists in six districts of central and eastern Kenya. PhD dissertation. Worcester, MA: Graduate School of Geography, Clark University

Downs, R. M. and D. Stea (1973) *Image and Environment: Cognitive Mapping and Spatial Behavior*. Chicago: Aldine

Ducsik, D. and T. D. Austin (1979) *Citizen Participation in Power Plant Siting: An Assessment*. Energy Studies Group Report no. 2. Worcester, MA: CENTED, Clark University

Dunlap, R., M. Kraft and E. Rosa (eds) (1993) *Public Reactions to Nuclear Waste: Citizens' Views of Repository Siting*. Durham, NC: Duke University Press

Dwivedi, O. P. (ed) (1988) *Public Policy and Administrative Studies*. Guelph, Ontario: Department of Political Studies, University of Guelph

Earle, T. C. and G. T. Cvetkovich (1984) *Risk Communication: A Marketing Approach*. Paper prepared for the NSF/EPA Workshop on Risk Perception and Risk Communication, Long Beach, California

Earle, T. C. and G. T. Cvetkovich (1995) *Social Trust: Toward a Cosmopolitan Society*. Westport, CT: Praeger

Easterling, D. and H. Kunreuther (1995) *The Dilemma of Siting a High-level Nuclear Waste Repository*. Dordrecht: Kluwer

Easton, D. (1965) *A Systems Analysis of Political Life*. New York: Wiley

Ebbin, S. and R. Kasper (1974) *Citizen Groups and the Nuclear Power Controversy*. Cambridge, MA: MIT Press

Edelstein, M. R. (1987) Toward a theory of environmental stigma. In J. Harvey and D. Henning (eds), *Public Environments*. Ottawa, Canada: Environmental Design Research Association, pp21–25

Edelstein, M. R. (1988) *Contaminated Communities: The Social and Psychological Impacts of Residential Toxic Exposure*. Boulder, CO: Westview

Edwards, W. and D. von Winterfeldt (1987) Public values in risk debates. *Risk Analysis*, vol 7, pp141–158

English, M. R. (1992) *Siting Low-level Radioactive Waste Disposal Facilities: The Public Policy Dilemma*. New York: Quorum

English, M. and G. Davis (1987) American siting initiatives: Recent state developments. In B. W. Piasecki and G. A. Davis (eds), *America's Future in Toxic Waste Management*. New York: Quorum, pp279–291

Erikson, K. T. (1994) *A New Species of Trouble: The Human Experience of Modern Disasters*. New York: Norton

Escano, C. R. and L. V. Buendia (1994) Climate impact assessment for agriculture in the Philippines: Simulations of rice yield under climate change scenarios. In C. Rosenzweig and A. Iglesias (eds), *Implications of Climate Change for International Agriculture: Crop Modelling Study*. EPA 230-B-94-003. Washington, DC: US Environmental Protection Agency.

Etzioni, A. (1990) *The Moral Dimension: Toward a New Economics*. London: Collier Macmillan

Fabryka-Martin, J. T., P. R. Dixon, S. Levy, B. Liu, H. J. Turin and A. V. Wolfsburg (1996) *Summary Report of Chlorine-36 Studies: Systematic Sampling for Chlorine-36 in the Exploratory Studies Facility*. Level 4 Milestone Report 3783AD. Los Alamos, NM: Los Alamos National Laboratory

Finucane, M. L., A. S. Alkahami, P. Slovic and S. M. Johnson (2000) The affect heuristic in judgments of risks and benefits. *Journal of Behavioral Decision Making*, vol 13, pp1–17

Fischhoff, B. (1985) Managing risk perception. *Issues in Science and Technology*, vol 2, pp83–96

Fischhoff, B., P. Slovic, S. Lichtenstein, S. Read and B. Combs (1978) How safe is safe enough?: A psychometric study of attitudes towards technological risks and benefits. *Policy Sciences*, vol 8, pp127–152

Flavin, C. (1987) Electricity in the developing world. *Environment*, vol 29, no 3, pp12–15, 39–45

Flynn, J. (1990) *Information from Three Surveys (Fall, 1989): Frequency Distributions and Preliminary Analyses for Selected Environmental and Repository Questions*. Carson City, NV: Nevada Nuclear Waste Project

Flynn, J., J. A. Chalmers, D. Easterling, R. E. Kasperson, H. Kunreuther, C. K. Mertz, A. Mushkatel, K. D. Pijawka, and P. Slovic with L. Dotto (1995) *One Hundred Centuries of Solitude: Redirecting America's High-level Nuclear Waste Policy*. Boulder, CO: Westview

Flynn, J., E. Peters, C. K. Mertz and P. Slovic (1998) Risk, media and stigma at Rocky Flats. *Risk Analysis*, vol 18, pp715–727

Flynn, J. and P. Slovic (1995) Yucca Mountain – a crisis for policy: Prospects for America's High-level Nuclear Waste Program. *Annual Review of Energy and the Environment*, vol 20, pp83

Flynn, J., P. Slovic and H. Kunreuther (eds) (2001) *Risk, Media, and Stigma: Understanding Public Challenges to Modern Science and Technology*. London: Earthscan

Flynn, J., P. Slovic and C. K. Mertz (1993) The Nevada initiative: A risk communication fiasco. *Risk Analysis*, vol 13, pp497–502

Forestier, K. (1989) The degreening of China. *New Scientist* (1 July), pp52–58

Frech, E. (1998) Low-level radioactive waste siting process in Canada: Then and now. Paper presented to the National Low-level Waste Symposium on Understanding Community Decision Making, March 4–5, Philadelphia

Freudenburg, N. (1984) *Not in Our Backyards: Community Action for Health and the Environment*. New York: Monthly Review Press

Freudenburg, W. R. (1988) Perceived risk, real risk: Social science and the art of probabilistic risk assessment. *Science*, vol 242, pp44–49

Freudenburg, W. R. (1992) Nothing recedes like success? Risk analysis and the organizational amplification of risk. *Risk: Issues in Health and Safety*, vol 3, no 3, pp1–35

Freudenburg, W. R., C. L. Coleman, J. Gonzales and C. Hegeland (1996) Media coverage of hazard events – analyzing the assumptions. *Risk Analysis*, vol 16, no 1, pp31–42

Friendly, J. (1985) Pesticide scare laid to communication gap. *New York Times*, 13 March, pA16

Funtowicz, S. O. and J. R. Ravetz (1990) *Global Environmental Issues and the Emergence of Second Order Science*. London: Council for Science and Society

Funtowicz, S. O. and J. R. Ravetz (1992) Three types of risk assessment and the emergence of post-normal science. In S. Krimsky and D. Golding (eds), *Social Theories of Risk*. Westport, CT: Praeger, pp251–274

Garling, R., A. Book and N. Ergezen (1982) Memory for the spatial layout of the everday physical environment: Differential rates of acquisition of different types of information. *Scandinavian Journal of Psychology*, vol 23, pp23–55

Geomatrix Consultants, Inc. and TRW (1996) *Probabilistic Volcanic Hazard Analysis for Yucca Mountain*. BA0000000-01717-2200-00082, Rev. 0

Gerlach, L. P. (1987) Protest movements and the construction of risk. In B. B. Johnson and V. Covello (eds), *The Social and Cultural Construction of Risk*. Dordrecht: Reidel, pp103–145

Gerrard, M. B. (1994) *Whose Backyard, Whose Risk? Fear and Fairness in Toxic and Nuclear Waste Siting*. Cambridge, MA: MIT Press

Gleick, P. H. (1989) Climate change and international politics: Problems facing developing countries. *Ambio*, vol 18, no 6, pp333–339

Goffman, E. (1963) *Stigma: Notes on the Management of Spoiled Identity*. Englewood Cliffs, NJ: Prentice Hall

Golding, D. (1989) *The Differential Susceptibility of Workers to Occupational Hazards*. New York: Garland

Golledge, R.G. and R. J. Stimson (1987) *Analytical Behavioural Geography*. London: Croom Helm

Goodey, B. (1973) *Perception of the Environment*. Occasional Paper no. 17. UK: University of Birmingham, Centre for Urban and Regional Studies

Goodey, B. (1974) *Images of Place: Essays on Environmental Perception, Communications, and Education*. Occasional Paper no. 30. Birmingham, UK: University of Birmingham, Centre for Urban and Regional Studies

Gould, P. R. (1966) *On Mental Maps*. Michigan Inter-University Community of Mathematical Geographers Discussion Paper no. 9. Ann Arbor: University of Michigan, Department of Geography

Gow, H. B. F. and H. Otway (eds) (1990) *Communicating with the Public about Major Accident Risks*. London: Elsevier Applied Science

Graedel, T. E. (1989) Regional and global impacts on the biosphere. *Environment*, vol 31, no 1, pp8–13, 36–41

Graham, J. and D. Shakow (1981) Risk and reward: Hazard pay for workers. *Environment*, vol 23, no 8, pp14–20, 44–45

Graham, J., D. Shakow and C. Cyr (1983) Risk compensation – in theory and in practice. *Environment*, vol 25, no 1, pp14–20, 39–40

Greber, M. A., E. R. Frech and J. A. R. Hillier (1994) *The Disposal of Canada's Nuclear Fuel Waste: Public Involvement and Social Aspects*. AECL-I0712. Pinawa, Manitoba, Canada: Whiteshell Laboratories

Greenberg, M. R., R. F. Anderson and K. Rosenberger (1984) Social and economic effects of hazardous waste management sites. *Hazardous Wastes*, vol 1, pp387–396

Gregory, R., J. Flynn and P. Slovic (1995) Technological stigma. *American Scientist*, vol 83, pp220–223

Groeneweg, J., W. A. Wagenaar and J. T. Reason (1994) Promoting safety in the oil industry. *Ergonomics*, vol 37, pp1999–2013

Grunhouse, S. (1988) French and Swiss fight about tainted cheese. *New York Times*, 1 January, p2

Handmer, J. and E. C. Penning-Rowsell (1990) *Hazards and the Communication of Risk*. Aldershot: Gower

Harris and Associates (1980) *Risk in a Complex Society*. Chicago: Marsh and McLennan

Harrison, P. and R. Palmer (1986) *News out of Africa: Biafra to Band Aid*. London: Hilary Shipman

Harvey, D. R. (2001) *What Lessons from Foot and Mouth? A Preliminary Economic Assessment of the 2001 Epidemic*. Working Paper no. 63. University of Newcastle upon Tyne, Centre for Rural Economy

Hattis, D. R., R. Goble and N. Ashford (1982) Airborne lead: A clearcut case of differential protection. *Environment*, vol 24, no 1, pp14–20, 33–42

Heising, C. D. and V. P. George (1986) Nuclear financial risk: Economy wide cost of reactor accidents. *Energy Policy*, vol 14, pp45–52

Hewitt, K. and I. Burton (1971) *The Hazardousness of a Place: A Regional Ecology of Damaging Events*. Department of Geography Research Paper no. 6. Canada: University of Toronto Press for the Department of Geography

Hibbing, J. R. and E. Theiss-Morse (1995) *Congress as Public Enemy: Public Attitudes toward American Political Institutions*. Cambridge: Cambridge University Press

Hill, A. (2001) Media risks: The social amplification of risk and the media debate. *Journal of Risk Research*, vol 4, pp209–226

Hilts, P. J. (1988) Radon tests urged for all houses: EPA, Surgeon General Note 'Urgency', Issue Joint Health Advisory. *Washington Post*, 13 September, ppA1, A16

Hohenemser, C., R. E. Kasperson and R. W. Kates (1977) The distrust of nuclear power. *Science*, vol 196, 1 April, pp25–34

Holling, C. S. (1986) The resilience of terrestrial ecosystems: Local surprise and global change. In W. C. Clark and R. E. Munn (eds), *Sustainable Development of the Biosphere*. Cambridge: Cambridge University Press, pp292–317

Holzheu, F. and P. Wiedemann (1993) Introduction: Perspectives on risk perception. In B. Rück (ed), *Risk is a Construct*. Munich: Knesebeck, pp9–20

Homer-Dixon, T. F. (1991) On the threshold: Environmental changes as causes of acute conflict. *International Security*, vol 16, no 2, pp76–116

Homer-Dixon, T. F. (1999) *Environment, Scarcity, and Violence*. Princeton, NJ: Princeton University Press

Homer-Dixon, T. F., J. H. Boutwell and G. W. Rathjens (1993) Environmental scarcity and violent conflict. *Scientific American*, vol 268, February, pp38–45

Hoos, I. (1980) Risk assessment in social perspective. In *Perceptions of Risk:* as presented at the National Academy of Sciences Auditorium, in celebration of the 50th anniversary of the NCRP. Washington, DC: National Council on Radiation Protection and Measurements, pp57–85

Hovland, C. J. (1948) Social communication. *Proceedings of the American Philosophical Society*, vol 92, pp371–375

Hunt, S., L. J. Frewer and R. Shepherd (1999) Public trust in sources of information about radiation risks in the UK. *Journal of Risk Research*, vol 2, no 2, pp167–180

IAEA (International Atomic Energy Agency) (1988) *The Radiological Accident at Goiânia*. Vienna: IAEA

ICSU (International Council of Scientific Unions) (1986) *The International Geosphere-Biosphere Programme: A Study of Global Change*. Paris: ICSU

Inglehart, R. (1988) The renaissance of political culture. *American Political Science Review*, vol 82, December, pp1203–1230

Inglehart, R. (1997) *Modernization and Postmodernization: Cultural, Economic, and Political Change in 43 Societies*. Princeton, NJ: Princeton University Press

Ingram, H. M. and S. J. Ullery (1977) Public participation in environmental decision-making: Substance or illusion. In W. R. D. Sewell and J. T. Coppock (eds), *Public Participation in Planning*. New York: Wiley, pp123–139

IPCC (Intergovernmental Panel on Climate Change) (2001) *Climate Change 2001: Synthesis Report*. Cambridge: Cambridge University Press.

Jackson, T., K. Begg and S. Parkinson (eds) (2001) *Flexibility in Climate Policy: Making the Kyoto Mechanisms Work*. London: Earthscan

Jacob, G. (1990) *Site Unseen: The Politics of Siting a Nuclear Waste Repository*. Pittsburgh, PA: University of Pittsburgh Press

Jancar, B. (1987) *Environmental Management in the Soviet Union and Yugoslavia: Structure and Regulation in Federal Communist States*. Durham, NC: Duke University Press

Janis, I. L. (1982) *Victims of Groupthink*, 2nd edition. Boston: Houghton Mifflin

Janis, I. L. and L. Mann (1977) *Decision Making: A Psychological Analysis of Conflict, Choice, and Commitment*. New York: Free Press

Jenkins-Smith, H. (1991) Alternative theories of the policy process: Reflections on research strategy for the study of nuclear waste policy. *Political Science and Politics*, vol 26, pp157–166

Johnson, B. B. and V. T. Covello (eds) (1987) *The Social and Cultural Construction of Risk*. Dordrecht: Reidel

Johnson, J. A. and D. V. Vogt (1996) *'Mad Cow Disease' or Bovine Spongiform Encephalopathy: Scientific and Regulatory Issues*. CRS Report for Congress, 96-644 SPR. Washington, DC: Library of Congress, Congressional Research Service

Johnson, K. M. (1982) Equity in hazard management: Publics, workers, and parathion. *Environment*, vol 24, no 9, pp28–38

Jones, E., A. Farina, A. H. Hastorf, H. Markus, D. T. Miller, R. A. Scott and R. de S. French (1984) *Social Stigma: The Psychology of Marked Relationships*. New York: W. H. Freeman

Kahneman, D., P. Slovic and A. Tversky (eds) (1982) *Judgment under Uncertainty: Heuristics and Biases*. New York: Cambridge University Press

Kaldor, N. (1939) Welfare propositions and interpersonal comparisons of utility. *Economic Journal*, vol 49, pp549–550

Kemeny, J. G. et al. (1979). *Report of the President's Commission on the Accident at Three Mile Island*. Washington, DC: US Government Printing Office

Kane, D. N. (1985) *Environmental Hazards to Young Children*. Phoenix: Oryx Press

Kasperson, J. X. and R. E. Kasperson (2001a) *International Workshop on Vulnerability and Global Environmental Change, 17–19 May 2001, Stockholm Environment Institute (SEI), Stockholm, Sweden: A workshop summary*. SEI Risk and Vulnerability Programme Report 2001-01. Stockholm: SEI

Kasperson, J. X. and R. E. Kasperson (eds) (2001b) *Global Environmental Risk*. Tokyo: United Nations University Press (London: Earthscan)

Kasperson, J. X., R. E. Kasperson and B. L. Turner, II (eds) (1995) *Regions at Risk: Comparisons of Threatened Environments*. Tokyo: United Nations University Press

Kasperson, R. E. (1977) Participation through centrally planned social change: Lessons from the American experience on the urban scene. In W. R. D. Sewell and J. T. Coppock (eds), *Public Participation in Planning*. New York: Wiley, pp173–190

Kasperson, R. E. (ed) (1983a) *Equity Issues in Radioactive Waste Management*. Cambridge, MA: Oelgeschlager, Gunn & Hain

Kasperson, R. E. (1983b) Worker participation in protection: The Swedish alternative. *Environment*, vol 25, no 4, pp13–20, 40–43

Kasperson, R. E. (1985) Rethinking the siting of hazardous waste facilities. Paper presented at the Conference on the Transport, Management and Disposal of Hazardous Wastes. International Institute for Applied Systems Analysis, Laxenburg, Austria, 2–5 July, 1985

Kasperson, R. E. (1986) Hazardous waste facility siting: Community, firm, and governmental perspectives. In National Academy of Engineering (ed), *Hazards: Technology and Fairness*. Washington, DC: National Academy Press, pp118–144

Kasperson, R. E. (1992) The social amplification of risk: Progress in developing an integrative framework of risk. In S. Krimsky and D. Golding (eds), *Social Theories of Risk*. Westport, CT: Praeger, pp153–178

Kasperson, R. E. and M. Breitbart (1974) *Participation, Decentralization, and Community Planning*. Commission on College Geography, Resource Paper no. 25. Washington, DC: Association of American Geographers

Kasperson, R. E., S. Emani and B. J. Perkins (1990) Global environmental change, the media and the publics: Preliminary data and observations. In *Sustainable Development, Science and Policy* (The Conference Report, Bergen, 8–12 May 1990). Oslo: Norwegian Research Council for Science and the Humanities, pp457–486

Kasperson, R. E., J. Emel, R. Goble, C. Hohenemser, J. X. Kasperson and O. Renn (1987) Radioactive wastes and the social amplification of risk. In R. G. Post (ed), *Waste Management '87, Volume 2, High-level Waste*. Tucson: Arizona Board of Regents, University of Arizona, pp85–90

Kasperson, R. E. and J. X. Kasperson (1996) The social amplification and attenuation of risk. *The Annals of the American Academy of Political and Social Science*, vol 545, pp95–105

Kasperson, R. E., J. X. Kasperson, C. Hohenemser and R. W. Kates (1988a) *Corporate Management of Health and Safety Hazards: A Comparison of Current Practice*. Boulder, CO: Westview

Kasperson, R. E., J. X. Kasperson, C. Hohenemser and R. W. Kates (1988b) Managing hazards at PETROCHEM corporation. In *Corporate Management of Health and Safety Hazards: A Comparison of Current Practice*. Boulder, CO: Westview, pp15–41

Kasperson, R. E., J. X. Kasperson, C. Hohenemser and R. W. Kates (1988c) Managing occupational and catastrophic hazards at the Rocky Flats nuclear arsenal plant. In *Corporate Management of Health and Safety Hazards: A Comparison of Current Practice*. Boulder, CO: Westview, pp79–99

Kasperson, R. E., J. X. Kasperson, C. Hohenemser and R. W. Kates (1988d) Managing occupational hazards at a PHARMACHEM Corporation Plant. In

Corporate Management of Health and Safety Hazards: A Comparison of Current Practice. Boulder, CO: Westview, pp43–56

Kasperson, R. E. and J. Lundblad (1982) Closing the protection gap: Setting health standards for nuclear power workers. *Environment*, vol 24, no 10, pp14–20, 33–38.

Kasperson, R. E. and J. V. Minghi (eds) (1969) *The Structure of Political Geography.* Chicago: Aldine

Kasperson, R. E., O. Renn, P. Slovic, H. S. Brown, J. Emel, R. Goble, J. X. Kasperson and S. Ratick (1988e) The social amplification of risk: A conceptual framework. *Risk Analysis*, vol 8, no 2, pp177–187

Kasperson, R. E. and P.-J. M. Stallen (eds) (1991) *Communicating Risks to the Public: International Perspectives.* Dordrecht: Kluwer

Kates, R. W. (1978) *Risk Assessment of Environmental Hazard.* SCOPE Report 8. Chichester: Wiley

Kates, R. W. (1985a) The interaction of climate and society. In R. W. Kates, J. H. Ausubel and M. Berberian (eds), *Climate Impact Assessment.* SCOPE 27. Chichester: Wiley, pp3–36

Kates, R. W. (1985b) Success, strain, and surprise. *Issues in Science and Technology*, vol 11, no 1, pp46–58

Kates, R. W. (1986) Managing technological hazards: Success, strain, and surprise. In National Academy of Engineering (ed), *Hazards: Technology and Fairness.* Washington, DC: National Academy Press, pp206–220

Kates, R. W. and B. Braine (1983) Locus, equity, and the West Valley nuclear wastes. In R. E. Kasperson (ed), *Equity Issues in Radioactive Waste Management.* Cambridge, MA: Oelgeschlager, Gunn & Hain, pp94–117

Kates, R. W., R. S. Chen, T. E. Downing, J. X. Kasperson, E. Messer and S. Millman (1988) *The Hunger Report: 1988.* Providence: Alan Shawn Feinstein World Hunger Program, Brown University

Kates, R. W., R. S. Chen, T. E. Downing, J. X. Kasperson, E. Messer and S. Millman (1989) *The Hunger Report: 1989.* Providence: Alan Shawn Feinstein World Hunger Program, Brown University

Kates, R. W., C. Hohenemser and J. X. Kasperson (eds) (1985) *Perilous Progress: Managing the Hazards of Technology.* Boulder, CO: Westview

Katzman, M. T. (1985) *Chemical Catastrophes: Regulating Environmental Risk through Pollution Liability Insurance.* Springfield, IL: R. D. Irwin

Kellogg, W. W. and R. Schware (1981) *Climate Change and Society.* Boulder, CO: Westview

Kellow, A. (1996) The politics of place: Siting experience in Australia. In D. Shaw (ed), *Comparative Analysis of Siting Experience in Asia.* Taipei: The Institute of Economics, Academia Sinica, pp115–130

Kemeny, J. G. et al (1979) Report of the President's Commission on the accident at Three Mile ISland. Washington, DC: US Government Printing Office

Kerr, R. A. (1996) A new way to ask the experts: Rating radioactive waste risks. *Science*, vol 274, November, p913

Kneese, A. V., S. Ben-David, D. S. Brookshire, W. D. Schulze and D. Boldt (1983) Economic issues in the legacy problem. In R. E. Kasperson (ed), *Equity Issues in Radioactive Waste Management.* Cambridge, MA: Oelgeschlager, Gunn & Hain, pp203–226

Knowles, R. N. (1995) Communicating with the public: Risk management and worst-case scenarios: The Kanawha Valley experience. Paper prepared for the

OECD Workshop on Risk Assessment and Risk Communication in the Context of Accident Prevention, Preparedness and Response, Paris, 11–14 July, 1995

Koller, M. (1988) Risk as a determinant of trust. *Basic and Applied Social Psychology*, vol 9, pp265–276

Kovats, R. S., B. Menne, A. J. McMichael, C. Corvalan and R. Bertollini (2000) *Climate Change and Human Health: Impact and Adaptation*. WHO/SDE/OEA/ 00-4. Geneva: World Health Organization

Krimsky, S. and A. Plough (1988) *Environmental Hazards: Communicating Risks as a Social Process*. Dover, MD: Auburn

Kunreuther, H., K. Fitzgerald and T. D. Aarts (1993) Siting noxious facilities: A text of the facility siting credo. *Risk Analysis*, vol 13, pp301–318

Kunreuther, H., L. Susskind and T. Aarts (nd) *The Facility Siting Credo: Guidelines for an Effective Facility Siting Process*. Philadelphia: University of Pennsylvania, Wharton School, Risk and Decision Processes Center

La Porte, T. R. (1996) High reliability organizations: Unlikely, demanding, and at risk. *Journal of Contingencies and Crisis Management*, vol 4, no 6, pp60–70

Lagadec, P. (1987) From Seveso to Mexico and Bhopal: Learning to cope with crises. In P. R. Kleindorfer and H. C. Kunreuther (eds), *Insuring and Managing Hazardous Risks: From Seveso to Bhopal and Beyond*. Berlin: Springer-Verlag, pp13–46

Langford, I. L. (2002) An existential approach to risk perception. *Risk analysis*, vol 22, pp101–120

Las Vegas Review-Journal (1990) 21 October

Lasswell, H. D. (1948) The structure and function of communication in society. In L. Bryson (ed), *The Communication of Ideas: A Series of Addresses*. New York: Cooper Square Publishers, pp32–35

Lavine, M. P. (1982) Industrial screening programs for workers. *Environment*, vol 24, no 5, pp26–38

Lawless, E. W. (1977) *Technology and Social Shock*. New Brunswick, NJ: Rutgers University Press

Lee, T. R. (1986) Effective communication of information about chemical hazards. *The Science of the Total Environment*, vol 51, May, pp149–183

Lesbirel, S. H. (1998) *NIMBY Politics in Japan: Energy Siting and the Management of Environmental Conflict*. Ithaca, NY: Cornell University Press

Lesly, P. (1982) The changing evolution of public relations. *Public Relations Quarterly*, vol 27, pp9–15

Leventhal, H. (1970) Findings and theory in the study of fear communications. In L. Berkowitz (ed), *Advances in Experimental Social Psychology*, vol 5. New York: Academic Press, pp119–186

Levy, M. A. (1995) Is the environment a national security issue? *International Security*, vol 20, no 2, pp35–62

Lewis, H. (1990) *Technological Risk*. New York: Norton

Lewis, J. D. and A. Weigert (1985) Trust as a social reality. *Social Forces*, vol 63, no 4, pp967–985

Li, L. M. (1987) Famine and famine relief: Viewing Africa in the 1980s from China in the 1920s. In M. H. Glantz (ed), *Drought and Hunger in Africa: Denying Famine a Future*. Cambridge: Cambridge University Press, pp415–434

Lichtenberg, J. and D. MacLean (1991) The role of the media in risk communication. In R. E. Kasperson and P.-J. M. Stallen (eds), *Communicating Risks to the Public: An International Perspective*. London: Kluwer pp157–173

Lichtenstein, S., P. Slovic, B. Fischhoff, M. Layman and B. Combs (1978) Judged frequency of lethal events. *Journal of Experimental Psychology: Human Learning and Memory*, vol 4, pp551–578

Lim, C. P., Y. Matsuda and Y. Shigemi (1995) Problems and constraints in Philippine municipal fisheries: The case of San Miguel Bay, Camarines Sur. *Environmental Management*, vol 19, no 6, pp837–852

Lindell, M. K. and T. C. Earle (1983) How close is close enough?: Public perceptions of risks of industrial facilities. *Risk Analysis*, vol 3, no 4, pp245–253

Linnerooth-Bayer, J. (1999) Fair strategies for siting hazardous waste facilities. In *Proceedings of the International Workshop: Challenges and issues in facility siting, January 7–9, 1999*. Taipei: The Institute of Economics, Academia Sinica

Lipset, S. M. and W. Schneider (1983) *The Confidence Gap: Business, Labor, and Government in the Public Mind*. New York: Free Press

Lipset, S. M. and W. Schneider (1987) *The Confidence Gap: Business, Labor, and Government in the Public Mind*. New Edition. New York: Macmillan

Lipsky, M. (1968) Protest as a political resource. *American Political Science Review*, vol 61, pp1144–1158

Liverman, D. M. (1990) Vulnerability to global environmental change. In R. E. Kasperson, K. Dow, D. Golding and J. X. Kasperson (eds), *Understanding Global Environmental Change: The Contributions of Risk Analysis and Risk Management*. Worcester, MA: The Earth Transformed Program, Clark University, pp27–44

Löfstedt, R. E. and T. Horlick-Jones (1999) Environmental regulation in the UK: Politics, institutional change and public trust. In G. Cvetkovich and R. E. Löfstedt (eds), *Social Trust and the Management of Risk*. London: Earthscan, pp73–88

Lonergan, S. and A. Swain (1999) Environmental degradation and population displacement. *AVISO*, 2 (entire issue)

Lowrance, W. W. (1976) *Of Acceptable Risk. Science and the Determination of Safety*. Los Altos, CA: W. Kaufmann

Luhmann, N. (1979) *Trust and Power: Two Works by Niklas Luhmann*. Chichester: Wiley

Luhmann, N. (1980) *Trust and Power*. New York: Wiley

Luhmann, N. (1986) *Ökologische Kommunikation*. Opladen: Westdeutscher Verlag

Luhmann, N. (1993) *Risk: A Sociological Theory*. New York: Aldine

MacGregor, D. G. (1991) Worry over technological activities and life concerns. *Risk Analysis*, vol 11, pp315–324

Machlis, G. E. and E. A. Rosa (1990) Desired risk: Broadening the social amplification of risk framework. *Risk Analysis*, vol 10, no 1, pp161–168

Malone, T. (1986) Mission to planet earth: Integrating studies of global change. *Environment*, vol 28, October, pp6–11, 39–42

Marris, C., I. H. Langford and T. O'Riordan (1998) A quantitative test of the cultural theory of risk perceptions: Comparisons with the psychometric paradigm. *Risk Analysis*, vol 18, no 5, pp635–648

Marris, C., B. Wynne, P. Simmons and S. Weldon (2001) *Public Perceptions of Agricultural Biotechnologies in Europe*. Final Report FAIR CT98-3844 (DG12-SSMI) (with contributions also from J. Cárceres, B. De Marchi, A. Klinke, L. Lemkow, L. Pellizzoni, U. Pfenning, O. Renn and R. Sentmarti). Brussels: Commission of the European Communities. www.pabe.net

Mathews, J. T. (1989) Redefining security. *Foreign Affairs*, vol 68, Spring, pp162–177

Maunder, W. J. and J. H. Ausubel (1985) Identifying climate sensitivity. In R. W. Kates, J. H. Ausubel, and M. Berberian (eds), *Climate Impact Assessment*, Scope 27. Chichester: Wiley, pp85–101

May, J. (2001) Lesotho, Uganda, Zambia and Maldives. In A. Grinspun (ed), *Choices for the Poor: Lessons from National Poverty Strategies*. New York: United Nations Development Programme, pp231–251

Mazur, A. (1981) *The Dynamics of Technical Controversy*. Washington, DC: Communication Press

Mazur, A. (1984) The journalist and technology: Reporting about Love Canal and Three Mile Island. *Minerva*, vol 22, Spring, pp45–66

Mazur, A. (1990) Nuclear power, chemical hazards, and the quantity of reporting. *Minerva*, vol 28, pp294–323

McCabe, A. S. and M. R. Fitzgerald (1991) Media images of environmental biotechnology: What does the public see? In G. S. Sayler, R. Fox and J. W. Blackburn (eds), *Environmental Biotechnology for Waste Treatment*. New York: Plenum, pp15–24

McGranahan, G., S. Lewin, T. Fransen, C. Hunt, M. Kjellén, J. Pretty, C. Stephens and I. Virgin (1999) *Environmental Change and Human Health in Countries of Africa, the Caribbean and the Pacific*. Stockholm: Stockholm Environment Institute

Melville, M. (1981a) Risks on the job: The worker's right to know. *Environment*, vol 23, November, pp12–20, 42–45

Melville, M. (1981b) *The Temporary Worker in the Nuclear Power Industry: An Equity Analysis*. Worcester, MA: Center for Technology, Environment, and Development, Clark University

Metz, W. C. (1996) Historical application of a social amplification of risk model: Economic impact of risk events at a nuclear weapons facility. *Risk Analysis*, vol 16, no 2, pp185–193

Midden, C. (1988) *Credibility and Risk Communication*. Paper presented to International Workshop on Risk Communication. Jülich, Germany: Nuclear Research Center, October

Mill, J. S. ([1863], 1961) *Utilitarianism*. New York: Bantam

Mitchell, R. C., B. Payne and R. E. Dunlap (1988) Stigma and radioactive waste: Theory, assessment, and some empirical findings from Hanford, WA. In R. G. Post (ed), *Waste Management '88: Proceedings of the Symposium on Waste Management: Vol 2, High-level Waste and General Interest*. Tucson, AZ: University of Arizona, pp95–102

Monastersky, R. (1994) Faults found at Nevada nuclear waste site. *Science News*, vol 145, April, p310

Monmonier, M. S. (1997) *Cartographies of Danger: Mapping Hazards in America*. Chicago: University of Chicago Press

Montreal Protocol (1987) *1987 Montreal Protocol on Substances that Deplete the Ozone Layer: Final Act*. Montreal: United Nations Environment Programme

Moore, R. and D. Nix (1997) Cochairs of the Western Interstate Energy Board. Letter to R. Milner, Office of Civilian Radioactive Waste Management, US Department of Energy, 13 January, 1997.

Morgan, G., B. Fischhoff, A. Bostrom and C. Atman (2001) *Risk Communication: A Mental Models Approach*. Cambridge: Cambridge University Press

Morgenstern, J., J. Durlak and P. Homenuck (1980) Making the evaluation of public participation programs feasible. In B. Sadler (ed), *Public Participation in*

Environmental Decision Making: Strategies for Change. Edmonton: Environment Council of Canada, pp121–139

Mushkatel, A. and D. Pijawka (1994) *Nuclear Waste Transportation in Nevada: A Case for Stigma-induced Economic Vulnerability*. Carson City, NV: Nuclear Waste Project Office

Mushkatel, A., D. Pijawka and M. Dantico (1990) *Impacts of the Proposed Nuclear Waste Repository on Residents of the Las Vegas Metropolitan Area*. Carson City, NV: Nuclear Waste Project Office

Myers, N. and J. Kent (1995) *Environmental Exodus: An Emergent Crisis in the Global Arena*. Washington. DC: Climate Institute

Nelkin, D. and M. S. Brown (1984) *Workers at Risk: Voices from the Workplace*. Chicago: University of Chicago Press

New Jersey Radioactive Waste Advisory Committee (1994) *Proposed Voluntary Siting Plan for Locating a Low-level Radioactive Waste Disposal Facility in New Jersey*. Trenton, NJ: New Jersey Radioactive Waste Advisory Committee

New York Legislative Commission on Toxic Substances and Hazardous Wastes (1987) *Hazardous Waste Facility Siting: A National Survey*. Albany, NY: New York Legislative Commission on Toxic Substances and Hazardous Wastes

Newman, L. F. (ed) (1990) *Hunger in History: Food Shortage, Poverty, and Deprivation*. Cambridge, MA: Blackwell

Nicholls, R. J. and S. P. Leatherman (1994) Sea level rise. In K. M. Strzepek and J. B. Smith (eds), *As Climate Changes: International Impacts and Implications*. Cambridge: Cambridge University Press for the US Environmental Protection Agency, pp92–123

Nicholls, R. J., N. Mimura and J. C. Topping (1995) Climate change in South and South-East Asia: Some implications for coastal areas. *Journal of Global Environmental Engineering*, vol 1, pp137–154

Nriagu, J. O. (1983) *Lead and Lead Poisoning in Antiquity*. New York: Wiley

Nuclear Fuel Waste Management and Disposal Concept Environmental Assessment Panel (1998) *Nuclear Fuel Waste Management and Disposal Concept*. Hull, Quebec: Canadian Environmental Assessment Agency

Nuclear Waste Strategy Coalition (1994) *Redesigning the US High-Level Nuclear Waste Disposal Program for Effective Management*. Draft report. St. Paul, MN: Minnesota Department of Public Service

O'Brien, C. (1996) Mad cow disease: Scant data cause widespread concern. *Science*, vol 271, March, p1798

OECD (Organisation for Economic Co-operation and Development) (1990) *Workshop on the Provision of Information to the Public and on the Role of Workers in Accident Preparation and Response*. OECD Environment Monographs no. 29. Paris: OECD

OECD (Organisation for Economic Co-operation and Development) (2001) *Highlights of the OECD Environmental Outlook*. Paris: OECD

O'Hare, M., L. Bacow and D. Sanderson (1983) *Facility Siting and Public Opposition*. New York: Van Nostrand

Ohkawara, T. (1996) Siting of nuclear power plants in Japan: Issues and institutional schemes. In D. Shaw (ed), *Comparative Analysis of Siting Experience in Asia*. Taipei: Institute of Economics, Academia Sinica, pp51–73

O'Keefe, P. and B. Wisner (1975) *The World Food Crisis: Issues*. Occasional Paper no. 1. Bradford: University of Bradford

Okrent, D. and N. Pidgeon (eds) (1998) Risk perception versus risk analysis. Special issue of *Reliability Engineering and System Safety*, vol 59, no 1, pp1–159

O'Riordan, T. and S. Rayner (1990) Chasing a spectre: Risk management for global environmental change. In R. E. Kasperson, K. Dow, D. Golding and J. X. Kasperson (eds), *Understanding Global Environmental Change: The Contributions of Risk Analysis and Management*. Worcester, MA: Clark University, The Earth Transformed Program, pp45–62

OSHA (Occupational Safety and Health Administration) (1983) Hazard communication: Final Rule. *Federal Register*, vol 48, no 228 (25 November), pp53280–53348

Ostrom, E. (1990) *Governing the Commons: The Evolution of Institutions for Collective Action*. New York: Wiley

Otway, H. (1987) Experts, risk communication, and democracy. *Risk Analysis*, vol 7, pp125–129

Otway, H., P. Haastrup, W. Cannell, G. Gianitsopoulos and M. Paruccini (1988) Risk communication in Europe after Chernobyl: A media analysis of seven countries. *Industrial Crisis Quarterly*, vol 2, pp3–15

Otway, H. J. and D. von Winterfeldt (1982) Beyond acceptable risk: On the social acceptability of technologies. *Policy Sciences*, vol 14, pp247–256

Palmer, C. G. S., L. K. Carlstrom and J. A. Woodward (2001) Risk perception and ethnicity. *Risk Decision and Policy*, vol 6, pp187–206

Parker, F. L., R. E. Kasperson, T. L. Andersson and S. A. Parker (1986) *Technical and Sociopolitical Issues in Radioactive Waste Disposal, 1986. Volume I: Safety, Siting and Interim Storage*. Stockholm: Beijer Institute

Parry, M. L. (1985) The impact of climatic variations on agricultural margins. In R. W. Kates, J. H. Ausubel and M. Berberian (eds), *Climate Impact Assessment*, Scope 27. Chichester: Wiley, pp351–368

Passmore, J. (1974) *Man's Responsibility for Nature*. New York: Scribner's

Patz, J. A., M. A. McGeehin, S. M. Bernard, K. L. Ebi, P. R. Epstein, A. Grambsh, D. J. Gubler, P. Reiter, I. Romieu, J. B. Rose, J. M. Samet and J. Trtanj (2000) The potential health impacts of climate variability and change for the United States: Executive summary of the report of the health sector of the US national assessment. *Environmental Health Perspectives*, vol 108, no 4, pp367–376

Peele, E. (1987) Innovation process and inventive solutions: A case study of local public acceptance of a proposed nuclear waste packaging and storage facility. In *Symposium on Land Use Management*. New York: Praeger

Pemetta, J. C. (1992) Impacts of sea-level rise on small island states: National and international responses. *Global Environmental Change*, vol 2, no 1, pp19–31

Pemetta, J. C. and G. Sestini (1989) *The Maldives and the Impacts of Expected Climate Changes*. UNEP Regional Seas Reports and Studies no. 104. Nairobi: United Nations Environment Programme

Pennock, J. R. (1979) *Democratic Political Theory*. Princeton, NJ: Princeton University Press

Perrow, C. (1984) *Normal Accidents: Living with High-risk Technologies*. New York: Basic Books. (2nd edition 1999, Princeton University Press)

Peters, E. and P. Slovic (1996) The role of affect and worldviews as orienting dispositions in the perception and acceptance of nuclear power. *Journal of Applied Social Psychology*, vol 26, no 16, pp1427–1453

Petterson, J. S. (1988) Perception vs. reality of radiological impact: The Goiânia model. *Nuclear News*, vol 31, no 14, pp84–90

Phillips, Lord, J. Bridgeman and M. Ferguson-Smith (2000) *The Report of the Inquiry into BSE and Variant CJD in the UK.* London: The Stationery Office, www.bseinquiry.gov.uk

Piasecki, B. W. and G. A. Davis (1987) *America's Future in Toxic Waste Management.* New York: Quorum

Piddington, K. W. (1989) Sovereignty and the environment. *Environment*, vol 31, no 7, pp18–20, 35–39

Pidgeon, N. F. (1988) Risk assessment and accident analysis. *Acta Psychologica*, vol 68, pp355–368

Pidgeon, N. F. (1997) *Risk Communication and the Social Amplification of Risk – Phase 1 Scoping Study.* Report to the UK Health and Safety Executive (Risk Assessment and Policy Unit), RSU Ref 3625/R62.076. London: HSE Books

Pidgeon, N. F., K. Henwood and B. Maguire (1999) Public health communication and the social amplification of risks: Present knowledge and future prospects. In P. Bennett and K. Calman (eds), *Risk Communication and Public Health.* Oxford: Oxford University Press, pp65–77

Pidgeon, N., C. Hood, D. Jones, B. Turner and R. Gibson (1992) Risk perception. In Royal Society Study Group (ed), *Risk: Analysis, Perception and Management.* London: The Royal Society, pp89–134

Pidgeon, N., R. E. Kasperson and P. Slovic (eds) (2003) *The Social Amplification of Risk.* Cambridge: Cambridge University Press

Pidgeon, N. and M. O'Leary (1994) Organizational safety culture: Implications for aviation practice. In N. Johnston, N. McDonald and R. Fuller (eds), *Aviation Psychology in Practice.* Aldershot: Avebury Technical, pp21–43

Pidgeon, N. and M. O'Leary (2000) Man-made disasters: Why technology and organizations (sometimes) fail. *Safety Science*, vol 34, pp15–30

Pocock, D. C. D. (1974) *The Nature of Environmental Perception.* UK: Department of Geography, University of Durham

Popper, F. J. (1983) LP/HC and LULUs: The political uses of risk analysis in land-use planning. *Risk Analysis*, vol 3, no 4, pp255–263

Portney, K. E. (1983) *Citizen Attitudes toward Hazardous Waste Facility Siting: Public Opinion in Five Massachusetts Communities.* Medford, MA: Tufts University, Lincoln Filene Center for Citizenship and Public Affairs

Postel, S. (2000) Redesigning irrigated agriculture. In L. Brown et al (eds), *State of the World, 2000.* New York: Norton, pp39–58

Putnam, R. D. (1993) *Making Democracy Work: Civic Traditions in Modern Italy.* Princeton, NJ: Princeton University Press

Putnam, R. D. (1995a) Bowling alone: America's declining social capital. *Journal of Democracy*, vol 6, no 1, pp65–78

Putnam, R. D. (1995b) Tuning in, tuning out: The strange disappearance of social capital in America. *PS: Political Science and Politics*, vol 28, no 4, pp664–683

Putnam, R. D. (1996) The strange disappearance of civic America. *The American Prospect*, vol 24, Winter, pp34–48

Quam, M. D. (1990) The sick role, stigma, and pollution: The case of AIDS. In D. A. Feldman (ed), *Culture and AIDS.* Westport, CT: Praeger, pp9–28

Quarantelli, E. L. (1988) Assessing disaster preparedness planning: A set of criteria and their applicability to developing countries. *Regional Development Dialogue*, vol 9, no 1, pp48–69

Rabe, B. G. (1994) *Beyond Nimby: Hazardous Waste Siting in Canada and the United States.* Washington, DC: The Brookings Institute

Rappaport, R. A. (1988) Toward postmodern risk analysis. *Risk Analysis*, vol 8, no 2, pp189–191

Rasky, S. (1987) Nevada may end up holding the nuclear bag. *New York Times*, 20 December, ppiv–4

Rawls, J. (1971) *A Theory of Justice*. Cambridge, MA: Harvard University Press

Rayner, S. (1984) Disagreeing about risk: The institutional cultures of risk management and planning for future generations. In S. G. Hadden (ed), *Risk Analysis Institutions, and Public Policy*. Port Washington, NY: Associated Faculty Press, pp150–169

Rayner, S. (1988) Muddling through metaphors to maturity: A commentary on Kasperson et al, 'The social amplification of risk'. *Risk Analysis*, vol 8, no 2, pp201–204

Rayner, S. (1992) Cultural theory and risk analysis. In S. Krimsky and D. Golding (eds), *Social Theories of Risk*. Westport, CT: Praeger, 83–115

Rayner, S. and R. Cantor (1987) How fair is safe enough? The cultural approach to societal technology choice. *Risk Analysis*, vol 7, no 1, pp3–13

Reich, M. (1994) Toxic politics and pollution victims in the Third World. In S. Jasanoff (ed), *Learning from Disaster*. Philadelphia: University of Pennsylvania Press, 180–203

Rempel, J. and J. Holmes (1986) How do I trust thee? *Psychology Today*, February, pp28–34

Rempel, J., J. Holmes and M. Zanna (1985) Trust in close relationships. *Journal of Personality and Social Psychology*, vol 49, pp95–112

Renn, O. (1986) Risk perception: A systematic review of concepts and research results. In *Avoiding and Managing Environmental Damage from Major Industrial Accidents*. Proceedings of the Air Pollution Control Association International Conference in Vancouver, Canada, November 1985. Pittsburgh: Air Pollution Control Association, pp377–408

Renn, O. (1991) Risk communication and the social amplification of risk. In R. E. Kasperson and P.-J. M. Stallen (eds), *Communicating Risks to the Public: International Perspectives*. Dordrecht: Kluwer, pp287–324

Renn, O. (1998) Three decades of risk research: Accomplishments and new challenges. *Journal of Risk Research*, vol 1, no 1, pp49–71

Renn, O., W. J. Burns, J. X. Kasperson, R. E. Kasperson and P. Slovic (1992) The social amplification of risk: Theoretical foundations and empirical applications. *Journal of Social Issues*, vol 48, no 4, pp137–160

Renn, O. and D. Levine (1991) Credibility and trust in risk communication. In R. E. Kasperson and P.-J. M. Stallen (eds), *Communicating Risks to the Public: International Perspectives*. Dordrecht: Kluwer, pp175–218

Renn, O. and B. Rohrmann (2000) *Cross-cultural Risk Perception: A Survey of Empirical Studies*. Amsterdam: Kluwer

Renn, O., T. Webler and P. Wiedemann (eds) (1995) *Fairness and Competence in Citizen Participation: Evaluating Models for Environmental Discourse*. Dordrecht: Kluwer

Riebsame, W. (1989) *Assessing the Social Implications of Climate Fluctuations: A Guide to Climate Impact Studies*. Nairobi: United Nations Environment Programme, World Climate Impacts Programme

Rip, A. (1988) Should social amplification of risk be counteracted? *Risk Analysis*, vol 8, no 2, pp193–197

Roberts, K. H. (1989) New challenges in organizational research: High reliability organizations. *Industrial Crisis Quarterly*, vol 3, no 2, pp111–125

Roberts, L. (1987) Radiation accident grips Goiânia. *Science*, vol 238, pp1028–1031

Rogers, K. (1994) Yucca site faults deeper than thought. *Las Vegas Review-Journal*, 24 May, pp1B, 4B.

Rogers, K. (1996) Nuke Waste Exec Cautions Scientists on Chlorine Reports, *Las Vegas Review-Journal*, 30 April, p2B.

Rosa, E. A. (1998) Metatheoretical foundations for post-normal risk. *Journal of Risk Research*, vol 1, no 1, pp15–44

Rosa, E. A. and D. L. Clark (1999) Historical routes to technological gridlock: Nuclear terminology as prototypical vehicle. *Research in Social Problems and Public Policy*, vol 7, pp21–57

Rosener, J. B. (1975) A cafeteria of techniques and critiques. *Public Management*, vol 57, December, pp16–19

Rosenzweig, C. and D. Hillel (1998) *Climate Change and the Global Harvest: Potential Impacts of the Greenhouse Effect on Agriculture*. Oxford: Oxford University Press

Ross, L. (1987) Environmental policy in post-Mao China. *Environment*, vol 29, May, pp12–17, 34–39

Rothbart, M. and B. Park (1986) On the confirmability and disconfirmability of trait concepts. *Journal of Personality and Social Psychology*, vol 50, pp131–142

Rothstein, H. (2003) Neglected risk regulation: The institutional attenuation phenomenon. *Health, Risk and Society*, vol 5, pp85–103

Rotter, J. B. (1980) Interpersonal trust, trustworthiness, and gullibility. *American Psychologist*, vol 35, pp1–7

Rourke, F. E., L. Free and W. Watts (1976) *Trust and Confidence in the American System*. Washington, DC: Potomac Associates

Royal Society (1992) *Risk: Analysis, Perception and Management*. London: The Royal Society

Ruckelshaus, W. D. (1985) Risk, science, and democracy. *Issues in Science and Technology*, vol 1, pp19–38

Ruckelshaus, W. D. (1996) *Trust in Government: A Prescription for Restoration*. The Webb Lecture to The National Academy of Public Administration, November 15

Sandman, P. (1985) Getting to maybe: Some communication aspects of siting hazardous waste facilities. *Seton Hall Legislative Journal*, vol 9. pp437–465

Schellnhuber, H. J., A. Block, M. Cassel-Gintz, J. Kropp, G. Lammel, W. Lass, R. Lienenkamp, C. Loose, M. K. B. Lüdeke, O. Moldenhauer, G. Petschel-Held, M. Plöchl, and F. Reusswig (1997) Syndromes of global change. *GAIA*, vol 6, pp19–34

Schneider, S. (1989) The greenhouse effect: Science and policy. *Science*, vol 243, pp771–781

Schneider, S. H., B. L. Turner, II, and H. Morehouse-Garriga (1998) Imaginable surprise in global change science. *Journal of Risk Research*, vol 1, no 2, pp165–185

Secretary of Energy Advisory Board, Task Force on Radioactive Waste Management (1993) *Earning Public Trust and Confidence: Requisites for Managing Radioactive Wastes*. Washington, DC

Sestini, G. (1992) Implications of climatic changes for the Nile Delta. In L. Jeftic, J. D. Milliman and G. Sestini (eds), *Climatic Change and the Mediterranean*. London: Edward Arnold, pp535–601

Sewell, W. R. D. and H. D. Foster (1976) Environmental risk: Management strategies in the developing world. *Environmental Management*, vol 1, no 1, pp49–59

Shapiro. S. P. (1987) The social control of impersonal trust. *American Journal of Sociology*, vol 93, pp623–658

Sharlin, H. I. (1985) *EDB: A Case Study in the Communication of Health Risk*. Washington, DC: Office of Policy Analysis, Environmental Protection Agency

Sharma, N. P., T. Dambaug, E. Gilgan-Hunt, D. Grey, V. Okaru and D. Rothberg (1996) *African Water Resources: Challenges and Opportunities for Sustainable Development*. World Bank Technical Paper 331. Washington, DC: World Bank

Shaw, D. (ed) (1996) *Comparative Analysis of Siting Experience in Asia*. Taipei: The Institute of Economics, Academia Sinica

Shoemaker, P. J. (1987) Mass communication by the book: A review of 31 texts. *Journal of Communication*, vol 37, no 3, pp109–131

Short, J. F. (1984) The social fabric of risk: Toward the social transformation of risk analysis. *American Sociological Review*, vol 49, pp711–725

Short, J. F., Jr. (1992) Defining, explaining, and managing risks. In J. F. Short and L. Clarke (eds), *Organizations, Uncertainties, and Risk*. Boulder, CO: Westview, pp3–23

Shrader-Frechette, K. S. (1985) Environmental ethics and global imperatives. In R. Repetto (ed), *The Global Possible*. New Haven: Yale University Press, 97–127

Shrader-Frechette, K. S. (1993) *Burying Uncertainty: Risk and the Case Against Geological Disposal of Nuclear Waste*. Berkeley, CA: University of California Press

Siegrist, M. and G. Cvetkovich (2000) Perception of hazards: The role of social trust and knowledge. *Risk Analysis*, vol 20, pp713–720

Siegrist, M., G. Cvetkovich and C. Roth (2000) Salient value similarity, social trust and risk/benefit perception. *Risk Analysis*, vol 20, pp353–362

Simon, P. J. (1983) *Reagan in the Workplace: Unraveling the Health and Safety Net*. Washington, DC: Center for Study of Responsive Law

Sinclair, M. (1977) The public hearing as a participatory device: Evaluation of the IJC experience. In W. R. D. Sewell and J. T. Coppock (eds), *Public Participation in Planning*. New York: Wiley, pp105–122

Singer, E. and P. M. Endreny (1993) *Reporting on Risk: How the Media Portray Accidents, Diseases, Disasters, and Other Hazards*. New York: Russell Sage Foundation

Sjöberg, L. (1999) Risk perception in Western Europe. *Ambio*, vol 28, pp555–568

Sjöberg, L. and B.-M. Drottz-Sjöberg (1994) *Risk Perception of Nuclear Waste: Experts and the Public*. RHIZIKON: Risk Research Report no. 16. Stockholm: Center for Risk Research, Stockholm School of Economics

Slovic, P. (1986) Informing and educating the public about risk. *Risk Analysis*, vol 6, no 4, pp403–415

Slovic, P. (1987a) Forecasting the adverse economic effects of a nuclear waste repository. In R. G. Post (ed), *Waste Management '87*. Tuscon: Arizona Board of Regents, University of Arizona, 91–94

Slovic, P. (1987b) Perception of risk. *Science*, vol 236, pp280–285

Slovic, P. (1992) Perception of risk: Reflections on the psychometric paradigm. In S. Krimsky and D. Golding (eds), *Social Theories of Risk*. Westport, CT: Praeger, pp117–152

Slovic, P. (1993) Perceived risk, trust, and democracy: A systems perspective. *Risk Analysis*, vol 13, no 6, pp675–682

Slovic, P. (1998) The risk game. *Reliability, Engineering and System Safety*, vol 59, pp73–77

Slovic, P. (1999) Perceived risk, trust, and democracy. In G. Cvetkovich, and R. Löfstedt (eds), *Social Trust and the Management of Risk*. London: Earthscan, pp42–52

Slovic, P. (2000) *The Perception of Risk*. London: Earthscan

Slovic, P. (2002) Terrorism as hazard: A new species of trouble. *Risk Analysis*, vol 22, pp425–426

Slovic, P., M. Finucane, E. Peters and D. G. MacGregor (2002) The affect heuristic. In T. Gilovich, D. Griffin and D. Kahneman (eds), *Heuristics and Biases: The Psychology of Intuitive Judgment*. New York: Cambridge University Press, pp397–420

Slovic, P., B. Fischhoff and S. Lichtenstein (1982a) Rating the risks: The structure of expert and lay perceptions. In C. Hohenemser and J. X. Kasperson (eds), *Risk in the Technological Society*. AAAS Symposium Series. Boulder, CO: Westview, pp141–166

Slovic, P., B. Fischhoff and S. Lichtenstein (1982b) Why study risk perception? *Risk Analysis*, vol 2, pp83–94

Slovic, P., B. Fischhoff and S. Lichtenstein (1986) The psychometric study of risk perception. In V. T. Covello, J. Menkes and J. Mumpower (eds), *Risk Evaluation and Management*. New York: Plenum Press, 3–24

Slovic, P., J. Flynn and R. Gregory (1994) Stigma happens: Social problems in the siting of nuclear waste facilities. *Risk Analysis*, vol 14, no 5, pp773–777

Slovic, P., J. Flynn and M. Layman (1991a) Perceived risk, trust, and the politics of nuclear waste. *Science*, vol 254, pp1603–1607

Slovic, P., J. Flynn, C. K. Mertz, M. Poumadère and C. Mays (2000) Nuclear power and the public: A comparative study of risk perception in France and the United States. In O. Renn, and B. Rohrmann (eds), *Cross-culture Risk Perception: A Survey of Empirical Studies*. Amsterdam: Kluwer, pp55–102

Slovic, P., M. Layman and J. Flynn (1991b) Risk perception, trust, and nuclear waste: Lessons from Yucca Mountain. *Environment*, vol 33, pp6–11, 28–30

Slovic, P., M. Layman, N. Kraus, J. Flynn, J. Chalmers and G. Gesell (1991c) Perceived risk, stigma, and potential economic impacts on a high-level nuclear waste repository in Nevada. *Risk Analysis*, vol 11, no 4, pp683–696

Slovic, P., S. Lichtenstein and B. Fischhoff (1984) Modeling the societal impact of fatal accidents. *Management Science*, vol 30, pp464–474

Sontag, S. (1978) *Illness as Metaphor*. New York: Vintage

Sorensen, J. H. (1984) Evaluating the effectiveness of warning systems for nuclear power plant emergencies: Criteria and application. In M. J. Pasqualetti and D. Pijawka (eds), *Nuclear Power: Assessing and Managing Hazardous Technology*. Boulder, CO: Westview, pp259–277

Sorensen, J. H. and D. S. Mileti (1987) Decision-making uncertainties in emergency warning system negotiations. *International Journal of Mass Emergencies and Disasters*, vol 5, no 1, pp33–61

Sorensen, J., J. Soderstrom, E. Copenhaver, S. Carnes and R. Bolin (1987) *Impacts of Hazardous Technology: The Psycho-social Effects of Restarting TMI-1* (SUNY Series on Environmental Public Policy, ed. L. W. Milbrath) Albany: State University of New York Press

Souter, D., D. Obura, and O. Lindén (eds) (2000) *Coral Reef Degradation in the Indian Ocean: Status Report 2000*. Stockholm: CORDIO, SAREC Marine Science Program, Department of Zoology, Stockholm University

Stallen, P.-J. M. and A. Tomas (1988) Public concern about industrial hazards. *Risk Analysis*, vol 8, pp237–245

Stallings, D. L. (1975) *Environmental Cognition and Land Use Controversy: An Environmental Image Study of Seattle's Pike Place Market.* Doctoral dissertation, University of Washington, Seattle

Stern, P. C. and H. V. Fineberg (eds) (1996) *Understanding Risk: Informing Decisions in a Democratic Society.* Report for National Research Council, Committee on Risk Characterization. Washington, DC: National Academy Press

Stever, D. W., Jr (1980) *Seabrook and the Nuclear Regulatory Commission: The Licensing of a Nuclear Power Plant.* Hanover, NH: University Press of New England

Susarla, A. (2003) Plague and arsenic: Assignment of blame in the mass media and the social amplification and attenuation of risk. In N. Pidgeon, R. E. Kasperson and P. Slovic (eds), *The Social Amplification of Risk.* Cambridge: Cambridge University Press, pp179–206

Susman, P., P. O'Keefe and B. Wisner (1983) Global disasters: A radical interpretation. In K. Hewitt (ed), *Interpretations of Calamity from the Viewpoint of Human Ecology.* Boston: Allen & Unwin, pp263–283

Svenson, O. (1988a) Managing product hazards at Volvo Car Corporation. In R. E. Kasperson, J. X. Kasperson, C. Hohenemser and R. W. Kates (eds), *Corporate Management of Health and Safety Hazards: A Comparison of Current Practice.* Boulder, CO: Westview, pp57–78

Svenson, O. (1988b) Mental models of risk communication and action: Reflections on social amplification of risk. *Risk Analysis*, vol 8, no 2, pp199–200

Tanaka, Y. (1999) *Is the Nimby Syndrome a Universal Phenomenon: Symptoms and Remedies.* Proceedings of the International Workshop: Challenges and Issues in Facility Siting, 7–9 January, 1999. Taipei: The Institute of Economics, Academia Sinica

Texler, J. (1986) *Environmental Hazards in Third World Development.* Studies on Developing Countries, no. 120. Budapest: Institute for World Economics, Hungarian Academy of Sciences

Thompson, K. (1969) Insalubrious California: Perception and Reality. *Annals of the Association of American Geographer*, vol 59, pp50–64.

Trumbo, C. W. (1996) Examining psychometrics and polarization in a single-risk case study. *Risk Analysis*, vol 16, pp429–438

Tuan, Y. (1979) *Landscapes of Fear.* New York: Pantheon

Turner, B. A. (1978) *Man-made Disasters: The Failure of Foresight.* London: Wykeham

Turner, B. L., II, W. C. Clark, R. W. Kates, J. F. Richards, J. T. Mathews and W. B. Meyer (eds) (1990a) *The Earth as Transformed by Human Action: Global and Regional Changes in the Biosphere over the Past 300 years.* Cambridge: Cambridge University Press with Clark University

Turner, B. L., II, R. E. Kasperson, W. B. Meyer, K. M. Dow, D. Golding, J. X. Kasperson, R. C. Mitchell and S. J. Ratick (1990b) Two types of global environmental change: Definitional and spatial-scale issues in their human dimensions. *Global Environmental Change*, vol 1, no 1, pp14–22

Turner, B. L., II and N. F. Pidgeon (1997) *Man-made Disasters*, 2nd edition. Oxford: Butterworth-Heinemann

Tyler, T. (1989) The psychology of procedural justice: A test of the group-value model. *Journal of Personality and Social Psychology*, vol 57, pp380–383

UK Interdepartmental Liaison Group on Risk Assessment (1998a) *Risk Assessment and Risk Management: Improving Policy and Practice within Government Departments.* London: Health and Safety Executive

UK Interdepartmental Liaison Group on Risk Assessment (1998b) *Risk Communication: A Guide to Regulatory Practice.* London: Health and Safety Executive

UNEP (United Nations Environment Programme) (1986) *The State of the Environment 1986: Environment and Health.* Nairobi: UNEP

USCIA (US Central Intelligence Agency) (2001) *Global Trends 2015.* Washington, DC: CIA

US Council on Environmental Quality (1980) *Public Opinion on Environmental Issues: Results of a National Opinion Survey.* Washington, DC: US Government Printing Office

USDOE (US Department of Energy) (1986) *Environmental Assessment: Yucca Mountain Site, Nevada Research and Development Areas, Nevada.* Vol 1, DOE/RW-0073. Washington, DC: DOE

USDOE (US Department of Energy) (1994*) Civilian Radioactive Waste Program: Program Overview*, Vol 1, DOE/RW0458. Washington, DC: DOE

USDOE (US Department of Energy) (1995*) Site Characterization Progress Report: Yucca Mountain, Nevada*, no 12, DOE/R44-4077. Washington, DC: DOE

USDOE (US Department of Energy) (1996) General guidelines for the recommendation of sites for nuclear waste repositories (Proposed Rule). *Federal Register* 61, no. 242 (16 December): 66157-66169

USEPA (US Environmental Protection Agency) (1987) *Unfinished Business: A Comparative Assessment of Environmental Problems.* Washington, DC: Office of Policy Analysis, Office of Policy Planning and Evaluation, EPA, February

USEPA (US Environmental Protection Agency) (1990) *Reducing Risk: Selling Priorities and Strategies for Environmental Protection.* Washington, DC: EPA

US Federal Highway Administration (1970) *Effective Citizen Participation in Transportation Planning.* Vol 2: A catalog of techniques. Washington, DC: US Department of Transportation

USGAO (US General Accounting Office) (1983) *Siting of Hazardous Waste Landfills and their Correlation with Racial and Economic Status of Surrounding Communities.* GAO/RCED-83-168. Washington, DC: GAO

USGAO (US General Accounting Office) (1987) *Nuclear Waste: Information on Cost Growth in Site Characterization Cost Estimates.* GAO/RCED-87-200FS. Washington, DC: GAO

USGAO (US General Accounting Office) (1997) *Nuclear Waste: Impediments to Completing the Yucca Mountain Repository Project.* GAO/RCED-97-30. Washington, DC: GAO

USNRC (US National Research Council) (1957) *The Disposal of Radioactive Waste on Land. Report of the Committee on Waste Disposal of the Division of Earth Sciences.* Washington, DC, National Academy of Sciences

USNRC (US National Research Council) (1980) *Disasters and the Mass Media.* Washington, DC: National Academy of Sciences Press

USNRC (US National Research Council) (1983) *Risk Assessment in the Federal Government: Managing the Process.* Washington, DC: National Academy Press

USNRC (US National Research Council) (1984a) *Hurricane Diana, North Carolina.* 10–14 September, 1984. Washington, DC: National Academy Press

USNRC (US National Research Council) (1984b) *Social and Economic Aspects of Radioactive Waste Disposal: Considerations for Institutional Management.* Washington, DC: National Academy of Sciences

USNRC (US National Research Council) (1984c) *Toxicity Testing: Strategies to Determine Needs and Priorities.* Washington: National Academy Press

USNRC (US National Research Council) (1989) *Improving Risk Communication.*

Washington, DC: National Academy Press

USNRC (US National Research Council), Board on Radioactive Waste Management. (1990) *Rethinking High-level Radioactive Waste Disposal*. Washington, DC: National Academy Press

USNRC (US National Research Council) (1999) *Our Common Journey: A Transition toward Sustainability*. Washington: National Academy Press

USNUREG (US Nuclear Regulatory Commission) (1975) *Reactor Safety Study*. WASH 1400, NUREG 75/014. Washington, DC: The Commission

USOMB (US Office of Management and Budget) (1996) *Statement of Administration Policy S. 1271 – Nuclear Waste Policy Act 1996*. Washington, DC: OMB

USOTA (US Office of Technology Assessment) (1982a) *Managing Commercial High-level Radioactive Waste. Summary*. Washington: OTA

USOTA (US Office of Technology Assessment) (1982b) *Technologies and Management Strategies for Hazardous Waste Control*. Washington, DC: OTA

USOTA (US Office of Technology Assessment) (1985a) *Managing the Nation's Commercial High-level Radioactive Waste*. OTA-O-277. Washington, DC: OTA

USOTA (US Office of Technology Assessment) (1985b) *Reproductive Health Hazards in the Workplace*. Washington, DC: OTA

USOTA (US Office of Technology Assessment) (1987) *Background Paper: Public Perceptions of Biotechnology*. Vol 2 of New Developments in Biotechnology. Washington, DC: OTA

US Presidential Commission on the Space Shuttle Challenger Accident (1986) *Report to the President*. Washington, DC: The Commission

US Secretary of Energy (1993) *Earning Public Trust and Confidence: Requisites for Managing Radioactive Waste*. Washington: DOE

Uzzell, D. L. (1982) Environmental pluralism and participation: A co-orientational perspective. In J. R. Gold and J. Burgess (eds), *Valued Environments*. London: George Allen and Unwin, pp189–203

van Konynenburg, R. A. (1991) Gaseous release of carbon-14: Why the high-level waste regulations should be changed. In *High-level Radioactive Waste Management 1991 : Proceedings of the Second Annual International Conference* (Las Vegas, Nevada, 28 April–3 May, 1991). La Grange, IL: American Nuclear Society and American Society of Civil Engineering, pp313–319

Vari, A., P. Reagan-Cirincione and J.L. Mumpower (1994) *LLRW Disposal Facility Siting: Successes and Failures in Six Countries*. Dordrecht: Kluwer

Vaughan, D. (1992) Regulating risk: Implications of the Challenger accident. In J. F. Short, Jr. and L. Clarke (eds), *Organizations, Uncertainties, and Risk*. Boulder, CO: Westview, pp235–254

Vaughan, D. (1996) *The Challenger Launch Decision: Risky Technology, Culture, and Deviance at NASA*. Chicago: University of Chicago Press

Vaughan, D. and M. Seifert (1992) Variability in the framing of risk issues. *Journal of Social Issues*, vol 48, no 4, pp119-135.

Vaughan, E. (1995) The significance of socioeconomic and ethnic diversity for the risk communication process. *Risk Analysis*, vol 15, no 2, pp169–180

Verba, S. and N. H. Nie (1972) *Participation in America: Political Democracy and Social Equality*. New York: Harper and Row

Viscusi, W. K. (1983) *Risk by Choice: Regulating Health and Safety in the Workplace*. Cambridge, MA: Harvard University Press

Vlek, C. A. and P.-J. M. Stallen (1981) Judging risks and benefits in the small and the large. *Organizational Behavior and Human Performance*, vol 28, pp235–271

von Winterfeldt, D. and W. Edwards (1984) *Understanding Public Disputes about Risky Technologies*. Technical report. New York: Social Science Research Council

Vyner, H. (1988) *Invisible Trauma: The Psychosocial Effects of Invisible Environmental Contaminants*. Lexington, MA: Lexington Books

Wahlberg, A. (2001) The theoretical features of some current approaches to risk perception. *Journal of Risk Research*, vol 4, pp237–250

Waterstone, M. (1985) The equity aspects of carbon dioxide-induced climate change. *Geoforum*, vol 16, no 3, pp301–306

Watson, R. T., M. C. Zinyowera and R. H. Moss (eds) (1998) *Regional Impacts of Climate Change: An Assessment of Vulnerability*. Cambridge: Cambridge University Press

WCED (World Commission on Environment and Development) (1987) *Our Common Future*. Oxford: Oxford University Press

Weick, K. E. (1987) Organizational culture as a source of high reliability. *California Management Review*, vol 29, no 2, pp112–127

Weinberg, A. (1977) Is nuclear energy acceptable? *Bulletin of the Atomic Scientists*, vol 33, no 4, pp54–60

Weinberg, A. (1994) *The First Nuclear Era: The Life and Times of a Technological Fixer*. New York: American Institute of Physics

Weingart, J. (1998) Comments presented at the symposium on understanding community decision making: Engaging the public in constructive dialogue. Philadelphia, 4–5 March

Weinstein, N. D. (1988) *Attitudes of the Public and the Department of Environmental Protection toward Environmental Hazards*. New Brunswick, NJ: Department of Human Ecology and Psychology, Rutgers University

Weiss, E. B. (1989) *In Fairness to Future Generations: International Law, Common Patrimony, and Ultergenerational Equity*. New York: Transnational Publishers and the United Nations University

Weiss, E. B. (1990) In fairness to future generations. *Environment*, vol 32, no 3, pp7–11, 30–31

Wenk, E., Jr (1986) *Tradeoffs*. Baltimore: Johns Hopkins University Press

Wildavsky, A. B. (1988) *Searching for Safety*. New Brunswick, NJ: Transaction

Wildavsky, A. B. and K. Dake (1990) Theories of risk perception: Who fears what and why? *Daedalus*, vol 119, pp41–60

Wilensky, H. L. (1967) *Organizational Intelligence*. New York: Basic Books

Wilkins, L. (1987) *Shared Vulnerability: The Media and the American Perspective on the Bhopal Disaster*. Westport, CT: Greenwood Press

Wilkins, L. and P. Patterson (1991) *Risky Business: Communication Issues of Science, Risk, and Public Policy*. Westport, CT: Greenwood Press

Williams, B. (1988) Formal structures and social reality. In D. Gambetta (ed), *Trust: Making and Breaking Cooperative Relations*. Oxford: Basil Blackwell, pp3–13

Williams, B. A. and A. R. Matheny (1995) *Democracy, Dialogue, and Environmental Disputes: The Contested Languages of Social Regulation*. New Haven: Yale University Press

Wilson, R. (1979) Analyzing the daily risks of life. *Technology Review*, vol 81, February, pp41–46

Winell, M. (1975) An international comparison of hygienic standards for chemicals in the work environment. *Ambio*, vol 4, no 1, pp34–42

Wisner, B. (1976) Man-made famine in Eastern Kenya: The interrelationship of environment and development. Discussion Paper no. 96. Brighton, England: Institute of Development Studies, University of Sussex

World Bank (1996) *Toward Environmentally Sustainable Development in Sub-Saharan Africa: A World Bank Agenda.* Washington: The World Bank

Wynne, B. (1984) Public perceptions of risk. In J. Surrey (ed), *The Urban Transportation of Irradiated Fuel.* London: Macmillan, pp246–259

Yankelovich, D. (1991) *Coming to Public Judgment: Making Democracy Work in a Complex Society.* Syracuse: Syracuse University Press

Younker, J. L., W. B. Andrews et al (1992). *Report of the Early Site Suitability Evaluation of the Potential Repository Site at Yucca Mountain, Nevada.* SAIC-91/8000. Washington, DC: US Department of Energy

Zinyowera, M. C., B. P. Jallow, R. S. Maya and H. W. O. Okoth-Ogendo (1998) Africa. In R. T. Watson, M. C. Zinyowera and R. H. Moss (eds), *The Regional Impacts of Climate Change: An Assessment of Vulnerability.* Cambridge: Cambridge University Press, pp29–84

Zucker, L. (1986) Production of trust: Institutional sources of economic structure, 1840–1920. *Research in Organizational Behavior*, vol 8, pp53–111

Index

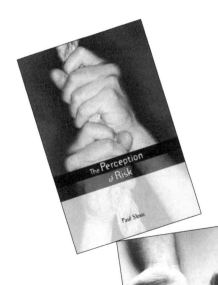

Global
Environmental
Risk

Edited by
Jeanne X. Kasperson and Roger E. Kasperson

Facility Siting
Risk, Power and Identity in Land Use Planning

Edited by
Åsa Boholm and Ragnar Löfstedt

If you're concerned about risk, you can't afford to be without Earthscan's series on **Risk, Society and Policy**. To find out more or to place your order, visit our website or give us a call:

www.earthscan.co.uk
Tel: +44 (0)20 7387 8558

...delivering sustainability